Politics in
FRANCE

*The Little, Brown Series*

*in Comparative Politics*

*Under the Editorship of*

**GABRIEL A. ALMOND**

**JAMES S. COLEMAN**

**LUCIAN W. PYE**

A COUNTRY STUDY

# Politics in
# FRANCE

Henry W. Ehrmann

*Dartmouth College*

*Boston*
**LITTLE, BROWN AND COMPANY**

*Published simultaneously in Canada*
*by Little, Brown & Company (Canada) Limited*

PRINTED IN THE UNITED STATES OF AMERICA

TO

A.G.        B.G.        F.G.

S.H.        G.L.        M.M.

R.R.        J.T.        *all of Paris*

AND TO

G.Z.        *of Berlin*

# Foreword

The Little, Brown Series in Comparative Politics has three main objectives. First, it will meet the need of teachers to deal with both Western and non-Western countries in their introductory course offerings. Second, by following a common approach in analyzing individual political systems, it will make it possible for teachers to compare these countries systematically and cumulatively. And third, it will contribute toward reestablishing the classic relationship between comparative politics and political theory, a relationship which has been neglected in recent decades. In brief, the series seeks to be global in scope, genuinely introductory and comparative in character, and concerned with broadening and deepening our understanding of the nature and variety of political systems.

The series has two parts: the Country Studies and the Analytic Studies. The Country Studies deal with problems and processes deriving from a functional, as compared with a purely structural, approach to the study of political systems. We are gratified that the participants, all mature scholars with original insights, were willing to organize their discussions around a common set of functional topics in the interest of furthering comparisons. At the same time, each author has been urged to adapt the common framework to the special problems of the country he is discussing and to express his own theoretical point of view.

An introductory book, *Comparative Politics: A Developmental Approach,* written by Gabriel A. Almond and G.

Bingham Powell, provides an analytic supplement to the Country Studies. It also opens our set of Analytic Studies, which will offer basic discussions of such topics as political change in the emerging nations, comparative analyses of interest groups, political socialization, political communication, political culture, and the like. We hope these books will prove to be useful and stimulating supplements to the Country Studies as well as points of departure in more advanced courses.

Henry Ehrmann's *Politics in France* is an interpretation of French politics based on a lifetime of creative scholarship on comparative, European, and French topics. The author of *French Labor from Popular Front to Liberation* and *Organized Business in France* presents his first full-length treatment of French politics in which he has utilized our system-functional scheme. One of the original features of Ehrmann's approach is his treatment of French political socialization as an ongoing process, continuing from childhood experiences to adult exposure to the media of communication, interest group membership, and political participation. A thoughtful conclusion attempts to assess the significance of modernization in French economy, society, and culture for the long-term prospects of French politics.

Gabriel A. Almond
James S. Coleman
Lucian W. Pye

# Preface

The Frenchman Montesquieu once remarked that those nations are happy whose annals of history are boring to read. To the extent that this is true, France is of course an "unhappy" country — for her history has been fascinating and turbulent, not boring. No wonder that the political systems under which she has lived have invited unending and frequently passionate comments by Frenchmen and foreign observers alike.

Such an abiding interest is caused in part by high expectations — expectations which the present leader of the French Republic is not the first to have voiced. Because the country has been the beacon of Western enlightenment, the performance of its political system is measured by exacting standards. There are puzzling inconsistencies in the political and social life of every nation. Those of France have frequently aroused irritation; explanations that have been offered are stubbornly contradictory because they fasten on different aspects of the country's internal contradictions. Does the turbulence of political life hide a pattern of basically undisturbed fundamental values? Or is, in a rapidly changing environment, an all too persistent adherence to basic values responsible for political explosions?

When discussing "Some Characteristics of Historians in Democratic Times," [1] Alexis de Tocqueville suggests that the lot of historians writing in an aristocratic age was an easy one. They were content simply to detach from the mass of general

[1] Alexis de Tocqueville, *Democracy in America* (New York: Vintage Books, 1954), Vol. II, pp. 90–93.

events "the particular influence of one man or of a few men."
Anyone trying to explain the present French regime cannot
quite fail to comment upon the "influence of one man." Yet
present-day political science fits well, as it must, the characteristics which Tocqueville attributes to the historians of democratic times. We seek, as he puts it, to "assign general causes"
to a mass of incidents and are "given to connect incidents together so as to deduce a system from them." Instead of attempting to discern the influence of individuals we prefer "talking
about the characteristics of race, the physical conformation of
the country, or the genius of civilization" — now conveniently
summarized under the heading of "political culture."

Just because France shares with other democracies many
political institutions which have worked adequately elsewhere
but have failed her, a discussion of the country's political culture as a major variable determining political behavior has always appeared to be particularly relevant. It also provides the
main theme of this book. To avoid the stereotypes which a
discussion of this kind easily invites, the functional approach
suggested in the writings of Gabriel Almond and common to
this series in comparative politics has proved particularly, and
to this author almost surprisingly, helpful. The categories here
employed seem to clarify where choice and where circumstances have shaped the structures of the French political system and how they have determined the functioning of these
structures. By sorting out what is unique and what is common
to societies of similar development, our classifications should
serve the purposes of comparison.

All comparative studies suffer from the limitations imposed
by the paucity of strictly comparable data. I do not share the
optimism of those who believe that the growing number of
comparative statistical studies of national politics are sufficient
to test general propositions. Where I have used such data I
have regarded them as suggestive illustrations, not as evidence.
Until quite recently most French statistics were notoriously
unreliable and were, for that reason alone, unlikely to mirror
reality better than subjective judgments. I have regarded polling and survey data, also, as suggestive illustrations. French
techniques in this field have been refined greatly and their results, too, provide interesting comments. But they "prove"
little and, as some French political scientists have shown, to me
convincingly, even less than in some other countries.[2]

[2] See Association Française de Science Politique, *Les Sondages et la
Science Politique* (Paris: Mimeographed, 1966).

This study is one of an old country undergoing rapid development. My footnotes should show how much I have profited from the literature on political development — some of which appears in this series. Circumstances have not permitted me to investigate in necessary detail the impact which the international environment has had on French domestic politics. It is obvious that the political development of a country such as France has been drastically affected by her frequent exposure to large-scale wars and more recently to the tensions caused by the cold war.

Yet however heavy the heritage of past events, whether generated within the national borders or outside, present-day France is not just a prisoner of its past. The "silent revolution" described on many pages of this book as taking place in many fields, would not be possible, if a nation's values were foreordained and unalterable. The limits and constraints conditioning the ongoing development must be clearly understood if France is to hold, as she has so often in the past, pertinent lessons for general and democratic political theory. But again Tocqueville reminds his disciples not to get embroiled too far in "doctrines of necessity" and, instead, to "acknowledge the strength and independence of men united in society." For, as he concludes, "the great object in our time is to raise the faculties of men, not to complete their prostration."

The research for and the writing of this book were substantially aided by Dartmouth College. Its generous leave policy, grants awarded by its Committee on Research, and altogether an atmosphere in which research and teaching are equally recognized made this study possible. But the book also owes much to my earlier musings and wanderings supported by the Social Science Research Council, the Rockefeller Foundation, and the Ford Foundation.

My colleagues and friends to whom this book is dedicated have contributed more than they might wish to acknowledge when they see the results of their counsel. Whether they have read, with great attention to ideas and details, parts of the manuscript, whether they have answered precisely my manifold inquiries or engaged with me, over many years, in lengthy discussions of French politics, their knowledge and understanding were indispensable. In the United States, Gabriel Almond, Lewis Edinger, and Richard Rose have commented helpfully and with acumen on parts of the manuscript. My colleague and friend at Dartmouth, Professor Howard Bliss has gone with great care over the entire manuscript. His thoughtful suggestions have resulted in many improvements of content and style. To be edited by as competent a staff as that of Little, Brown and Company is an intellectual joy. The efficiency of the staff of Baker Library at Dartmouth and especially of its Order Department should prove attractive to any scholar.

One of my students, Mr. Roger Witten of the Dartmouth Class of 1968 proved his mettle as an untiring research assistant. Mrs. Louise Spiess can only be described as a paragon among secretaries. The reader is bound to profit from Mrs. Joan Erdman's skill as a judicious indexer.

My wife Claire made no suggestions whatsoever, nor did she proofread. She did not even read. Ever since we met more than thirty years ago in Paris — to be sure in the midst of acute political crisis — we have talked, lived, and breathed French politics, with a frown or a smile, in France and from afar. This book will teach her nothing. But all through the writing process she fulfilled her usual and indispensable function. She never ceased insisting that there are broader horizons and more urgent problems in the world at large than a work-centered author will admit. For this my undivided thanks go to her.

Henry W. Ehrmann

Hanover, New Hampshire, March 1968

When the gravest crisis yet to befall the Fifth Republic broke out, this book was ready to go to press. A study such as this has no ambitions to run after the newspapers' headlines. The publisher and author decided not to change a word in the text as originally written but rather to add a postscript and maintain the existing production schedule. This necessitated a hurried trip to France for closer observation of a bewildering and intricate situation.

Since this reconnaissance and writing had to overlap, I needed more than ever the intellectual and material help of my French colleagues to whom this book is dedicated. This help was gallantly offered in spite of the pressures and harassments to which the events were submitting them. The Postscript was written in the venerable building of the Paris "Sciences Po" while students had occupied it and had hoisted over its entrance the black and red flags of protest.

H. W. E.

Paris, Rue St. Guillaume, July 2, 1968

# Table of Contents

*Chapter I*

Origins and History of the System  . . . . .  *1*

*A nation of patriots — divided. Tension between representative and plebiscitarian traditions. Tensions between bureaucratic traditions and individualism. Consequences for the political system.*

*Chapter II*

The Economic and Social Setting  . . . . .  *18*

*The impact of recovery.  "France without peasants?"  The entrepreneurial system.  A modern welfare economy.*

*Chapter III*

Political Socialization  . . . . . . . . .  *43*

*Political socialization and political culture.  Religious and antireligious traditions.  Family and class.  Education.  Associations.  Conclusion.*

*Chapter IV*

Political Participation . . . . . . . . .    *81*

> *The citizen in local politics.    Voting in parlia-*
> *mentary elections.    Voting in plebiscitarian con-*
> *tests: referendum and presidential elections.*

*Chapter V*

Recruitment and Style of Decision-Makers . .   *119*

> *The phenomenon of the "political class."    The*
> *phenomenon of the bureaucracy.    The phenom-*
> *enon of Charles de Gaulle.*

*Chapter VI*

Political Socialization Through the Mass Media   *152*

> *The flow of communications. Governmental*
> *control of information.*

*Chapter VII*

Articulation of Values and Interests:
The Interest Groups . . . . . . . . .   *169*

> *Interest representation in a fragmented society.*
> *Means of access and style of action.    Mutation in*
> *the group universe?*

*Chapter VIII*

Aggregation of Values and Interests:
Political Parties . . . . . . . . . . .   *196*

> *The party system.    Present-day parties.    Conclu-*
> *sion: mutations in the party system?*

*Chapter IX*

## Policy Processes — I . . . . . . . . . . 245

*The President of the Republic: multiplicity of functions and omnipotence. The government: rule making and rule application. The civil service: motor or instrumentality?*

*Chapter X*

## Policy Processes — II . . . . . . . . . 276

*Parliament: the National Assembly — from omnipotence to impotence. Parliament: which upper house? The future of parliamentary government.*

*Chapter XI*

## Political Modernization and Legitimacy . . . 303

*The dynamics of modernization in France. Legitimacy for the new institutions? A modern democracy? — chances and shoals.*

## Postscript: Summer 1968 . . . . . . . . 321

*The explosions of May. Restoration without revolution. Perspectives.*

*Suggestions for Further Reading, 344*

*Chronology of Events, 346*

*The French Constitution of 1958, 349*

*Index, 359*

# CHAPTER I

# Origins and History
# of the System

## A NATION OF PATRIOTS — DIVIDED

As one of the oldest nation-states of Europe, France has been free of many of the tensions characteristic of countries which have found their national unity and identity only in more recent times. Many of her borders are not determined by natural barriers as are those of the British Isles. Yet, except for some relatively minor though hotly contested frontier areas, France's territorial limits were determined far earlier than those of other continental countries. Brought together over centuries by accidents of history rather than by facts of geography or of ethnical origin, Frenchmen have developed a strong sense of national identification. Theirs is an adult "civilization," a term which to them is more meaningful than "culture" or *"Kultur."* It not only denotes a long-term achievement but also encourages missionary zeal to spread its values.

Geographically the country is at once Atlantic, Continental, and Mediterranean, and hence occupies a unique place in Europe. Ethnically, no such thing as a French race exists. "We are a race of half-breeds," a French historian has written; but he added wistfully: "Mongrels are often more intelligent than purebred dogs." [1] Which of their gifts and deficiencies French-

[1] Charles Seignobos, as quoted in André Siegfried, "Approaches to an Understanding of Modern France" in Edward M. Earle (ed.), *Modern France. Problems of the Third and Fourth Republics* (Princeton: Prince-

men owe to the Latins, the Celts, or the Germanic tribes is far
less significant than the fact that in a nation fashioned by
common historical experience, neither regional nor linguistic,
nor even differences between Catholics and Protestants, are
divisive factors as they have been for all of France's neighbors.
Moreover, the existing diversities have been encompassed by a
strong national unity.

The French monarchy played an outstanding role in national integration. It also gave to French national feeling some
of its distinguishing characteristics. Unlike other European
monarchs, the French kings claimed and received, for close to
a thousand years, sacerdotal and religious dignity. Such status
has marked not only French Catholicism but all concepts of
authority.[2] A French monk described the first crusade as *Gesta
Dei per Francos:* the Franks were presented as the chosen
instruments of God. There are other nations that from time to
time have claimed to be pacesetters for the rest of the world.
But among Frenchmen a belief in the universal value of their
own civilization has remained strong whatever the setbacks of
their national destiny. Only recently André Malraux, one-time
left-wing intellectual and now the Fifth Republic's Minister of
Cultural Affairs, voiced the conviction that "with the exception of the Revolution [!] the universal calling of France has
never been as striking as at present."

Claims that attribute general significance to a national
civilization have been common to the political Right and Left.
The very term nationalism in its pejorative sense was coined
to reproach the Jacobins for their all too burning desire to export ideals at the point of French bayonets. In 1793, at the
height of the Terror, "patriotism" described the resolve not
only to defend the soil of *la patrie,* but also to cultivate civic
and republican virtues and to share with other nations the
blessings of the Revolution. The Paris Commune of 1871,
hailed by Karl Marx as the harbinger of a world-wide class
struggle, was in fact an act of defiance addressed to the "Prus-

ton University Press, 1951), p. 4. In some respects Siegfried's article contains still valid generalizations about the political culture of the country.

   [2] Ernst Robert Curtius, *The Civilization of France* (New York: Vintage
Books, 1962), pp. 72 ff.

sian" Bismarck as well as to the bourgeois government at Versailles. The language and thought of Communist and Socialist resistance movements during the Second World War showed the same amalgam of patriotism and democratic values.

Even an insistence on the nation's greatness, its *grandeur,* is not the monopoly of any particular political orientation, for it is raised in the name of a civilization rather than in defense of martial ventures. Jules Michelet, influential historian of the Revolution, wrote sweepingly that the concept of French national *grandeur* belonged to a tradition which was common to the National Convention of 1792 and to St. Louis, the first Bourbon king. More recently, the opening sentences of General de Gaulle's memoirs have given to such a mythology of the nation an expression that already has become classical.

> All my life I have thought of France in a certain way. This is inspired by sentiment as much as by reason. The emotional side of me tends to imagine France like the princess in the fairy stories or the Madonna in the frescoes, as dedicated to an exalted and exceptional destiny. . . . In short, to my mind, France cannot be France without *grandeur.*[3]

However deep the roots of a common national mythology, Frenchmen are divided by conflicting views as to which political system is most appropriate to attain the goal of greatness. If every Frenchman loves France, this does not preclude his little concealed contempt for the Frenchmen outside of his own immediate or political family. When the momentary destiny of the country appears mediocre, he is inclined to impute this to the faults of his fellow-citizen, while the genius of the land remains unimpaired in his eyes.

In all nations, historical events that have created deep divisions have produced a political culture in which the citizens are full of mutual mistrust and low in agreement on fundamentals.[4] It was natural enough that the Revolution of the eighteenth century opened long, drawn out controversies be-

[3] Charles de Gaulle, *War Memoirs,* I: *The Call to Honour* (New York: The Viking Press, 1955), p. 3.

[4] See the observations by Sidney Verba in Lucian W. Pye and Sidney Verba (eds.), *Political Culture and Political Development* (Princeton: Princeton University Press, 1965), p. 556.

tween monarchists and republicans. But it also shook and
split, on the most sensitive level, the conscience of elites and
common people. The Revolution amounted not merely to a
collective apostasy from the Catholic Church, but to such a
violent break with Christianity as, prior to the bolshevik
seizure of power, no other European nation had experienced.
From then on France became the champion of emancipated
reason and yet remained a refuge for Catholic faith.[5] The
sharp political discontinuities, the revolutions and counter-
revolutions of the nineteenth and twentieth centuries, were
in part a consequence of the rift between believers and non-
believers, although they also added new sources of conflict.

The more vividly the conflicts of the past are remembered,
the more heavily they weigh on the behavior of political actors and onlookers. Edmund Burke spoke of society as "a
partnership . . . between those who are living, those who
are dead and those who are to be born." French society appears frequently overcommitted to the experiences of past generations. A habit of historical thinking can prove a bond, but
also — as the American Civil War shows — a hindrance to
consensus. Frenchmen are so fascinated by their own, admittedly exciting, history that the feuds of the past are constantly
superimposed on the conflicts of the present. The passionate
use of historical memories, resulting in seemingly inflexible
commands and warnings, narrows the scope of authoritative
and private decision-making. The old country that is France is,
again in de Gaulle's words, "weighed down by history." [6]

The very nature of political conflicts is in part determined
by the style which defines them. "Politics are ideas," a modern
French writer has claimed.[7] Hence at least at a certain level,
the style of politics will remain as ideological as it became in
the age of the enlightenment when the Old Regime, in order
to compensate for the servile condition to which it had confined the educated classes, left them free to voice their views

---

5 Curtius, *op. cit.,* p. 123.

6 Charles de Gaulle, *op. cit.,* III: *The Salvation* (New York: Simon and
Schuster, 1960), p. 330.

7 Albert Thibaudet, Les Idées Politiques en France (Paris: Stock, 1932).

on many topics. Philosophy, religion, ethics, and even politics could be discussed provided the discussion remained on a general and abstract plane. At about the same time, the bourgeoisie was compelled to abandon those local administrative functions which it had exercised previously. Hence its political initiation, sophisticated though it was, was derived entirely from men of letters and philosophers. "Thus alongside the traditional and confused, not to say chaotic, social system of the day there was gradually built up in [these Frenchmen's] mind[s] an imaginary ideal society in which all was simple, uniform, coherent, equitable, and rational in the full sense of the term." [8]

Since then the urge to discuss a wide range of problems, even the most trivial ones, in broad philosophical terms has not diminished; nor has the endless search to find a solution to the problems of the day in a system, a doctrine, or a faith. In all countries conservatives seek the Platonic idea to which they want to make society conform. But in France the enemies of the republican regime have gone to the extreme of defining their image of France as the *"pays réel,"* the real country, compared to which the existing institutions deserve the contemptuous label of the *"pays légal,"* the merely legal institutions. Yet their opponents can be just as bigoted and doctrinaire when they reject a compromise between conflicting ideologies as an offense to the cartesian method. (There are undertones of this when as lucid a critic of the present political system as Pierre Mendès-France insists on describing the Fifth Republic as a "non-regime.")

Symbols and rituals perpetuate the political style. A pretender to the throne, the Comte de Chambord, might have been able to restore the monarchy in 1873 had he been less unyielding on the issue of a flag for the nation. Today, two rural communities which fought on opposite sides in the

[8] Alexis de Tocqueville, *The Old Régime and the French Revolution* (New York: Doubleday Anchor Books, 1955), pp. 64, 146. For a succinct analysis of the political and social situation during the decades preceding the Revolution, see also Gabriel Almond and G. Bingham Powell, Jr., *Comparative Politics: A Developmental Approach* (Boston: Little, Brown and Company, 1966), pp. 320 f.

French Revolution, pay homage to different heroes nearly two centuries later. In the eyes of an American observer who knows them both, they have no real quarrel with each other. Yet inherited symbols have kept them apart so that their political and religious habits have remained disparate.[9] Formal symbols to which all Frenchmen respond are not entirely lacking but rare. After 1940 the Vichy regime found it necessary to replace on every public building the time-honored "Liberty-Fraternity-Equality" with another triad. In every town and city a considerable number of streets change names with every change in political fortunes. Whether a Paris street should bear the name of Maximilien Robespierre became quite recently the subject of a passionate debate in the Municipal Council.

Abiding faiths create deep hatreds. Since the Jacobins denounced their opponents as "enemies of the people," such accusations have belonged to the arsenal of French political polemics (long before they entered the terminology of modern totalitarianism). In every democratic country, a scandalous mistrial such as that of Captain Dreyfus with its backdrop of intrigue, motivated by antisemitism and caste spirit, would have provoked indignation and possibly prolonged unrest. What was characteristically French was the fact that at the turn of the century *L'Affaire* became a violent conflict over values among the country's elites. Both sides went to fanatical extremes; guilt or innocence of Dreyfus was not a question of evidence but of unshakable dogma. The legacy bequeathed by the upheaval and its aftermath was the confinement of the officers corps and a majority of the practicing Catholics for many decades to a political ghetto, in which they lived apart from the mainstream of national life.

For all its drama, the Dreyfus affair was only one, if characteristic, episode in the political history of a nation united by almost universal admiration for a common historical experience yet divided by conflicting interpretations of its meaning.

[9] Laurence Wylie, "Social Change at the Grass Roots," in Stanley Hoffman *et al., In Search of France* (Cambridge: Harvard University Press, 1963), p. 230.

## TENSIONS BETWEEN REPRESENTATIVE
## AND PLEBISCITARIAN TRADITIONS

Although the controversies between monarchists and republicans have continued well into our century, their effect on the various political systems that have emerged in rapid succession since the Revolution has been less significant than the opposition between the temptations of two other patterns of government. One is identifiable with a representative tradition of democracy, the other with a plebiscitarian.

In the early days of the Revolution, mere lip service was paid to Rousseau's concept postulating the direct participation of the citizenry in the political process. The system then established was based on a belief, shared by most of the middle-class deputies to the National Assembly, that the intentions of the sovereign people could be expressed validly only through its elected representatives; that legislative as well as constituent power should be exclusively in their hands. But a few years later, the constitution of 1793 rejected such views, and denouncing "representative despotism," it tried to organize the general will by annual elections and referendums. But before this Constitution could come into existence it was superseded by revolutionary rule which climaxed in Napoleon's rise to power.[10] His rule set the pattern for a system which was as hostile to the representative ideas of Abbé Sieyès, of the American Constitution, and of the parliamentary monarchies of Europe, as it was to the absolute monarchy of the Old Regime. It was more than a device of political cleverness that for several years French coins bore the double inscription: "French Republic — Napoleon Emperor." Bonaparte claimed to continue the Revolution rather than to abrogate it.

Hence France, just freed from its old shackles, experienced within the short span of a decade two novel and different forms of authority. They were to form the opposite poles be-

[10] The historical background of the two traditions is traced in greater detail by Henry W. Ehrmann, "Direct Democracy in France," *American Political Science Review*, LVII:4 (1963), pp. 883 ff. Cf. also Stanley Hoffmann, "Paradoxes of the French Political Community," in *In Search of France*, p. 14.

tween which French political life has moved ever since, even if
some of the sixteen constitutions under which Frenchmen have
lived since the Revolution have aimed at combining elements
of both traditions. Almost invariably, political life under a
given regime has been determined by one or the other of the
major trends. With each change of regime the tradition which
was temporarily eclipsed lived on as a strong undercurrent
creating perpetual internal tensions.

Since Napoleon Bonaparte was the first to develop the pattern of a political system which claimed that its rule was
sanctioned by the voice of the sovereign people, practices of
direct democracy in France are easily identified with bonapartism. Shorn of all accidentals, the theory and practices of
the two Napoleons scorned intermediaries in state and society
which might stand between the unorganized masses and the
popularly acclaimed head of the executive. There was in their
system room neither for a totalitarian party nor for voluntary
associations. Accordingly, the role of the legislative branch
was reduced; the political life of the nation was carefully circumscribed and potentially extinguished. Any infringement of
constitutional and other laws by the ruler could be given legitimacy by popular approval. The Napoleonic plebiscites combined the threat of social chaos which would follow the demise
of the providential leader with the flattery of the people by
giving them the opportunity of choosing their master directly —
or of perpetuating his rule. The temper of the regime was anti-
individualist: Napoleonic codes and legislation strengthened
the authority of the head of the family, of the employer, of the
administrative official.[11]

What distinguishes French bonapartism from other forms of
caesarism is the allegiance it paid to certain Jacobin traditions
of the Revolution. At all times, Napoleon's appeals to the
masses over the heads of the traditional notables had egalitarian undertones. During the Hundred Days, the returning
emperor discovered the possibilities of a "people's bonapart-

[11] For the plebiscitarian ideology of bonapartism cf. Robert Michels,
*Political Parties* (New York: Collier Books, 1962), pp. 212–219 and the
excellent recent treatment by René Rémond, *La Vie Politique en France,
1789–1848* (Paris: Armand Colin, 1965), pp. 221–247.

ism." From then on the Napoleonic legend, on which Napoleon's nephew Louis Bonaparte would draw in his campaign for a popularly elected republican presidency, was distinctly tinged with egalitarian socialism — or at least with its terminology. The constitution of the Second Empire (as would that of the Fifth Republic) explicitly referred to the "principles of 1789" and boasted of having given the constituent power back to the people.

With the demise of Napoleon III, the opposite, representative tradition established itself firmly and exercised its sway with only short interruptions until turmoil in Algeria returned General de Gaulle to power. But during every crisis of the Third and Fourth Republics, the critics of the existing system liked to argue in terms established by bonapartism. All political parties were condemned as hampering the expression of a general will — assumed to be unequivocal on all major political decisions. Parliament was likened to a broken mirror misrepresenting the true interests of the electorate. Popular sovereignty should be reestablished by giving the voters the amending power and the right to vote in referendums. The executive should be enabled to rule efficiently above and despite political and social divisions. Such detailed and fundamental criticism of the parliamentary regime, to be sure came either from a vocal minority of intellectuals and publicists or from men that put themselves forward as an alternative to the existing regime. But antiparliamentary feelings, both vague and vehement, were at times quite widespread and frequently associated with longings for a strong-man rule. The tenacity of this mood even during the height of the representative regime tended to put the latter's protagonists on the defensive and drove them to exaggerations.

To the authentic spokesmen of the representative tradition, the essence of democratic government consisted in the close control of an ever-suspected executive and in the defense of constituency interests, however fragmented they might be. For such tasks the deputy, "entrenched, fortified and undefeatable in his constituency like the feudal lord of old in his castle," [12]

[12] Alain, *Éléments de la Doctrine Radicale* (Paris: Gallimard, 1925), p. 42. The (unfortunately untranslated) writings of the curious philosopher-

was superbly qualified. He could be counted upon to decide
for himself, without directives from an extraparliamentary
body — even a political party — how best to resist authority.
Any direct appeal to the people was viewed as a manifestation
of "supreme decadence." In fact, historical experiences had
instilled in deputies and senators such fear of executive leadership and of the popular acclaim it might seek, that they
frowned upon any address by a political leader which was not
made either from the tribune of parliament or within the
narrow confines of his small constituency. Paul Reynaud,
perennial deputy throughout three republican regimes, gave
perfect expression to this tradition during the debate on President de Gaulle's proposal for a constitutional referendum. He
condemned the very idea of consulting the French electorate
on a question of constitutional revision. "For us republicans,"
he scorned, "France exists only here [in parliament] and nowhere else."

It will be explained below (Chaps. V and VIII) why republican France has never developed a modern party system of
the kind which, in other democracies, has accomplished the
necessary transformation of parliament "from the representative corporation which it was into a plebiscitary expedient." [13]
In the absence of such a system, the tensions created by the
oligarchic deformations of the representative traditions and
the caesaristic temptations of plebiscitarian regimes have never
been resolved.

### TENSIONS BETWEEN BUREAUCRATIC
### TRADITIONS AND INDIVIDUALISM

To both distrust government and expect much from it is a
widespread ambivalence of modern times, which might well
betray some unresolved inner conflict about the interaction

---

journalist Alain are indispensable for an understanding of the French
version of the representative system and of the period during which it
flowered, i.e., the first thirty years of the present century. For a recent
evaluation of Alain's significance, see Roy Pierce, *Contemporary French
Political Thought* (London and New York: Oxford University Press, 1966),
pp. 4–10.

[13] Gerhard Leibholz, "The Nature and Various Forms of Democracy,"
*Social Research*, VII (1938), p. 99.

of government and society.[14] In most countries this ambivalence is a consequence of the rise of the modern service-state
which is unavoidably burdened with ever new tasks. But in
France such feelings can again be traced to centuries-old traditions. The Old Regime, and especially the long reign of Louis
XV, gave the country a rigidly centralized administration,
recruited and operated according to functional criteria. Its
activities reached deep into many phases of economic and social life. It proved so all pervasive that it "deprived Frenchmen of the possibility and even the desire to come to each
other's aid. When the Revolution started it would have been
impossible to find . . . even ten men used to acting in concert and defending their interests without appealing to the
central power for aid." [15] What sheltered the individual from
constant interference by governmental authorities was, in an
age of underdeveloped communications, the relative remoteness of the central government which had not abolished the
existing patchwork of local privileges and traditions of lax
enforcement.

The Jacobins and Napoleon took over the techniques and,
frequently, the men which the monarchy had bequeathed to
them and used them for their political ends. The egalitarian
temper of sans-culottism, bent as it was on uprooting privileges wherever they had survived, became soon hostile to
hopes for a federal structure of government alive during the
early days of the Revolution. The demand for equality was
to be satisfied by the greatest possible uniformity of rules,
over which an ever stronger, better qualified, and more centralized administration was to watch. The more significant the
central power became, the more tenacious grew the fight for
its control. Because the stakes were high, political forces not
only denied the wisdom of their opponents, which is normal,
but contested the very legitimacy of their power or of their
claim to power.

The French citizen's fear and distrust of authority and his
simultaneous need for strong authority feed on both his indi-

---

[14] Cf. Felix Frankfurter, *The Public and Its Government* (New Haven:
Yale University Press, 1930), pp. 3–4.
[15] Tocqueville, *op. cit.*, p. 206.

vidualism and his passion for equality. In France social mobility has remained steady if limited; a preindustrial mentality
shared by the peasantry and the bourgeoisie has persisted
(for details see Chaps. II and III). Such a country produces a
self-reliant individual who is convinced that he owes to himself (and perhaps to his immediate family) what he is and
what he may become. In his eyes the obstacles in his way are
created by the outside world, the "they" that operate beyond
the circle of the family, the family firm, the village. Most of
the time, however, "they" are identified with the government.

> The government is made up of incompetents, swindlers or
> fools, who are usurping the function of the state. The govern-
> ment is that which prefers someone else. The government is
> that which threatens the family property through taxes. The
> government is that which threatens the established order
> through partisan legislation. The government is that authority
> which must be checkmated or exploited through seduction, si-
> lence and systematic obstruction.[16]

A stock of memories reaching possibly all the way from the
eighteenth century through the most recent wars is used to
justify a state of mind which is one of latent, even if seldom
actual, insubordination. If the government is nefarious, it
must be controlled and is not looked upon as a possible source
of reform. The authentic republican tradition is again exemplified by Alain's "radical doctrine": the government deserves
distrust without revolt, and obedience without commitment.
A strong government is considered *ipso facto* reactionary, even
if it pretends to follow a politically progressive course of action. Such deeply ingrained beliefs explain why, over the span
of history, authoritarian regimes have originated more fundamental transformations of society and state than representative regimes.

Since the citizen feels that no one but himself can be entrusted with the defense of his interests, he is inclined to shun
constructive cooperation. He fears that the discipline involved
in any cooperation might put social constraints on him. Where

[16] Jesse R. Pitts, "Continuity and Change in Bourgeois France," in *In
Search of France,* p. 260.

he participates in public life, he hopes to weaken authority rather than to encourage change, even when change is overdue.

At times this commitment to individualism is tainted with outright anarchistic tendencies. Yet, inasmuch as it is wedded to a sharp sense of equality, it is quite able to accommodate itself to bureaucratic rule. Especially on the lower level of administration, the government may act through incompetent civil servants whom the citizens are wont to criticize as unjust masters. Another French philosopher, Charles Péguy, has spoken sarcastically of that one true division between Frenchmen, more marked than all class division — the one between those who wait in front of an official's window and those who sit behind it.

But however despised the government and its officials, the abstract entity that is the state is indispensable since it safeguards the uniform rulings which guarantee equality of treatment. The farther removed and hence the more centralized that entity is, the more acceptable are the solutions which it imposes from above. They permit the citizen to escape responsibility for resolving conflicts and to avoid face-to-face relationships with either his peers or his superiors.[17] This in turn gives to the administration enough leeway to stand firm amidst the vagaries of the political system. Its rulings might meet with the derision and bitterness of the citizenry; they will still be condoned as guaranteeing egalitarian standards. This explains the often noted paradox that traditionally France, the country of weak governments, appears as a strong state until an acute crisis reveals the feebleness of state and government.

Thus individualism and administrative centralization, both fostered by the same Jacobin temperament, are complementary and able to mitigate their mutual effects. The pattern of authority created thereby is neither liberal nor totalitarian, but has been characterized as the coexistence of *limited* authoritarianism and *potential* insurrection against authority.[18]

[17] All the writings of Michel Crozier have emphasized with fascinating details, the basic avoidance of face-to-face relationships in French society. They are summarized and expanded in his study, *The Bureaucratic Phenomenon* (Chicago: The University of Chicago Press, 1964), esp. pp. 220 ff. For more detailed treatment see below, esp. Chaps. III and VI.

[18] Hoffmann, *op. cit.*, p. 8.

The attitudes of the deliberately distrustful French are quite different from those of the British who in their political attitudes reflect the basic trust characteristic of their social relationships. In neither (and no) society is equality fully achieved. But in England it is often not valued as a goal,[19] while in France the concern for equality far outranks the value placed on liberty.

## CONSEQUENCES FOR THE POLITICAL SYSTEM

There have been long-standing discussions among Frenchmen and among foreign observers of the French political scene as to the moment when the political system became unable to deal successfully with the tasks incumbent upon it. The apparent contradictions in the behavior of individuals and of groups are, in fact, the result of tensions, themselves the consequence of historical experiences reaching back to the period of the absolute monarchy.

Even though in fact the Revolution of 1789 did not effect as complete a break with the past as is commonly believed, it has conditioned the general outlook on crisis and compromise, on continuity and change. Sudden rather than gradual mutation, dramatic conflicts couched in the language of opposing and mutually exclusive, radical ideologies — these are the experiences that excite Frenchmen at historical moments when their minds are particularly malleable. Even at the end of the nineteenth century, history itself appeared to an illustrious French historian, Ernest Renan, as a "kind of civil war." In fact, what appears to the outsider as permanent instability is a fairly regular alternation between violent crises and more or less prolonged periods of routine.

It is perhaps noteworthy that in France there is an abundance of political biographies of the figures of exalted times, but hardly any of the great parliamentary leaders, to say nothing of administrators or judges. To contend that Frenchmen, whether illustrious or humble, "love" crisis may be invidious. But they have become accustomed to think that no thoroughgoing change can ever be brought about except through a

[19] Richard Rose, *Politics in England* (Boston: Little, Brown and Company, 1964), pp. 39, 43.

major upheaval. Since the great Revolution, every adult Frenchman has experienced — usually more than once in his lifetime — occasions of political excitement followed by disappointment. This leads periodically to moral exhaustion and almost permanent and widespread scepticism regarding any possibility of change. The aphorism that "The more things change, the more they stay the same," may be quite worn, but it still expresses general feelings.

In addition to the factors discussed so far wars and other pressures from the international environment have constantly sharpened crises. Before the Revolution the very development of the French nation and state was closely related to many of the dynastic conflicts of Europe. Since then many of the political upheavals and constitutional breaks were caused by, or at least connected with, wars in which the country became embroiled. Whether they originated within the country or were brought about by international conflicts, each of the frequent national emergencies has resulted in a constitutional crisis. Each time the social and political forces emerging temporarily triumphant codified their norms and philosophy, usually in a comprehensive document. Hence, to give only a few examples, the constitutions of 1791, 1830, 1875, and 1946 enshrined the representative principle and Montesquieu's precepts; those of 1793 and of 1848 belong partly, those of 1852 and of 1958 (especially as amended in 1962) more frankly to the plebiscitarian tradition. Because of such practices, constitutions have never played the role of fundamental charters, nor have they laid down generally accepted rules for the political game. Their conflicting norms are satisfactory only to one segment of public opinion and are hotly contested by the others. This in turn invites a lack of respect for fundamental norms that are viewed as being forever in flux.

The highly ideological and historically oriented language of politics has deepened the chasm between actual and declared policies. To wrap the political discontent of the day in metaphysics, to give to the tritest discussion the dignity of philosophy, has not furthered the French contribution to political theory, in spite of some brilliant thinkers.

The prevailing style of debate has encouraged a proclivity

for "false conflicts." To the degree that behavior of the political actors and of the electorate corresponds to past alignments,
it is unsuited to the solution of actual conflicts. On the other
hand, when finding solutions and accommodating conflicting
interests by compromise finally becomes unavoidable, such
agreements are reached without any reference to fundamentals.
This increases the contempt not only for politicians but for
the political way of life itself as seemingly betraying the principles by which men ought to live. Middle-of-the-road politics
are considered a "swamp": the center is an eternal *"marais"*
which muddies every forthright action. As far as possible, the
political system is put outside the rational and emotional
loyalty of the citizens, which strengthens their nonparticipa-
tory disposition. "Turbulence on the one side," a French sociologist has concluded, "and a nearly unbelievable tolerance
of the provisionary and the confused on the other, are evidence that the French do not take social situations seriously." [20]

The high sensitivity of the public at moments of crisis and
its withdrawal into apathy during periods of unexciting routine are again only different aspects of the same phenomenon.
Although the pulling back of the public from the political
game and its exclusive devotion to private life is observed not
only in France, the absence of a modern party system mediat-
ing between the public and its government, the insensitivity of
parliament and of the administration to currents of public
opinion has at different periods rendered the alienation of
the French citizen more acute than in other modern democracies, even though electoral participation remains generally
high. An approaching major crisis is usually foreshadowed
rather precisely by a lack of support for the regime, a lack
which sometimes is expressed in the flash successes of extremist
parties,[21] in tax evasion or outright resistance to tax collection,
and in fiery debates on the next, and better, constitution.

[20] François Bourricaud, "France" in Arnold M. Rose (ed.), *The Institutions of Advanced Societies* (Minneapolis: University of Minnesota Press,
1958), p. 520; cf. also Otto Kirchheimer, "France from the Fourth to the
Fifth Republic," *Social Research*, XXV:4 (1958), pp. 382–83.

[21] In all elections held between 1947 and 1956, extremist parties,
opposed to the very foundations of the existing order, obtained about 40
per cent of the votes.

That Frenchmen are people difficult to govern is a common-place voiced in over-quoted statements by Caesar, Tocqueville, and, most recently, by one of the country's present preceptors, the first Prime Minister of the Fifth Republic, Michel Debré. Historical events have brought this about. The subsequent chapters will show in greater detail the mutual influence of values and beliefs, of political institutions, and of the economic and social setting.

# CHAPTER II

# The Economic and
# Social Setting

## THE IMPACT OF RECOVERY

Unevenness in economic development and strains in the social structure resulting from such unevenness, have their impact on the political process and the political culture of any given country. In the case of France it is no longer necessary to argue whether or not in economic terms the country is a perennially retarded developer. She was regarded as such when for nearly eighty years her economic growth was the slowest of all developed countries (about 1.1 per cent annually). But the economic vitality manifest during much of the Fourth Republic and consolidated since then has put France into the ranks of the highly industrialized countries of Western Europe. There is little likelihood that she will lose that position even if political instability were to overtake her again.

Explanations for the massive recovery and rapid modernization vary as greatly as did those for the earlier sluggishness. For this and other reasons a valid political analysis of present-day France cannot dispense with a discussion of the setting in which the resurgence of the economy has taken place. It is especially necessary to determine, however summarily, the respective roles which changes in attitude and transformations of the institutional setup have played; what have been the impulses coming from the international environment and which have been domestic in origin. That such mutations as have occurred are not uniform and that therefore the modernization process remains uneven, is not peculiar to France. As elsewhere, but probably more than elsewhere, the behavior of Frenchmen as producers and consumers is intimately related to their general value and belief system. Hence it is useful to analyze at which point traditional attitudes prevail or are replaced, and where such attitudes are likely to spill over into political behavior.

In terms of per capita gross national product, France at present ranks among the wealthiest nations of Western Europe (in 1965: $1,922, as compared with $2,724 in the U.S.), right behind Germany but ahead of the United Kingdom, and nearly twice as prosperous as Italy. Since 1950, the annual rate of economic growth has always been close to 5 per cent. Equally satisfactory and steady has been the average annual increase in productivity since 1950 — 4.5 per cent.[1]

What should not be forgotten is that in large part such growth is merely a catching up on past retardation. While the record of the interwar years had been altogether undistinguished, the decade preceding the outbreak of hostilities in 1939 had been catastrophic for economic development; then the German occupation brought new disaster. Statistically, economic development profited from a low starting point. Altogether, and especially in comparison with other Common Market countries which in general have advanced more steadily, French progress has been more than respectable without reaching the proportions of an "economic miracle."[2]

Economists and demographers will continue to argue about the respective significance of population trends and economic growth at various stages of economic development. For France

[1] These and most of the following statistical data are from Bernard Mueller, *A Statistical Handbook of the North Atlantic Area* (New York: The Twentieth Century Fund, 1965); U.N. Statistical Yearbook 1966 (New York: United Nations, 1967) or from Institut National de la Statistique et des Etudes Economiques, *Annuaire Statistique de la France, 1964* (Paris: Imprimerie Nationale, 1965).

[2] This point is made in what I consider the most careful study of French economic development, A. Cotta, "La Croissance de l'Economie Française, 1945–1975," *Analyse et Prévision*, II:1–2 (1966), pp. 519–560, at p. 533.

there is no doubt that the slow growth of her population since 1850, a declining birth rate and a net reproduction rate below the level of replacement, had not only an adverse economic but, even worse, a disastrous psychological effect. Widely publicized pictures of the age pyramid showed quite dramatically the direct and indirect effect of the First World War: the total population deficit (composed of the dead and of the children that were not born because of the war) amounted to over three million people, i.e., 7–8 per cent of the prewar population. Until quite recently, conversations about the future of France turned frequently to the consequences of this tragic loss for the country's vitality, for its labor force, and leadership. And, the losses that had been sustained were not made up during the interwar period. The population grew at a rate less than half that of Germany, becoming almost stagnant with the depression. The continuation of interwar trends would have meant a population of 39 million by 1960 and 36.9 million by 1970. Instead, and in spite of substantial new losses caused by the Second World War, the population reached the 50 million mark in 1967 (at about the same time the United States population rose to 200 million) and it is estimated it will be 51.2 million by the beginning of the next decade. The annual increase is likely to level at about half a million per year. Within the age pyramid, the proportion of those under twenty years of age expands so fast that France today is one of the "youngest" nations of Europe.

Part of this upswing is undoubtedly due to a systematic policy of material inducements, such as family allowances and other devices. Since 1939, with unusual consistency every successive regime enacted measures favorable to population growth. There is, however, ample evidence to show that the drastic upward swing in the size of families is due principally to a change in attitudes towards procreation. Demographic malthusianism was particularly widespread among the bourgeoisie and the peasants. To them too numerous a progeny meant the dividing up of land, of business property, and of inheritance. By limiting the possibilities for a better education, it might destroy class status or upward mobility. Worse yet, it might upset the carefully preserved equilibrium of society at large. If now former restraints are being overcome and a new view of family life prevails, this seems to be indicative of a "more trustful and future-oriented view of the human condition." [3]

It must not be forgotten, however, that in spite of impressive increases France remains lowest in population density among the six Common Market countries. In the "garden that is France" (and French children are commonly taught to think of their country in this way) there live only 221 persons per square mile, as compared with 571 in West Germany and 783 in Belgium. If France had the same population density as other major European powers, there should be more than 125 million Frenchmen — and in fact, both President de Gaulle and Michel Debré have at times evoked the ambitious vision of a nation of one hundred million!

Apart from the population increase itself, the most remarkable demographic development since the war has been the mobility of this growing population. Geographical and professional mobility have supported each other; while both have been an important stimulus to modernization, they also have unavoidably generated certain tensions contingent upon it. Many developments which other Western societies have been undergoing since the end of the last century have been taking place in France only since the last war. Some of them, such as the exodus from the countryside, have occurred with such rapidity that census figures have surprised even the best-informed.

On the eve of the war, the proportion of the active population employed in agriculture was still at a high 37 per cent; twenty-five years later it is now below 20 per cent. Industry employs now 38 per cent as against 30 per cent, while employment in the tertiary sector (commerce, services, and administration) has risen from 36 to 42 per cent. (In as highly developed a country as the United States, it is true, the corresponding figures for the three sectors are 8 per cent, 30 per cent, and 56 per cent respectively; in both West Germany and Great Britain industrial employment amounts to 47 per cent). At the same

[3] Crozier, *op. cit.,* p. 307, and Charles P. Kindleberger, "The Postwar Resurgence of the French Economy," in *In Search of France,* pp. 131–135.

*The New Regional Organization of France*

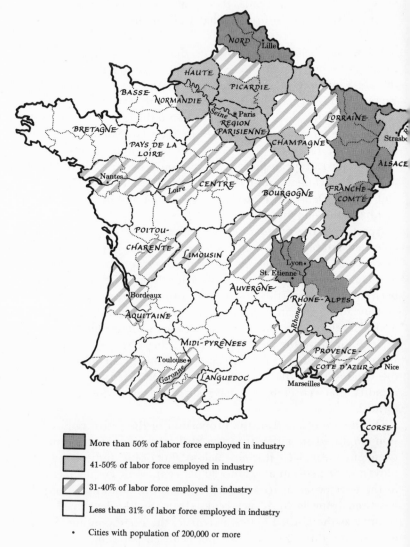

More than 50% of labor force employed in industry

41-50% of labor force employed in industry

31-40% of labor force employed in industry

Less than 31% of labor force employed in industry

• Cities with population of 200,000 or more

Adapted from *Atlas Historique de la France Contemporaine 1800-1965*
(Paris: Colin, 1966), pp. 38, 47

*Geographical Distribution of "Yes" Vote in the Referendum of October 28, 1962*

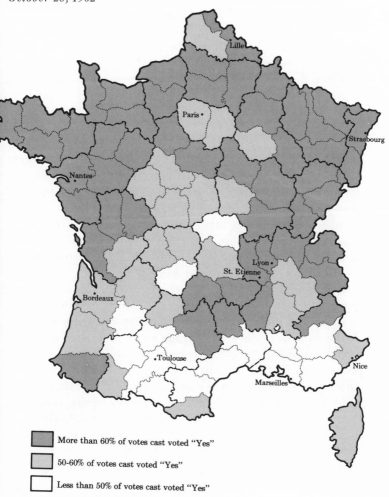

More than 60% of votes cast voted "Yes"

50-60% of votes cast voted "Yes"

Less than 50% of votes cast voted "Yes"

time, the proportion within the total labor force of employers, self-employed, and unpaid family workers is steadily declining, while that of wage and salary earners rises to figures that are average for Western Europe — a striking development for a country that traditionally has been one of small enterprises and of independent farmers.

Before the war 48 per cent of the population lived in rural communities of fewer than 2,000 inhabitants; only 38 per cent do so at present. Villages of less than 1,000 population are being deserted, especially by the young, at such a rate that in certain parts of the country this movement is toppling local social and economic structures. At the other end of the scale the development is almost as striking: In 1936, there were in the entire country only 16 cities with a population of more than 100,000. At the time of the last census (1962) there were 30 such cities, and now almost one Frenchman in five lives in one of these metropolitan areas. But only ten cities have more than 200,000 inhabitants (as against 26 cities of this size in West Germany and 20 in Great Britain).

If compared with other industrialized countries of Western Europe French urbanization appears slow, it has already had an important impact on French mentality and living habits — all the more so as the growth of big and middle-sized cities has brought many people still living in rural communities into professional and social contact with urban life and preoccupations. A recent national sample reveals that geographical mobility has reached proportions that are quite novel for France: at present 20 per cent live in a region different from that in which they were born; 15 per cent have moved from another community within the last five years, and 15 per cent expect not to stay for the rest of their lives in their present place of residence.

Population shifts and a corresponding redistribution of national wealth have, on the whole, accented rather than mitigated traditional differences. The increase in population has profited only one-third of the country; more than two-thirds of the ninety departments into which the country is divided have now a lower population than in 1950. As early as the seventeenth and eighteenth centuries, royal edicts tried to put a stop to the growth of Paris; present-day attempts are similarly unsuccessful. By 1965, 9.2 million people, i.e., close to one-fifth of the entire French nation and more than one-fourth of its total urban population, lived in the metropolitan region of Paris. The yearly increase, especially in the outlying districts, is now almost two and one-half times that of the rest of the country. This creates, as in other metropolitan areas of the world, staggering problems on every level. But in a country with centuries-old traditions of administrative, economic, and cultural centralization, it has also produced a dramatic gap in human and material resources between Paris and the rest of the country. The per capita income of individuals in the Paris region is about 60 per cent higher than the national average; the regions that rank next in wealth are barely reaching that average. The difference between them and the capital is about twice as great as that between them and the poorest region of France. "Paris and the French desert," was the alarming catchphrase used to describe the imbalance that had developed. However, vigorous economic growth and the progressive development of other urban centers have alleviated the situation somewhat.

Another economic division of the country, dating back at least to the Second Empire, also continues to exist. So far, efforts to overcome it have proven hardly more fruitful than the attempts to halt the population influx into the Paris region. France west of a line that runs from Le Havre to Grenoble and thence to Marseilles is, in comparison to the rest of the country, as underdeveloped as is the south of Italy. The western part of the country comprises 56 per cent of its territory and 37 per cent of its total population. But 80 per cent of the country's industrial production and 76 per cent of industrial employment are located east of the line. In the East where farming is intensive, only 15 per cent are employed in agriculture. In the West live 35 per cent or two-thirds of the entire agricultural population. Here the massive flight from the countryside can be expected to continue, while in the East the optimum distribution between the various occupations may have been reached.

Traditionally and, as we will see, politically, the division of

the country north and south of the Loire River has been a
salient factor. Now, growing differences and tensions, breaking occasionally into open revolts, arise between the rapidly
developing regions northeast of the Le Havre–Marseilles line
and the regions which are losing population and are lagging in
investment, productivity, and, with some expectations, new
industries. The demands of the dynamic and the static parts
of the country are in conflict, and governmental intervention
cannot easily reconcile them without slowing down overall
growth.[4]

### "FRANCE WITHOUT PEASANTS?" [5]

As we have seen, by comparison with other highly developed
industrial countries, the agricultural sector of France remains
both economically and politically important. Cultivated acre-
age amounts to about half of that of the six Common Market
countries combined; agriculture furnishes still about 9.2 per
cent of the gross domestic product (as against 4.2 per cent in
the United States). Between 1954 and 1962, more than 1.3 million people left agricultural employment, and the movement is
expected to continue at an annual rate of at least 120,000 —
about every ten minutes a farm closes down as an independent
unit of production. Nonetheless, agricultural production does
not decline. In (constant) francs, its value has almost tripled
over the last seven years; the number of tractors in use and the
consumption of fertilizers have soared; and the increase of
productivity in farming is far higher than in the rest of the
economy.

Yet, in spite of modernization and intensified cultivation,
the average net income of the drastically reduced agricultural
population is just about half that of the rest of the nation. In
fact, because specialization and productivity progress at very
different rates in different regions, such averages distort reality
even more than usual. An executive of the most important

[4] See François Goguel, "Six Authors in Search of a National Character,"
in *In Search of France*, pp. 380 ff.

[5] This is the suggestive title of a useful book which discusses the agri-
cultural situation, past and present, with a great amount of data — Michel
Gervais, Claude Servolin, Jean Weil, *Une France sans Paysans* (Paris:
Editions du Seuil, 1965).

farmers' organization told his constituents that in the country as a whole one out of every three farms, i.e., a total of almost 800,000 farms, are too small to be economically viable. These units also lack the resources and the technical knowledge to adapt to market conditions.

Even those who rightly refuse to explain the unimpressive performance of the French economy in the past by single facts agree that the survival of the marginal family farm played an important role in the economic backwardness of the country. "The peasant destroyed the feudal regime [at the time of the Revolution]," it has been said, "but he consolidated the agrarian structure of France." [6] When towards the end of the last century the multicrop, nonintensive production methods of the small family farm had become obsolete, the French peasants were not driven off the land as was the case in Great Britain. The republican government and its Minister of Agriculture, Jules Méline, came to their aid with massive measures of protectionism. Behind sheltering tariff walls French farmers (as well as small businessmen) were able to cling to established routines.[7] In a sense, France never repealed its corn laws.

Although French agriculture was favored by soil and climate, it fell behind other European countries. Schoolbooks as well as eminent writers exalted the peasantry as the mainstay of a harmoniously balanced economy and society. In fact, a web of protective regulations, including exorbitant tariffs and other privileges, isolated the rural sector of the economy from the mainstream of national life. At different periods protectionism took on different forms. But the mentality which originated in the Méline era has not everywhere run its course.

Modernization, underway since the last war, has brought a "silent revolution" to the countryside. The Planning Commissariate gave it its impetus (see below); now the European Common Market offers certain sectors of French agriculture

---

[6] Georges Lefebvre, "La Révolution Française et les paysans," *Etudes sur la Révolution Française* (Paris: Presses Universitaires, 1954), p. 256.

[7] For background and details of this politically all-important legislation, see Gordon Wright, *France in Modern Times* (Chicago: Rand McNally, 1960), pp. 346 ff.

expanded possibilities for export. Where this is true the rural sector can overcome its previous isolation from other parts of the French economy and from other countries. In many places even the most stubborn individualism seems to be waning; new habits of cooperation are observed which are unlikely to turn, as they have in the past, into restrictive corporatist practices. The rural interest groups have brought to some key posts men that represent the younger generation and the poor regions of mixed agriculture. (For details see Chap. VII.) Together with a number of influential civil servants and backed by the government, the younger peasant leaders have drafted legislation which seeks a new solution to the old problems of ensuring parity between the farmers and other sectors of the economy. While price guarantees and market supports have by no means disappeared, more attention is paid to "group agriculture" — for instance the joint exploitation of adjoining family farms, or the cooperative processing and marketing of products. The consolidation of marginal holdings, the improvement of a particularly inadequate technical education, and further mechanization and experimentation are used as avenues for long-range structural reforms. As yet, the success of these ambitious reforms is in doubt.

What might prove most important and in the end decisive is a change in mentality, observed by some, doubted by others. Instead of an inheritance and a property title, farming is considered by many members of the young generation a profession for which proficiency can and must be acquired. When a leased farm promises more certain gain than the family farm, the latter should be abandoned. If such concepts spread, the silent revolution is likely to transform much of rural France. "The great mass of precapitalist peasants [would be replaced] by a smaller, more coherent, more prosperous stratum of independent farmers, rather like those of Britain or the American Middle West." [8]

---

[8] Gordon Wright, *Rural Revolution in France. The Peasantry in the Twentieth Century* (Stanford: Stanford University Press, 1964), p. 179. For the best up-to-date account of the development of French agriculture in the Fifth Republic, see François-H. de Virieu, *La Fin d'une Agriculture* (Paris: Calmann-Lévy, 1967).

## THE ENTREPRENEURIAL SYSTEM

The complement of the family farm is the French family firm. More than half of the 770,000 industrial enterprises belong to individuals; another third are classified as *"entreprises artisanales"* (craftsmen). Close to 80 per cent of the commercial firms do not employ a single salaried employee, only 17 per cent of them employ more than fifty. In industry over one-third of all wage earners work in firms employing from 1 to 50, another third in firms employing between 51 and 500. Although the number of joint stock and limited liability corporations has more than doubled during the last ten years, the family firms and partnerships still claim a considerable share of total business transactions. Large concerns are not lacking, and in several sectors (automobiles, chemicals, electricity) they dominate. In a single recent year (1965), consolidations and concentrations increased fourfold over earlier years. But firms doing a yearly business of $2 million amount to less than 2 per cent of the total number of firms (up from 0.14 per cent ten years ago) and are practically nonexistent in many sectors which in other countries are controlled by large concerns. The annual sales of the largest French corporation ranks fifty-fifth among American firms, eighteenth among European firms. General Motors and Standard Oil combined do an annual business equal to the total business of the 500 largest French firms.

But size, dispersion, and concentration are not the only factors that determine the efficiency of an economy. Past discussions have emphasized the obstacles which the mentality of the patrimonial employer, his extreme individualism, and his concern for secretiveness and stability have put in the way of economic development. On the whole, and brilliant exceptions notwithstanding, the performance of the family firm has been found mediocre both in terms of technical innovation and of support given to economic growth. Fears of glutting the market were stronger than willingness to expand. Vigorous competition was considered inadvisable since bankruptcies might upset the social status of other bourgeois families. Business associations, though never as strong as in fully developed capitalistic countries, had usually enough authority to enforce a price level which permitted inefficient high-cost producers to stay in business.[9] (Even today, the average age of industrial firms is about four times that of concerns in other developed countries.) These attitudes limited domestic demand and closed foreign markets to firms that were never export minded to begin with.

While a scarcity of investment capital might in part have been caused by such practices of "economic malthusianism" (a term quite common in France), the continuing scarcity also perpetuated these practices since savings were either hoarded or placed abroad. The outcome was that the country was saddled with many of the problems of industrialism without fully enjoying its material benefits.

Until recently, society did not fully reward success in business ventures, though it regarded failure as justification for the relatively low esteem in which the business community was held. Much of this was due to a belief, not uncommon in Catholic and Latin cultures, that moneymaking lacked nobility. Hence the most talented sons of the bourgeoisie sought careers in the professions or in the civil service. Only as a last resort might they turn to running the family enterprise.[10]

Since prerevolutionary times, entrepreneurial timidity was partly compensated for by the role which the French state played in technological innovation and economic development. The royal *fermiers,* Colbert's mercantilism, and the way in which Napoleon III's entourage interpreted the doctrines of Saint-Simon created traditions which considered government the motor, not a parasite, of the national economy. In terms of Max Weber, a "politically oriented capitalism" emerged and was accepted with the same ambivalence which characterizes French attitudes towards authority in general: protection and promotion by the state were at the same time expected and dreaded. The tradition bound patrimonial em-

[9] For a detailed treatment see, Henry W. Ehrmann, *Organized Business in France* (Princeton: Princeton University Press, 1957), *passim.* It should, however, be noted that much of the material in this book is now dated.
[10] See Cotta, *op. cit.,* p. 534. The abundant literature, mostly American, on this subject has recently been ably summarized and critized by Crozier, *op. cit.,* pp. 272 ff. See also Kindleberger, *loc. cit.*

ployer, producing or distributing for a local or at best regional market, felt harmed, not benefited, by governmental intervention and regulation. On the other hand, the managers of modern and larger enterprises had long accepted the positive role of government, notwithstanding certain flamboyant pronouncements to the contrary.

At present the situation in industry is not unlike that in agriculture. The old structures, many of them essentially pre-capitalistic, have by no means disappeared and are evolving only gradually; pressures for change are emerging from the modernized sectors of the economy, both public and private, from the new European institutions, and from the younger generations in business and the bureaucracy; the respective values of stability and of competition, of privilege and of innovation, of individual achievement and of cooperation, are under scrutiny.

As often in French history, a major crisis was needed to set an overrigid system in motion. The Second World War and its aftermath provided the crisis. It compelled the communities which make up French society finally to accept the conditions of a modern welfare economy, even where these conditions run counter to long established traditions.

## A MODERN WELFARE ECONOMY

The French economy of today has been characterized as being "less capitalistic and more socialistic than the economies of other European nations." [11] While essentially true, such a diagnosis needs elaboration and refinement before its political implications can be understood.

Government operated business enterprises have existed in France since before the Revolution in widely diversified fields — fields which in other countries of Western Europe are under private ownership. For centuries France has illustrated the proposition that the relationship of public to private enterprise in a society is more a function of a country's cultural heritage than of its level of development. Contingencies of politics and

[11] Raymond Aron, *France, Steadfast and Changing.* (Cambridge: Harvard University Press, 1960), p. 62. Recently the French Prime Minister Georges Pompidou made a similar statement.

of leadership rather than the degree of modernity determine the way in which public regulation of enterprise is exercised.[12]

The strongest impulses for a wider public sector arose during the periods of the Popular Front (1936–37) and after the Liberation (1944–45). For mixed reasons, economic, political, and ideological, the legislature proceeded with a great number of nationalizations.

At present, the government operates all or part of the following: railroading; almost all energy production (mining, electricity, etc.) and telecommunication (radio and television); most air and maritime transport; most of the aeronautic industry; 60 per cent of bank deposits; 40 per cent of insurance premiums; one-third of the automobile industry; one-third of the housing industry — in addition to the old state monopolies of post, telephone, telegraph, tobacco, match and salt manufacture, and sundry less important activities. Public concerns account for more than 10 per cent of the gross national product; their investments represent more than one-third of the gross capital formation of all enterprises. Fifteen per cent of the total active population, or 27 per cent of all salary and wage earners (agricultural labor not included), are paid directly by the state either as civil servants or on a contractual basis. Their income comes close to one-third of the total sum of wages and salaries.

It is impossible to generalize on the ways in which so large a public sector is run. There exist substantial differences in legal structure, control, and management personnel among the various enterprises. After difficult beginnings during the immediate postwar period, political influence in the newly nationalized industries has all but vanished. In terms of productivity and modernization, the record of the nationalized firms is far more favorable than in Great Britain. Massive investments have helped to make many nationalized concerns pacesetters for an entire industry or branch of industry, and governmental banking institutions are playing an important role in the otherwise still limited financial market.

[12] C. E. Black, *The Dynamics of Modernization* (New York: Harper & Row, 1966), pp. 17–18. For a general view of government control of French industry since the war, see John Sheahan, *Promotion and Control of Industry in Post-War France* (Cambridge: Harvard University Press, 1963).

Most important is the fact that the public sector is now thoroughly integrated with the economy as a whole. Private business, especially corporate management, has abandoned its initial hostility and clearly settled for cooperation. In the most optimistic view (not shared by all) the symbiosis that has taken place has reduced both bourgeois and bureaucratic traditions and has furthered the emergence of a new managerial spirit in both elite groups.

The effect which the comprehensive social security system has had on the redistribution of wealth is controversial. Its total expenditure, in comparison with the gross national product, is slightly higher than in Great Britain and Sweden but lower than in West Germany and Belgium. Because of the piecemeal fashion in which many of the reforms have been introduced, parts of the social security system have strengthened rather than overcome economic disparities among different categories of the population — especially among the various regions. Its beneficial effect on population growth and on the health of families is undeniable. Many of its weaknesses stem from an overly bureaucratic structure which, with time, has only increased in weight.[13] Yet public opinion polls show that after twenty years of operation 73 per cent of the population believe that the system has worked well; only 20 per cent are outrightly critical. Given the French temper, this is a remarkably favorable judgment passed on a governmental institution which must necessarily hurt the interests of some.

Economic planning in postwar France has extended to all branches of the economy and to all regions. When in 1945 General de Gaulle, then President of the Provisional Government of the Fourth Republic, entrusted to Jean Monnet, a former businessman, the task of preparing a Plan of Modernization and Equipment, he accepted the alternative which Monnet had put before him: "modernization or decadence." [14] Since then the General Commissariat for the Plan has elabo-

---

[13] Cf. the overall evaluation in Pierre Laroque *et al., Succès et Faiblesses de l'Effort Social Français* (Paris: Armand Colin, 1961), pp. 345–49.

[14] In order to show the importance which he attributes to this decision, General de Gaulle included the memorandum prepared by Jean Monnet and "adopted by the General" into the documentary part of his wartime memoirs. See *op. cit.*, III: *Documents*, p. 369.

rated a series of four-year plans; the Fifth Plan covers the period from 1965 to 1970. From an era of shortages and rigid regulation, through alternating periods of inflation and deflationary stagnation, and now amidst prosperity, the numerous governments of the two Republics have allowed the Commissariat to carry on.

None of the leaders of the Fourth Republic, not even when they were socialists, has spoken about the Plan in as enthusiastic and emphatic terms as have General de Gaulle and his onetime Premier and present Finance Minister, Michel Debré. For the former, the Plan is an instrument for realizing, through a "gigantic renovation," the "capital ambition" of France of becoming a strong industrial power, a necessary condition for great power status. Debré invokes freely Richelieu and Sully, Colbert and Turgot, as forerunners of state planning in France. He assigns to the Plan the task not only of beating back the claims of special interests, but also of indicating where the State should create new enterprises and generally of committing the nation to a policy of economic expansion.[15]

In the opinion of most, the actual role of the Commissariat over the last twenty years has been far more modest. But whatever its effect on economic growth, its exemplary and possibly lasting significance for change in economic and political behavior should not be underestimated. Each Plan has set goals for overall production and productivity as well as for the development of the various branches of the economy. Numerous modernization commissions made up of members of the planning staff and representatives of the interests concerned prepare the Plan. To check the inconsistencies which unavoidably result from such decentralized procedures, the projections of the commissions are fitted into national-income accounts, previously unknown in France. As the French are committed to a flexible process of planning, the objectives laid down in the Plan are merely an indication of what is deemed desirable and possible. No individual firm or trade

[15] See de Gaulle's speech of May 6, 1960, in *L'Année Politique, Economique, Sociale et Diplomatique* (abbreviated hereafter as *A.P.*), 1961, pp. 656–57 and sundry remarks in later press conferences; Michel Debré, *Au Service de la Nation* (Paris: Stock, 1963), p. 30; and *Jeunesse, quelle France te faut-il* (Paris: Plon, 1965), p. 172.

association faces sanction if it fails to reach the goals which it had originally accepted. Even the Plan's program of public investments is only indicative; binding decisions concerning investments are made by the Ministries concerned.

Nonetheless, it is erroneous to liken the activities of the Planning Commissariat to "revivalist prayer meetings," just because its proposals and projections lack binding force.[16] The role which the planning staff has played in propagating information to all public and private centers of economic decision-making is considerable and has had far-reaching effects: before the war, the absence of such information and in many fields the lack of reliable statistics were a severe handicap to economic development. In addition, the planning staff and its working methods have established communication between sectors of the economy which previously were rigorously separate and hence ignorant of each other's production and investment plans. In many instances, such confrontation as has taken place has led to the mediation of claims, has brought present-day rationality into historically frozen positions, and clarified the options to be incorporated into the Plan. Such communication, to be sure, does not by itself propagate economic growth. But it is its precondition.

The institutionalized contacts afforded by the planning process between public officials and the world of business and agriculture are in many respects a departure from the traditional political style. There is no commitment to a definite ideology of either comprehensive planning or economic liberalism. Carefully elaborated but easily modified compromises on means — an empiricism which takes full cognizance of changing market conditions and psychological imponderables — are different from the political "deal" of the past in two respects: they are not considered a betrayal of previously proclaimed principles because such principles are not involved; they have none of the onus of a secret bargain since they have been reached in the give-and-take of open

[16] This is the view expressed by Kindleberger, *op. cit.*, p. 155. A far more positive appreciation, which I share, is that of Michel Crozier, "Pour une analyse sociologique de la planification française," *Revue Française de Sociologie*, VI (1965), pp. 147–163, and by François Bloch-Lainé, "Réflexions sur les Explosifs," *Esprit*, XXX:308 (1962), pp. 59–64.

discussions, witnessed by third parties. As was the case in the nationalizations, a definite change in climate has taken place since the early postwar years. Distrust and antagonism between most business representatives and officials of the Planning Office have given way to an understanding of mutual positions, based on sharing information. This in turn has facilitated agreement on objectives.

Novel also is the relationship between the Commissariat and other sectors of public administration. Contrary to bureaucratic traditions, the number of staff members in the Commissariat has been kept deliberately small. Placed under the immediate responsibility of the Prime Minister, the staff members rely for expertise and technical knowledge on their colleagues in the amply staffed administrative bureaus. The outlook and working methods of the planning staff enjoy the esteem of at least the younger generation of ranking civil servants. In their judgment, the Commissariat may provide the model for overcoming some of the gravest shortcomings of the traditional administrative style (to be discussed below, Chap. V).

A closely connected concept, dating from the early days of the planning effort but further developed since, is that of the "concerted economy" (*économie concertée*). The new attitudes toward cooperation and planning and the systematization of encounters between business and bureaucracy in their routine contacts are, hopefully, winning over both to a new kind of rationality. What has happened within the rather limited realm of the Commissariat's activities is expected to extend to broader sectors of economic life — wherever the two managerial elites, the private and the public, interact.

A continuing and acknowledged weakness of the planning process is that certain organized interests, among them the labor unions, participate in it perfunctorily at best. This impairs the validity of a pattern of decision-making which seeks to replace formerly bureaucratic regulation by contractual agreement. That the interest which the public shows in the Plan as a whole remains confined to a relatively small group is not surprising. At the start of the Fifth Plan in 1965, about 40 per cent of those consulted in a public opinion poll still seemed to ignore the Plan. While 30 per cent believed that their standard of living depended on its success, an equal number denied this. Such an appraisal is significantly different from opinions about the social security system.

The current Plan hopes to see the GNP increase annually by 5 per cent. Taking into account the population growth, this would permit a 4 per cent rise in per capita wealth. At the end of this period, in 1970, consumption by the French would be comparable to that of the most highly developed industrial nations; production would be diversified; and techniques would reach a level never before attained. The obstacles still standing in the way of such developments are, at least in part, structural and institutional and closely attuned to political and social attitudes.

Since much is expected from the government and since its own objectives are ambitious, public expenditures are, in proportion to the GNP, the highest of all countries in the North Atlantic area. In 1963 they amounted to 33.8 per cent, and this percentage has been rising steadily since 1950. Investment in private industry has remained unsatisfactory. For several years it has been altogether stagnant and is now, since the government froze prices and wages in 1962 in order to forestall inflationary pressures caused by the overheating of the economy, lower than in any other Common Market country. The structure and the habits of the family firm, the urgency of public investments, and the financial needs of the state weigh heavily on a capital market with antiquated structures. Under such conditions, the reluctance of the distrustful domestic investor has not been overcome, and a profit margin that in comparison with other countries of similar development remains rather small, limits the possibilities for self-financing by business concerns.

Since Tocqueville's classical description of the devious ways by which the French peasant, under the Old Regime, evaded the "arbitrary, not to say ferocious, methods of taxation," [17] the legacy of a peasant mentality has been blamed for the low tax morale of Frenchmen. Insufficient tax revenue and a tax structure fit to protect the unproductive are often held respon-

[17] Tocqueville, *op. cit.*, p. 127.

sible for the narrowness of the capital market. Also blamed is
a dearth of civic virtue. There is little doubt that the survival
of so many small units in industry and agriculture which uni-
versally, not only in France, are able to conceal part of their
earnings, magnifies the problem of evasion. French sources
have estimated that fraud is practiced by more than one-third
of those with taxable incomes, a far higher figure than in the
United States and Great Britain.

Yet, as a percentage of gross national income, taxes collected
in France amount to almost 34 per cent — a tax burden higher
than that of England or West Germany. Because of the high
rate of evasion practiced by some, this burden must fall heavily, and sometimes too heavily, on the individual wage earner
and on the modern firms which have only limited, if any,
possibilities for evasion. In all modern countries, industry con-
tributes most to income from taxes. Since in France the industrial sector is still considerably narrower than for instance in
England or Germany, it has to carry a proportionately heavier
weight than in other countries. Indirect taxes, often inequi-
table and likely to drive up prices, constitute a far greater
share of total tax income than in other countries of similar
development: 46.6 per cent compared with 38.8 per cent in
Germany and 34.5 per cent in the United States.

Since the inauguration of the Fifth Republic the number of
tax declarations has soared and the rate of revenue has risen;
the broadening of the base of some taxes has put an end to the
previous penalization of some of the most productive enterprises. Nonetheless, because of resistance from many sides, the
government has been unable to introduce a reform which
would attack the basis of the uneven tax burden. The problem
of how to combat systematic tax evasion and how to devise a
more productive system of taxation is undoubtedly one of the
foremost problems not only of economic but also of social and
political development in France.

In city and countryside, the adaptation of the economy and
of the social structure to new conditions has provoked tensions
and stresses which prove more stubborn than General de
Gaulle admits when in his periodic press conferences he paints
a bright picture of the situation. Obviously, the Fifth Republic

has inherited many of the limiting conditions under which it operates. Many of the barriers to modernization can be attributed to traditional strains rather than to failings of the new regime. Conversely, it is true, much of the vitality and many of the mutations for which the Fifth Republic claims credit result from attitudes that took root and from reforms that were accomplished or well on the way before General de Gaulle's return to power.

The challenge of modernization which has caused, directly or indirectly, the existing tensions and stresses derives from closely intertwined internal and external factors. Among them the competition from France's partners in the Common Market is only one, albeit an important, element. The regime has reacted to the challenge by deferring the solution of certain economic and social problems. Whatever its justification, the political impact of this policy will undoubtedly be felt in the future.

The concern that an inflationary rise in costs and prices might get out of hand is understandable enough since France has experienced, ever since the end of the First World War, the consequences of a nagging inflation and of several devaluations of the currency. The need to keep industry competitive, not only in the European market where customs barriers are soon to disappear but also elsewhere, has made it even more imperative to maintain price and monetary stability. To obtain such a stability under conditions of full employment and in the face of long-postponed consumer demands is possible solely if there occurs a dramatic rise in productivity which can only be achieved with massive investments and a rapid process of concentration. For reasons discussed earlier neither of these is to be expected for the time being. Moreover there are political limits for foreign investment in France. A regime which constantly proclaims the need for "independence" from all foreign countries, and particularly from the United States, cannot look with sympathy on foreign participation. The government frowns upon it even in fields where French industry, for technological or other reasons, is clearly not competitive.

Under such conditions it has been impossible to withstand

all inflationary pressures. Official statistics admit a rise in the
cost of living during the seven years of General de Gaulle's
first presidency of about 25 per cent; the leaders of the opposition read the same statistics differently and claim that the rise
has been at least 34 per cent (as compared with about 40 per
cent in the last seven years of the Fourth Republic). Since 1965
prices have continued to climb moderately. In order to limit
their rise, the government has frequently been compelled to
sacrifice expansion to stability. Incapable of altering the structures which are largely responsible for the high costs of production, the government has proceeded in predictable ways.
For the sake of austerity, it has imposed immediate sacrifices
on those ill-prepared or -equipped to defend their share of
the national wealth. For the sake of modernity, it has withdrawn shelter and subsidies from the least efficient producers,
exposing them thereby to the chilling winds of internal or
foreign competition to which they might well succumb. Only
some examples can be given here.

Dissatisfaction with available housing continues to have a
direct influence on political attitudes. In the past, the slow
rate of construction, particularly striking in comparison with
neighboring countries, and the continued overcrowding of
obsolete, substandard lodgings, helped to maintain extremist
parties and movements. The country which in number of
passenger cars per inhabitant outranks all European countries except Sweden, ranks thirteenth in number of new lodgings built (here West Germany occupies the first place). In
fact, France's position is even worse: one-third of the dwellings
constructed since the war have gone to replace those which
have had to be abandoned because of old age or lack of re-
pairs. At present, about 20 per cent of existing housing is considered overcrowded by any standard.

The dramatic neglect which these figures betray has its
origin partially in emergency legislation dating from the First
World War and not yet fully rescinded. Conscious that in
many fields it would be too weak to control inflationary price
rises, the government kept rents frozen since the early twen-
ties. Such artifices, while keeping down the cost of living, took
most housing out of the regular market, and suited the style

of living of a population which had long preferred to spend most of its budget on food and other "perishables."

From appearances the construction paralysis seems to have ended: in many towns and around every larger city, modern dwellings are rising. However official figures indicate that the increase in new housing from year to year just about· keeps pace with the growth of the GNP, which means that housing is not yet being given the priority it needs. Since 1958, the share of housing in total investments has actually diminished substantially, year after year. In order to cut the dreaded budgetary deficit, low-rent, subsidized housing, for which the need is greatest, continues to lag behind demand and often behind plans. In part this is due to real estate speculation which the government in spite of its vaunted vigor has been unable to stop, and which has been denounced as "the scandal of the Gaullist regime." At the present rate of construction, it would take a quarter of a century to fill the reasonable needs of a growing population no longer content to live in overage dwellings. The dearth of housing might well be considered the open wound of the French social fabric. That wound is not soon going to heal, yet no strong current of public opinion, no effective interest group, has undertaken the defense of those who have been called the "disinherited of living space."

In contrast there has been no lack of protest, and frequently of violence, in defense of the peasants who suffer from the decline in governmental price supports. Many of the technologically backward farmers, especially in Brittany, in other Western areas, and in the center of France, who have been unable or unwilling either to modernize or to abandon their holdings, feel that prosperity has passed them by and that neither the government nor the rest of the country understands their problems.[18] For a few years protest movements abated when the government claimed that it was rising constantly to the defense of French producers in hard bargaining with the country's Common Market partners. But it turned

[18] See the findings of a public opinion poll undertaken for the Ministry of Agriculture in *Sondages*, XXVI:1 (1964), pp. 13 ff. and the interesting article by Lawrence Collins and Dominique Lapierre, "France's Small Farmers Never Had It So Bad," *New York Times Magazine*, December 24, 1967.

out that benefits from the Common Market accrued only to the most efficient producers and that the lowering of the protecting walls spelled new disaster for the marginal farms. This realization is not only costing the government electoral support, but new revolts are assuming an ever more political character, and interest groups are becoming "colonized" anew by Communist front groups and other extremists. (For details see Chaps. VII and VIII.) Anti-European feelings and latent xenophobia are easily aroused.

What is dramatically true in agriculture is widely felt: social and economic inequalities have been aggravated by rapid economic development even though the psychological effect of this phenomenon has been mitigated by a general upward movement. Since earnings have risen faster than prices, the global purchasing power has indeed increased. But such increases have varied greatly for different categories. At the bottom of the ladder earnings have barely kept pace with the cost of living; the earnings of skilled workers have risen eight times as fast as those of unskilled labor; and workers in private industry have fared far better than the millions employed in public enterprises since the government has wanted to keep public outlays down. This has led to periodic but rather ineffectual strikes in the public services. If the total income of all farmers has kept pace with the wages of the average worker, this is solely due to the sharp decrease in farming population. In fact, the earnings of both farmers and unskilled workers have risen less than has national wealth, and their relative position has therefore deteriorated.

These inequities are but some of the consequences of a policy that seeks to postpone the solution of urgent problems in the hope that progress and modernization will alleviate unavoidable but hopefully temporary maladjustments. In a society which puts high value on equality of treatment (see Chap. I), the bitterness created by such policies can easily be exploited politically. If governmental authority were to weaken, this could endanger the steady growth of the economy — a precondition of its modernization.

# CHAPTER III

# Political Socialization

## POLITICAL SOCIALIZATION AND POLITICAL CULTURE

This volume, like others in the Comparative Politics Country Series, attempts to explain a country's politics by explaining the political attitudes and political behavior of its citizens. Such an emphasis does not exclude an analysis of governmental institutions (see Chaps. IX, X), nor that of the political infrastructure — formed mainly by interest groups and parties (Chaps. VII, VIII). Yet, we assume that the way people act within the political system is of foremost importance both for the functioning of the system and for an adequate explanation of how it functions.

Like all human beings, Frenchmen of all ages play many roles, not all of them relevant to the political system. Which roles they play and how they perform depends on a variety of objective factors, as well as on their values, beliefs, and emotions. Many social scientists, dissatisfied with a narrow and legalistic interpretation of politics, have studied the basic values existing in a society to explain political behavior and through it the political system. These studies, however, have sometimes led to erroneous generalizations [1] or to high-level abstractions with little explanatory force.

To understand the particularities of the political realm, we

[1] Cf. the trenchant remarks by the French author François Goguel, in *In Search of France*, pp. 374 ff., commenting on such generalizations by two American social scientists, appearing in the same volume.

need not be concerned with all the ideas that swirl around in a society, nor with all the patterns which mold the individual and determine his conduct. What matters is the individual's political socialization — his attitudes towards the political system, towards the institutions through which the system functions, and towards the values by which it lives.[2]

Every political system, at all its levels, allocates authoritatively the resources at its disposal. (The discussion of the present French economic setting in Chap. II provides examples of a far more general phenomenon.) Attitudes towards the political system are therefore concerned with specific orientations towards authority and the forms in which authority manifests itself. How Frenchmen view authoritative decisions — how they accept or resist them, and how they distinguish between those to be obeyed and those to be circumvented.

Socialization is a learning process which proceeds by observing and experiencing authority. But authority patterns, i.e., the way people look at those giving them orders, do not only exist in the political life of a nation. They are observed and experienced first and, at least in a democracy, foremost in the family and other primary groups, in the church and the schools, on the job and in associations. Participation in social activities often provides training for roles assumed in political life. The subsequent sections of this chapter will therefore deal with various social settings.

Like any learning process political socialization passes on from one generation to the next a "mixture of attitudes developed in a mixture of historical periods." [3] What tensions the peculiarly French "mixtures" have created not only between Frenchmen but often within the same individual have been described above (Chap. I). Centuries ago Montesquieu spoke of the composite of values, emotions, and beliefs as "the general spirit, the morals of a nation." More recently several

[2] This line of thought owes much to Gabriel A. Almond and Sidney Verba, *The Civic Culture* (Boston: Little, Brown and Company, 1965), esp. Chaps. I and XII, as well as to the other writings by these two authors quoted therein.

[3] Sidney Verba, "Comparative Political Culture," in Pye and Verba (eds.), *Political Culture and Political Development* (Princeton: Princeton University Press, 1965), pp. 512 ff.

authors have defined this composite as political culture.[4] It is important to consider this not merely a residual concept ("What one cannot adequately define nor describe is political culture") but to understand the relationship between political culture and political socialization.

Any political culture provides the link between what happens in the mind of the individual (and in the primary groups to which he belongs) and politics. Its study is equally important to the student of micropolitics focusing on the individual and his attitude, and to the student of macropolitics, mostly concerned (as we are here) with the structure and function of a political system as a whole. There is constant interaction between a country's political culture and its citizens' political socialization. If one thinks of political culture as an alphabet, then the process of arranging the letters into words is determined by the process of socialization which the citizen has undergone. The way a Frenchman looks at political events, especially at the decisions of his own government, has much to do with the attitudes he has observed and learned in both the social and in the political realms. Conversely, the capabilities of the political system, whether it can act forcefully or must temporize and maneuver, often depends on the behavior of the citizens. Their actual or presumed reactions to specific events or general policies may condition the content and style of political decisions.

An understanding of the limitations which an inherited political culture imposes on political development is of particular importance in studying an old country such as France. More than a century ago Tocqueville spoke of his compatriots as "a people so unalterable in its *primary instincts* that it is recognizable in its portraits drawn 2,000 or 3,000 years ago . . ."[5] Political institutions, even if they are seemingly created *de novo,* are shaped by the political culture. Hence change and mutation cannot adequately be understood without ac-

[4] See the writings by Almond and Verba, but also the important discussion by Samuel H. Beer, *Patterns of Government* (New York: Random House, 1958), esp. pp. 32 ff.

[5] Tocqueville, *op. cit.,* pp. 210–11. Emphasis supplied: what Tocqueville called "primary instincts" overlaps the two present-day terms, "socialization" and "political culture."

counting for the influence which values and beliefs bring to bear on any attempted reform.

The Frenchmen who after the Second World War gave a new constitutional framework to the Fourth Republic had the mandate to establish a regime totally different from that which led the country to the disaster of 1940. Most of them honestly believed that this was what they were doing. Yet, in spite of past experiences and of great differences in the *texts* of the constitutional laws, it soon turned out that the Fourth Republic was unable to avoid the pitfalls of the Third. The attitudes and beliefs not only of the political actors inside and outside parliament but also of the French citizens as voters, as members of interest groups, etc., frustrated the intended change.

Yet Tocqueville himself went on to ascribe unforeseen changes in the country's destiny to the changeability of the "moods (and) . . . tastes" of Frenchmen. Today, the contrast between politics in the Fourth and Fifth Republics shows that constitutional texts are not necessarily devoid of political effect. The experiences accumulated since the war and the acute crisis precipitated by the fighting in Algeria opened the way for changes which were manifestly impossible twelve years before. Yet, as will be shown (see Chaps. IX and X), also the constitution of 1958 was altered by the impact of the political culture.

The style in which political roles are acted out is another illustration of the intimate relationship between the socialization of the individual citizen and the political culture. It is true that at various periods the style of the political actors, and more generally of a country's elites, may be quite different from that of its citizens, either as individuals or as members of groups. There is, for instance, serious doubt as to whether the orientation of a majority of French voters towards politics is any more ideological than that of the American voter (see Chap. IV). Public opinion polls are an important source of information for a political profile or a nation by indicating the major groups which make up the nation. But in any public opinion sampling the number of intellectuals and political leaders is obviously too small to be statistically relevant. The style of a community (as an expression of the political culture) can neither be deduced solely from answers to a questionnaire, nor from the mere pronouncements of the elite. This is one of the major difficulties in any attempt to make the findings of micro- and macropolitics mutually relevant.

If one sets out to construct a model of basic values which will presumably explain the major manifestations of political life, one should guard against giving undue weight to the ideological orientation of one stratum of society. In fact, in each country there is a pluralism of values, a plurality of cultures and styles. This is particularly true of France, a country of divided elites. It is therefore necessary to investigate as concretely as possible the socialization process of citizens and of leaders alike. Only by looking subsequently at the political process, as it unfolds at a particular historical moment, will it be possible to determine what values and beliefs (or to draw once more on Tocqueville, what "sentiments" and what "principles") are dominant.

**RELIGIOUS AND ANTI-RELIGIOUS TRADITIONS**

France is at once a Catholic country — at least 92% of Frenchmen now living are baptized in the Catholic faith — and a country which the Church itself considers as "dechristianized." Until well into the present century, the opposition between believers and non-believers has been one of the main determinants of the political culture. Since the Revolution, it has divided society and political life at all levels.

In 1789, very few people started with the idea of making war on religion. But a series of historical accidents achieved an early split between the Revolution and the Church. The forces of counterrevolution based their legitimacy on a religious faith for which unquestionable authority and ecclesiastic discipline were more central than in some other countries, while the double revolt against King and Church gave to the democratic creed a rationalist basis whose purest French expression was voltairianism. (It has been said of Voltaire that only a Catholic country could produce him.) Just as for Catholic Frenchmen the Revolution was the work not just of erring or

evil men but of Satan, antireligious beliefs took the form of a
militant faith. The Jacobin-inspired cult of reason was indeed
a "cult," which lives on in spirit though no longer in form.
This explains why the secularized state and its institutions
have never been given sacral dignity: there is no reference to
God in any of the republican constitutions, no prayer at
official functions, no "In God we trust" on the coins, no religious oath for office holders. Such practices, quite common in
many countries that respect the separation of church and state,
would have been sacrilegious to both camps in France.

Whether the evolution of French society under the Orleanist
monarchy and the Second Empire might have offered chances
for a religious reconciliation is a moot question. For with the
establishment of the Third Republic, the gulf between the
political cultures of Catholicism and anticlericalism reopened
and deepened further. After a few years the errors of its enemies permitted militant anticlericalism to take over the Republic.

Parliament rescinded the centuries-old concordat with the
Vatican, expelled most Catholic orders, and severed all ties
between Church and state, so that "the moral unity of the
country could be reestablished." There was a time when the
hostility between Catholicism and anticlericalism almost broke
out into generalized violence. In those rural regions where
Catholic observance had already become an expression of
habit rather than of genuine faith, dechristianization spread
when the new legislation deprived the Church of all official
prestige.[6] From the rostrum of parliament Viviani, Premier at
the outbreak of the First World War, boasted that his generation had extinguished forever in the minds of the oppressed
classes all hopes for salvation by divine providence. At the
same time, representatives of the small town bourgeoisie which
had replaced the *haute bourgeoisie* as political leaders, swelled
the membership of the organized "antichurch" — the Freemasonry.

French Freemasonry, like that of other Latin countries, had
broken earlier with the religious and political conservatism,
and even the deism, of Anglo-Saxon Masonry. During the

6 Wright, *France in Modern Times*, p. 332.

formative years of the Third Republic, its agnosticism turned into fervid anticlericalism. Its lodges, especially those of the influential Great Orient, functioned as the nurseries of much of the political and the administrative personnel of the Republic. The views of the membership on political and economic problems varied widely and evolved over time. But the commitment of every Freemason to an unrelenting fight against the Catholic creed and the Church as an institution proved a strong cement. To the Freemasons and their middle-class sympathizers, religion was a vehicle of political oppression, just as to the majority of the working class it was an instrument in the service of economic exploitation. The number of Freemasons was estimated never to have exceeded 50,000. But since they were intentionally distributed over many organizations, both public and private, they exercised, at least until 1914, a greater influence on the minds of republican Frenchmen than their number would suggest.

The intransigeance of the republican regime was matched by that of the Pope who excommunicated every deputy who had voted the separation laws. Faithful Catholics were driven into a political ghetto. Regular attendance at mass by army officers (reported by Freemasons converted into amateur spies) became a hindrance to promotion. A feeling of being besieged from outside the walls of their faith was given expression in many Catholic publications of the period. The faithful saw no other way than the overthrow of the existing political regime to overcome their isolation.

The Catholic subsystem existing within the republic drew its strength from a well-developed network of private education and associations (see this chapter and Chap. VII). The mass-pilgrimages to cathedrals or shrines were not ordinary church services but rites of communion: the sermon-speeches held at such occasions stressed the distinctiveness of those assembled and denounced the sins of those outside the community of faith.

A keen observer of the prewar political stage maintained that he could distinguish between political conventions held in the same region by devout Catholics and by anticlerical republicans merely by looking at the features of the partici-

pants: the faces of the former resembled wooden sculptures of
the thirteenth and portraits of the fourteenth and fifteenth
centuries; the others had stepped out of nineteenth century
paintings, many could have been Daumier's models.[7] Such
visual impressions indeed confirmed that there were then two
French nations rather than one.

The opposition between the political Right and Left was frequently determined by attitudes towards the Catholic Church.
In rural regions where religious practice continued to be lively
and where the advice of the local clergy counted on election
day, conservative candidates carried the vote. But even governments of the center usually did not invite the support of conservative deputies whose anticlerical lineage was dubious. For
a total of sixty years (1879 to 1939), with rare exceptions no
practicing Catholic obtained cabinet rank in any of the numerous Ministries. The political isolation of the Catholics has
correctly been compared to that of the Communists since 1947,
when every government left of center has found it necessary to
disclaim communist support even though offered.[8] The existence of such political ghettos of whatever kind necessarily narrows the basis of representation.

The experiences of national unity during the First World
War and the reconciliation of believers and nonbelievers in
the resistance movement of the Second World War were bound
to erase many of the political differences which religious divisions created. Today the interaction of religious and political
forces has been transformed in many respects, yet past alignments still determine, in many cases, the role which religious
beliefs or agnostic convictions play in the socialization of the
individual.

Indifference towards religious practices continues to be fairly
widespread among Frenchmen baptized in the Catholic faith.
Although 62 per cent consider themselves "practicing Catholics," only 38 per cent of them attend religious services at
least every Sunday, 36 per cent go to church occasionally, and
26 per cent never attend church services. A comparable inquiry

7 Thibaudet, *op. cit.*, pp. 36–37.

8 See François Goguel and Alfred Grosser, *La Politique en France* (Paris:
Colin, 1964), p. 25.

among young people between sixteen and twenty-four years of age shows some but not very significant differences, here the figures are 37 per cent, 42 per cent, and 20 per cent.[9] But these national averages hide enormous geographical and social disparateness as well as differences between the sexes. In rural France, parts of Flanders, Alsace-Lorraine, and those regions which for geographic, administrative, or economic reasons have been relatively isolated (the Northwest, especially Brittany, some of the Alps, and some of the countryside south of the *Massif Central*), have withstood dechristianization. Where social hierarchies have remained strong, religious practices are more firmly rooted: this is true in the border regions of the North where family life is close and in the West where nobility and clergy have long been a determining factor in village life.[10] Everywhere the wealthier farmers attend church service far more assiduously than the owners or tenants of marginal farms, sharecroppers, or laborers.

The rapid progress of urbanization might soon deprive these data of all but historical interest. However, it is as yet impossible to predict what mass emigration will do to the religious practices of the newly urbanized population, especially if it were to come from such regions as the underdeveloped West where the Church still has a strong hold.

In the Middle Ages, Christianity was propagated from the urban agglomeration. Now the large cities and the lines of communication between them seem to contribute most to dechristianization. From a survey of young people, it appears that the attitudes in city and country will continue to differ: 59 per cent of those living in large urban centers believe that for their generation religion is less important than for their parents; only 42 per cent of those living in communities of less

[9] For these and all other statistical data on religious attitudes see "L'Eglise Catholique et les Prêtres," *Sondages*, XXIX:1 (1962), pp. 23 ff.; "Religion et Politique," *ibid.*, XXIX:2 (1967), pp. 7 ff.; Jacques Duquesne, *Les 16–24 Ans* (Paris: Le Centurion, 1963), pp. 202–231, and the comments by A. Coutrot and F. Dreyfus, *Les Forces Religieuses dans la Société Française* (Paris: Colin, 1965), *passim*.

[10] Edward R. Tannenbaum, *The New France* (Chicago: The University of Chicago Press, 1961), p. 41, and his entire chapter on Catholic practices, significantly entitled "Children of the Past."

than 2,000 population think so. For the cities, regional variations remain important: in Strasbourg there are more than
33 per cent practicing Catholics, in the Mediterranean harbor
of Marseilles less than 11 per cent go to church with any
regularity.

Most telling are the differences among the social classes in
big cities. In the Paris region, which the clergy considers as
"mission territory" because of low church attendance, 19 per
cent of the managerial group but only 1.7 per cent of workers
go to mass. In less dechristianized cities such as Lille, 3 per
cent of the unskilled, 8 per cent of the skilled workers, but
60 per cent of the professional group are churchgoers. On a
national level, almost half of all Frenchmen who have severed
church ties belong to the working class. The estrangement between the working class and the Church, in spite of the renewed vitality of Catholic workers' organizations, remains a
central fact of religious and cultural life.

The urban bourgeoisie continues to be traditionally divided: at various historical periods, especially the nineteenth
century, contradictory experiences have deposited here a layer
of devout Catholicism, there an unrepentant voltairianism.
Sometimes the divisions run within the same family. But by
and large, church services in the urban centers are mostly attended by the upper and middle classes, with a definite predominance of women and young girls.

The difference between the religious attitudes of men and
women is far more pronounced in France than in other countries of similar development. A far higher proportion of men
have severed all church ties, a far greater number of women
attend church with regularity. Among those who find the
church an institution that deserves "outright criticism," 64
per cent are men and only 36 per cent women. Only 47 per
cent of the men, but 62 per cent of the women who believe
that the church still has considerable political influence in
France approve of this situation. Such differences, even though
to a varying degree, are common to all classes, all regions, to
the rural as well as to the urban milieu.

Of course, church attendance is only one manifestation of
religious or agnostic feelings. Other factors, more difficult to

gauge and less suited to generalization, must be considered. According to a detailed study of a village community situated in a region of about average religious practices and considered in many respects typical, mass, religious weddings, and funerals have little religious significance. Those who do attend these rites are there mostly from habit and for social reasons. They look upon the priest as they look upon the mayor: each fulfills different public functions.[11] Religious faith is regarded as something beyond the reach of the uninitiated: it is the clergy's business.

In a representative national panel, only 38 per cent of regular churchgoers conceive the role of the church in exclusively spiritual and evangelical terms, to 35 per cent of them the functions of the church are predominantly mundane: it defends the established order, inculcates respect for morality, etc.

When young Frenchmen in all parts of the country were asked to list the values they cherished most and whose loss they would most regret, there were no significant differences between the first three preferences of religious youth and of nonreligious youth. Both groups listed health, money, and love, though not quite in the same order. For those who attended church regularly, religious faith occupied fourth place, while it appeared at the bottom of everybody else's list. On the basis of these and other answers to similarly critical questions concerning public and private morality, a study has concluded that less than 12 per cent of the youth can be classified as convinced Catholics — far less than the number of churchgoers in the total population. On the other hand, it is significant that on many problems the current thinking of the faithful and of the faithless coincides rather than diverges. Two-thirds of the students in Catholic schools approve of divorce "in certain cases," as against three-quarters of students in public institutions.

There are also indications that the separation of church and state is losing some of the rigidities which have so far characterized the secular character of a republican regime in France. While the constitution of the Fifth Republic was being writ-

[11] Lucien Bernot and René Blancard, *Nouville, un village français* (Paris: Institut d'Ethnologie, 1953), pp. 239, 299.

ten, a public opinion poll asked whether the electorate would
be in favor of inserting into its preamble a reference to "God
the Creator and the Father of all mankind": 37 per cent approved, 33 per cent disapproved, 22 per cent declared to be
indifferent to the question. (No such reference was included
in the actual text of the constitution, which still affirms that
the republic is *laïque*.) The classical Left, composed of Communists, Socialists, and Radicals, still disapproved of the proposition in far greater numbers than other voters. Yet, with the
exception of the Communists, even here the percentage of
those who declared to be "indifferent" to the question appears
astonishingly high to those who remember the passionate
fights at the beginning of the present century.

The development which became manifest as soon as political life reawakened in 1946 has been continued: there are no
more walls built around the religiously devout; he is no longer
barred from careers; he may be different but he is no longer
estranged from the world that lies beyond his own community
of faith. Finally, lines of political division are not drawn primarily according to religious orientations. Believers and non-
believers are to be found in many political camps, their values
and interests are represented by a variety of organizations
which no longer appear invariably on the Right or Left of
the political spectrum. In a recent public opinion poll 51
per cent of the respondents classified politically active Catholics with the Right, 14 per cent with the Left, while a significant 35 per cent declined to answer.

The changes that have thus occurred are a consequence
both of shifts in the general environment and of mutations in
French Catholicism. The groundwork for the latter had been
prepared during the interwar years. In fact, traditions of a
nonauthoritarian, democratic, and socially conscious Catholicism which had been quite lively during the middle of the
nineteenth century dried up during the Second Empire and
the struggles with the anticlerical republic.

After the Second World War the diverse Catholic movements and the Church hierarchies changed outlook and methods of action and did much to accomplish the rehabilitation
of Catholicism. In a pluralistic society, Catholic organiza-

tions, publications, and teachings became themselves pluralistic and gave expression to a wider range of social and political choices.[12] A new style and better defined role assigned to lay members enabled Catholic action groups to become more effective as innovators in a variety of fields.

In the organizations of farmers, workers, and employers, and among intellectuals, in certain administrative bureaus (such as that of the Plan), there now exists a novel (and entirely informal) "freemasonry" of those who have been active in the various branches of the Catholic youth movements. (For details see Chap. VII.) It is estimated that more than 3,000 (of a total of 38,000) mayors of local communities have such a background. The use which the Church, Church-affiliated educational institutions, and the multiple Catholic organizations make of the mass media shows little of the sectarianism of earlier days.[13]

After the war, the experience of the worker-priests holding mass in factories and slum dwellings was the most widely noted and most dramatic sign of a novel orientation. Yet upon orders of the Vatican this form of missionary work had to be abandoned, at least temporarily, when it turned out that when placed in a working class milieu many of the priests admitted that they were overwhelmed by the justifications of communist ideology. (Manual workers are still little inclined to attend church services or to participate in any religious activities.[14]) But such limits to success do not invalidate the result that an earlier, sharply defined subsystem has overcome much of its former isolation. This in itself has transformed the socialization of Catholic Frenchmen.

This socialization also has had its impact on the attitude of

[12] See the interesting remarks by Otto Kirchheimer, "Private Man and Society," *Political Science Quarterly*, LXXXI:1 (1966), p. 21; as well as Pitts, *op. cit.*, pp. 279–288; Hoffman, *ibid.*, pp. 36–37.

[13] See Coutrot and Dreyfus, *op. cit.*, pp. 292–305, and William Bosworth, *Catholicism and Crisis in Modern France* (Princeton: Princeton University Press, 1962), esp. Chaps. IV–VII.

[14] For a careful inquiry into the present relationship between the church and the working class, see Gérard Adam and Marc Maurice "L'Eglise catholique et le monde ouvrier," in Société Française de Sociologie, *Tendances et Volontés de la Société Française* (Paris: S.E.D.E.I.S., 1966), pp. 285–321.

antireligious or non-Catholic forces. Freemasonry has no longer to be reckoned with as an important influence in political life. The vanishing significance of the unifying fight against clericalism has brought out the weakening fissures in the Masonic lodges. From time to time in the public at large, specific issues can still activate anti-clerical feelings which then erupt volcano-like. In 1960, presumably 11 million signatures were gathered within a short time and especially in rural regions to oppose new legislation generalizing public subsidies to parochial schools. It was the first, and for a long time the only, interruption of the lethargy that has characterized political life under the Fifth Republic. Subsequent events, especially the rather smooth working of the new legislation, seem to indicate that the protests drew on a body of traditions which has in fact lost political and even ideological vitality.

French Jews (numbering since the recent exodus from North Africa about 500,000 most of whom live in urban centers) are politically so integrated that they do not need to be discussed as a separate element of the political culture, even though there exists a latent antisemitism among certain groups of the population.

By contrast the Protestants (800,000 or 1.6% of the total population) have, at least until recently, lived somewhat apart — a heavy concentration in Alsace, in the Paris region, and in some regions of the center and of the southeast of France has been characteristic of this small religious minority. About two-thirds of its members belong to the upper bourgeoisie — business, banking, the civil service, journalism, and the professions are heavily represented — so that Protestant sermons are frequently of a much higher intellectual level than those in Catholic churches. Socially and even economically a clannishness and a rather deliberate style of life mark the Protestant milieu, well exemplified by Gaston Defferre, the Socialist Mayor of Marseilles, who for a time was considered the most serious opponent of General de Gaulle in the presidential election of 1965. Politically, until recently the separateness of the French Protestants was expressed by the fact that they usually voted much further to the left than others in the social milieu to which they belonged or the regions in which they resided.

They identified themselves with the advanced opinions of republicanism, not because of an explicit political influence of their churches which has been minimal, but because of the corresponding identification of Catholicism with the political Right and antirepublican movements. If the Protestants were faithful, even though culturally different, republicans, the republic did not confine them to a ghetto: on the contrary, the number of Protestants in high public positions was and remains very large in proportion to their number in the country.

The new alignments which the recent mutations of French Catholicism have made possible, have had a corresponding impact on the beliefs and attitudes of Protestants. Since the liberation it can no longer be said that Protestants vote "Left" with any consistency. Their electoral behavior, like their activities in cultural and economic associations, is now determined by other factors than religious affiliation. They too, and for the first time in almost 300 years, have been fully integrated in the mainstream of French political culture.

**FAMILY AND CLASS**

For Frenchmen who view their neighbors and their fellow citizens with distrust and the institutions around them with considerable cynicism, the family group is a safe haven. Balzac's novels, among others, illustrate how the immediate family (parents-children) was embedded in the larger extended family, how both supported each other and might be ruthless in assuring family well-being. To the outsider, French or foreign, the Frenchman was always sociable, especially when met on neutral ground such as restaurants and other people's salons for the purposes of stimulating conversation. But otherwise distance was maintained and intimacy rarely granted: people had a tendency of barricading themselves in their homes as if they were fortresses.[15] Concern for stability, safe income, property, and continuity (including rational calculations as to matrimony and conception) were the characteristics common to bourgeois and peasant families: the urban and

[15] André Siegfried, *France. A Study in Nationality* (New Haven: Yale University Press, 1930), pp. 12–13. In what respects Siegfried's "classic" is now outdated, see below.

rural proletariat were excluded from this pattern which was sanctioned by legislation and highly valued as a generalized standard.

The belief that the family must remain the foremost training ground for acculturation was matched by a resolve of all competent family members — parents, older siblings, and others — to contribute to the training of the child. Close supervision, incessant correction, threatened and applied sanctions (though usually little physical punishment), and a rather authoritarian style were characteristic of family life. "No use discussing," "that's how it is," etc. were accepted formulae. But the great difference from authoritarian family life elsewhere, e.g., in Germany, was that in general little more than outwardly conforming behavior was required. The child and adolescent were free to withdraw emotionally and intellectually into their own thoughts and build, if they were so inclined, their own value system.[16] The fear of face-to-face relationships which, as we shall see, characterizes the French administrative and political style was and remains prevalent in many families before it is reproduced and strengthened by the educational system.

The structure of the family has recently undergone a number of important changes. Patriarchy was always mitigated by the fact that in France both lines of kinship — the father's and the mother's — were considered important for the nuclear family and its protection. Although their actual effect is controversial, a variety of factors seemed to have weakened the authority of the French father. Family allowances paid to each family with two or more children and the special compensations for nonworking mothers are quite normally considered to be the wife's rewards — they might be higher than the husband's wages. In the rapidly urbanizing society of higher mobility which France has become, prolonged absences of the father from home are more frequent. Because of better training and new experiences, the sons of farmers or of small businessmen no longer accept unquestioningly the outmoded working methods of their fathers.

[16] These processes within a family of the upper bourgeoisie are masterfully described in Roger Martin du Gard's great novel *The Thibaults* (New York: The Viking Press, 1939).

These factors have shaken seriously, and in quite different milieus, the patriarchal authority of the head of the family. There is a corresponding inclination of the young of both sexes to feel that they have far better personal relations with their mothers than with their fathers, even though outright and permanent conflicts with the latter are not too frequent. The desire on the part of young people to assert their independence by leaving the family residence altogether is on the increase. In part, this is an aspect of the rural exodus but happens also in the large cities.

What is most striking is a general change in atmosphere. In a dynamic society, family members, including children, bring into the family circle the results of their varied experiences, instead of merely passing on and receiving traditions. Leisure time activities, especially travel by parents and children, have influenced the style of family living and often the relationship of the family with the world outside. The search by the family group for equilibrium and balance is, of course, not abandoned. But to enable the family to continue its role as one of the molders of individual motivations, a fresh equilibrium is sought to take into account the new forces pressing from the outside. André Siegfried's characterization of the French family as fundamentally "anti-social," stated 35 years ago, is no longer a valid generalization.[17]

To what extent the French family subjects its members to political socialization in a narrower sense is altogether uncertain. A number of recent investigations,[18] though not strictly comparable, agree that in most families political (and religious) discussions are extremely rare. This seems to be less symptomatic of a general lack of interest in political questions than of a desire to avoid possible controversy and of an unwillingness to impose parental opinion in such matters (as distinguished from rules concerning behavior). Only 29 per cent of French voters knew anything at all about the political

[17] See above, n. 15.
[18] Duquesne *op. cit.*, Philip E. Converse and Georges Dupeux, "Politicization of the Electorate in France and the United States," *The Public Opinion Quarterly*, XXVI:1 (1962), 89–90; and an inquiry among children in the Grenoble region: C. Roig and F. Billon-Grand, *La Socialization politique des enfants* (Paris: Colin, 1968).

orientation of their fathers, as compared with 91 per cent of American voters. This enormous difference can be explained only in part by the complications of the French party system. Secretiveness, another mark of individualism, is not only practiced by the family cell (and the family firm) in its relations with the outside world, it also colors intrafamily relations.

Such muteness might explain the rather surprising results of the recent inquiry conducted among younger children in the Grenoble region. Although they came from widely varying family backgrounds, the children's outlook on important historical events and personalities was fairly uniform, a finding one would expect from a society high in consensus. It hardly reflected the divisiveness which historical memories and issues are known to provoke in the adult world.

However democratic and egalitarian a society pretends to be or actually is, families (and schools) can never be run democratically.

> One of the most basic and indispensable functions in any social system . . . must therefore always be to some extent out of tune with democratic patterns, and potentially at odds with them.[19]

But in the adult world the degree of and feelings about class stratification produce different attitudes towards authority. These attitudes shape a society's authority pattern and have thereby a direct impact on the style in which authority is actually exercised in both the social and the political realm.

Frenchmen, like Englishmen, are very conscious of living in a society that is divided into classes. But since in France equality is valued more highly than in England, deference towards the upper classes — an important element of the British political culture — is far less developed and indeed a resentful antagonism is widespread. The number of those who are conscious of belonging to a class remains high, the solidarity within the same group intense. In a 1964 public opinion poll, 59 per cent declared that they belonged to a class, 29 per cent denied it, the rest gave no answer. But 82 per cent of those who classified

[19] Harry Eckstein, *Division and Cohesion in Democracy. A Study of Norway* (Princeton: Princeton University Press, 1966), p. 237 and, for the following, p. 135.

themselves as workers felt solidarity with other members of that group; 89 per cent of the peasantry and 73 per cent of the "middle classes" expressed similar feelings.[20]

When asked whether in their opinion "class struggle" was still a reality, 44 per cent of all respondents answered in the affirmative, 37 per cent denied it, and 19 per cent gave no answer. Remarkably enough, the answers did not vary greatly according to political preferences, except that avowed Communists were somewhat more likely to believe in an ongoing class struggle.

The sense of belonging and being loyal to a class is matched by a generalized lack of communication between the classes. Sensibility to social precedence, rather than deference, and a spontaneously produced particularism of collective behavior lead to far greater differences in the style of living than the disparity in financial means would warrant. Eating places, cafés, weddings, dances, sports, and funerals cater to different classes and have different rites. They are manifestations of separateness, rarely of common folklore.

The nation's elites continue to be recruited from an extremely small sector of the society.[21] Upward social mobility exists but is frequently awkward and slow, especially into the ranks of the upper bourgeoisie. In general, it is not enough for an individual to cross the barrier, not only he but his entire immediate family must gain entry and must adopt the standards and style of the class to which access is sought. In general this will take more than one generation, especially since money is not the only deciding factor. According to a recent testimony: "The bourgeoisie accepts in its ranks only those whom it considers worthy, those who resemble its own sons and who have the same mentality." [22] An examination

[20] See an (unpublished) poll by the French Institute of Public Opinion of July 1964. Different data on class identification and mobility have been discussed by Natalie Rogof, "Social Stratification in France and the United States," *American Journal of Sociology*, VIII:4 (1953), pp. 347–57, but they have been widely criticized on various grounds.

[21] See the valuable study, rich in empirical data, by Alain Girard, *La Réussite Sociale en France. Ses caractères — ses lois — ses effets* (Paris: Presses Universitaires de France, 1961), p. 350.

[22] J. Gagliardi and P. Rossillon, *Survivre à de Gaulle* (Paris: Plon, 1959), p. 107.

of successful careers reveals very few self-made men. Just as in Tocqueville's time, social promotion by marriage out of the class remains infrequent, which is a testimony to the continuing solidity of the bourgeois family.

It is true that partly because of the prevalent egalitarian ideology classes have the function not only of serving as barriers but also of leveling.[23] Once an individual has overcome the obstacles that barred his access to a higher class, his humble origin will be forgiven and forgotten. He will usually find that he has obtained more than mere legal equality. The peer group not only exercises pressure to obtain a degree of outward conformity, it also grants protection by insisting that its members, new or old, be accorded that *considération* (esteem) which creates the desired barriers against lower classes. Although this particular pattern of stratification was initiated by the elite group of a bourgeois society, it has shaped relations between other social classes and categories.

The deep fissure between bourgeoisie and working class has molded the social history of the country for more than a century. Such problems as church-state relations have invited temporary political alignments between part of the middle classes and the proletariat. Nonetheless the struggle between the classes is the more permanent fact and has resulted in antagonistic values and beliefs, i.e., a divided political culture with different symbols, flags, and holidays. The legislation and policies of the Third Republic evoked rather than compensated for the memories of the working class massacre in 1848 and especially of the bloody and revengeful suppression of the Paris *Commune* in 1871. In both houses of parliament, a majority, made up of the defenders of small business and the family farms, delayed social legislation for so long that the much decried reforms of the Popular Front in 1936 did little more than catch up with developments in other industrialized

[23] The phenomenon is described in these terms and with interesting, though partially dated details, by Edmond Goblot, *La Barrière et le Niveau, étude sociologique de la bourgeoisie française moderne* (Paris: Alcan, 1925), see esp. pp. 4, 6, 16. For a recent inquiry into these questions, see Claude Durand, "Mobilité Sociale et Conscience de Classe," in Darras (ed.), *Le Partage des Bénéfices* (Paris; Editions de Minuit, 1966), pp. 275–293.

countries. Protectionism, slow economic growth, and the resulting difficulties in obtaining credit were not propitious for
the social promotion of workers. Nor were they apt to instill
in the worker an esteem for the functioning of the capitalist
system.[24]

As a reaction, the industrial working class, numerically weak
by comparison with other countries, opposed to the bourgeois
society a counterfaith appropriately called *ouvriérisme:* workers should never entrust their defense to members of the bourgeoisie, not even to those who in parliament mouthed the
cause of socialism; to send workers into parliament was acting
the part of a mother who sold her daughters into a house of
prostitution. Deprived of expectations of individual social promotion, the proletariat was reduced to harboring apocalyptic
dreams of collective emancipation. At the end of the last century, the ugly working-class suburbs of Paris and the elegant
*beaux quartiers* of the capital had become symbols of two
hostile civilizations facing each other.

More recently, the old traditions of an almost instinctive
*ouvriérisme* were revived when it turned out that the hopes
aroused by the Popular Front and later by the Liberation had
been vain. These experiences, because they were interpreted
as a chance for revolution that had been missed, gave to the
political style of the postwar years a superficially revolutionary
tone. Certainly, the continuing strength of communism in a
society that has otherwise produced changes in working class
attitudes must be explained in part by such traditions and
experiences.

During the last decade large groups of wage earners have
seen their real income sufficiently increased so as to live in a
style that was previously unobtainable and was therefore
taunted as "bourgeois." The availability of durable consumer
goods and the development of consumer credit, the "motoriza-
tion" of almost everybody, the rapid spread of television, the
high value placed on leisure time activities — and the correspondingly high budget for the month-long paid vacation — all

[24] See, also for the following, Val Lorwin, "Reflections on the History of
the French and American Labor Movement," *Journal of Economic History,*
XVII:1 (1957), pp. 25–44.

have produced attitudes which have upset the ingrained habits
of individuals and groups. As class distinctions lose some of
their former sharpness, a new egalitarianism no longer stops
at class borders. The common patterns of a mass culture are
changing at last — even the style of celebrations and of sports
events.

Nonetheless, as careful observers have pointed out, it is
necessary (and in France probably more so than in other modern industrial societies) to distinguish between the spheres of
consumption and of production.[25] As a consumer, the worker
has ceased to live apart or in a class ghetto; once he leaves the
factory he no longer regards himself as a worker. But as a
producer, the fundamental characteristics which have always
distinguished the working class from other social strata have
remained unchanged, or at any rate are perceived as unchanged: hierarchism, inequality, and an authoritarian style
are resented as before. However only a small minority of
workers still reacts to the situation by an articulate opposition
to capitalist organization, mainly through certain trade union
activities. The vast majority has resigned itself to an acceptance of industrial work and its conditions, interrupted by a
protest vote for the Communist ticket on election day.

Hence most workers are almost completely cut off from former working class traditions. Among the young hardly anything
is left of a specific working class culture.[26] On such questions
as antimilitarism, internationalism, and collective action for
class emancipation (all problems on which the *ouvriérisme* of
former days took a violently nonconformist stand), young
workers do not think differently from other Frenchmen of
their age group. Their knowledge of labor movement history
or even of social history is nil, which seems to indicate that at
least in certain fields the French "habit of historical thinking"
is vanishing.

[25] Serge Mallet, *La Nouvelle Classe Ouvrière* (Paris: Editions du Seuil,
1963), pp. 9, 31, and 32; Andrée Andrieux and Jean Lignon, *L'ouvrier
d'aujourd'hui* (Paris: Rivière, 1960), p. 189 and *passim*. For a comparative
discussion see also T. B. Bottomore, *Classes in Modern Society* (New York:
Panthéon, 1966).

[26] See Duquesne, *op. cit.*, pp. 140–41, and the results of other inquiries
quoted there.

## EDUCATION

"All national educational systems indoctrinate the coming generations with the basic outlooks and values of their political order." [27] Education is the foremost process by which a community preserves and transmits its physical and intellectual characteristics. At a dramatic moment of its history, France was ruled by a man who recognized the central significance of education for the perpetuation of his values. In the second half of the twentieth century, the French educational system remains an imposing historical monument — in the unmistakable style of the First Empire.

The edifice which Napoleon I erected integrated education at all levels, from primary school to postgraduate professional training, both public and private, into one centralized and strictly structured corporation: *the* imperial university. Its function was to teach the "national doctrine"; the teachers were to have, according to Napoleon, the Jesuit mentality, but that of secularized Jesuits free from Rome and devoted solely to defending the public interest. A "Grand Master" presided over the entire institution; he insured the uniformity of programs at the various levels and the conformism of students and teachers at all levels. The development of secondary education and the training of its teachers became a particular and personal concern of Napoleon. The lycées and collèges, selecting their pupils at an early age, were invaluable in recruiting the elites for a regime unwilling to rely solely on privilege or birth. Both an egalitarian temper and the need to develop rapidly a nontraditional loyalty shaped the structure and the program of these training grounds for the future servants of civil and military society. Enforced by strict military discipline, enlivened only by vulgar patriotism, an otherwise deliberately abstract instruction used Latin, rhetoric, logic, and mathematics as vehicles for molding what was called the "cultivated" mind.[28]

[27] V. O. Key, *Public Opinion and American Democracy* (New York: Knopf, 1961), p. 316.

[28] For the description of the napoleonic origins of the system and of its later development see Hippolyte Taine, *Les Origines de la France Contemporaine. Le Régime Moderne,* II (Paris: Hachette, 1894), pp. 153 ff.

Succeeding regimes have loosened disciplines; the outwardly military style has disappeared; the tides of clerical and anti-clerical influence have advanced and receded. But whether imperial, royal, or republican, all regimes discovered that the machinery created by Napoleon was an admirably convenient and coherent instrument for dispensing the changing or permanent values of French civilization. Hence the centralized imperial university has never been dismantled. The "Grand Master" commandeering, through government appointed rectors, the twenty-three academies into which the country is divided for purposes of educational administration is nowadays the Minister of National Education.

Habits of centralization and devotion to a special kind of egalitarian ideology feed on each other and create a lasting solidarity among teachers of all ranks in the public education system. The curriculum and teaching methods, the criteria for the selection and the advancement of pupils and teachers, the content of examinations, and the perpetual changes of all of the foregoing continue to be centrally imposed, usually by the Ministry in Paris. It may no longer be true as it once was that the Minister can determine merely by looking at his watch which verse of Vergil is being translated in all third-year Latin classes of the realm. But in the Fifth Republic, to give a present-day example, the songs used to recruit voice teachers in all public schools are still designated annually by ministerial ordinance. Such authoritarian practices, even when they are devoted to the propagation of emphatically nonauthoritarian concepts, leave little room for administrative or pedagogic initiative at any level. Local authorities, educational associations, parent-teachers organizations, and teachers unions are now rather active as legitimate interest groups. But they leave the discussion and determination of educational policies to the administrative hierarchy. When a new field of academic concern is added, on whatever level, standards of uniformity demand that it be introduced almost everywhere without consideration for needs or resources.

The practice of making the individual's advancement at every step dependent on an appropriate examination is not peculiar to France. But nowhere has there developed such a widespread cult of competitive examinations, a cult which draws its strength from an obsessive belief that everybody is equal before an examination. In one important respect there is little difference between the certificate of studies delivered at the county seat to the 14-year-old upon leaving school, the *baccalauréat* sanctioning secondary studies, the senselessly specialized *agrégation* needed for a professorship, or the various *concours* by which the administrative elite of the nation is selected: success or failure in the examination shake not only the candidate and his family but the entire milieu to which he belongs. The walls of many a cathedral are hung with votive tablets imploring or thanking the Virgin Mary for assistance in examinations. French society is strewn with individuals to which failure or a lower than expected rank have inflicted irreparable psychological damage. Some rigidities of earlier times may have been overcome, but a voluntarily centralized and anonymous system still offers little opportunity to judge candidates by any other performance than their answers in an examination and the jury's appreciation of them.

On the other hand, there is no mechanism to ensure or control a continuing high performance once the prize is won. This may result in increased bureaucratic rigidity and, in the educational system, intellectual sclerosis. Moreover, the seemingly egalitarian process of selection frequently hides outright corporatist practices, such as the co-optation of university professors by secret faculty ballot.

Altogether it would be wrong to assume that the educational system is tyrannical because it is so vastly different from the schools and universities that train for the "civic culture" in England and the United States. Beginning with Napoleon's times, the centralization of authority in a far-removed national government has often resulted in a wholesome weakening of controls and in a lessening of community pressures which because of their closeness might have become offensive. Since the demise of the Empire, there has developed within the framework of uniform rules considerable freedom of expression in the classrooms and lecture halls. Such freedom was backed early by tenure rules which satisfied both libertarian and egalitarian convictions. Education as an effective weapon for emancipation and social betterment has been more than an official ideology — farmers' and workers' families regard the instruction of their children (and a better instruction than they had) as an important weapon for fighting "them," which includes the authorities organizing the instruction. In the past, the moving of rural youth into the ranks of elementary school teachers has been of great importance for the two-step social promotion discussed earlier.

The French child and adolescent is trained primarily in those arts of living which profit the critical and civilized individual who is an island unto himself. A vivid and sometimes quite ruthless competitiveness isolates him from his fellow students. The generally authoritarian stance of his instructors is not conducive to warmth in the teacher-pupil relationship, and the mutual fear of the face-to-face relationship determines the climate of most classrooms. Rote learning rather than insight into the learning process, a minimum of oral discussion and hence passivity on the part of the students, in the secondary schools, at least, an almost undiminished emphasis on rhetoric and logical presentation, are still widely accepted pedagogic methods. A curriculum which prides itself on being abstract and nonpractical bears the distinct marks of the Jesuit pedagogy which was Napoleon's paradigm.

A French social psychologist has described the causes and consequences of these educational and intellectual traditions in revealing terms:

> [The Frenchman's] love of clarity results simultaneously from a certain laziness which turns him away from a deeper search and complications; from a desire never to be fooled and from the example set by an elite group which has been trained for two millennia by the exercises of composition and by dialectics. The love for order is in the classical tradition: the Romans have imparted it to the Gauls, the lasting influence of the rhetors, the Justinian and Aristotelian renaissance, humanism, the Jesuit program, and later the [Napoleonic] University have reinforced ancient traditions. The qualities of the French mind are a precious gift for the entire world. . . . The risk is that taken altogether, a certain superficiality neglecting the shadowy zones of thought simplifies decisions excessively or complicates them

by an excess of abstract logic. It sometimes resolves a difficulty with an elegant sally.[29]

Until recently, the prominent place given Latin in the curriculum of secondary education and the other requirements of the *baccalauréat*, the sole means of access to higher education, were designed as barriers between the bourgeoisie and the other classes.[30] Although various lycées now offer some alternate curricula, traditional educational goals have not been abandoned. After the child has reached the age of fourteen, any attention to pedagogical methods is deliberately discarded as being alien to secondary and higher education.

But with forty to fifty students in each of the many terminal classes of the secondary schools and hundreds in the lecture halls of the universities, such a system suits and profits only that self-motivated individualist for whom it was designed originally. It even works to the disadvantage of the gifted child who comes from other than the bourgeois milieu. The distance between teacher and pupil, the absence of pedagogy, and the emphasis on the cultivated use of language widen the cultural gap further. The obstacles which children of various milieus face after they have gained admission to a lycée are illustrated by the findings of a recent inquiry: after six years of secondary schooling, 86 per cent of the children of bourgeois families were admitted to the final examinations, 55 per cent of those with a lower middle class background, but only 35 per cent of farmers' and 21 per cent of workers' children.[31] The others had fallen by the wayside, although all of them had proven talented enough to transfer to the secondary level.

His singular success in an educational system which is uniquely suited to the milieu from which he comes convinces the young bourgeois that his position in society is due to an inborn talent. In his opinion, few others will be able to ac-

[29] Gabriel Le Bras, "Psychologie de la France," *Revue de psychologie des peuples* (1952), quoted here from Michel Beaujour and Jacques Ehrmann, *La France Contemporaine* (New York: Macmillan, 1965), p. 70.

[30] Although the book by Goblot (see above n. 23) is now outdated in many respects, it remains entirely and significantly up to date in its description of the role which the *baccalauréat* plays in the bourgeois family.

[31] See Raymond Poignant, *L'Enseignement dans les Pays du Marché Commun* (Paris: Institut Pédagogique National, 1965), p. 105.

quire the necessary knowledge, or the privileges which his knowledge affords. Postwar reforms have tried to counter such class snobbery by facilitating the transition between the various branches of the educational system and by moving the teaching personnel more freely from one to the other. Hence a certain amalgamation of methods and outlook is on the way. But in many instances efforts to provide, on the secondary level, for a mixing of children from different social backgrounds have run afoul of ingrained custom. Bourgeois families (with the aid of sympathetic school administrators and teachers) always find a way of sending their children to the old, established, "class-segregated" *lycées,* leaving the newer institutions and their more modern curricula to the "upstarts."

Yet even before the raising of the compulsory school age from fourteen to sixteen years — a reform constantly delayed for budgetary reasons — the proportion of French youth pursuing studies at various levels is higher than elsewhere in Europe. At age seventeen, close to 17 per cent of the population is engaged in studies which correspond to the academic curriculum in an American high school. If one adds technical instruction and the like, more than one-third of this age group in France are full-time students, more than twice as many as in Germany or in England, even though substantially fewer than in the United States. For the age group between twenty and twenty-four, France ranks equally high among its European neighbors. In 1956, close to 6 per cent were enrolled in institutions of higher education and now this figure reaches probably more than 7 per cent (as compared with about 4 per cent in England and Germany and 27.2 per cent for the United States).[32]

These data indicate that in spite of the difficulties which have been discussed education in France more than elsewhere in Europe remains a vehicle of social promotion, even though it is far from providing the social mobility that might be desirable. Table I illustrates the wide disparities in the class composition of the student body. In some schools that are

[32] *Ibid.,* pp. 146, 155; Ministère de l'Education Nationale, *Informations Statistiques,* No. 74–75 (1965), p. 414; and J. F. Dewhurst (ed.), *Europe's Needs and Resources* (New York: The Twentieth Century Fund, 1961), p. 315.

TABLE I  *Social Origin of Students (in percentages)*

| | Farmers | Agri-cultural workers | Em-ployers industry | Em-ployers, trade | Crafts-men | Profes-sions, manage-ment, and high civil service | Lower civil service and middle manage-ment | White collar workers | Manual workers | Service per-sonnel | Diverse other cate-gories | Total |
|---|---|---|---|---|---|---|---|---|---|---|---|---|
| Enrolled in secondary schools preparing for higher education | 6.5 | 1.3 | 1.9 | 8.0 | 5.1 | 15.1 | 15.0 | 16.5 | 20.3 | 1.3 | 9.0 | 100.0 |
| Enrolled in institutions of higher education | 5.4 | 0.5 | 3.0 | 8.5 | 3.8 | 29.5 | 17.7 | 8.6 | 7.7 | 1.0 | 14.3 | 100.0 |
| Percentage in the total labor force | 15.7 | 4.3 | 0.4 | 6.6 | 3.2 | 4.0 | 7.8 | 12.6 | 36.7 | 5.4 | 3.3 | 100.0 |

Compiled from *Informations statistiques du Ministère de l'Education Nationale*, Nos. 74–75 (1965), p. 435, and *Annuaire Statistique de la France 1963* (Paris: Imprimerie Nationale, 1964), p. VIII.

strategically important for the training of the country's political and administrative elites, the students are now more exclusively of bourgeois origin than they were during the immediate postwar years.

The role of the schools in that particular form of socialization which trains either directly or indirectly for citizenship has varied over time. In the early days of the Third Republic, and especially during its period of virulent anticlericalism, the government had no difficulty in relying on the teacher for the propagation of the rationalistic, positivistic faith. In all classrooms, but particularly in those of the countryside, such teaching was also imbued with an emotional patriotism that drew its strength from anti-German feelings, and from the belief that France remained the epitome of civilized humanity. Objectively, the revered history textbooks of the period are almost disarmingly ethnocentric. For many a young Frenchman they provided an early introduction to the dichotomy of an abstract, ideal *patrie* and a generally despised government, of a country in whose defense one was willing to die but whose political institutions were considered badly suited to daily life.

After the First World War the teachers in the public schools turned from patriotism to internationalism and pacifism. An entire generation, especially of rural youth, bore the impact of such convictions imparted to them. The vagaries of the interwar period, the dissensions created by Vichy and Free-France, and the deep cleavages of the postwar period which divided the teaching profession as much as anybody else, now have created an unfavorable climate for any political discussions. In the classical curriculum of the secondary schools, citizenship training has always been as alien as any empirical social science. History instruction usually combines stress on humanistic values with resigned determinism. "Civic instruction," as prescribed by ministerial directives, has generally been turned into a farce.[33] Most decisive, however, is the fact that, at least in the lycées, the human climate and the educational atmosphere are isolating and therefore in essence anticivic.

While the number of students in nonpublic institutions of

[33] For a general but still too favorable picture see "L'Education du Citoyen," *Cahiers Pédagogiques*, XIV:12 (1959), pp. 1–148.

higher learning is insignificantly small, private schools continue to play a definite if declining role on the primary and secondary levels. They are overwhelmingly Catholic: of 1.8 million pupils in private schools, 1.7 million are enrolled in Catholic parochial institutions. In the primary grades, less than 15 per cent of the total school population frequent such schools, on the secondary level about 34 per cent (as compared with 45 per cent in 1945). But as could be expected from what has been said earlier about the well defined regionalization of religious practice and of dechristianization, Catholic schools are very unevenly distributed throughout the country.[34]

The times when Catholic schools were "ghetto" schools, highly valued as transmitters of a threatened tradition or bitterly fought as an alien body within the republic, are over. Since the war, the usual issue at stake was the allocation of public funds to the parochial institutions which the Catholic community was unwilling to rescue from financial starvation. Even in such terms the controversy quickly took an ideological turn. Reopening old wounds, the fight over subsidies, transmitted to parliament by the feuding organized interests was one of the reasons for governmental instability under the Fourth Republic. In the Fifth Republic, presidential authority was needed to accredit a compromise solution which might not have displeased Napoleon: to receive financial assistance parochial schools must submit to the administrative authority of the state. If the compromise works, another ideological conflict of long standing will be liquidated.

For many years and in many quarters, far more fundamental reforms have been discussed in order to change the style of all, but particularly of secondary, education and to make higher education more easily accessible to broader strata of the population. Here the Fifth Republic has been no more successful than its predecessors. An overabundance of frequently contradictory reforms of details has not been matched by a needed overhauling of structures and mentality. Both the exorbitant centralization of the system and the leverage which

[34] For the above data, see Coutrot and Dreyfus, *op. cit.*, pp. 43–45 and 224–25; and *Sondages*, XXIV:1 (1962), p. 51. The figures given here are not strictly comparable.

vested interests have inside and outside the Ministry of Education have frustrated the reformers. Even when enacted, their prescriptions are often unable to change reality, a phenomenon about which educational reformers in France have complained for generations. Education more than anything else is the reason for the lag between the traditional style of authority and the needs of a modern society in development.[35]

It is now widely believed that the mere pressure of numbers will explode the old structures, modify methods, and transform the style. A secondary school system that in 1970 is expected to provide instruction for four million children cannot remain identical to one which at the beginning of the century trained two hundred thousand. Between 1950 and 1965, the number of students in higher education has risen ten fold to 550,000, and this before the demographic bulge has made itself fully felt. The student body is expected to have doubled again by 1972, yet at present there exist only nineteen universities and an equal number of other institutions of higher learning. Today a good third of all students are still concentrated in Paris, but some of the provincial universities are finally able to expand because the traditional methods of selecting the teaching staff for higher education are breaking down in some places.

Critics of the present government point out that in spite of substantial increases budgetary allocations for educational equipment and personnel are constantly compressed and dramatically insufficient because year after year other objectives are granted priority. Only in the field of education does the majority party, the U.N.R., formulate annually sharp grievances against the government which it supports. An increasing body of opinion calls for a reexamination of the role of education in society beyond the allocation of resources and beyond partial reforms. But there are legitimate doubts as to whether the weight of population pressures and of economic and technological needs will, as it were, automatically transform an archaic system.

[35] Hoffmann, *op. cit.*, p. 73, and in a strikingly similar vein more than half a century earlier, Emile Durkheim, *Education and Sociology* (Glencoe: The Free Press, 1956; originally published between 1903 and 1911), pp. 135 ff.

## ASSOCIATIONS

Many observers, the French sociologist Durkheim among them, have deplored that France is weak in secondary groups standing between the state and the individual and able "to drag them [the citizens] into the general current of social life." [36] It is no longer true, if it ever was, that the system lacks interest groups aggregating and defending innumerable material and immaterial interests and values. (For details see Chap. VII.) But it remains correct that neither interest groups nor other associations, numerous though they are, play as significant a role in the socialization of the citizen as they do in other countries.

A negative bias against authority might have encouraged association if the egalitarian thrust and the competition between individuals did not cast suspicion on those who recommended that efforts be combined. The ambivalence towards participation in group life is not merely negativistic apathy, but a lack of belief in the value of cooperation.

Nonetheless, there exists now a fairly dense network of organizations concerned not only with interest representation but also with leisure time activities, social life, and the like, and membership in these associations is quite widespread and frequent, even though it reaches nowhere near American levels. For example, a not entirely reliable survey undertaken in 1951 concluded that only 41 per cent of French adults belonged to any kind of association. But while, on the one hand, this included political parties, on the other, it did not account for multiple memberships.[37] More recent inquiry is concerned

[36] Emile Durkheim, *The Division of Labor in Society* (New York: The Macmillan Company, 1933, originally published in 1893), p. 28.

[37] Arnold M. Rose, "Voluntary Associations in France" in Arnold M. Rose (ed.), *Theory and Method in the Social Sciences* (Minneapolis: University of Minnesota Press, 1954), pp. 74–75. Professor Rose's findings have been criticized on the basis of empirical research by Orvell R. Gallagher, "voluntary Associations in France," *Social Forces*, XXXVI:2 (1957), pp. 153 ff. Duncan MacRae, Jr., *Parliament, Parties and Society in France, 1946–1958* (New York: St. Martin's Press, 1967); p. 30 presents an interesting table comparing associational membership in the United States and France. One only wished that his basic data were more reliable and more comparable.

respectively, with the sixteen to twenty-four and the fifteen to
twenty age group found that only between 28 per cent and 35
per cent belonged to any association open to either young or
adult, of these a good half to sports clubs.[38] Even such numbers are considered inflated by some observers.

However, these and similar data are not too meaningful if
one wishes to assess the importance of associations in the life
of the individual. It is not enough to count associations or
membership affiliations. They play a role in the socialization
process only when they determine activities and emotions of
the citizens. Here, as to a lesser extent in the United States,
social class makes a difference. The upper urban bourgeoisie
appears to have the most active associational life in a style that
frequently imitates the mores of the nobility. But various community studies that have been undertaken agree that outside
that limited circle formally organized associations have little
importance and cut very little into the lives of their members.
The need for human fellowship is satisfied either within the
family or, depending on class and environment, in such un-
structured gatherings as the *salon,* the café, or, for the young,
the *bande* (not to be confused with a gang). The individual's
reluctance to get involved finds justification in the fact that in
a highly centralized political system grass roots associations are
generally ineffectual. Neither the promotion of reforms nor the
defense of established situations seem to be the proper domain
of community action — influence has to be exercised at the
seat of power.

This has encouraged and facilitated the politization of a
wide range of associational activities. Since Frenchmen feel
that they are unable to control the immediate environment,
those who wish to be active concentrate their efforts on trying
to make over society at large; at the very least they hope to
save their souls by striving for a well defined cause. Student
associations and other youth movements are politically committed and hence periodically divided, sometimes over the
question as to whether or not a political orientation is desir-

[38] Duquesne, *op. cit.,* pp. 216 ff., and pp. 138–41, and Rapport d'Enquête
du Ministère de la Jeunesse et des Sports, *Jeunes d'Aujourd'hui* (Paris: La
*Documentation Française,* 1967), pp. 179 and *passim.*

able. Every religious denomination (and the nonreligious *laïques* as well) has its own scout movement. Trade unions are split into several splinter and four major confederations. In many respects the labor movement offers a particularly striking example of the gap that exists between the purposes and the realities of associational life (for details see Chap. VII).

Of late there are indications that associative life is becoming denser and more rewarding. Its value is no longer assessed merely in terms of the associations' success in the interest group arena. Modern mass media (see Chap. VI) have encouraged a flowering of cultural clubs, mostly but not only among the young; they have often swept aside the traditional barriers of class, of denomination, and of political conviction. The organizations of young farmers already mentioned have usually preserved their twofold function as interest groups and organs of cooperation. Their fairly wide acceptance is all the more remarkable as they are the outgrowth of a Catholic movement. In other milieus similar activities are noted. "What characterizes all these organizations," a French sociologist has written in a statement which, it is true, some would consider too sweepingly optimistic, "is the need to make contact between category and category, between spiritual family and spiritual family, the horror of a priori formulas and systems, the passion for reform and the ideology of participation." [39]

Young workers and white-collar employees, young farmers, young businessmen and students, express their intention of affiliating with their professional associations, trade unions, etc., in significantly greater numbers than their elders. Most of them are also convinced that their contemporaries are more interested in such associations and in their future role than is the older generation. At the same time, it appears that this role is viewed differently now than in the past: associations are regarded as necessary and normal elements of modern society rather than as "movements" or standard bearers of a cause.

If such attitudes were to be accepted widely, associational life might furnish a far more important contribution than

[39] Michel Crozier, "The Cultural Revolution: Notes on the Changes in the Intellectual Climate of France," in Stephen R. Graubard (ed.), *The New Europe* (Boston: Houghton Mifflin, 1964), p. 624.

heretofore to the learning process of elites and of common man.

## CONCLUSION

From our discussion of the ongoing socialization of French-men, it has become clear why an often noted contradiction in the behavior of Frenchmen is more apparent than real. Why, it is frequently asked, is a nation whose history has frequently been an inspiration to free peoples everywhere and which is made up of self-reliant, rational, and mature individuals, un-able to establish a stable democracy? The answer to this ques-tion may be found in the fact that the values which the individual Frenchman has learned to accept as normal and which many of them cherish are often in conflict with the needs of a political system combining freedom and authority.

Tensions between the desire to assert the "uniqueness" of the individual and centuries-old experiences with a centralized bureaucratic control of society have produced ambiguous atti-tudes towards authority. They request that strict rulings treat everybody and everything alike in order to minimize possibili-ties for capricious discretion and discrimination. Since one suspects that the "others" — the authorities or the peers — will flout these rules in the interest of privilege, not willing obedi-ence but only a minimum of commitment, of outward compli-ance with community rules, can be expected. Hence, again in the words of Michel Crozier, "the disproportion between the authority which seems to us indispensable to govern a hu-man group and the authority that we can accept as members of a group." [40]

The distrust of others as a threat to individual self-fulfill-ment demands the distrust of, indeed wherever possible rebel-lion against, conventions and beliefs established by others.[41] As another French sociologist has remarked: whereas many Americans believe that self-fulfillment consists in adjustment

[40] "La France, terre de commandement," *Esprit,* XXV:12 (December 1957), pp. 779–97.

[41] The table published under the heading "Trust in Others" by Eck-stein, *op. cit.,* p. 222 makes it appear as if a higher percentage of French-men than of Americans trust their fellow-citizens. It rather points to the dubious value of such comparative polling data.

to a society whose basic values are not challenged, Frenchmen think that man is himself only when he rebels.[42] "I revolt, therefore we are," Albert Camus has written to dramatize the universality of protest. Since such protest is raised in the name of principle, since it is seen as a phase in the struggle against the forces of evil, it is usually highly moralistic — which is again fundamentally different from what has been described as the "unmoralistic" character of most Americans.[43]

The insistence on authoritatively enforced rules and the simultaneous distrust of established authority and of the peer group produce a political culture that expects little from co-operation or a broad-based participation in decision-making. The individual is self-confident enough not to expect strength from cooperation with others. Face-to-face relationships without which no cooperative form of action is possible are avoided as a possible source of friction. Intransigeant insistence on one's own position is regarded as more promising to conflict solution than bargaining. Typically enough, French dictionary definitions of the equivalent of bargaining and of compromise are all slightly pejorative. Only the arbiter who forces the conflicting parties to accept his verdict for a binding *compromis* earns prestige. The field of industrial relations is one of many where all partners show a preference for the imposed rather than the mutually agreed balance of interests.

It is obvious that such reservations against direct negotiations are likely to perpetuate the estrangement between groups and classes. "Every fraction of the social body," complains a progressive employers' organization, "has the — frequently justified — feeling that it is not understood by all the others. No group has the monopoly of this obsessional fever which one sometimes diagnoses solely among the working class. . . ."[44]

---

[42] Raymond Aron, as quoted by Stanley Hoffmann, "Protest in Modern France," in M. A. Kaplan, ed., *The Revolution in World Politics* (New York: John Wiley, 1962), pp. 69 ff.

[43] Cf. Robert E. Lane, *Political Ideology* (New York: The Free Press, 1962), p. 344.

[44] Association des Cadres Dirigeants de l'Industrie pour le Progrès Social et Economique, "Rapport sur l'Activité de l'Association en 1953," *Bulletin,* No. 78 (March 1954), p. 86.

The overall result of such mental attitudes has frequently been *incivisme,* that lack of solidarity and of civic sense which many Frenchmen deplore even while they are practicing it. When it results in a stalemate which stalls overdue changes, the nation is likely to turn to an authoritarian pacifier to solve the crisis. To accredit the solution which he imposes, he will frequently resort to a heroic style which in such a situation appears far more acceptable than the humdrum of laborious bargaining.

In spite of superficial similarities, this setting is not identical with the one in which a people try to be saved by a totalitarian rule from themselves which they are unable to control. Since the confidence which Frenchmen have in themselves as individuals is not impaired, they do not see the need for totalitarian manipulation of their minds. They still distrust their government as well as their neighbors and want to voice their distrust. The freedom left for such criticism and the unwillingness to enforce conformity distinguish the authoritarian from the totalitarian regime. The present Fifth Republic is as little totalitarian as was the liberal empire of Napoleon III to which it has been correctly compared. But the French authoritarian regimes of the past have never been able to get to the roots of the citizens' perennial ambiguity towards authority. Subsequent chapters will discuss whether or not the institutional framework created since General de Gaulle returned to power in 1958 promises to interrupt the alternation of either a lack or too great a concentration of power.

From the perspective of this study, the search for the "perfect" institution is vain. What matters most is whether the transformation of the political culture will overcome those traditions in the socialization of Frenchmen that have proven an obstacle to political modernization and to a mature democracy.

# CHAPTER IV

# Political Participation

IN A DEMOCRATIC SOCIETY the citizen's participation in the process by which political decisions are made influences both his political socialization and his political recruitment. When he takes part, directly or indirectly, in the selection of candidates for political office, when he votes in local or national elections, he experiences at first hand manifestations of the political system to which he belongs and he thereby undergoes further socialization. The process started in the family, the school, associations, and the like continues, but by getting involved in this kind of elementary political activity, the citizen also performs a political role and is therefore recruited into the system.

Hence socialization (discussed in the preceding chapter), political participation discussed in the present chapter, and the recruitment into active decision-making positions (to be treated in the next chapter) are tied together by the role which the citizen might play in any or all of these processes.

## THE CITIZEN IN LOCAL POLITICS

The concept of "grass-root democracy" is not peculiar to Anglo-American political systems. The notion that a viable democratic society must have a solid grounding in democratic institutions at the local level is widespread and generally realistic, even though occasionally tinged with romanticism. "The strength of free nations is rooted in their local governments,"

Tocqueville has written. When after the last world war the Allied Powers were responsible for the rebuilding of democratic institutions in Germany and Japan, they soon entrusted local officials with the discharge of public functions and authorized local elections as the first manifestations of a renascent political will.

In France, as elsewhere, politics at the local level play a multiple role in the socialization of the citizen. They continue the process of civic education which home and school have begun, at least interstitially. They offer possibilities for political participation beyond but including casting a ballot for local officials. They are a vantage point from which the political process can be watched at first hand and without some of the distortions which the observation of distant national politics entails. In many countries, and France among them, the local scene also provides the training ground for the political activist, for those who seek and find fulfillment in local government as well as for those who move on to a wider stage. All of these functions are interconnected. Whether and how effectively local politics can discharge them depends on the place of local government in the institutional framework of the total political system, and on the political culture surrounding both.

A marked characteristic of the French system is the extreme diffusion of local government units.[1] There are close to 38,000 *communes* (the basic area of local administration), or about as many as in the other five Common Market countries and Great Britain together. For comparison: there are fewer than 35,000 local school boards in the United States! But more than 35,000 French communes have less than 2,000 inhabitants, or an average of 450. The average population of all communes, including the large cities, is 1,300. This administrative structure is inherited from the Revolution and Napoleon, and in part goes back to the parishes of the *Ancien Régime*. It has survived stubbornly the economic and social transformations

[1] The best, nonlegalistic descriptions of local government has come from the pen of British authors: Brian Chapman, *Introduction to French Local Government* (London: Allen and Unwin, 1953), and F. Ridley and J. Blondel, *Public Administration in France* (New York: Barnes and Noble, 1965), pp. 85–122.

which an erstwhile agricultural country has undergone since then. In merely quantitative terms, it offers unrivaled opportunities for political socialization and participation. Since every commune is administered by a municipal council elected by universal suffrage and composed of between nine and thirty-seven [2] members, there are a total of almost 470,000 municipal councilors in France — 1.8 per cent of the electorate. This is not much less than the dues-paying membership of all political parties taken together. It has been estimated that three-fourths of the members of the Radical Party and one-half of the Socialists have at one time been municipal councilors!

The communes are combined into ninety departments, an upper-tier unit of local government, created during the Revolution from a desire to give France a uniform and rational structure that would eliminate the dangers of a centrifugal pull by the old provinces. The elective body presiding over the department, the *Conseil Général,* wields less power than does many a municipal council in its area, but the higher body opens additional avenues to elective office.

The formal equality bestowed on the local government units recognizes no legal difference between a metropolis and a mountain hamlet, between a department of five million or one of 82,000 inhabitants. As could be expected, discrepancies have increased considerably since 1789. Yet if there was artificiality when the structure was created, its very age has lent legitimacy to the established units. Whether communes and departments are, under present conditions, still efficient entities of local government, whether their legal equality is more than a hampering fiction, will be discussed below (see Chap. IX). But for citizens' identification, departments and communes have become natural, because traditional, entities of local government upon which to center political attention.

Another characteristic of French local government differs sharply from American and British practice; it also affects

[2] Only the city councils of Paris, Marseilles, and Lyons are larger. But in order to forestall any such autonomy as the Paris Commune assumed in the bloody uprising of 1871, neither Paris nor its twenty boroughs have a mayor.

fundamentally the roles of all of the main actors on the local
political scene. Because of governmental centralization, municipal government possesses no constitutional autonomy beyond
the right of existence. All the powers exercised by the local
government units are granted by the national government.
Such decentralization as is practiced means merely that local
officials have the legal right to exercise "their" powers. What
these powers actually consist of is determined by the central
government.[3] And the manner in which such centrally decreed
decentralization is made operational is of great importance.
Bureaucratic and representative institutions function side by
side; every individual operating on the level of either the department or the commune acts in a dual capacity. Whether
they are elected by the citizens, as are the mayors of the communes, or appointed by the Minister of Interior in Paris as are
the administrative heads of the ninety departments, the prefects, their every act is both that of a local government official
and of an agent of the national government. (Whenever the
mayor acts in an official capacity, such as marrying the
couples appearing before him, he dons the tricolor sash,
symbolizing state authority.)

The instrumentality tying together bureaucratic and representative institutions is the "tutelage" (*tutelle*), in principle,
and largely also in practice, quite different from the hierarchical supervision within a governmental administration. Political tutelage is exercised in two directions: control over the
personnel of the decentralized authorities and control over their
decisions. The elected local authorities are chosen by the
electorate without the intervention of the state; yet under
certain conditions they can be dismissed, and, more impor-
tantly, their decisions can be annulled as illegal by the prefects
to whom they must be submitted for approval.

The level of local taxation is determined by the local councils; but for fear of incompetence and dishonesty local taxes

---

[3] See Mark Kesselman, *The Ambiguous Consensus: A Study of Local
Government in France* (New York: Knopf, 1967), pp. 171 ff. This work is
largely based on excellent direct observation, but its material is mostly
drawn from small villages and towns.

are collected by the central government which permits, among other things, the complete audit of local finances by the national administration. In the total budget of local finances, grants-in-aid by the national government are of increasing importance, especially for all long-range investments. A commune which wants to float a loan will in general turn to one of the institutions controlled by the state, since, except for the very large cities, the market for municipal bonds is extremely limited. Even more restricting is the fact that local government authorities are not even expected to finance expenditures of certain local operations. Neither education (except for the buildings and for janitorial help) nor the police forces (except for the *garde champêtre*) are financed out of the local budget. This means that local government authorities have no control over these services. It might well be argued that such control is the test of local autonomy.

There are frequent and generally justified complaints about the tutelage as an instrument of archaic paternalism and of centralization; the prevailing system of finances is criticized as obsolete and inimical to economic growth and modernization.[4] Nonetheless, the present setup is far from being entirely inefficient, it profits from being a local adaptation of the traditional pattern of authority.

The established centralization does not regularly result in a slow and impersonal process. For the partner of the local authorities is not some ministerial bureau in Paris but the prefect and even more frequently the subprefect presiding over one of the 450 *arrondissements* into which the 90 departments are divided. If the entire system of local government is characterized by strong executive power, both the elected mayor, and the appointed prefect are strong executives. It is quite true that many initiatives for change come from above (in rural regions mostly from the subprefect), and that all initiatives starting from below become effective only with prefectoral

---

4 Cf. Roger Aubin, *Communes et Démocratie,* I: *Tâches et Moyens de la Commune* (Paris: Editions Ouvrières, 1965), pp. 221 f. The two volumes of this handbook are a mine of up-to-date information on local government and politics.

approval. But this does not condemn the mayor to passivity. It rather means that the mayor and his immediate assistants are expected to bargain incessantly with the authorities of the state for such approval.

The tone of prefectural directives may often be harshly authoritarian, and the mayor will never cease complaining about the lack of understanding shown by the representatives of the state, but more often than not relations between local authorities and their partners representing the central government are quite close and cordial. Within the commune an effective mayor emerges as the powerful executive which law and custom permit him to be. But at the same time the tutelage authorities value him as the link between the myriad of human problems within every commune and the abstract power of the state. This is not less true of the communist mayors than of others. (In 1960 of the 150 largest cities and towns, 25 were administered by Communists.)

In public opinion polls the mayor or the persons to whom he delegates functions, such as an assistant and especially the town clerk, are usually singled out as the "most important" or the "most useful figure around here," outranking deputies to the national parliament and civil servants. It is true that in most cases the other members of the municipal council, though they have elected the mayor from their own midst, do not amount to much. For all the informality of proceedings, the mayor resembles a local potentate in the midst of his council of elders and vassals.[5]

In many cases the authority of the mayor does not depend on his skill. He rather corresponds to the image of a traditional and often quite authoritarian father figure, acting out on the stage of local politics the role not only of the paterfamilias but also that of the head of family firm and family farm. This explains why conservative methods, or an acknowledged Conservative, are successful even in those communes which otherwise feel and vote to the left. It also explains why, barring a scandal, an incumbent mayor gets re-

[5] See Kesselman, *op. cit.*, pp. 66 ff., and pp. 38–52 for an excellent composite "portrait of mayor."

elected as long as he wishes to serve. There are municipalities where the office of the mayor has remained in the same family for many generations.

As that of an elected notable in the commune, the mayor's authority has increased with the decline in influence of the public school teacher and of ascriptive local notables, especially of the land-owning gentry. Many a *châtelain,* in the past often a mayor himself, has no longer the means to keep up his château and has consequently lost his interest in the welfare of the community.[6] Modern mass communication and the pull of urbanization have uprooted the teacher — formerly wedded to his rural school, acting as adviser to the families of his pupils, and frequently indispensable as town clerk. Quite apart from the feminization of the teaching profession, the duties of the town clerk have become too arduous to be handled by the teacher. But a full-time clerk, without an independent basis of authority, is nothing else but the mayor's agent, however indispensable his clerical services might become to the citizen enmeshed in the intricacies of a bureaucratized existence.

The prestige of local office is enhanced by the fact that the *cursus honorum* for a political career on the national scene starts usually in the commune and in the *Conseil Général* of the department. If in fact local government does not always provide a suitable training ground, it serves nevertheless as jumping-off point for the ambitious. To be taken seriously in Paris, a politician must have the credentials of local success. Whenever a new political regime is established, such as the Fourth Republic in 1945 and the Fifth in 1958, attempts may be made to cut such close ties in order to facilitate the access to national prominence for persons who had neither the time nor inclination to climb the ladder of local politics. But it never takes long before some of the normal career requirements are reestablished even if that means that the new men of power sink local roots *post hoc.*

Traditionally the combining of the functions of a deputy or a senator with those of a mayor has been one of the goals

[6] For a typical case see Wylie, *op. cit.,* p. 186.

of a political career. More than two-thirds of all deputies elected between 1900 and 1940 had been elected to local office before becoming representatives of the nation.[7] Vincent-Auriol, frequently Minister and finally President of the Republic, claimed that none of the offices he held gave him as much satisfaction as did that of Mayor of the town of Muret (pop. 6,800 and close to his birthplace), "our little *patrie*." Undoubtedly, such interlacing of national and local elective office has had a stabilizing influence on both levels. Flash political movements whose activists had no local ties have usually lost momentum after a short time. Municipal affairs are not seriously disrupted by sudden upheavals: in the local elections that took place one year after General de Gaulle's return to power, three-fourths of the mayors that had been in office under the defunct regime were reelected.

But so close a relationship is also unsettling. The deputy or senator who knows that he will be judged on the basis of his success in commune or department will frequently spend much of his energy in obtaining satisfaction for local demands. The Deputy Mayor of Bordeaux, speaker of the National Assembly and a staunch Gaullist, boasted quite recently that he would find the millions which Bordeaux needed for housing — but not in the pocketbooks of the people of Bordeaux. In this way the national representative, "ambassador" of his commune in Paris, brings constant local pressures into the national scene. Parish pump politics and centrifugal interests complicate further the working of the system. Another consequence has been that because of their strong local basis, political personnel become immovable and stability turns into stagnation. Needed reforms of structure and finances of local government, placed before the national legislature, are likely to be defeated by those representatives whose position benefits from the *status quo*.

French and foreign observers alike are uncertain in their evaluation of the French citizen's interest in local politics.

[7] In 1955, 176 *députés-maires* and 123 *sénateurs-maires* sat in the two houses of parliament. Although the first elections in the Fifth Republic (1958) brought many new men into the national arena, the number of *députés-maires* increased to 221.

A British author concludes that although local authorities possess greater power in his country, there is more interest in local matters and more vitality in local government in France. French political scientists believe that, among other symptoms, a high level of abstentions in local elections indicates that at present local politics fulfill very inadequately the function of inducing citizen participation.[8] In part such divergences result, of course, from the difficulty of generalizing about experiences in more than 38,000 local units which are different in everything but their legal structure — even average election figures are not too meaningful, the less so as the electoral system varies with the size of the communes. In rural communities participation is sometimes considerably higher in municipal than in national elections. In the large urban centers the situation is reversed. Just as the citizens of large American cities know that they must turn to the Federal Government rather than to the State Houses, French urban voters realize that the elective bodies of local government (either the municipal councils or the *Conseils Généraux*), conceived for the administration of an agricultural society, are inadequate for the solution of present-day problems.

However, electoral participation is not the only yardstick by which to measure political interest. Bonds of sympathy between the elected local authorities and their constituents are quite strong. In an opinion poll held shortly before the municipal elections of 1965, only 23 per cent of the voters wished to see their council members replaced by others, although the six years since the preceding elections had brought important changes to the entire nation. As we will see, there was during the Fourth Republic no circuit of confidence between the voters and an omnipotent National Assembly. Yet in local government despite its limited powers, there was such a circuit between representatives and people.[9]

[8] Cf. Chapman, *op. cit.*, p. 221, with Goguel and Grosser, *op. cit.*, p. 58. The question of the turnout in local elections is treated in detail by Kesselman, *op. cit.*, pp. 19 ff.

[9] See "L'Opinion Publique au début de l'année 1965," *Revue Française de Science Politique* (abbreviated hereafter as *RFSP*), XV:3 (1965), pp. 534–36, and Philip M. Williams, *Crisis and Compromise: Politics in the Fourth Republic* (1966 ed., Garden City: Doubleday and Company, Inc., 1966), p. 332.

The confidence that exists is based mostly on a record of efficient and capable administration, independent of the political color of the incumbent. But it is enhanced by the fact that municipal administration is the natural symbol for a community of local interests which are forever threatened by the central government — and frequently also by a neighboring town. The commune thus becomes a bastion manned by the mayor and his "team." Because of the narrow limits within which it must move, the achievements of local government often fall short of expectations. The central government will regularly be blamed for this, and in the next national election the citizen might react by casting a vote of protest against the regime. Hence the interest of the citizenry in the affairs of local government can sometimes be as disturbing for the stability of the system as the strong local roots of the representatives. Where civic involvement is exclusively determined by a parochial commitment, it might in the end produce effects which are inimical to a cohesive civic culture.

Since the local government is regarded above all as a dispenser of effective administration and as the focus of communal solidarity, a nonpartisan stance is fairly widespread both in elections and in the behavior of the elected. In the smaller communities the political labels which the candidates wear are quite meaningless. Sometimes the opposing candidates represent mere local factions. Often lists "For the Defense of Local Interests" are considered more attractive than party lists. They resemble frequently the "balanced ticket" of an American municipality: representatives of various economic interests and social groups, local notables, sometimes representatives of minority groups are all given a place. When an incumbent mayor stands for reelection, he enjoys an almost complete freedom from the institutional restraints which well organized political parties might place on the selection of candidates and the determination of programs. The mayor, aided by his assistants, fulfills the party's function all by himself, which is, however, quite different from being the boss of a local machine.

In cities over 30,000 the political label of the mayor is usually somewhat more distinct. But even when the mayor is a national political figure, the local election campaign will de-emphasize as far as possible his party affiliation. The Gaullist Mayor of Bordeaux weathered in his city administration the years during which the Gaullist movement touched rock bottom. Gaston Defferre, leader of the Socialist group in parliament and for a time prospective candidate in the presidential elections, sought to distance himself from his own party when he campaigned for reelection as mayor of Marseilles. "Things are different from parliamentary elections," he declared. Candidates would not behave in this way if the voters did not approve of keeping party politics out of municipal affairs. Recently, 46 per cent of the voters declared that the attitude of local candidates towards General de Gaulle's policies was of no concern to them. Significantly, the proportion of those who were unconcerned was highest among farmers (57 per cent) and in rural communities generally, while in the big cities and especially in Paris the political orientation of the respective municipal councilors became a somewhat weightier factor.

By and large not only the elected representatives but also the "tutelage" authorities take the nonpartisan character of local government at its face value. This explains in part the success of communist-administered communes flourishing under regimes which have for twenty years pushed communism to the outer reaches of the political system. If communist mayors complain more frequently that the prefects suspend their decisions and interfere with their projects, this merely indicates that their administrations are trying to break out somewhat more boldly from the narrow confines of French local government.

The price that has to be paid for nonpartisan harmony on the municipal level is, at least in the small rural communities, frequently quite high. A constantly renewed effort not to destroy the consensus often discourages dynamic action and indicates more interest in equilibrium than in progress. Political activity and problem solving are not carried to the market place where opposition would have to be faced and where bargaining would have to take place in public. Instead, success and failure depend on personal relations, many of which are hierarchically ordained.

Such arrangements have in turn their effect on the participatory attitudes of the citizens. Once the elections are over, the citizenry in many communes pays scant attention to the activities of their local representatives. The meetings of the city council are hardly ever attended by the public. Nothing of importance seems to happen there since most mayors prefer to make decisions and take action behind closed doors. If citizens feel aggrieved they will assemble to protest in front of the buildings housing the prefect or subprefect rather than lay their case before the city council. In fact, local government is "representative" government in the strict sense which does not permit the electorate to interfere in any way with its work. A municipal code for all of France, enacted in the dying days of the Fourth Republic and not modified by the new regime, forbids all referenda on local matters or even straw voting. This suits most mayors who, once elected, wish to behave like little monarchs ruling both their constituents and the city council with a strong hand.

The rules set by the council, most of whose members are quite inactive, are accepted as rulings coming from above, i.e., from the conjunction of the two strong executives: the mayor and the prefect. Such a system is hardly suited to teach citizens the art of solving problems together. Here again generalizations are hazardous, especially since traditional attitudes seem to be giving way in more than a few localities. There are municipal councils that organize themselves so as to give a hearing before appropriate subcommittees to a variety of interests. Citizen groups are invited to cooperate with the local authorities either on a functional or geographical basis.

Of late, local politics are sometimes becoming the battleground for the struggle between generations. For many members of the younger generation, political activity means entering the municipal council and aspiring to be elected mayor. To overcome isolation, they will establish contact with like-minded elements in other communes. With the flatness of the political landscape in a regime where political prominence is reserved to the presidency, the office of mayor remains one of the few places where authority and ability are still visible.[10]

The style and behavior of these new local leaders is often incompatible with traditional attitudes. Where the "old" mayor sought distinction by living within a limited budget, the "new notables" do not shy away from imposing new tax burdens on their constituents. In cities and towns with an expanding economy the electorate approves of such efforts and is willing to shoulder additional obligations. (Another characteristic of such municipalities is that their candidates for local government office shun party commitment even more emphatically than others.)

The defeat which in the municipal elections of 1965 a slate of such new notables inflicted on both the Gaullist incumbent and on the Communists in Grenoble (pop. 233,000) has been hailed as an indication of future trends in local government. This victory, paralleling less dramatic events in other regions of rapid development, was in part due to a mobilization of the managerial strata and activists from *all* of the existing trade union movements. The victorious candidates appeared more committed to the practices of a participatory local democracy than their rivals. But it is as yet impossible to judge whether what has happened was an event of considerable political importance or a mere episode.[11]

Whether changes occurring elsewhere in local government are apt to overcome that ambivalence of attitudes and institutions which until now has made it so difficult to assess the role of local politics in the socialization of the French citizen remains equally uncertain.

## VOTING IN PARLIAMENTARY ELECTIONS

Writing in 1910 Alain, philosopher-preceptor of classical French republicanism, stated that election day had only one

[10] See Philip Williams, "Party, Presidency and Parish Pump in France," *Parliamentary Affairs*, XVIII:3 (1965), p. 257.

[11] For a cautious and thoughtful evaluation see Georges Lavau, "Réflexions sur le 'Mythe' de l'Election Grenobloise," *RFSP*, XV:5 (1965), pp. 958–63.

significance: the citizen designated the deputy best suited to
resist the ever encroaching power of the central government.
Parliament was not there to launch reforms which in the end
would only result in more infringements upon the rights of
the individual. Its mandate was rather to submit to the authorities, like the States-General on the eve of the French
Revolution, the citizens' complaints against unending arbitrariness.[12]

As in most of his writings, Alain when giving such advice did not prescribe novel attitudes but admonished his
fellow Frenchmen not to forget old, established traditions. All
through the Third and Fourth Republics, with the exception
of a short interlude between 1945 and 1947 when a modern
party system seemed to be in the making, the French voter
looked upon his representative in parliament as his personal
"ambassador" in Paris. By his vote he entrusted him with the
defense of constituency interests, caring little as to how a
coherent national policy could emerge when the cleavages of
society were faithfully reproduced in parliament. France remained the classical example of an atomistic representative
system, conceived for another age. In this sense, a deputy who
harassed every government until he could finally destroy it
by a vote of censure was carrying out the assignment which
his constituents had given him.

In other Western parliamentary systems, the emergence of
structured and disciplined parties has modified (in the age of
mass democracy), the earlier system of representation. Binding
instructions from party or parliamentary groups leave to the
representatives little room for independent decisions based
on constituency considerations, but determine instead the
course of action for government or opposition. In the United
States, where the parties do not wield such power, not the
congressional but the presidential elections give to the electorate a voice in deciding who should govern and who should
be replaced at the helm of the government. In republican
France, neither disciplined parties nor popular elections of
the executive allowed that involvement of the electorate which

[12] Alain, *Politique* (Paris: Presses Universitaires, 1952), pp. 2, 7.

has elsewhere given strength and legitimacy to representative institutions.[13]

In the words of an astute and close observer of French parliamentarianism:

> They [the French voters] were not consulted on concrete problems, as might have been the case if elections had been able to establish a clear sanction for durable and coherent government administration and a choice between specific programs. They were not even consulted on the way the Parliamentary "game" was played between elections. . . . The weakness of the political parties and their narrow oligarchical organization was such that it was impossible to assume that they represented the opinion of most Frenchmen.[14]

This explains the long-standing ambivalence of the French voter towards the parliamentary system. As the guardians of constituency interests, deputies and senators still commanded respect. Either as an individual or as the member of an interest group, the voter would lay his grievances before "his" deputy either in writing or during the deputy's frequent tours of his constituency. But when the deputies engaged in what de Gaulle has called the "games, poisons and delights" of the system, when they made and unmade governments, seemingly and in fact without any regard for the "popular verdict" of the preceding elections, popular contempt engulfed both the representatives and the system. The electorate felt that it was "absent," kept away from meaningful participation and outside the centers where policy alternatives were decided. Such feelings were at the root of a basic antiparliamentary bias on the part of many regular voters, a bias that was noted even at a time when cabinet instability was not yet disturbing the basic equilibrium of a "stalemate society." [15]

When contrary to expectations the Fourth Republic was as unable as its predecessor to make elections meaningful for

13 For more details, see Henry W. Ehrmann, *Direct Democracy*, pp. 885 f., and the authors there quoted.

14 Goguel, in *In Search of France*, p. 396. The author is the Secretary General of the French Senate.

15 The term was coined by Stanley Hoffmann, *op. cit., passim.*

determining the policies of rapidly shifting majorities, the circuit of confidence between the electorate and its representatives was totally interrupted. Electoral participation did not flag, but shortly before the last elections of the Fourth Republic, 33 per cent of the voters were convinced that their vote would have no influence whatsoever on future political developments. At that time not more than 2 per cent designated the premier who assumed office after the election as their choice for that post. Only 11 per cent were in favor of retaining the prevailing system under which the deputies were at liberty to overthrow the government at will without themselves being threatened by a dissolution of parliament. If 39 per cent were unable or unwilling to express any preference for either the existing setup or proposed alternatives, 31 per cent were, even then, in favor of a direct election of the chief executive.[16]

Popular attitudes towards the proper functions of parliamentary elections underwent a rather drastic change during the postwar years; they remained, however, as contradictory as they had always been. In 1944, shortly after the liberation, 72 per cent of the voters were of the opinion that votes should be cast on the basis of programs put forward by the political parties; only 16 per cent said that they would vote "for a man." In January 1958, shortly before General de Gaulle re-entered the political scene, only 27 per cent of the voters (overwhelmingly Communists) wished to decide on the basis of sympathies for a party, for 52 per cent the "man" would determine their vote.[17]

After the fall of the Fourth Republic, the insistence of the new leadership that the old parties were unrepresentative was widely accepted by the citizens whenever an electoral contest pitted the traditional parties against the new regime. In the opinion of the voters this did not mean that a democratic system could do without parties: only 26 per cent thought so

16 See *Sondages,* XVII:4 (1955), pp. 11, 18, and XVIII:3 (1956), p. 54. According to experienced French observers these as well as the public opinion data which follow should be evaluated with caution, since both questions and answers were often ambiguous.

17 *Ibid.,* XX:3 (1958), pp. 56–57.

in 1962 and 20 per cent in 1965, after the Fifth Republic had been in power for seven years.[18] Yet in the same opinion poll the respondents showed little inclination for a disciplined party system: only 18 per cent believed that a deputy should vote with his party; 50 per cent wished to see him reach his own individual decisions in each case; for 21 per cent the answer would vary according to the question to be voted upon. Whether those who answered in this way were conscious of it or not, their preferences indicated how deeply rooted were the traditions of a system of atomistic representation. To them parties and elections were to disperse power rather than to gather its segments and to yield them as one.

It has often been argued, by Frenchmen and foreigners alike, that the electoral systems as practiced in France have been responsible for the weakness of the party system, for cabinet instability, and thereby ultimately for the voters' ambivalence towards parliamentary elections and represent-ative institutions. It is true that since direct and general manhood suffrage was introduced in 1848 (women won the franchise only in 1945), French men have never voted under the system practiced in both the United States and Great Britain. In these two countries single member constituencies in which the leading candidate is elected, whether or not he has won an absolute majority, have apparently been an im-portant factor for the emergence of a two-party system. Could one not have expected the same development in France, if a similar voting system had been adopted in time?

Ever since parliamentary institutions were introduced in France, the electoral system "has been treated as a weapon in the struggle between different political camps and between different political forces for the control of State and so-ciety." [19] Since the establishment of the Third Republic in 1871, about a dozen different electoral laws governing na-tional elections have been adopted and tried; in between a number of abortive reform proposals have given rise to

[18] *Ibid.,* XXVIII:1 (1966), p. 37.
[19] See Peter Campbell, *French Electoral Systems* (Hamdon: Archon Books, 1965), p. 17.

passionate debates in parliament. The mode of local elections has also frequently been tampered with. Only once has a national electoral system survived for thirty years (1889–1919); none of the others was used for as long as ten years before being considerably changed or completely discarded. Obviously, such constant modifications have not lent to any system that legitimacy which comes from permanence. Instead these modifications have fostered the voters' cynicism and their feeling of being used for the ends of a "political class" over which they had no control.

Nonetheless, the proposition that a single-ballot, simple-majority system would have bestowed greater stability to French politics is untenable. If such a solution has not been adopted by now it is largely due to the fact that the two camps which must be formed to make such a system work never had sufficient cohesion. The divisions which have existed within the Right and the Left were not created by the electoral systems. Rather, the electoral systems which were tried appeared unavoidable because of existing divisions. In order to reduce the vote of the people to a simple alternative, their representatives should have been able to reduce their differences to simpler terms — such a simplification has never appeared to be within reach.[20]

The two major electoral systems that have governed all parliamentary elections, albeit with innumerable variations, have mirrored rather faithfully a divided body politic. During the Fourth Republic proportional representation was practiced, a system which in the Scandinavian countries and now in the Federal Republic of Germany has not prevented strong parties and stable government coalitions. In France it was soon in need of modification because if the extremist parties on the Right and the Left had been represented in accordance with their electoral strength, no government whatsoever would have been possible. Most elections in the Third Republic were held under a system in which run-off elections were necessary unless one of the candidates obtained an absolute majority of the votes cast. Because of the multiplicity of

[20] See Raymond Aron, "Electeurs, Partis et Elus," *RFSP*, V:2 (1955), p. 252.

groups and factions few seats were won in the first ballot. Since in the second ballot a plurality of votes was sufficient to win, the less successful candidates withdrew in favor of their competitors, which gave to the earlier ballot some of the characteristics of an American primary. But political results were different. The coalition of factions or parties which obtained between the two ballots in order to reach agreement on the most promising candidate, never persisted for long in parliament: fundamental divisions reappeared. Except on the extreme Left, there were no organized parties that could exact voting discipline from the representatives.

If under the present regime greater stability has prevailed, this cannot be attributed to the method by which the deputies to the National Assembly are elected. For in essence it is the same system, slightly modified, which was in force during the most troubled years of the Third Republic, and which had been discarded after the war for its parochial and "log rolling" effects. If in 1958 General de Gaulle designated it as his personal preference, to the surprise of many of his closest collaborators, he did so in the tradition of all electoral reformers in France: he wished to promote short-range goals, in this instance to prevent the strong expression of any one current of opinion in parliament, which he preferred to keep divided. As has happened before, the outcome was quite different from what had been expected, for politics are shaped by factors other than the electoral system.

Important though possibly temporary changes in electoral participation and electoral behavior have indeed occurred since the return to power of General de Gaulle. But hardly any of the changes can be traced to the reintroduction of an electoral system which in the Third Republic was associated with an entirely different style of politics.

In both the Third and the Fourth Republics general disenchantment with parliamentary institutions never prevented a high turnout at national elections. Since the consolidation of republican institutions in 1885 (and with the one exception of the somewhat abnormal post-World War I election of 1919), electoral participation never fell to less than 71 per cent of registered voters. In most elections participation was much

higher; in the last election of the Third Republic (1936) it
rose to 84 per cent and, twenty years later, in the last election
of the Fourth Republic to 83 per cent. Actually, voting by the
male population since the Second World War must have been
considerably more intense than before. For women accounted
for about two-thirds of the nonvoters, and yet overall electoral
participation did not substantially decline after the introduction of woman suffrage.[21]

As in other countries, social class, age, and education were
important factors in determining the degree of electoral participation: the least educated, the lowest income groups, and
the youngest and the oldest age groups voted less. Among
women, those employed voted more frequently than those at
home.

More pronounced than in other countries, however, was the
difference between rural and urban constituencies. Quite generally, voting was heavier in the countryside than in the cities
to the point of offsetting other determinants, such as education and income. This was generally attributed to the greater
personal intensity experienced by the rural voter during the
campaign and afterwards in his relation with *his* deputy. During the electoral campaign, the smaller the districts the more
fascinating became the personal confrontations of the candidates, their mutual accusations in the election materials, and
the equally vehement discussions among their followers. Local
antagonisms usually had the effect of mobilizing voter interest.

If one measures political participation in terms of voting
alone, a regional difference appeared and continues to exist:
south of the Loire River abstention is generally higher than
in the North. But if one also takes into account other "participatory" factors, such as attendance at electoral meetings, reading of the posters, political discussions, then the rural voters
in the South as well as elsewhere appear far more involved
than the urban population.[22] This, however, holds true only
of men, not of women.

21 For estimates of women voters' behavior see Mattei Dogan and
Jacques Narbonne, *Les Françaises face à la Politique* (Paris: Colin, 1955),
esp. pp. 85–87 and the inquiries therein cited.
22 For details see Georges Dupeux, "Citizen Participation in Political
Life, France," *International Social Science Journal*, XII:1 (1960), pp. 41 ff.

Altogether, the frustrating results of most elections notwithstanding, the political mobilization of the citizenry by the election process remained strong all through the lives of the now defunct republics. Constituency interests and an individualized appeal to the voters kept tension and hence interest high.

The first two parliamentary elections held in the Fifth Republic (1958 and 1962) took place under such extraordinary circumstances that it was impossible to draw any conclusions regarding a possible change in voting behavior. By French standards, the number of abstentions was unusually large: 31 per cent abstentions in 1962 represented a high since 1881. But the high voter participation in the presidential elections of 1965 (see below), and the fact that in the third parliamentary elections in 1967 there were only 19.1 per cent abstentions makes it clear that Frenchmen, even under vastly changed circumstances, still attach value to that form of political participation which consists of casting a ballot.

The first two elections of the Fifth Republic took place within weeks of a national referendum of great importance. Both in 1958 and in 1962 the electorate had accepted by referendum the constitutional proposals put before it by General de Gaulle. After this many voters were known to have felt that the die was already cast and that in an election all they could do was to corroborate their earlier "yes" or "no" vote. Such an act of confirmation obviously elicited less interest, hence the high rate of abstentions which was of about equal proportion for all parties.

In 1967 the situation was radically different. No constitutional, political, economic, or diplomatic crisis loomed on the horizon. The situation was more "normal" than it had been for any election during the preceding forty years. This, however, does not mean that the political significance of the parliamentary elections of 1967 and the voters' attitude towards them can be likened to the situation which had prevailed at

---

The findings of this often quoted and interesting article are seriously doubted. The author himself admits that the attempt to emulate, in the interest of comparison, inquiries developed in the U.S. yields at times unconvincing results.

election time in the Third and Fourth Republics. Probably even more than the first two elections in the new republic, the most recent contest was clearly national in character. From the very beginning, and in spite of the fact that for the first ballot more than two candidates were standing in each constituency, the electorate was asked to decide between General de Gaulle's government and the forces opposed to it. The personalization of the national contest was matched by a depersonalization of the individual campaigns. Candidates still made public a traditional "confession of faith," i.e., a statement of goals. But for the Gaullist side the pronouncements became stereotyped, if they were not simply copying a model. For the opposition forces, the theme crowding out all others was a defiance of "personal power." In the second ballot, only two candidates faced each other in the vast majority of constituencies. (For the distribution of votes and of seats in parliament, see Chap. VIII and Table IV.)

Campaigning and political propaganda have acquired a national dimension, even though they are still decentralized to fit the anachronistic forms imposed by the electoral system. But voters and candidates alike had much earlier come to look at traditional electioneering as obsolete and superfluous rites. The attendance at electoral meetings has steadily fallen off, except in certain rural areas of the South where verbosity is still enjoyed. The individual billboards placed throughout the constituency and on which each candidate is entitled to post his personal appeal to the electorate, no longer draw much attention. Even the American style neighborhood campaigning, previously quite customary in France, appears to yield diminishing results. This does not mean that local electioneering has ceased entirely, but it addresses itself to a different audience.[23] Quite systematically many candidates seek out local notables, foremost among them the mayors, which is additional evidence of the political vitality of local government. Candidates grant interviews to interest group representatives in their districts; they send out circular letters, often with an appeal for contributions, to diversified mailing lists.

[23] For an example of party instructions to local candidates see Goguel and Grosser, *op. cit.*, pp. 59 ff.

The national and regional press, radio and television, uniform tracts and posters for the entire nation, at most slightly altered to fit local needs, put candidates and issues before the voter. The professionalization of campaigning has made rapid progress: the use of public opinion polls and of public relations experts, and the systematic observation of electioneering in other countries have become widespread.

All this represents a rather radical departure from the past. The fact that, in 1967, voters went to the polls in great numbers and amidst real political excitement, seems to indicate that they accept the logic of the new institutions. Popular elections of the President and of the lower house of parliament, even when they are separated as was the case this time by a considerable time span,[24] were seen as two closely connected modes of electoral participation, and as such both have won approval. Whether the plebiscitarian character which the parliamentary elections have assumed so far will characterize future contests also, especially after General de Gaulle's demise, remains to be seen. It might depend on the personality of future presidential candidates and on the chances for a transformation of the party system, a problem to be discussed below (see Chap. VIII).

## VOTING IN PLEBISCITARIAN CONTESTS: REFERENDUM AND PRESIDENTIAL ELECTIONS

During the seventy years of the Third Republic, proposals for the direct appeal to the electorate were weapons in the arsenal of antirepublican and bonapartist critics of the regime (see Chap. I). It came therefore as a surprise when shortly after the liberation of the country, in a climate of democratic frenzy, General de Gaulle proposed to consult the electorate on the problem of the new constitution. Even before the Provisional Government, headed by de Gaulle, had assumed control of the country, the leader of the Free French movement had manifested his predilection for a direct appeal to the

---

[24] The regular term of presidential office is seven years, that of the National Assembly five. The death of a president or the dissolution of parliament, which may take place at almost any time, can narrow or widen the time gap between the two elections.

people. His radio addresses requesting loyalty to the Free French cause and encouraging manifestations of such loyalty were designed to create a bond between leader and people. They also established a habit for both.

When the first tiny island was wrested from Vichy rule, General de Gaulle, not unlike Napoleon III when France incorporated Nice, organized a regular plebiscite among the population. As always under such circumstances, 98 per cent of the votes cast expressed their allegiance to him. During the progressive liberation of French territory by the Allies, de Gaulle took the spontaneous acclamations he reaped wherever he appeared as the popular endorsement he had striven for since the dark days of 1940.

The postwar decision to give constituent powers to the electorate was motivated by a similar desire to invest the political order with legitimacy after the interruption of war and occupation. The political atmosphere in which the three referendums were held in 1945 and 1946 seemed to clear them of plebiscitarian or bonapartist suspicions. Only later General de Gaulle did interpret the first ballot which Frenchmen were invited to cast after the war as a mark of confidence in his person and as a condemnation of "party omnipotence." [25] In the midst of the material harshness of the postliberation period, 80 per cent of the voters cast their ballots in the first two direct consultations of the electorate since the declining days of the Second Empire. Massive abstentions in the third referendum, when only a minority of registered voters adopted the constitution of the Fourth Republic, were not due to a lack of interest. As later, in the referendum of 1962, conflicting pressures resulted in hesitations to cast either a negative or an affirmative vote. In parliamentary elections held barely a month later, voting participation was back to normal.

There were many indications that an electorate for which constituency concerns had long blotted out the symbolic value

[25] *War Memoirs*, III, p. 270. In the referendum the electorate rejected in fact the ultra-representative constitution of 1875 and at the same time accepted the proposal to submit the text of the new constitution, after its elaboration by a Constituent Assembly, to a popular referendum.

of elections as manifestations of a national political will, approved of nation-wide consultations, at least in time of crisis. In a public opinion poll held in 1945 only one-fifth of the electorate criticized the use of the referendum for the proposed ends. Nonetheless, the Fourth Republic returned to the undiluted representative traditions cherished by deputies, senators, and local notables. When de Gaulle founded his own party in 1947 to combat the regime and to question its very legitimacy (see Chap. VIII), the new party soon called for the extensive use of the referendum on constitutional amendments, major legislation, and international treaties. But by then such demands were once more regarded as expressions of an authoritarian assault on the republic.

The constitution of the Fifth Republic, as enacted in 1958, was far more modest in its departures from a classical representative regime. It is true that the constitution itself was submitted to the electorate for approval. But the direct appeal to the voters which it permitted under carefully circumscribed conditions (art. 11 and art. 89 of the constitution) was hedged by parliamentary controls. The government gave official assurances that the referendum would never be used by the executive as a means of arousing popular opinion against the elected assemblies. Moreover, parliament remained the sole, directly elected trustee of the sovereign nation. The popular election of the President of the Republic was explicitly rejected in favor of his designation by an electoral college of some 80,000 local government officials.

In fact, an extensive use of the referendum, the introduction of direct popular suffrage for presidential elections, and the attitude of the electorate towards such novel modes of consulting the voters, permitted the thorough transformation of political institutions. It also had a possibly profound impact on the style of electoral participation.

Between 1793 and 1962 the French electorate has been convened fifteen times to vote in a national referendum. (As mentioned earlier, there exist no local referendums.) It has been said correctly that all but the two consultations in 1946, when subsequent drafts of a constitutional text were submitted to the voters, have in fact been not referendums but plebiscites.[26] A referendum (such as practiced in the American states and the Swiss cantons), is a device, handled with more or less political felicity, but always inviting the voters to arbitrate between equally available solutions. By contrast, a plebiscite requests the voters to endorse an already established policy from which the return to the *status quo ante* either is impossible or can be obtained only at a seemingly exorbitant price. Usually a providential leader (in France the two Bonapartes and now General de Gaulle) demands an act of faith from the electorate by declaring that he could not continue at the helm without a massive vote of confidence. He thus raises the specter of political or social chaos as the alternative to his continued rule. In the eighteenth century, Jean-Jacques Rousseau assigned to the leader the task of formulating correctly the few questions which were to be put before the people in such a way that the general will would "see things as they are (and) sometimes as they ought to appear to it." With the approach of mass democracy, the nineteenth century Swiss historian Jacob Burckhardt had stated that the "future belongs to the masses and to the men that can explain things simply to them." Since in fact political problems have become immensely more intricate rather than simpler, this means that issues may be simplified to the point of distortion. Moreover, by wrapping several propositions into one, the plebiscite not only maximizes chances for approval but also usually ties the sanction of an irretrievable past to the acceptance of dimly specified future policies.[27]

On all these grounds the four referendums organized since 1958 qualify as plebiscites. (For the results, see Table II.) In 1958, a vote against the new constitution might in fact have brought the country back to the civil war which it had narrowly escaped a few months earlier. Forty per cent of the gen-

[26] See Gilbert Bortoli, *Sociologie du Referendum dans la France Moderne* (Paris: Librarie Générale de Droit et Jurisprudence, 1965), pp. 2 ff. There is *ibid.,* p. 9, a useful table of all the referendums held in France between 1793 and the present.

[27] For the difference between a true referendum and a plebiscite, see Otto Kirchheimer, "France from the Fourth to the Fifth Republic," *Social Research,* XXVI:4 (1958), p. 403.

TABLE II  *French Referendums, 1958–1962, and Second Ballot of Presidential Elections, 1965 (Voting in Metropolitan France)*

| Date | Registered voters (In millions) | Abstentions | | Yes-votes or votes for de Gaulle as President | | | No-votes or votes for Mitterand for President | | |
|---|---|---|---|---|---|---|---|---|---|
| | | (In millions) | % of registered voters | (In millions) | % of registered voters | % of votes cast | (In millions) | % of registered voters | % of votes cast |
| 9/28/58 | 26.61 | 4.01 | 15.06 | 17.67 | 66.41 | 79.25 | 4.62 | 17.38 | 20.74 |
| 1/ 8/61 | 27.18 | 6.39 | 23.51 | 15.20 | 55.91 | 75.26 | 5.00 | 18.37 | 24.73 |
| 4/ 8/62 | 26.99 | 6.59 | 24.41 | 17.51 | 64.86 | 90.70 | 1.79 | 6.65 | 9.29 |
| 10/28/62 | 27.58 | 6.28 | 22.75 | 12.81 | 46.44 | 61.75 | 7.93 | 28.76 | 38.25 |
| 12/19/65 | 28.22 | 4.36 | 15.45 | 12.64 | 44.79 | 54.50 | 10.55 | 37.39 | 45.49 |

eral electorate declared they reached their decision on the
constitutional project on the basis of its intrinsic values, 41
per cent because of the personality of General de Gaulle.
However, for the floating voter (corresponding roughly to the
"independent voter" in the United States), the figures were
39 per cent and 47 per cent respectively.[28] The two following
referendums prepared or endorsed in highly ambiguous terms
the peace settlement of the unending Algerian war, isolating
successfully the diehards who by their rebellion threatened
both order and prosperity. During the summer of 1962, 73
per cent of the voters declared that they could not or would
not name anyone in whom they had confidence as de Gaulle's
successor. Hence, even with the ending of the Algerian war
the sway of the providential leader remained decisive.

For General de Gaulle the direct consultation of the electorate had the merit of eliciting that "confident adherence of
the citizenry" which he had often sought in his early speeches.
It also brought about as if by a "miracle" the manifestation
of a "national conscience," which in his opinion lay dormant
so long as parties and other "intermediaries" could manipulate the voters' choice. He therefore stressed in all of the referendum campaigns that he was addressing each citizen as an
individual, above, and sometimes in violent opposition to, all
intermediaries. In his words every referendum was a "personal
affair" between himself and the nation; "the clearest, the
frankest, and the most democratic of procedures." Moreover,
an appeal which told each citizen that his personal decision
was invited and that the fate of the country was thus entrusted to him flattered the egalitarian instincts so readily
aroused in France.

De Gaulle's preference for the referendum as an instrument
of direct democracy has been shared at almost all times by an
important majority of citizens: 68 per cent of those who answered questions concerning the use of the referendum between 1958 and 1962 approved of it; 64 per cent believed that
as a general practice the people rather than parliament should

---

[28] See *Sondages,* XXII:4 (1960), p. 44. The French Institute of Public
Opinion classifies as floating voters all those who declare that in the next
elections they would vote for another party than in the last.

have the decisive voice on problems of major national interest. Important variations between the sexes, between age and socio-economic groups indicated where the support for plebiscitarian practices was strongest, at least as long as General de Gaulle has control: among women (75 per cent), people over sixty-five, the shopkeepers, the retired, and the lowest income group. A significant difference characterized the attitude of those with university education: slightly more than half of them approved of the past referendums, but only one-third of this group believed that in the future questions of great national concern be laid before the electorate.[29]

Undoubtedly the frustrations of the voters, who in the past had felt that parliamentary elections provided no leverage for major policy directives, account in large part for the popularity of the referendum. The political participation which the plebiscites invite is at best fleeting and frequently a sham, since the decisions on which the electorate is ostensibly consulted have been reached beforehand. But where the confiscation of power by the members of parliament has been resented, a similar confiscation by the providential leader is accepted as commensurate with the prevalent style of authority. In a society where face-to-face relationships have been traditionally disliked, the referendums free the citizens from active participation in bargaining practices required of group decisions. The concentration of power in the hands of the leader is tolerable because the distance between him and his followers is far greater than that between the voter and his deputy. Except for a few dramatic occurrences, the leadership of the Fifth Republic is intentionally keeping public opinion at arm's length. It provides what has been called a "counter-pedagogy" of which the ambiguity of deceptively simple questions put before the electorate in the referendums is only one example.[30] At present such counter-pedagogy profoundly marks the ongoing socialization process.

As a new form of electoral consultation, the referendum

[29] See Bortoli, *op. cit.*, pp. 343 f. For the special situation prevailing at the time of the referendum of October 1962, see below.

[30] On this point see Georges Lavau, "Réflexions sur le Régime Politique de la France," *RFSP*, XII:5 (1962), p. 820, and Hoffmann, *op. cit.*, p. 101.

has considerably softened, and in many cases largely restruc-
tured, the traditional alignment of voters. In none of the referendum campaigns has the government appealed to party
loyalties when asking for an endorsement of its position. But
since most organized political forces in the country had lined
up behind the new constitution in 1958 and behind the Algerian peace terms in 1962, voter approval by 80 per cent and
90 per cent respectively did not give evidence of new alignments, except that in 1958 not more than one-fifth of the
traditionally Communist voters seemed to have followed their
party's injunction to vote against the constitution. But in
October 1962, all of the "old parties" were massed against
de Gaulle when he proposed to amend the constitution. They
opposed the constitutional novelty of electing the President
by direct suffrage; they also had no difficulty in denouncing as
illegal the form in which the amendment was submitted: the
amendment procedures of the constitution permitted a call
for a referendum only after a concordant vote of the two
houses of parliament, which the government had neither
sought nor obtained. (For details see Chap. X.)

In the first elections of the Fifth Republic, the parties
which only four years later, in 1962, campaigned for the "no,"
obtained no less than 82 per cent of the votes; yet the actual
"no" vote in the referendum amounted to only 38 per cent.
Public opinion polls indicated that most parties were poorly
followed by their habitual electoral clientele. "No" votes were
most numerous in the traditional strongholds of the Left,
south of the Loire River, where they outweighed the "yes"
votes in 14 departments (see map p. 23). On the other hand, it
has been demonstrated rather convincingly that in spite of the
strength of left-wing traditions in the working class, 50 to 55
per cent of the workers must have answered "yea" to de
Gaulle's proposed amendment, while at least one-third of the
"no" vote came from non-working-class elements.[31]

Moreover, there is little doubt that the yes votes in the
referendum of October 1962 (46 per cent of the registered

[31] For details see Mattei Dogan, "Le vote ouvrier en France: analyse
écologique des élections de 1962," *Revue Française de Sociologie*, VI:4
(1965), p. 442.

voters and 62 per cent of those actually voting) were an insufficient expression of the extent of popular support for the election of the President by direct suffrage. Because the form in which the amendment was proposed violated the constitution and because the government and General de Gaulle conducted the campaign in authoritarian tones, memories of bonapartism were evoked: Napoleon III had risen to imperial power through a popular majority in presidential elections. In both the Third and the Fourth Republic the President was, therefore, elected by the two houses of parliament, convening as one body for this occasion. But shortly after the war, in 1945, a public opinion poll revealed that, at least at that time, a majority of the electorate was quite willing to see the executive strengthened, even at the price of relinquishing the institutional preferences of French republican traditions. Fifty per cent declared in favor of a popularly elected president, only 40 per cent wished to see him designated by parliament.[32]

Neither the constitution of the Fourth nor, in its original form, that of the Fifth Republic opted for the solution preferred earlier by the voters. But in 1961, before the question had become tainted by the circumstances under which the referendum took place, 52 per cent were in favor of electing the President by universal suffrage "like the deputies." Only 17 per cent were opposed to the reform, with 31 per cent undecided at that time. Once the reform was approved by referendum and at the approach of the first presidential elections three-fourths of the voters expressed their preference for popular elections. During the campaign itself, four-fifths favored popular elections, far more than were to vote for General de Gaulle as President. Young voters, including those who were to cast their ballot for de Gaulle's opponents, had even more definite sympathy for the new institution than the older generation.[33] The great and rapidly increasing popularity of

[32] Michel Brulé et J. Piret, *Les Transformations Sociales de la France Contemporaine. Réflexions sur 20 Années de Sondages Politiques de l'I.F.O.P.* [Institut Français d'Opinion Publique] (mimeographed), p. 9.

[33] For these and all following data on the presidential elections see *Sondages*, XXVII:4 (1965), pp. 7 ff. A highly sophisticated attempt to explain voters' attitudes in the presidential elections on the basis of public opinion data grouping the voters according to traditional political orien-

a reform, apparently hotly contested so shortly before, seems
to prove that a long frustrated electorate was elated with elections which permitted its participation in the process of choosing the executive.

Many facets of voting behavior in the presidential elections
of December 1965 evoked surprise, both on the side of the
government and on that of the opposition. Not the least of
these surprises was the high level of participation: 85 per cent
voted in the first ballot, 84.5 per cent in the run-off elections.
Only three years after parliamentary elections in which abstentions had been at an all-time high, abstentions now reached
an all-time low, giving the lie to earlier speculations about
the ebbing of political interest, the "depolitization" of the
electorate.

Another surprise, though foreshadowed for the informed
public by preelection polls, was the decline in popular support for the distinguished incumbent, General de Gaulle.
Since in the first ballot in December 1965 he was 7 per cent
short of the majority of votes cast (winning the approval of
only 37 per cent of the registered voters), run-off elections between the two top candidates became necessary. But as late as
June 1965, no less than 64 per cent of the voters had still
expressed their satisfaction with the President of the Republic
in a public opinion poll, and a few months after the election
his popularity had climbed back to approximately the same
level. The temporary but quite dramatic drop in popularity
immediately before the election (20 per cent in six weeks) was
quite obviously connected with the different ways in which
he and the electorate viewed the elections.

Faithful to his concept that relations between the government and the governed should essentially be reduced to
periodic consultations in which the ruler seeks the approval
of an undifferentiated and unorganized electorate, de Gaulle
regarded the elections as another plebiscite. Prior to the first
ballot he refused to present himself as a political candidate,

tations is made by Emeric Deutsch, Denis Lindon, and Pierre Weill, *Les
Familles Politiques Aujourd'hui en France* (Paris: Editions de Minuit,
1966), pp. 55–77.

let alone as the leader of the majority which had controlled the government during the preceding years. The electorate saw it otherwise, with the result that de Gaulle fell into the trap of the institution which he himself had created. Instead of merely confirming the powers of a president whose behavior during the campaign clearly irritated them, the voters judged him on his past record, including his personality, and subjected the promises and the personalities of his competitors to the same test. Unlike the preceding referendum, the voters did not decide on a single issue (or on an artificial amalgamation of issues prescribed by the government), but on the totality of issues the French political community faced at the time of the elections (Europe and the atomic bomb, wages and prices, housing and executive stability, etc.). Their preferences on the first as well as on the second ballot reflected their views on these issues. (Between the two ballots de Gaulle, in a skillfully conducted television interview, consented to play the role of a political — and attractive — candidate, although this single appearance might not have determined the final outcome.) If in the end a majority of the total electorate decided for de Gaulle's reelection, this amounted to a lack of confidence in the anticipated performance of his opponent, François Mitterand, a candidate without definite party commitment but endorsed by all parties left of center, including the Communists. Of those who decided to vote for de Gaulle in the second ballot, 51 per cent declared that they did so because of personal confidence in him, 19 per cent because they approved of his ideas, 26 per cent out of distrust of his opponent. For the Mitterand voters, the corresponding, but significantly reversed, figures were 20 per cent, 52 per cent, and 24 per cent. This permits the conclusion that the contest had become neither less nor more plebiscitarian in character than the American presidential or the British parliamentary elections. If de Gaulle, like the American President, is now once more incarnating national unity, he does so because a majority (55 per cent) of the voters (45 per cent of the registered electorate) approved of his past record as a political leader.

During the election campaign the voters clearly enjoyed its serious and dignified style. Interest in the performance of the candidates on television and the radio was consistently high. But the voters derived their greatest satisfaction from knowing that, unlike in past parliamentary elections, national and not parochial alignments were at stake and that they were invited to pronounce themselves effectively on such issues. The traditional and at one time deeply rooted attitude that the only useful vote was a vote against the government no longer made sense when almost everybody knew that the task at hand was to elect the head of an executive endowed constitutionally with strong powers, for a normal term of seven years.

If the new mode of elections gave the voters a new sense of participation, their alignment behind the major candidates in the two ballots showed that consistency in French voting patterns which careful observers have always detected behind an apparent volatility. Such volatility as did exist led, in the past, to the ephemeral success of flash movements which, in a parliamentary system, added to the instability of the regime without however really disturbing long-term trends. For all their novelty, the presidential elections reproduced traditional voting patterns rather faithfully, modified mostly by the particular attractiveness of General de Gaulle for voters older than 65, and for all women, excepting those in large cities. (For some details see Table III.)

The division between Right and Left, crystallized since the establishment of manhood suffrage in 1848, largely determined the distribution of votes between the major candidates in both ballots.[34] Mitterand did best in urban centers and in the countryside south of the Loire, which had always given a majority of its votes to the Left. He failed, however, to carry all of the traditional left-wing vote in the industrial areas of the North and in the working-class suburbs of Paris. In these constituencies de Gaulle did far better than the parties of the Right and Center had ever done and the vote for Mitterand was often lower than it had been for Socialists and Commu-

[34] For an excellent analysis of the election results, on which I have drawn heavily, see Philip Williams, "The French Presidential Elections of 1965," *Parliamentary Affairs*, XIX:1 (1965–66), pp. 14–30. Additional data and an overall evaluation are found in François Goguel, "L'Election Présidentielle Française de Décembre 1965." *RFSP*, XVI:2 (1966), esp. pp. 242–44.

TABLE III   *French Presidential Elections, 1965*

*First Ballot*

| | |
|---|---:|
| Total Voting | 28,233,167 |
| Abstentions (per cent of registered voters) | 14.98 |
| | % of Votes Cast |
| De Gaulle | 43.7 |
| Mitterand (Left of Center) | 32.2 |
| Lecanuet (Center) | 15.8 |
| Tixier-Vignancour (Extreme Right) | 5.3 |
| Marcilhacy (Moderate) | 1.7 |
| Barbu (Indefinite) | 1.2 |

| *Breakdown of vote in Second Ballot* * | *De Gaulle* | *Mitterand* |
|---|---|---|
| Men | 49% | 51% |
| Women | 61 | 39 |
| Ages: | | |
| Voters between 20 and 34 years of age | 49 | 51 |
| Voters between 35 and 49 years of age | 55 | 45 |
| Voters between 50 and 64 years of age | 55 | 45 |
| Voters 65 and older | 65 | 35 |
| Occupations: | | |
| Farmers | 59 | 41 |
| Businessmen | 67 | 33 |
| Executives and professionals | 63 | 37 |
| White collar, lower civil servants, etc. | 55 | 45 |
| Workers | 45 | 55 |
| Retired and without profession | 60 | 40 |
| Places of Residence: | | |
| Rural Communities | 57 | 43 |
| Towns of less than 20,000 population | 53 | 47 |
| Towns of 20,000 to 100,000 population | 47.5 | 52.5 |
| Towns of more than 100,000 population, Paris excluded | 57.5 | 42.5 |
| Northwest | 61 | 39 |
| Northeast | 58.5 | 41.5 |
| Southwest | 47.5 | 52.5 |
| Southeast | 52 | 48 |
| Region of Paris | 51 | 49 |

* According to a poll conducted between the two ballots and forecasting accurately actual election results. (See *Sondages,* XXVII:4 (1965), pp. 36–37.)

nists in the preceding parliamentary elections. Of the 2.8 million votes by which Mitterand bettered his record between the two ballots, a rather substantial portion came from those who at first had voted for the extreme, rightist candidate, Tixier-Vignancour. Refugees, driven out of Algeria, poor, and settled in the South where leftist traditions are dominant, acted mostly out of hatred for de Gaulle when they cast their ballots for his opponent.

De Gaulle, and in the first ballot Lecanuet as well, got their largest votes in the traditional strongholds of conservatism, especially in the Northwest and the East of the country. Previously a senator elected on the lists of the moderately progressive, Catholic-oriented M.R.P., Lecanuet, who was little known before his television appearance and a public-relations inspired campaign, drew support away from de Gaulle among voters who must have voted "yes" in the 1962 referendum. Whether discontent with the government's European or rather with its agricultural policies drove voters to Lecanuet remains controversial. In the second ballot, in which the de Gaulle vote increased by 2.2 million, most of Lecanuet's voters returned to de Gaulle's fold.

Sometimes the point is made that Gaullism, especially since it has made some inroads into the working class vote, owes its majority to the economically dynamic sections of the country, while the Left and Mitterand recruit a following primarily in "underdeveloped" regions of stagnant economy and declining population. But there are on both sides many exceptions to such a generalization which distinguishes insufficiently between economic and historical differences. It is rather that part of France, industrialized or not, in which republican traditions and the distrust of personal power have long been most outspoken that has given strongest support to Mitterand.

In terms of social stratification, the elections failed to shatter established alignments. De Gaulle's support was still lowest in the working classes and highest among businessmen and shopkeepers. (See Table III.) The following of the major candidates was also quite clearly differentiated according to religious habits: of the practicing Catholics, de Gaulle attracted 66 per cent, Lecanuet 20 per cent, and Mitterand 8 per cent; of the nonbelievers only 18 per cent voted for de Gaulle, 5 per cent for Lecanuet, and 72 per cent for Mitterand.[35] On the whole, this meant simply a reappearance and confirmation of the established relationship between religious practices and political orientation. (See Chap. III.)

Altogether, and this was perhaps the ultimate surprise, the elections were a victory for the new institutions of the Fifth Republic and at the same time a reinstating phenomenon — resuscitating the traditional outlines of the French political landscape. Because of this coincidence it can be assumed that the institution of the popularly elected presidency has won a legitimacy which is likely to outlast the present incumbent. (See also Chap. XI.)

However one issue which the past contest left wide open was the role which the political parties would play in future presidential elections. There was the possibility that the institutional needs of the new form of elections would force the traditional parties into new grooves. The American experience (repeated in some other nations) seems to prove that political parties are indispensable in elections of this kind: they either create the candidate or the candidate captures the party in order to legitimize his campaign.

Actually all the candidates in the presidential election of 1965 found it necessary to cut themselves loose from existing parties; with the possible exception of Jean Lecanuet, none of them could really be considered as a party "regular" to begin with. Once a candidate had declared, there was no choice for the existing political formations than to endorse the one least objectionable to them, but no party played a decisive role as an organizational base. That de Gaulle ran far ahead of the Gaullist party, the U.N.R. was nothing new. The Communist Party kept its voters behind Mitterand but did not retrieve those it had lost to de Gaulle with the advent of the Fifth Republic. In general, each candidate did relatively worst where the parties which sponsored him seemed strongest and best where the parties were weakest. The future of the U.N.R., tied as it is exclusively to one personality, remains too uncertain to evaluate its significance for the party system (see

[35] *Sondages*, XXVIII:2 (1966), p. 17.

Chap. VIII). The other parties have emerged weakened rather than solidified by a contest which on other grounds has definitely strengthened democratic procedures and attitudes. How this disjunction between the electoral process and political parties will affect long-term voter orientation and future political participation remains to be seen.

# CHAPTER V

# Recruitment and Style
# of Decision-Makers

## THE PHENOMENON OF THE "POLITICAL CLASS"

A study seeking to explain the facts of political life must determine not only who the leading actors on the political scene are, how they got there and where they came from, but also how they wield their power. Therefore, an analysis of their own socialization and recruitment, of their background, and of their style of action is needed. Besides the decision-makers' origin many other factors, particularly the milieu in which the politicians act and interact, explain their particular style.

How to reconcile the existence of a political elite, comprising both those who live for politics and those who live off politics,[1] with the original assumptions underlying a democratic polity is a ubiquitous problem. Many modern critics of representative regimes, especially Mosca, Pareto, and Michels, have questioned the realism of democratic theory by pointing to the existence of an elite holding a near-monopoly of decision-making. In their writings they both scorn and praise the "political class," usually in the same moralizing tone in which Jean-Jacques Rousseau denounced the dangers inherent in all political representation. Because of their polemic use of the

[1] The distinction is made by Max Weber in "Politics as a Vocation," in *Essays in Sociology* (New York: Oxford University Press, 1958), p. 84.

119

term, the designation of the political decision-makers in a democratic society as a "political class," has generally become the earmark of an antidemocratic bias.

However, in modern France, and especially since the beginning of the constitutional crisis of the 1930s, not only the "elitist" enemies of the representative regime speak of a "political class" when they wish to criticize those who in their opinion have succeeded in "confiscating the theoretical sovereignty of the people as expressed in universal suffrage." [2] Even before the First World War, Robert de Jouvenel in a still widely quoted statement, referred to a few thousand political decision-makers who use their monopoly of political power not to control each other, which they are supposed to do, but to further each other's ends.[3]

Then as today (or at least until the advent of the Fifth Republic), the basic nucleus of this decision-making group were members of parliament. For in France it was less possible than in some other Western democracies to make a significant political career outside the national legislature. Besides members of parliament the holders of elective offices in municipalities or departments, some local party leaders, and perhaps some journalists of national renown were counted among the political class — which altogether totaled not more than fifteen or twenty thousand persons. All of them, whether already elected to parliament or not, gravitated towards the halls of the lower or the upper house, the National Assembly or the Senate. Hence, when analyzing the recruitment and the style of this group of decision-makers, it is justified to center attention on the elected representatives.[4]

[2] As quite typical see François Goguel, in *In Search of France*, p. 395. The term is also widely used by intellectual spokesmen for the political Left, such as Professor Duverger, and by liberal newspapers and periodicals, such as *Le Monde* and *Esprit*.

[3] Robert de Jouvenel, *La République des Camarades* (Paris: Grasset, 1914), p. 262. For an excellent more recent description of the French parliamentary system and its mores, see Roger Priouret, *La République des Députés* (Paris: Grasset, 1959).

[4] For reasons of space this discussion is limited to the deputies, i.e., the members of the lower house. *Mutatis mutandis* much of what is said here applies also to the upper house, the Senate. Some of the institutional problems of the Senate will be discussed below, Chap. X.

It has been described above (see Chap. IV) how loosely organized parties, voting habits, and electoral laws combined to cut the deputies loose from any expression of political will on the part of the electorate. Isolated in their legislative chambers ("the house without windows" a scornful comment on ·the, perhaps symbolic, architecture of the parliamentary building), the deputies exercised a seemingly limitless power. Their ritualistic style has been criticized from within no less than from the outside. Decades before General de Gaulle denounced it, the Socialist leader Léon Blum, shortly before he himself became a deputy, spoke about the depressing, shut-in atmosphere of parliament and linked it to the monotonous quarrels of married couples. "If only we had in France political parties," he sighed, "and if these parties had an organization and a doctrine!" And he concluded (as early as 1917!) that the understandable reactions of the electorate towards the mores of parliament were rapidly becoming a "public danger." [5]

In the closed circuit to which it was confined, the incessant struggle for political power in parliament was actually little more than a reshuffling of cards.

The style in which this game was played — the rules according to which the roles were distributed — was sometimes criticized as overly dogmatic and ideological, sometimes as recklessly opportunistic. In fact they were both.[6] Without clear mandates from either the electorate or political parties, but with the traditional mission of rebelling against authority, decisions were postponed by the endless debates on matters of principle rather than bargaining realities. But when, periodically, circumstances would tolerate no further delay, then last minute compromises required turnabouts without any reference to previously announced metaphysical convictions. The professed egalitarianism resulted in a passion for anonymity

[5] "Lettres sur la Réforme Gouvernementale," *Revue de Paris*, VI (December 1, 1917), pp. 453–54.

[6] Jacques Fauvet (political editor of *Le Monde*) in *The Cockpit of France* (London: Harvill, 1960) stresses the ideological character of French politics; an American observer, Nathan Leites, in his *On the Game of Politics in France* (Stanford: Stanford University Press, 1959) sees the political class committed to "games" rather than to doctrines. Both books make a convincing case and both are one-sided, the work by Mr. Leites outrageously so.

and made it difficult to build a stable leadership. Yet there developed here another dichotomy between an egalitarian style and reality. Those likely to qualify for a cabinet post, especially those who had already been members of a government, formed a group quite distinct from the ordinary deputies or senators. Only if they violated the unwritten rules by too forthright an exercise of authority they would incur sanctions, such as their elimination from further ministerial office. Responsibility was further diluted by the fact that constantly shifting majorities gave most deputies the impression that they were simultaneously in power and in opposition.

Before the First World War, the esoteric games played by the representatives were not considered incongruous by the outside world since politics itself was believed to be a game and not a condition shaping men's lives. But when the crisis of the Thirties changed this, the behavior of its representatives became meaningless and irritating to the French nation, outside the restricted circle of an all but autonomous political class.

For the political culture of a democracy it is crucial that there be confidence in the persons and the role of the political actors. Such confidence, commanding loyalty not only to the men but also to the system, was lacking, and therefore the nation was estranged from its own affairs as transacted in parliament. A natural affinity between the participating actors exists also in the American Senate and in the British House of Commons. But in France it became suspect, as evidence of collusion. In an age when for various reasons political power becomes more and more personalized and when therefore utmost visibility is expected, the French representatives' emphasis on anonymity further increased the suspicion that their highly stylized practices hid malfeasance.

The frequently heard stereotype contrasting a stable country with its instable parliamentary system was likely to conceal the fact that talent, skill, and character are by no means lacking among the parliamentary personnel. In all countries, professional politicians develop special characteristics which amount to their personal equation. But because the activities in which French politicians had to engage were energy consuming and paralyzing, the mores of parliament "tended to magnify the occupational traits into an absurd caricature." [7]

It has already been noted (see Chap. IV) that the normal *cursus honorum* of the French deputy (and senator as well) begins in elective offices on the local or departmental level. During the last forty years of the Third Republic, more than two-thirds (two-fifths in the Fourth Republic) of the deputies held such offices before their election to the Chamber. Even in the crisis elections of 1958, which swept many newcomers into parliament, less than one-fourth of the deputies had never held local or departmental office. Because of their structural weakness, most political parties do not provide a sufficiently large and solid base for the recruitment of aspirants to a parliamentary seat. Hence a career in local government serves as the selection process, and the local implantation of deputies and senators is far stronger than in Great Britain or Germany.

The local notables, however, do not only furnish a reservoir for the political class, they also function as the necessary desirable link between the social and the political cadres. Where, under special circumstances, a candidate has been "parachuted" into a constituency from the outside, he will hasten to sink solid roots into local political life after his election to national office. The consequences of such a strong commitment by the representative to local and departmental affairs have already been described. (See Chap. IV.)

This is not to deny that the parties have a role in the recruitment or formal nomination process. Especially for the Socialist and Communist candidates previous party activity is a condition of endorsement, although even for them local notoriety is a strong recommendation. But if the Fourth Republic had intended to replace a republic of local leaders by one of party activists, it soon turned out that it had failed. Party endorsement of those seeking election to parliament was necessary, especially under the then prevailing list system of proportional representation. In general, however, such endorsement was given to those who had proven their worth on the local scene. The political weight of party leaders who for

7 Raymond Aron, *France Steadfast and Changing* (Cambridge: Harvard University Press, 1960), p. 23.

whatever reason were not deputies or senators was and continues to be insignificant. Socialists and Communists expected, very few deputies have started their political career in party office.[8]

The regular career of the political class may be modified in times of crisis. In the immediate postwar elections of 1945 and 1946, the very small group of people that had been active in the resistance movement against the German occupiers and the Vichy regime furnished 80 per cent of the deputies; it is true that some of them had already been politically active before the war but at lower party echelons. Their sudden rise to prominence was in part an indication that political parties identified with the resistance movement exercised temporarily a stronger influence on the selection and recruitment process. Even in later elections, including those of 1958, resistance activists represented about two-thirds of the membership of the lower House. But because their chances for reelection increased in proportion to their activities in local government, this group that had started outside the normal *cursus honorum* joined it afterwards.

The first elections in the Fifth Republic also occurred in a crisis situation. But in terms of the normal political antecedents of a parliamentary career they hardly amounted to an upheaval. Of the total 202 deputies which a new party, the Gaullist U.N.R., elected in 1958, less than 30 had never held some political office beforehand. A majority of the U.N.R. deputies who were new to parliament had been mayors or members of municipal and departmental councils.[9]

If a political class there is, an inherited political career is very rare. There are increasingly fewer families for which elective office is a tradition as it is still in Great Britain. The chronological age of the deputies reflects, as is to be expected the breaks that occur when one regime succeeds the other. In

[8] See the data in Aubin, *op. cit.*, II, p. 206, and Léo Hamon, "Members of the French Parliament," *International Social Science Journal*, XIII:4 (1961), pp. 547 ff. In my opinion this author attributes too great an importance to the role of parties in the nomination of candidates.

[9] See Mattei Dogan, "Changement de Régime et Changement de Personnel," in *Le Référendum de Septembre et les Elections de Novembre 1958* (Paris: Colin, 1960), esp. pp. 260–62.

1936, after the last elections of the Third Republic, 120 deputies were younger than forty, and 250 older than fifty. In the
first parliament of de Gaulle's Republic, the under-forty out-
numbered the over-fifty. But the average age of the deputies,
while lower than in the last elections of the Fourth Republic,
was still higher than after the war in 1946. The average age of
the deputies elected to the National Assembly in 1967 is 53
years, with little difference between the various parties.

Political longevity, however, is of greater significance than
chronological age. For a successful political career it is not
sufficient to be elected a deputy; it is necessary to remain
one.[10] Between 1877 and 1932, the classical era of the French
representative system, two-fifths of all deputies were reelected
between three and ten times. Three per cent of the deputies
were in at least seven legislatures and typically kept their
seats for about a third of a century. Certain deputies were
seated, without interruption, from their first election to the
end of their last mandate. Paul Reynaud, who lost his seat in
1962 when he led the fight against General de Gaulle's constitutional referendum, had been a deputy since 1919, with only
short breaks after temporary defeats.

Comparisons with the Fourth Republic are misleading since
there were five legislative elections during a period of thir-
teen years. But relative longevity persisted: almost half of all
deputies were elected three to five times. It is typical of the
French party system that the group of deputies who could not
be classified politically because they really did not belong to
any party made up, also in the Fourth Republic, the highest
percentage of those who were constantly reelected, with the
Communists next in political longevity.

Continuity in time and fixity of locale were intimately
linked. An incumbent who sought reelection in his constituency could hardly ever be dislodged. This, together with the
particular candidate's activity and experience in local affairs,

---

[10] See, also for the data following in the text, Mattei Dogan "Political
Ascent in a Class Society: French Deputies, 1870–1958" in Dwain Marvick
(ed.), *Political Decision-makers* (New York: The Free Press, 1961), pp.
57–90 and the same author's "Le personnel politique et la personnalité
charismatique," *Revue Française de Sociologie*, VI:3 (1965), pp. 305–24.

usually provided great familiarity with constituency interests and competence in defending them. But, especially in times of crisis, such longevity as prevailed reinforced the voters' distrust for the political class as a self-perpetuating clique. The French version of "throw the rascals out" (*Sortez les Sortants*) was thus heard at least at each change of regime, and frequently between.

In 1958, 406 incumbent deputies were not reelected, but 62 of them had chosen not to run. Such a hecatomb of politicians had not occurred since the beginning of the Third Republic. On the benches of the new parliament, 146 carry-over members encountered four hundred and six new arrivals. However, as has been explained, only a small fraction of the latter were new to political careers. The renewal of parliamentary personnel has continued in the elections of 1962: just half of the deputies who won a seat in these elections were not incumbents (two hundred and forty-two out of four hundred and eighty-two). If this indicates a new trend in parliamentary turnover, the recruitment pattern is but little modified. Only slightly over one-fourth of the nonincumbents were truly new to elective office. The others had belonged to parliament in the past, or, most frequently, had held posts in local government. In the elections of 1967 the number of freshmen deputies declined to 164.

The professional and especially the social origin of members of parliament has changed significantly since the establishment of the Third Republic in 1871. Then the nobility and the upper bourgeoisie had furnished respectively 34 and 36 per cent of the deputies; in the first elections after the First World War, only 10 per cent and 30 per cent of the deputies could be assigned to these social categories. The middle and the small bourgeoisie were now represented by 35 per cent and 15 per cent respectively of the deputies.[11] Since then the same trends have continued. Compared with the British House of Commons, the membership of the lower house of the French parliament has been of more modest social origin. From about

[11] See Georges Dupeux, *La Société Française 1789–1960* (Paris: Colin, 1964), p. 188, and Wright, *Modern France, op. cit.*, pp. 356 f.

1879 on, the representatives of the middle bourgeoisie dominated parliament and cabinets but later began to be edged out
of this dominant role by men of yet lower middle-class origin.
Since then, an amalgam of these two groups has become dominant, before the First World War furnishing about one-third
of the deputies, during the interwar period one-half, and in
the Fourth Republic about 70 per cent. The upper bourgeoisie,
which in England until recently formed the backbone of the
Conservative Party, exercised political influence in France
only indirectly: through interest groups and the bureaucracy.
On the other hand, the number of deputies with working
class background is smaller than in the House of Commons.
It has never risen to more than 15 per cent, partly because the
syndicalist tradition of the French labor movement frowned
upon the assumption of parliamentary seats by trade union
leaders. In more recent times, the number of deputies with a
working class background has depended on the number of
Communists elected to parliament. This in turn has fluctuated
not so much with the voters' sympathies but with the electoral
tactics of the Communists and their neighboring parties.

Among the political actors inside and outside of parliament,
the number of intellectuals has always been greater in France
than in other countries, their political activities more visible
than elsewhere. Perhaps one should call Voltaire the first
French "intellectual in politics." In the nineteenth century
such traditions continued. In the short-lived Second Republic,
a poet (Lamartine) and a scientist (Raspail) were candidates
for the presidency of the republic. Subsequently, Victor Hugo
and Emile Zola participated actively in politics. More recently,
a number of outstanding writers (Gide, Barrès, Malraux,
Sartre, and Mauriac) have let their voices be heard in the
political market place both on the Right and on the Left.

In parliament, the number of "intellectuals" (in a broad
sense) — teachers and professors, journalists, doctors, high
civil servants, etc. — has usually been higher than in other
countries: about 31 per cent before the Second World War,
35 per cent in the Fourth and 40 per cent so far in the Fifth
Republic. One account of the political regime spoke in 1927

of the "Republic of the Professors." [12] The highly revered
*Ecole Normale* in Paris, training ground for many university
professors, especially in the humanities and in the social sciences, also functioned for many generations as a "political
seminar." Many parliamentary leaders, predominantly those
of the Left, discovered and sharpened their political ambitions
while they were students at the school. Undoubtedly, the ideological style characteristic of political life inside and outside
parliament must in part be ascribed to the high proportion of
intellectuals in the political class.

> In France, at least, it was the intellectuals who were most
> impassioned in political debates in the Assembly under the
> Fourth Republic as under the Third. They were often the most
> intransigent ideologues. . . . they were apt to pose problems
> abstractly, with more or less sincerity, and often to expound
> them with ability. But this aptitude meant that they often
> proposed unrealistic solutions; and that they fixed upon sub-
> tleties and neglected essentials, thus uselessly complicating and
> prolonging parliamentary debates by inventing false problems
> and disagreeing among themselves. [13]

That lawyers have always made up the largest single professional group in parliament is a fact that is common to
France and other representative regimes. Before the Second
World War, the legal profession supplied one-fourth of all
deputies, many of them prominent, so that lawyers actually
accounted for more than one-third of the cabinet posts. There
were some brilliant members of the Paris bar among them.
But the vast majority were local notables, trained in law and
experienced in local administration. Rural constituencies,
seldom represented in parliament by farmers, usually preferred lawyers over other candidates. [14] Frequently not less competent than the heads of administrative bureaus, these lawyers

[12] Albert Thibaudet, *La République des Professeurs* (Paris: Grasset,
1927). In France secondary school teachers are also usually "professeur."
[13] Dogan in Marvick, *op. cit.,* p. 67.
[14] Figures indicating that in the Fourth Republic 12 per cent and in
the Fifth Republic between 8 and 10 per cent of the deputies are *agriculteurs* are misleading since most of these are not farmers but the owners
of large estates and often absentee owners at that.

imposed their style on the regime and formed the backbone of a parliament which considered the exercise of the tightest possible control over the cabinet and the bureaucracy to be its foremost mission.

Since the Second World War, the number of lawyer-deputies has decreased rather drastically, a trend that has continued in the Fifth Republic. In the parliament elected in 1967 members of the teaching profession furnish once more the largest contingent (71), followed by members of the medical profession and by civil servants on leave (51 and 57 respectively). The number of attorneys is now reduced to 34. An outstanding new development in the social composition of parliament seems to be a relatively large increase of businessmen, engineers, and industrial managers. But quite apart from the fact that this group is not as homogenous as for instance the teaching profession, a merely quantitative approach to this question is misleading. Many of those classified as businessmen, sales representatives, and the like play a very minor role in the halls of parliament, while most of the lawyers and "individuals" are prominent members.

With the new institutional arrangements of the Fifth Republic radically reducing the powers of parliament (see Chap. X), the decline in parliamentary prestige and influence has turned some of the best talents towards other political or administrative activities, and it has not been easy to persuade the most dynamic elements of the younger generation to stand for election. The new regime has increased the remuneration of the deputies and, at the same time, has reduced their powers. But this has not made up for the frustrations (and still considerable cost) of a deputy's seat in Paris.

The ties between national and local political careers, far from being broken, have probably been reinforced. The traditional local leaders may lose their footing, yet they are replaced on both the local and the regional level by younger activists (see Chap. IV and Chap. IX). The new notables soon discover that as before their achievements will remain precarious without assistance from the national government. To obtain such assistance, a seat in parliament still offers the best access and leverage.

As under previous regimes, in such cases a parliamentary career becomes the consecration of notoriety obtained elsewhere. Should this traditional amalgamation continue, parliament will remain an important means for the identification and further development of the most talented, if not of primary recruitment. This in turn would return to parliament some of its lost prestige and its attractiveness to a revived political class.

There is, however, one rather disparate group — one might best characterize it as a milieu — which is highly involved in political issues but as yet little in politics, and which so far has shunned any parliamentary career. These "aspirants" [15] to the political class are usually between thirty-five and forty-five years of age; their political orientation might vary widely. Many of them have been active in the resistance movement, or if too young for that, in contact with it through their families. Others became known to each other during the few months when the government of Pierre Mendès-France seemed to give a new style to the politics of the Fourth Republic. So far their political activities have been confined to the local level, to various interest groups and political clubs — a phenomenon largely of the Fifth Republic. (See Chaps. VII and VIII.) Whether or not they actually participated in the earlier resistance movement, they are in many respects the intellectual heirs of the resistance. A passion for reform and for intensive thinking about the correct strategy for achieving reform in France is common to them. In a country of divided elites, communication between elites is the contribution they wish to make to modernization. They hope to guard against the temptations of technocratic ambition by a commitment to an ideology of democratic participation, which they seek to submit to the test of practicality.

Whether and how these aspirants will be able to penetrate the political class in depth might determine to a considerable extent the future recruitment of political actors and their style.

[15] The term was coined by Roy Macridis, in Karl W. Deutsch *et al., France, Germany and the Western Alliance* (New York: Scribner's, 1967), pp. 31 ff.

## THE PHENOMENON OF THE BUREAUCRACY

More than a century ago, Tocqueville remarked that "since 1789 the administrative system has always stood firm among the debacles of political systems." [16] He personally had known top administrators who had entered the ranks of the bureaucracy before the storming of the Bastille and who retired at the end of an uninterrupted career long after the Bourbons had been restored to power. Since Tocqueville wrote, it has become axiomatic that the vagaries of the actors on the political stage have been balanced and thereby rendered largely innocuous by a stable bureaucracy. It is quite true that some of the anarchic and demagogic tendencies of the political system could be indulged in only behind the protective shield of a seemingly regular pattern of administrative behavior. But the latter never did neatly balance the former so that a satisfactory equilibrium could be established. Indeed, since they relied on each other, there was symbiosis as much as opposition between the two systems.

In the judgment of a recent French observer, in many ways a latter-day Tocqueville, "the bureaucratic system of organization of French public administration is certainly one of the most entrenched of such closed systems of social action that has existed in the modern world." [17] This came about not only because an administration, burdened as it was with tasks which it shares in other representative regimes with the political leadership, sought strength in isolation. An intense dislike for all outsiders of whatever social origin had been a characteristic of the civil service under the *Ancien Régime*. Later, both the elected representatives, the "political class," and the bureaucrats waxed intolerant of individuals and associations who wished to take independent action, removed from the aegis of either administration or parliament. The decision-makers' aversion to a participatory political culture was deepened by the citizens' ingrained and "learned" incapacity for cooperation and participation. Hence there was in the end congruence between French society and its admin-

[16] *The Old Regime,* p. 202.
[17] Crozier, *The Bureaucratic Phenomenon,* p. 308.

istrative style. Such congruence goes far to explain the singular success of French bureaucracy in the political system, as well as its shortcomings. A comparison of the pattern of French administration and of its success with that of other countries highlights not only a difference in techniques, in recruitment, and in style. It permits comparing different political cultures on an all-important level.[18]

There are between 3,000 and 10,000 high civil servants in France whose functions correspond by and large to those of the administrative class of the British civil service. (For the total number of civil servants, see Chap. IX.) Among the high civil servants a few hundred can be singled out as active and often daily participants in the process of political decision-making. In French they are sometimes call the *grands fonctionnaires,* while their next-ranking colleagues are merely high (*hauts*) administrators.

The selection of even the highest (as well as of the lowest) civil servants takes place by rigorous competitive entrance examinations, in which elaborate rites guard against all favoritism, and give the appearance of upholding the passion for equality. When Napoleon I founded the *Ecole Polytechnique,* which still produces the top administrators with an engineering background, and when after the Second World War Michel Debré (who in 1959 was to become the first Prime Minister of the Fifth Republic), established the *Ecole Nationale d'Administration,* the training ground of most of the other prestige corps of the bureaucracy, they both wanted to open the civil service to "talent," whatever its economic standing or family background. In 1945, the demands for infusing the political and administrative elites with new blood had been particularly strident. In order to democratize the ranks of the high civil service, it seemed opportune to break the *de facto* monopoly which the *Ecole Libre des Sciences Politiques* had held over the preparation for entrance examinations to the top positions. That school, founded in 1871, in the aftermath of another floundering political regime, recruited its successful students almost entirely from among the uppermost Parisian bourgeoisie, with an admixture of aristocratic ele-

[18] The work by Ridley and Blondel, *op. cit.,* is implicitly comparative.

ments. This led to a recruitment for the top level of the bureaucracy which was vastly different from that of the American civil service. By and large it can be said that even today in the United States the bureaucracy, both federal and state, represents a cross section of society and is therefore likely to reflect its values. This never has been the case in France. In order to democratize recruitment without abandoning the customary high standards of performance, the new School of Administration (known as the E.N.A.) was to open its training facilities not only to all qualified students, but in equal number to those already serving in the less exalted echelons of the civil service. By their admission to the school they could prepare for advancement to the apex of the bureaucratic pyramid.

The new school has had a considerable impact on administrative developments.[19] But as an instrument of social promotion it has largely failed. Today, between 60 and 65 per cent of the school's trainees and 68 per cent of the most successful among them are the children of high civil servants or come from families with a professional or managerial background (a group which in the total population amounts to 3.1 per cent). The middle and lower middle classes furnish less than another third — a slow increase in their number is the only transformation that has taken place. Farmers and working class families are hardly represented at all.[20] Most striking is the fact that the number of candidates from inside the civil service has constantly declined. Moreover, many of those who now enter in this way usually stem from almost the same milieu as the other trainees. The predominance of candidates of

[19] A good if incomplete analysis of the E.N.A. is provided by François Gazier, "The National School of Administration: Semblance and Reality," *International Review of Administrative Sciences*, XXXI:1, 1965, pp. 31–34; VIII–IX.

[20] The interesting comparative table established by V. Subramaniam in "Representative Bureaucracy: A Reassessment," *American Political Science Review*, LXI:4 (1967), p. 1016, shows that the social origin of high civil servants in France is far different from that found in developed Western democracies, but resembles that of Turkey and India. Slightly differing data are provided by Girard, *op. cit.*, p. 308; Club Jean Moulin, *L'Etat et le Citoyen* (Paris: Seuil, 1961), p. 138; and the very informative article by F. F. Ridley, "French Technocracy and Comparative Government," *Political Studies*, XIV:1 (1966), pp. 34 ff.

Parisian origin has somewhat diminished. But 93 per cent of the students admitted in a recent year had previously attended the Paris School of Political Science, and that school enrolls once again more upper middle class students than it did in the immediate postwar years.

The social composition of the student body preparing for the highest administrative positions at the E.N.A. is almost identical to that of the rest of the student population (see Table I). Only to a small extent is the absence of a solid system of grants and fellowships responsible for the absence of trainees with other backgrounds. Far more important is the fact that the entrance examinations like most other academic tests in France put a far higher premium on traditional knowledge, elegance of exposition, familiarity with and adjustment to the dominant humanistic culture, than on original thinking and on "raw" native ability.

The one, possibly significant, change which has occurred in recent years is the decrease in the number of candidates by one-third for the same number of openings in the administration. Such decline in interest is generally taken as an indication that the milieu from which the aspirants to these positions have come no longer values the *mandarinat,* as the top level of the bureaucracy is significantly called, as highly as it did in the era of stagnant economy. Whether this, together with the planned reforms in higher education, will eventually lead to a greater influx of candidates from other social strata cannot yet be foretold.

Since its establishment, the E.N.A. has furnished some 1,200 men and women to the highest echelons of the bureaucracy. Others in this category have, as before, come from the renowned *Grandes Ecoles,* such as the *Ecole Polytechnique,* the School of Agronomy, etc., which prepare the state engineers in various specializations not only for technical but also for leading administrative careers. The most brilliant of the state engineers exercise controlling functions in the manifold nationalized enterprises. Many others change relatively early to positions in private industry. The phenomenon of transferring from public to private employment (in administrative circles called *pantouflage* — one puts on the "soft slippers" of jobs outside the civil service) has traditionally deprived the French civil service of some of its best and most experienced personnel. For about a decade it was relatively rare among the graduates of the E.N.A. but is now again practiced widely.

More than 40 per cent of those who have graduated from the E.N.A. are attached to and dominate the services of the Ministry of Finance and Economic Affairs, 20 per cent are in the Foreign Service. Among the latter and among other graduates who are distributed over many administrations, a sizable number is concerned with economic matters.[21] Whether this indicates that the new School and the training it affords furnishes the bureaucracy, and thereby society at large, with something like a "freemasonry" specializing in economic change and modernization is a highly controversial question. Their common training and especially a common and acute feeling of superiority provides for all E.N.A. graduates a bond of which the publications of their alumni association are one expression. But the traditional particularism which has divided the high bureaucracy and has created elites within the administrative elite has in no way been overcome.

Besides the Foreign Service, the *Corps* of the Inspectors of Finance, of the Council of State, and of the Court of Accounts offer the most coveted civil service positions to the few hundred who have graduated at the top of their classes.[22] Even during their training period there develops an intense rivalry between members of the same class, which might be normal under extremely competitive conditions, but which also develops a stark snobbery among those who have reason to believe that they will end up in exalted positions. Their classmates will often be assigned to the less "noble" administrations, for ministries are invariably graded according to the quality of their services and their personnel. Sometimes graduates who

[21] See the comprehensive account in Jean-François Kesler, "Les Anciens Elèves de l'Ecole Nationale d'Administration," *RFSP*, XIV:2 (1964), pp. 258 and *passim;* and the same author's "L'Influence de l'Ecole Nationale d'Administration sur la rénovation de l'administration et ses limites," in *Tendances et Volontés, op. cit.,* pp. 257–67.

[22] Prior to the establishment of the E.N.A., candidates for the *Grands Corps* prepared individually for exacting entrance examinations, different for each Corps.

are not members of the elite corps are recruited for a highly rated administration, but theirs may be a routine function which makes little use of their previous training and intellectual ability. Little by little their identification with the ministries to which they are assigned tends to outweigh their affinity to their fellow-graduates of the E.N.A. Typically, the low-prestige administrations (among them the Ministries of Agriculture, of Public Health, and of National Education) recruit their top personnel from graduates with a middle-class background rather than from the ranks of the high bourgeoisie.

By contrast, the members of the *Grands Corps* are ubiquitous and mobile. Considered the reservoir for highest talent, they serve not only the administrations to which they are formally attached, but are sent on a virtually unlimited number of exacting assignments. They occupy top positions — the coveted places of *directeur* — in the important ministries. They frequently head up the personal staff of a Minister or of the President of the Republic (on the overall functions of these staffs or *cabinets* see Chap. IX). They are in charge of the numerous interministerial committees entrusted with laying the groundwork for the preparation of important decisions. If they do not always have direct control over decision-making, they consider themselves, and with much justification, the "intellectuals" in the administrative machinery.

If the members of the *Grands Corps* are a somewhat self-conscious caste within the larger group of the high civil servants, the different *corps* are also divided among themselves. Every *corps* is both a fortress and a prison for its members whose rivalries and controversies stem from a different perspective on what needs to be done. Here decisions are fought over in a passionate and often almost chauvinistic style. This kind of particularism tends to interfere with overall effectiveness and adds instability to the system. Contrary to original expectations, the common training at the E.N.A. has been unable to overcome either the particularism which separates the *corps* from each other, nor the sort of "feudalism" which divides them from the rest of the administrative class (in the British sense of the word). This particularism is largely due to the fact that the reform of administrative training has not been matched by a reform of the administrative system. The latter continuously reproduces the divisions created by divergent functions and by an exaggerated centralization.

Because of the high degree of centralization, general policy-making in France continues to be characterized by a constant transfer of decision-making to the highest administrative echelons. In many situations, and especially in times of crisis, the *Grands Corps,* together with certain other top civil servants, have provided the personalities that are capable of imposing the necessary reforms on the administration. They have become the agents of change for the entire system.[23] Hence their mentality and the way in which they view their own role in the process of change need to be considered here.

The education and training which future high civil servants receive both before and after their admission to the E.N.A. is in many ways different from that of pre-war times. Many still earn a law degree, but there is in their course of study less emphasis on the formalities of civil law. Although, according to the opinion of many close observers, training in economic science is still inferior to that afforded in Great Britain and the United States, the principles and refinements of Keynesian economics occupy more time than previously and less attention is given to a more narrowly circumscribed fiscal and accountant's knowledge. The hold which the tenets of economic laissez-faire once had has given way, as has much of the passion for system-building based on abstractions. The discourse between instructors and trainees and among the trainees themselves is pragmatic and deliberately unideological. A modified case method and an attempt to provide an integrated social science knowledge are characteristics of the instruction. While the training shies away from providing much "administrative science," it includes a good deal of administrative practice. Altogether, it is probably true to say that it is now more "managerial" and less "upper class." [24] Much of this is new and, in the opinion of old practitioners,

23 See, also for what follows, Crozier, *The Bureaucratic Phenomenon,* pp. 197, 309.

24 See Ridley, *op. cit.,* p. 38, and T. B. Bottomore, *Elites and Society* (London: C. A. Watts and Co., Ltd., 1964), p. 82.

adds significantly to the abilities which their future colleagues must demonstrate before gaining admission to the E.N.A.

Other aspects of training and mentality remain more traditional. They characteristically correspond to the values of the rather homogeneous milieu from which the top civil servants and the members of the examining boards are recruited. The brilliant and well balanced exposé, product of that "solitary preparation for mastery" which has been described earlier as an educational ideal (see Chap. III), often hides the fact that the trainees are insufficiently informed about available alternatives for action. The abstract cult of humanist values is seldom matched by a sensitivity for human relations, so that the civil servant is oftentimes an inept interlocutor of his partners outside the bureaucratic universe. An exclusive commitment to economic and administrative efficiency might lead to unjust solutions. If the administrator has confidence in what he calls the scientific approach, his confidence is frequently based less on technical knowledge than on logical analysis.

The ethos of the top-ranking bureaucrat has always included the strong conviction that he is the principal if not the sole defender of the public interest. His latent or open hostility towards parliament might not be more virulent than that of the ordinary citizen, but it is more focused. He resents parliamentary institutions and their personnel as disintegrating forces because, under the assault of special interest and of particularism, they are apt to dismantle the reform proposals hatched in the administrative bureaus. In the eyes of the bureaucracy, the intermediaries between the state and society become the enemies of a rational society. Administrative centralization, even if excessive, is regarded as a necessity since only at the top can enough sense of the public interest be generated to resist successfully arbitrariness and the pressure for privilege. An intended, if seldom achieved, remoteness from such pressures has given to the bureaucrats a somewhat abstract perception of a mission entrusted to them by the State, rather than the feeling of being the servants of a concrete community. Planning and "prospecting" for 1970 or 1985 they are sometimes apt to overlook the needs and troubles of their contemporaries.

For all his desire to see problems of public policy taken out of the realm of "politics," the French public servant is frequently politically less neutral than his British colleague. The "colonization" of certain ministries by political parties which occurred after the Liberation was a short-lived phenomenon. With the advent of the Fifth Republic, no large-scale takeover of the administration by proven Gaullists has taken place. But past and present civil servants have run for elective office and have identified themselves with certain outstanding politicians without being prevented from resuming afterwards their administrative careers.

It has frequently been assumed that the Fifth Republic with its frank emphasis on the prestige and procedures of the administrative state would promote the image of the high bureaucracy as a powerful and self-sufficient caste. Certainly, many of the pronouncements of one of the most articulate spokesmen of the regime, Michel Debré, have exalted technical expertise and depreciated politics. They betray a mentality reminiscent of Claude-Henri Saint-Simon, would-be reformer of the early nineteenth century, who has long been the apostle of many civil servants. (Debré himself, before entering politics, belonged to the *Corps* of the Council of State, as did the Socialist leader Léon Blum.) It is also true that even those civil servants who were inimical to Gaullism on political grounds have greeted the restoration of governmental authority with satisfaction.

Yet, if it has amplified existing tendencies, the new republic has hardly made the high bureaucracy into an autonomous and unified technocracy. The fragmentation of the top civil service into splinter bureaucracies, described previously, is only one reason why diversity rather than uniformity has prevailed. The great problems which the national collectivity had and continues to face (the Algerian problem and decolonization; European integration, foreign and defense policies; desirable priorities in economic and social policies) have divided the bureaucracy as they have other elites. Before long, seemingly technical conflicts turn into political disagreements, themselves the result of polarizations concerning fundamentals or personalities. The greater pragmatism that prevails generally has in fact led many civil servants to take a less exalted view of their role as infallible arbiters. In their contacts with interest groups they seek to conform to a new image of a representative bureaucracy which reflects better than hitherto the society within which they act.[25] What emerges is a managerial elite which tends to assume leading positions in the state and, after their *pantouflage,* in the economy as well, but certainly not a unified technocracy.

Whereas in other countries the administration frequently reacts to innovating impulses originating elsewhere,[26] the French bureaucracy continues to be the main originator of innovation. A close and astute observer of the administrative scene in France has distinguished two different role conceptions which prevail among present-day civil servants. One group firmly believes that the state and its administrative machinery should bring about, by persuasion if possible, by force if necessary, needed structural reforms. "The state can do everything it wants to do," they argue — it can overcome all obstacles that stand in the way of progress. Many of them are almost fanatic about "prospective" thinking: long-range vision and planning appear as remedies for all temporary setbacks. A second group sees as its foremost mission the protection of the equilibrium between contending forces and values. While they are in no way averse to progress, they are anxious to see the necessary mutations proceed in orderly fashion. At all times the state must be able to control the forces which the dynamics of group pressure might let loose.

Both groups are distributed, even though not evenly, throughout all the administrative *corps* and are represented among different age groups in the administration. What they have in common is a decidedly apolitical bent. "For one group among the highest civil servants, the state is the carrier of progress, for the other an important arbiter, but in the eyes

25 For details, see Henry W. Ehrmann, "French Bureaucracy and Organized Interests." *Administrative Science Quarterly,* V:4 (1961), pp. 534–55, and "Bureaucracy and Interest Groups in the Decision-Making Process of the Fifth Republic," *Faktoren der politischen Entscheidung, Festgabe für Ernst Fraenkel* (Berlin: Gruyter, 1963), pp. 273–93.

26 See Almond and Powell, *op. cit.,* p. 158.

of both the state is authoritarian and paternal and free from all political ferment." [27]

Whatever their personal outlook, the traditional structures within which bureaucrats have to operate and the administrative style which emphasizes impersonal and hierarchical relations often impede the role of the bureaucrats as agents of change; a role both self-assigned and publicly imposed. It is therefore significant that a growing number of civil servants admittedly are losing faith in the classical French bureaucratic model. They are conscious that their knowledge of economics, domestic and international, and their insight into human and group relationships are far greater than that of their predecessors. But they are dubious as to whether such knowledge can really be made fruitful as long as the old style prevails and excessive compartmentalization is continued. The increasing prestige which the personnel and the working methods of the Planning Office command (see Chap. II) could indicate that a slow conversion is underway. If it were to spread to a larger number of top civil servants, it would affect not only the role of the bureaucracy in the process of change, but its working methods and possibly its recruitment as well.

Inasmuch as French judges are without exception civil servants, their role and outlook should be considered here briefly. Training, mentality, and again tradition isolate them to a high degree from the political milieu, including the local politicians, from the business world, and even from administrative circles. A strong adherence to legalism means that adjudication, as they see it, should be based exclusively on legislative texts and on other statutory enactments. There is supposedly little, if any, room for considering the intentions of the legislators, the social context, or immutable or changing principles. Nonetheless, like any judiciary, the French judges by the decisions they render cannot help playing a political role. "Judges are not 'sold to the bourgeoisie,'" a high judge, writing anonymously, has stated, "they are part

[27] Bernard Gournay, "Un Groupe Dirigeant de la Société Française: Les Grands Fonctionnaires," *RFSP*, XIV:2 (1964), pp. 229–31. The entire article deserves close study.

and parcel of it." [28] But their role is far more *sub rosa* than elsewhere, with the possible exception of the administrative judges who by training and prestige are closer to the high bureaucracy than are the judges sitting on civil or criminal courts.

In the past, the higher ranks of the judiciary came usually from the same social milieu as top civil servants. The main difference was regional: together with the upper bourgeoisie of the capital, a few other urban centers — mostly south of the Loire River and often situated in regions of mediocre economic development — contributed to judicial recruitment. A slow but fairly steady lowering of prestige has resulted in a greater number of high judges from the middle classes and, above all, in the "feminization" of the profession. Today about two-thirds of the Paris candidates for judicial posts are women.

It is quite characteristic that the professional journals of the judiciary are full of complaints about the career chances of the judges and critical of their place in society. But, especially in comparison with the high bureaucracy, the will for change has been slow in emerging. Nevertheless the present regime has carried out rather drastic reforms of the judicial system while it has so far left administrative structures at the national level almost untouched.

### THE PHENOMENON OF CHARLES DE GAULLE

What follows here is not intended as a political biography or a psychological study of one of the most complex personalities of our times. But an analysis of the recruitment and the style of decision-makers in present-day France cannot ignore the man who has dominated the political scene for more than a quarter of a century, either in the center of the stage or in the wings. Moreover, unusual a man though he is, his own "recruitment" into the political role he has assumed, his re-

---

[28] Casamayor, *Les Juges* (Paris: Editions du Seuil, 1959), p. 143. For interesting details on the relationship between political authority and the judiciary see Georges Lavau, "Le Juge et le Pouvoir Politique," in Louis Trotabas (ed.), *La Justice* (Paris: Presses Universitaires, 1961), pp. 59 ff.

flections on this role, as well as his style of action are intimately conditioned by and connected with the French political
process past and present. Finally, the reactions of Frenchmen,
elites and masses, to the phenomenon of de Gaulle are by
themselves politically significant. (For de Gaulle's exercise of
the office of President of the Republic, see Chap. IX.)

Son of a history teacher in a Jesuit school, Charles de Gaulle
has always refused to consider himself part of the French
bourgeoisie and of its acquisitive culture. His ancestors were
impecunious and learned men, many of them servants of the
church or of the state, faithful Catholics and monarchists at
heart. While he would not object to being classified with the
minority of Frenchmen who are "practicing Catholics," de
Gaulle's orientation towards his faith is Gallican rather than
Roman: he has never been known for accepting advice or
suggestions from the hierarchy of the Church.

As a cadet at the French West Point, the School of St. Cyr,
and later as an officer, he was appraised by his superiors as
"intelligent, cultivated, and serious." But his "incontestable
qualities" were considered spoiled by an "excessive assurance
of himself, too rigorous a judgment of the opinion of others,
and altogether his attitude of a 'king in exile.' " [29] The still
young officer paid his critics back when in his first book (in-
corporating lectures delivered at the War College) he contrasted the true leader of men and the "stuffed dummies" of
the military and civilian hierarchy.[30] In a single sentence he
praised Alexander, Galilei, Columbus, Richelieu, Boileau,
Napoleon, Lesseps, Bismarck, and Clemenceau for having done
great deeds without concern for "low prudence" or "cowardly
modesty."

Royal and aristocratic though he was in personal bearing,
de Gaulle shed early the vestiges of monarchical convictions

[29] Jean Lacouture, *De Gaulle* (New York: New American Library, 1966),
p. 28. This small essay is so far the best and most judicious biography of
de Gaulle.

[30] Charles de Gaulle, *The Edge of the Sword* (New York: Criterion
Books, 1960), p. 63. This book has appropriately been called a "handbook
for heroes." See the fine article by Peter J. Larmoun, "De Gaulle and the
New France," *Yale Review*, LX:4 (1966), p. 502.

germane to the milieu from which he hailed. As a military expert, convinced that a armored and mechanized professional army was necessary to avoid catastrophe, he engaged in discussions with liberals and nonconformist fellow officers. He rubbed shoulders with republican politicians, such as the Socialist Léon Blum and the Conservative Paul Reynaud, to win them to his cause by the lobbying methods that were customary in the Third Republic. As an intellectual in uniform (a not uncommon phenomenon in France), he was imbued with the manifold traditions of French philosophical and political thought and committed to a belief in the civilizing mission of its many strands.

What had been a groping search during the interwar years became a definite orientation under the conditions which turned the military expert and gifted essayist into the political leader of the Free French. The support from many political quarters which he drew in London and in underground France, combined with the responsibilities incurred by the French elites for the defeat of 1940, made it clear to de Gaulle that in order to bestow legitimacy on his new role he had to represent the whole national past and not only part of it.

Egocentric visionary though he was to be in the eyes of his wartime allies, de Gaulle never departed from the insights he had won as a student of military strategy: what counted was to reach limited objectives with the help of available resources. "There exists," he has written, "no absolute truth, either in politics or in strategy. There are only the circumstances." [31] In his youthful lectures he had pointed out that it is the mark of the leader to dominate the events. A combination of intuition, instinct, and intelligence was necessary to master "the circumstances." All his life de Gaulle has been fascinated by the permanent tension between reflection and action, by the use of principled language as a spring of action. But what mattered most was — *die Tat* [32] — the mastery of events, rather than a mere reaction to them — and the prag-

[31] *War Memoirs*, vol. III, p. 136.

[32] The citation from Goethe's *Faust:* "In the beginning there was not the word but the deed," is one of the mottoes of the *Edge of the Sword*. De Gaulle also quotes admiringly Napoleon's prescription: "On s'engage, puis on voit" (One gets involved and then sees what comes of it.)

matic recognition of the realities within which action had to move. This explains his frequent references to seemingly inalterable givens of history. ("Frenchmen as they are and will be" . . . "The world being what it is," etc.) It also explains why, especially in comparison with the younger technocrats in his entourage, he resembles more often than not the successful politician of classical republican tradition.

In his *Memoirs,* to be sure, de Gaulle expresses his conviction that France was "dedicated to an exalted and exceptional destiny." But he immediately contrasts the "genius of the land" with the "mediocrity" which often "shows in her acts and deeds." And he admits, in language that the historian Ernest Renan used before him, that calamities and obstacles, more than memories of past glories, are apt to force the country into the greatness that is her lot. For only when "exemplary misfortune" befalls them are Frenchmen able to find that cohesion which de Gaulle has at all times admired as the solid base of the British state.

De Gaulle's concept of *grandeur* has been judged an antiquated and hence quixotic disturbance for present-day international relations. But its function is also, if not primarily, domestic: designed to heighten pride and belief in a great destiny, it is an antidote to disunity and a diversion from discord. After the Third Republic had ignominiously collapsed in 1940, and the Fourth had become the "sick man of Europe" in the Fifties, France had to be healed of a dangerously low self-esteem. The great leader, de Gaulle, had to become the healer, enabling France to live up to her "exalted destiny." His speeches as a wartime exile or as the President of the Republic are to many outsiders — and to critical Frenchmen as well — at times exasperating because they heap exaggerated praise on the nation and its leader for past achievements. But, the speaker frequently treats Frenchmen as if they had already done things which remain to be done. His exhortations are designed to coax his listeners into efforts and changes of which he believes them to be capable, with proper guidance.[33] There

---

[33] On this point see the excellent essay by Stanley Hoffmann, "De Gaulle's Memoirs. The Hero as History." *World Politics,* XIII:1 (1960), p. 151.

is a parallel here to the way in which the young officer described the ideal man of character in the *Edge of the Sword.* In this anticipatory autobiography de Gaulle attributed to the ideal man all the qualities he wished to acquire for himself: foremost among them passion and self-confidence.

The instrumentality which the hero needs to fulfill his mission of saving the nation from mediocrity is the strong state. When de Gaulle reentered the political scene in the spring of 1958, his first pronouncement painted the preceding twelve years as a "disastrous process . . . of a degradation of the state," with its dismal consequences for "national independence" (the key-word in his foreign policy strivings). When he entered liberated Paris in 1944, his first concern was to install himself at the seat of state power, the Ministry of War, while the members of the resistance movement were waiting to greet him at the City Hall. In pages that equal in beauty of prose the writings of Michelet, the extraordinary historian of the Revolution, de Gaulle described later his solemn entry into the capital, where every building reflected for him the "majesty of the state under two emperors and two monarchies," but also the "miracles of national conscience."

An astute observer has remarked that de Gaulle regards the French state with the eye of a "great jacobin cardinal" [34] — his views represent indeed a mixture of Richelieu and Robespierre. Such cult of the state has nothing in common with the obsolete dreams of monarchists and counterrevolutionary doctrinaires, such as Maurras and the *Action Française,* influential in the traditionalist milieu into which de Gaulle was born.[35] He is out of sympathy with their longings for corporatist organizations in a decentralized state. To him not only parties but also all other organized intermediaries standing between the citizen and the state are what the "categories" were to Richelieu, the "particular societies" to Jean-Jacques Rousseau, and the parties to Napoleon: disturbers of the

[34] Lacouture, *op. cit.,* p. 170.

[35] It is true that the present royal pretender applauds de Gaulle's constitutional thinking as a blend of the traditions of the Capetian kings and of the general will, "antidote to caesarism and dictatorship." See H. W. Ehrmann, "Direct Democracy," p. 897.

national interest and particularly disastrous in a nation full of volatile centrifugal trends.

His views explain de Gaulle's gross unfairness to the resistance movement which, during the harsh war years, had united behind him and bestowed on him a measure of that legitimacy which he sought. If he belittled its contribution, it was partly because the resistance movement was a potential competitor for power. But de Gaulle also wanted to rebuke the members of the resistance as representatives of a reemerging pluralist, and hence naturally divided, society.

The "profound" legitimacy which he claims for himself, his "assumption of French sovereignty," was in his opinion not based on "multiple representation" but on the "instinct of the country . . . ," on "sentiments and hopes which unite" rather than divide.[36] This, he declares, is the reason why he cares less for the support of the elites which failed France in 1940 and at numerous other occasions, than for the approval of the undifferentiated public. The elites are divided, the people can be "assembled (*rassemblé*)," another key-word in de Gaulle's political vocabulary. Like Rousseau, he is convinced that there is a dormant general will which only needs awakening, that the people want what is right even if they are not always able to see what they want without proper guidance. Like Napoleon, he admonishes his compatriots, of whatever political camp, to be "good Frenchmen with him." The resolve to take major questions of national concern out of the political realm, to "depoliticize" them as de Gaulle's Premier Michel Debré has put it, denotes of course a definitely political purpose. It is a policy which before de Gaulle not only the first Bonaparte but also Napoleon III vowed to pursue.[37]

The leader and the people need each other to do great things "together," de Gaulle has reminded the electorate in many a political campaign. Since such legitimacy is based on

---

[36] See *War Memoirs*, II, p. 390, and de Gaulle's speech at the funeral of René Coty, last president of the Fourth Republic, *A.P.*, 1961, p. 688.

[37] See Marcel Merle, who speaks about "organized depolitization" in his article "Inventaire des apolitismes," *Association Française de Science Politique, La Dépolitisation, mythe ou réalité?* (Paris: Colin, 1961), pp. 48 ff.

popular approval, it is cleansed of all suspicion of personal power. In his letters and writings, de Gaulle has analyzed perspicaciously the brittleness of modern dictatorship, except for the constitutional assumption of emergency powers during a period of temporary distress. To him, a "natural contract between greatness and liberty" is the foundation of an authentically French, and hence of his own, regime. His style waxes most lyrical each time he describes or experiences contact with the masses. A voluntarily lonely and melancholic de Gaulle is transformed and invigorated when he moves through cheering crowds, French or foreign.

Because he claims to incarnate popular sovereignty, de Gaulle is careful not to neglect authentically republican symbols and models. When he returned to France after the war, he frequently invoked "père" Clemenceau, popular hero of the First World War. When he presented the constitution of the Fifth Republic, he chose a place and date connected with memories of Gambetta, key-figure in the republican Ministry that chased Napoleon III from power. It is true that the republican lineage on which the regime insists seems often in contradiction with de Gaulle's personal style, which has nothing of the Jacobin and is far more reminiscent of Louis XIV than even of the first Napoleon.

But for a leader who wishes to incorporate many and divergent strands of French tradition, such a posture, whether genuine or feigned, is very useful even though sometimes easy to ridicule. According to Bossuet, France "learned to know herself" under Louis XIV, and to freethinkers and Catholics alike this epoch has remained the "great age" and, at least in some respects, has given permanent form to the national spirit.[38]

De Gaulle's "singular preoccupation with his own fortune," which so exasperated Winston Churchill, is in his own eyes the natural preoccupation of the leader with his mission. To him a totalitarian personality cult is as vulgar as the exalted position of the extraordinary leader is historically necessary. National policy, he wrote in his *Memoirs,* means action, and action is the work "of one alone" — echoing almost verbatim

38 See Curtius, *op. cit.,* p. 77.

a dictum of Max Weber's.[39] The voluntary distance and isolation of the "one" have become part of de Gaulle's carefully built mythology, according to which the great leader must periodically withdraw from the banalities of political decision-making in order to return to the sources of his strength. Thus removed from innuendos and surprises, distance and impenetrability enhance the possibilities for effective action and for the attainment of the objectives prescribed by political strategy.

The *Edge of the Sword* first spoke of the sudden retreats of the great leader. The *Memoirs* describe melodramatically how de Gaulle sought the solitude of the seashore before announcing his withdrawal from power in 1946. During the various referendum campaigns since 1958, the threat of a similar withdrawal was used as an effective means of political persuasion. Its success legitimized the continued exercise of power. The oracular pronouncements concerning the future of Algeria confused and divided the forces opposed to the solution adopted by de Gaulle until Algerian independence could be imposed. An apparently baroque rhetoric serves the purpose of disguising thoughts rather than clarifying issues until the moment comes when their clarification is apt to change reality, such as the incorporation of the Sahara and its oil wells into Algeria, the veto of England's entry into the Common Market, the denunciation of NATO's command structure, or the announcement of the constitutional changes in 1962. It might well be the judgment of future historians that some of de Gaulle's autobiographical writings descend to the level of sheer apologia, common to the literature of this genre. Yet the version of historical events which he seeks to accredit serves the writer's plans for the future and supports his claims of consistency.

It has been said that all Frenchmen have been, are, or will be Gaullists, or at least admirers of the General. But not all are so inclined at the same time, and certainly not all for the same reasons. In part this consensus, however staggered, may

[39] *War Memoirs,* II, p. 179. For Max Weber's dictum "Only the great single man can set positive political goals for the nation," see the excellent article by Gilbert Ziebura, "Ideologische Grundlagen der Aussenpolitik de Gaulle's," *Europa Archiv,* VIII (1965), p. 277.

be due to the secretiveness surrounding de Gaulle's intentions leading to a variety of interpretations. More important might be the fact that his policies are characterized most of the time by a mixture of innovation and of tradition, and of many different traditions at that. This allows for a maximization of support and for the confounding of the opposition. Many nonconformist intellectuals and ranking civil servants feel attracted by de Gaulle's foreign policy orientation, while his economic and financial course is generally reassuring to conservatives. If the consular republic installed and headed by a Catholic general arouses uneasiness on the Left, the same Left finds consolation in the thought that only the situation not the man is bonapartist. To others, his monarchical style is outrightly pleasing.

For the citizenry at large, the charismatic personality and the high degree of symbolic capability might be decisive factors. Waves of sympathy in de Gaulle's favor have been quite extraordinary: in September 1957 only 10 per cent of the electorate considered him the best choice for the chief executive; a mere nine months later, in June 1958, 70 per cent expressed confidence in him for the task of reforming the constitution and the political institutions. Such an opinion was strong among voters of all parties with the sole exception of the Communists who furnished almost all of the 8 per cent that expressed open distrust.[40]

Since his installation as President of the new republic, de Gaulle, in all of his contacts with the outside world, has manipulated symbolic signs and values with great dexterity, such as radio and television addresses, press conferences, tours of the French provinces, and travel abroad. His success in such manipulation was facilitated by the extreme paucity in the preceding regime of powerful, unifying, and popular symbols.[41] Realist that he is, he recognizes well what his country lacks today in "naked power." This insight, however, provides

[40] *Sondages*, XX:3 (1958), p. 66, and XX:4 (1958), p. 8.
[41] On the importance of symbolic outputs see Almond and Powell, *op. cit.*, p. 200. On the paucity of symbols in the Fourth Republic John E. Sawyer, "Strains in the Social Structure of Modern France," E. Earle (ed.), *op. cit.*, p. 298.

added motivation to use to the fullest the psychological and political strength that can be derived from symbols.

Both the maximum use of symbols and the low ideological content of General de Gaulle's pronouncements and style of action serve his objectives. Since conflicting ideologies have long divided Frenchmen, the deliberate pragmatism which suits de Gaulle's temperament and way of thinking discourages useless remembering of past strife. Since it has long been true (see Chap. IV) that the electorate is far less given to ideological commitment than the political class and the elites in general, the leader's anti-ideological stance provides additional leverage for discrediting traditional political forces. And at least for a time the constant evoking of unifying rather than divisive symbols is soothing a widely felt longing for the common good.

# CHAPTER VI

# Political Socialization
# Through the Mass Media

## THE FLOW OF COMMUNICATIONS

"All of the functions performed in the political system — political socialization and recruitment, interest articulation, interest aggregation, rule-making, rule application, and rule adjudication — are performed *by means* of communication." [1] Some of these processes have been described in previous chapters, others will be discussed in subsequent parts of this study. The present chapter explaining the role of the mass media in France tries to find out, in the words of Harold Lasswell: "Who Says What, In Which Channel, To Whom, With What Effect," [2] a paradigm which directs us towards many important political problems, only a few of them involving the mass media.

There are as many "channels" of information and communication as there are political learning processes — families and class rooms, playing fields and meeting halls, interest groups and parties. The mass media of modern society "do not simply displace or supersede other channels; rather, they link existing networks while giving rise to a host of dependent nets which

[1] Gabriel Almond, "Introduction" in Gabriel Almond and James Coleman (ed.), *The Politics of the Developing Areas* (Princeton: Princeton University Press, 1960), p. 45.

[2] Quoted here from Richard R. Fagen, *Politics and Communication* (Boston: Little, Brown and Company, 1966), pp. 4, 5.

service, disseminate, and frequently transform their product." [3] In an established polity such as France, the potentialities and the limitations of the communications process as used by the mass media, are often determined by the way in which Frenchmen appraise the integrity of this process. Indeed their appraisal will be one of several factors indicating their faith in or their cynicism about the political system.[4]

In many of the political crises of the past, the French press played a dramatic role. During major campaigns, and great scandals or *"affaires,"* newspapers politicized the elites and mobilized the masses. They were used, and often subsidized, by the antagonists. In the absence of strong political parties and of sufficient revenue from advertising, business firms, tycoons, and governments (both French and foreign), habitually backed major newspapers. The widespread and largely justified belief that much of the press was run by "occult forces" seriously impaired its function as a channel of political communication.

When during the Second World War the resistance movement developed blueprints for the future, quite naturally much attention was given to the future status of press and radio. As a matter of course, the newspapers which had continued to publish in France during the German occupation were to be replaced by the organs of the resistance movement. In addition, a nationalized enterprise was to allocate printing presses and other resources to all existing political forces; the sources of information were to be kept clean and lean. For as the spokesmen for the resistance movement declared solemnly: "The press is free only when it depends neither on the government nor on the moneyed powers, but solely on the consciences of journalists and readers."

The realities of postwar politics soon did away with such aspirations. Today, the press operates under the same conditions as it does in other Western democracies, except that revenue from advertising remains comparatively low. In becoming more like newspapers elsewhere in the West, the French

[3] *Ibid.,* p. 45.
[4] See Lucien W. Pye, *Communications and Political Development* (Princeton: Princeton University Press, 1963), p. 8.

press has departed in many respects from its prewar structure and approach. Most important among such departures are the fusion of many newspapers and the deemphasis of their political commitment.

In spite of a growth in population the circulation of daily newspapers in France declined between 1946 and 1959 from 15.1 to 9.6 million a day. Since then there has been a slow, steady, and possibly significant, increase (12.8 million in 1966).[5] The decline in readership, a common phenomenon in most Western democracies, may be partly the result of a decline in the number of newspapers. In 1964 Paris had only 14 dailies as against 28 in 1946 and 57 before the First World War. Outside the capital, their number has decreased in the years since the last war from 175 to 93. According to public opinion polls, 75 per cent of Frenchmen are regular readers of the daily press; 12 per cent admit that they never look at it. In a representative youth panel, the corresponding figures are 45 per cent and 21 per cent. Among the farming population non-readers make up 22 per cent, and in the least developed regions 39 per cent of the total adults.

The most striking difference from prewar days is the emaciation of the party press. The Communist *Humanité,* the national newspaper of a party which had five million voters in the 1967 elections, has a circulation of little over 200,000 copies, as against close to one million copies for the two Communist dailies after the liberation. Only the far less politically and more culturally oriented Sunday edition of the *Humanité* still holds close to the half-million mark. The Socialist Party with more than two million voters, and the U.N.R. — the government party which in 1962 and 1967 attracted a larger percentage of votes than any French party in history — publish their dailies, *Le Populaire* and *La Nation,* in just a few thousand copies, mainly so that their editorials can be quoted on radio and television. But during the fifties and early sixties

[5] Bruce M. Russett, *et al., World Handbook of Political and Social Indicators* (New Haven: Yale University Press, 1964), p. 108, ranks France nineteenth in circulation of daily newspapers, behind most other countries of similar development. Unfortunately, at least for France, the figures do not correspond to the data given here and gained from reliable sources, see *A.P.,* 1966, pp. 393 ff.

the two foremost nonpartisan Paris newspapers which shun an editorial opinion on many issues, the *Parisien Libéré* and *France-Soir,* have skyrocketed to a total of 2.1 million copies, or almost 45 per cent of all papers presently published in the capital. The two papers that come next in reader appeal, even though at a considerable distance, *Le Figaro* and *L'Aurore* (between 400,000 and 500,000 copies each) have a somewhat more definite political orientation; both are conservative, but they too shun all party affiliations.

The provincial press has the same characteristics. Unlike England, the newspapers in the various regions of France have stood the competition from the capital quite well. There are seventeen provincial newspapers that print more than 150,000 copies each; one of them, *Ouest-France,* is the third most important daily in the country. Others hold a quasi-monopoly in their respective regions, after having absorbed many of the strictly local papers. But while before the war some of the regional papers, especially in the South, were the mainstay of political parties, such ties are now cut. Their appeal is clearly directed to the reading public in its entirety. Hence it is not astonishing that their readership, and that of the two most successful Parisian dailies as well, reflects faithfully the social composition of the adult population at large. Half of the readers of the *Parisien Libéré* are workers who were obviously not unduly disturbed about the bias their daily paper showed when it expressed sympathy for the rebellious generals in Algeria. Other Paris newspapers appeal, by their presentation and style, to one social group over others.[6] But their audience is differentiated according to socio-economic status, not by political opinion.

Since most dailies feel compelled to offer to a politically undifferentiated clientele a product which antagonizes none, they tone down information that might prove divisive and avoid, as far as possible, controversial comments. Pressure from the reading public as perceived by circulation figures results in conformism of the newspapers, and such conformism

[6] See *A.P.,* 1963, p. 382, to compare changes that have occurred in the distribution of readers with data from 1949 in *Sondages,* XVII:3 (1955), p. 59.

reinforces the political indifference of their readers.[7] Responsible journalists complain about the "self-censorship" which their papers exercise; they acknowledge that present trends were underway long before the present regime was installed. Where before the war the financial backers expected most newspapers to be sympathetic to their own political preferences or economic interests, the concern now is for general innocuousness. The earlier policy aroused frequent opposition, the present invites indifference and at worst boredom. "Letters to the Editor" on any but trivial issues remain rare — one of many indications that politics is still regarded as a spectator sport. Typically, a provincial paper will print side by side national and international news and items of local or regional interest. What is generally missing, in striking contrast with corresponding American newspapers, are references to political organs and processes that intervene at the various levels; efforts of local authorities on the national scene, cooperation between local and national interest groups, etc. Such activities are going on (see Chap. IV), but are seldom considered newsworthy.

There are no reliable data as to the proportion of readers that turn to their dailies in search of political information. Twenty-one per cent of all readers, 37 per cent of women, and 45 per cent of the farmers admit that they never pay attention to political news in the dailies.[8] It is doubtful whether for this group radio and television have become the sources of political information which they simply may not seek.

Two Parisian dailies occupy a special place as communication media: *La Croix* (circulation 115,000) and *Le Monde* (325,000). The former, issued by an important Catholic publishing house which also circulates about twenty other periodicals with a much wider reader appeal than the daily, was founded to combat the institutions of the Third Republic with all the violence it could muster. Today its columns give limited space to religious information as such. Not committed

[7] Goguel and Grosser, *op. cit.*, pp. 155 ff.

[8] See Philip E. Converse and Georges Dupeux, *op. cit.*, p. 6. Their comparative data, which indicate a much greater political interest on the part of the American newspaper reader, are noteworthy but not quite convincing.

to any party and open to divergent opinions, it seeks none-theless to develop a coherent stand on major political and social issues and to represent and possibly develop a dominant trend in modern French Catholicism.

The influence of *Le Monde* is far wider than its circulation. It recruits readers and enjoys respect in many political camps, and it provides food for daily reflection, a basis for discussions, and a working tool for intellectuals, professionals, students, and especially the political and economic elite. Its editorial and reportorial staff are of unusually high quality; the covering of such events as political elections is unequaled by any American paper. Its editorial policy is as critical of the present regime as it was of the defunct Fourth Republic, yet it has no sympathy for political radicalism of any kind. Its *Tribune Libre* solicits divergent opinions. There is wide agreement that — compared with the prewar press — daily newspapers have lost much of the political interest and tension they used to convey, but it is also conceded that none of the prewar dailies enjoyed the independence of *Le Monde*.

Some of the needs for political controversy and partisan information are filled by certain weeklies, representing all shades of opinion. Their audience is fairly small, but they function as an important channel of communication for information not otherwise available, even though their information is not always reliable. While there is no lack of thoroughly cause-oriented weeklies, nor of periodical publications with wide mass appeal, such publications as the British *Economist* and the *Observer,* the German *Zeit,* or the Sunday supplements of certain American newspapers devoted to political information and discussion but devoid of shrill partisanship, do not exist as yet.

As to the publications destined for the broad public, France is now as well provided as other countries and with the same wares. Circulation figures increase steadily even if they do not yet reach the density in coverage of similar American periodicals. Noteworthy is the fact that in "dechristianized" France *L'Echo de Notre Temps,* a monthly which addresses Catholic women in an unsectarian style, leads (with 1.6 million copies) the circulation record of all periodical publications, with the exception of a weekly listing the television programs (2 million copies).

As we have seen, the press had lost much of its political coloring before the advent of the Fifth Republic. Nonetheless, the institutions and the style of the new regime have changed the role of the government in the communication process rather drastically. The flow of information from the centers of decision-making to the printed media has been redirected, its substance altered. In the past, parliamentary debates and even more the communiqués and intentional leaks of committee members and other representatives furnished a great deal of political information to the peripheral public. A deputy or senator who had become a cabinet minister did not break off his cordial "working" relationship with journalists. Discreetness was expected to a far lesser extent from him than, for instance, from a member of the British Cabinet.

Parliament is no longer a center of decision-making (see Chap. X) and has therefore lost most of its importance as a source of information. Deputies that belong to a seemingly solid majority no longer need the press to further their political or personal ends. The ministers, even those with a political rather than administrative background, are chary of confidences. After each cabinet meeting, a communiqué informs the press about the decisions that have been reached; the accompanying commentaries of the Minister of Information are short of enlightening. The secretiveness that has long been considered characteristic of the French businessman has now become the earmark of government operations as well. As a result, newspapermen must prod the immediate collaborators of the Minister and certain members of the bureaucracy to piece together the details of conflicts and political struggles that underlie decision-making, now as before. But because of the official pretense of unanimity, the rumors gathered in such a way by even the most responsible newspaperman are spotty and often misleading. As a result, the level of political information has declined further. "Finally one wonders," an outstanding journalist has written, "whether . . . one does not hear anything because nobody says anything, whether one does not know anything because nothing happens, or whether the regime is able to mask everything, to mute everybody." [9]

Remarkably enough, such dilution of information occurs at a time when the press enjoys, at least since the end of the Algerian war, almost complete freedom from interference and censorship — except for the self-censorship that has been mentioned. Outright support of the regime by major newspapers is spotty. In several of his press conferences, General de Gaulle commented sarcastically on the hostile attitude which the press had shown towards him "for the past 25 years." But he also expressed quiet confidence that in due time this would change, implying that the present "aloofness" of the printed media was in no way disturbing to him or the regime.[10] It is quite true that criticism, even where it is not discredited by the unreliability of the information on which it is based, proves generally ineffective in eliciting from the government a justification or a fuller explanation of its policies.

Dissatisfaction of the general public with the amount of information it receives about governmental decisions and policies is relatively widespread. In 1964, 43 per cent complained about a lack of information while 42 per cent thought they knew enough. But among men complaints amounted to 54 per cent and rose to 62 per cent among those with a college education, a degree of criticism not easily matched on any question at any time.[11]

The deliberate secretiveness which surrounds government operations corresponds to General de Gaulle's style of authority. (See Chaps. V and IX.) The period of icy silence which generally precedes the announcement of major decisions gives communications between the centers of decision-making and the public an aura of suspense, surprise, and drama. A constant flow of information with little gradation

[9] Pierre Viansson-Ponté (leading political columnist of *Le Monde*), "Vingt Ans d'Information Politique (1946–1966)," *La Nef*, XXII:27 (1966), p. 50. The entire issue of this magazine is devoted to a discussion of political information in present-day France.

[10] See especially the remarks made during the thirteenth and fourteenth press conferences (February and October 1966). An English translation of all press conferences is published by and obtainable through the Ambassade de France, Service de Presse et d'Information.

[11] *Sondages*, XXVI:3 (1964), pp. 38–39.

as to the importance of the news would impair the desired effect. Unlike a totalitarian government, the regime appears little concerned with enlisting active mass support for its policies and hence explains them only sporadically.

Each of General de Gaulle's carefully spaced and staged biannual press conferences has been used as an important occasion to communicate to the French and the international public major decisions ranging over a broad field of questions. The content and form of such communications are determined unilaterally, since questions addressed to the Chief of State are either prearranged or, if inappropriate, ignored. The press is free to explain and comment on the announced decisions. But nothing is known of how and under what assumptions the decisions have been reached — except that it sometimes appears that the government itself has not had advance information.

Under prevailing conditions, the newspapers are hardly a sufficient source of information for a government that wishes to gauge public attitudes. To a certain extent, the elected representatives, especially the deputies of the majority, still serve as transmission belts between their constituents and the authorities (see Chap. X). The routine contacts between high-ranking civil servants and the representatives of organized interests fulfill the same function and are particularly valuable in a country where, until recently, the cult of secrecy has obscured official statistics.

During the reigns of the two Bonapartes, the regular reports of prefects and other officials kept the government informed about the state of mind of the public. Nowadays, opinion polls fill the gap in information. Considered with diffidence for a long time, polling has now become a major and generally accepted operation; its results are widely publicized by the press. The high accuracy of election prediction justified confidence in the reliability and the techniques of the pollsters — until a number of errors in prognosticating the final outcome of the 1967 elections (erring in favor of the government) discredited somewhat their operations. Most of the polling operations are private and competitive but live to a considerable extent on government contracts. As in the United States, popularity curves exist for the President and his principal collaborators. But in addition there are searching inquiries into attitudes, opinions, and habits which, traditionally, Frenchmen have carefully concealed even from members of their families. If French society is becoming less opaque, this is to a considerable extent due to the vogue for opinion polling.

Polling enables the government and numerous public administrations to gather data without the help of the intermediaries who serve as channels of information in a classical parliamentary democracy. Hence the pattern of a more direct democracy, which the Fifth Republic has sought to establish, is well served by the wide use of public opinion polls; just as in commercial polling, they are based on the plebiscitarian assumptions of "one citizen, one vote, one value." [12]

As to the communication flow in the opposite direction, the modern mass media such as radio and television are similarly appropriate to the style of the regime. It was, of course, a historical accident that General de Gaulle's appeal of June 18, 1940, in which he exhorted his compatriots to continue the fight against Nazi Germany, was broadcast from London to France. But to have entered history by appealing directly to the undifferentiated masses of radio listeners suited de Gaulle well. It was another accident that television, which was developing slowly in France, began to expand rapidly about the time General de Gaulle was called back to power in 1958. Neither de Gaulle nor Castro created the mass media channels which they both have used to widen and continue the bases of their charismatic relationship with the masses.[13] But in France the popularity of television and the techniques employed by the government in handling the new medium has become so outstanding that the regime is sometimes spoken of as a "Telecracy." Those who describe the Fifth Republic as "De Gaulle plus Television" wish to point to the existing institutional shapelessness.

During election and referendum campaigns, the President

[12] On this point see Stein Rokkan, "Comparative Cross-National Research: The Context of Current Efforts," in Richard L. Merritt and Stein Rokkan, *Comparing Nations: The Use of Quantitative Data in Cross-National Research* (New Haven: Yale University Press, 1966), p. 16, and the authors there quoted.

[13] See the pertinent remarks on Cuba in Fagen, *op. cit.*, p. 68.

of the Republic has found the publicly owned radio and television stations an excellent means of communication between leader and nation, over the heads of traditional local leaders. Even more characteristic were his appeals to the nation (in General's uniform rather than in a double-breasted suit) when mutinous settlers or officers threatened the republic from Algeria. On these occasions, the hero invited the citizens to share with him not only the experience of exciting events but also the responsibility of resolving the crisis. In fact, twice a rebellion collapsed shortly after almost the entire population watched de Gaulle's television appearance. The effective use of modern communications made the rebels realize that the national community was intact, and proved far more decisive than the *post hoc* utilization of presidential emergency powers (see Chap. IX).

Almost all households possess a radio. The number of households with television amounted to about half of the total in 1965 (more than 6 million sets as against 53,000 only 12 years earlier). TV is estimated to reach between twenty-one and twenty-three million people. In the villages, television has frequently and drastically transformed leisure time habits and social life. At least a partial socialization of the village population into the broader national or regional community is taking place all the more easily because the diffident French farmer has always trusted what he can "see" more than what he reads or is told.

All existing television chains (two national and twenty-two regional relays) are a public monopoly and do not carry commercial advertising. Since the war, there are no private radio stations broadcasting from French territory. But the so-called peripheral stations, covering all of French territory from border zones and until recently privately controlled, have a far more recognized status than the "pirate" stations in Great Britain. On the other hand, the official French radio has never acquired the significance or the prestige of the British B.B.C. As late as 1963, government radio could count on little more than one out of every ten listeners. Since then a concerted effort to improve its appeal has enlarged its audience to about 38 per cent of the total. The continuing predominance of the private stations is due principally to their frank catering to popular tastes. However, it is also true that "listening to the news" means for many distrustful Frenchmen tuning in on the newscasts of the private rather than the publicly owned stations.[14] This seems to indicate that Frenchmen still have the same doubts about the integrity of the communications process which made them widely critical of the prewar press. It is true that to check on televised news, the public must turn to the private radio stations.

Because of the rapid expansion of television, the problem of governmental control of the mass media is one of the most ardently discussed questions in the public life of the Fifth Republic. By 1972, the normal date of the next presidential elections, it is estimated that the number of television sets will have almost doubled and will reach 90 per cent of the population. "The regulation of broadcasting and television," a moderate deputy of the opposition has written, "becomes more important than the articles of the Constitution."

## GOVERNMENTAL CONTROL OF INFORMATION

The regulation of information is by no means peculiar to the present regime; it antedates the wide diffusion of television. In Great Britain, parliamentary inquiries into the operations of the B.B.C. have concerned themselves with the quality of its radio and television operations; there never was any doubt that the network was free from governmental interference. By contrast, whenever the annual budget of the information services was debated in the parliament of the Fourth Republic, bitter and justified complaints were voiced about the manner in which each of the short-lived cabinets was using the government controlled communications systems to further its political ends. To conceive of the mass media as a public service, which was to be put at the disposal of all political forces, remained a difficult concept for a political community in which government and opposition contested

[14] According to (unpublished) opinion polls, 23 per cent consider the political information over the official radio partial, 33 per cent impartial, with 44 per cent expressing no opinion, probably because they never listen to political newscasts.

each other's legitimacy. Each majority, however ephemeral, claimed to speak in the name of all and therefore saw no virtue in permitting dissonant voices to be heard over the publicly owned air waves. Such practices rapidly created a body of precedents which every government used when it wished to interfere with the presentation of political and often, of general information.

An additional obstacle to objectivity is the habit common to all French journalism of fusing news report and editorial comment. To present the news without coloring it with the opinion of the reporter is considered dull and would probably by now be rejected as uninteresting by the reading and listening public. The long years of the Algerian war, during which the government considered the radio a weapon in the fight against internal and external foes, further discredited the state controlled channels, with the result that the private, peripheral stations soared in popularity.

With the advent of the Fifth Republic the situation worsened. There was no competition to the government monopoly in the field of television. The government was also known to have acquired shares, and in some cases a controlling majority, in the private radio stations. Moreover, there was no longer that cascade of rapidly succeeding governments which in the past had checked the one-sidedness of information. The Minister of Information declared from the tribune of parliament that to use radio and television for the almost exclusive presentation of the government's case was justified because this did no more than establish a necessary balance to the press which in his opinion remained overwhelmingly critical of the regime.

The reorganization of broadcasting and television which the government undertook by ministerial ordinance in 1959 met with widespread criticism, as did the use of the mass media by the government during the referendum and election campaigns of 1962. Under pressure, which in this case included the advice of the Constitutional Council (see Chap. IX), the government finally submitted to parliament a bill for the creation of a new agency, the *Office de Radiodiffusion-Télévision Française* (O.R.T.F.). During the lively parliamentary debates bitter criticism against past operations was once more voiced, but the government easily defeated all amendments which would have made the agency truly autonomous in the manner of the B.B.C., or the public chains in the Federal Republic of Germany.

Nevertheless, the new law, as finally voted, strikes a somewhat better balance between concerns for governmental control and for independence; it offers at least a framework for a liberalized policy.[15] The Minister of Information supervises but no longer administers O.R.T.F.; a Board of Directors has been given seemingly broad powers to direct general policy and to supervise the general standards of programs — it is empowered to check on the accuracy and objectivity of information and to insist on a balanced presentation which should give to "the principal trends of thought and the important currents of opinion" access to the mass media. Parliamentary representatives and program committees, composed of qualified laymen, assist the board in the discharge of its functions. However, high civil servants are in a majority on the board — other members represent the public, the press, and O.R.T.F. personnel. What might prove decisive is that neither the Director General of the O.R.T.F. nor his principal assistants are designated by the Board. They are appointed, and their appointments can be revoked at will by the government. This means that, in spite of the controls that have been introduced, the personnel responsible for the actual management of the agency and of its financial resources depend as before directly on the government. Under these conditions, the staff may be tempted to pay unquestioning allegiance to the Director General who himself is at the government's mercy.

Not enough time has elapsed to test whether the new set-up will permit broadening the free flow of information through the official media. Their newscasts suffer from the same self-censorship to which much of the press is subjecting itself. There are still complaints from many sides that on the

[15] For a detailed analysis of the present legislation and its history, see P. M. Gaudemet, "Le régime de la radiodiffusion et de la télévision en France" (with an extensive summary in English), *International Review of Administrative Sciences*, XXXI:1 (1965), pp. 15–23; IV–VI.

national and on the regional networks information of great public interest is being omitted when it is considered inappropriate by the authorities. In fact, an interministerial committee makes frequent suggestions as to which topics should be treated lightly; entire programs are known to have been deleted. Since many in the management of the O.R.T.F. are very close to the centers of decision-making, no binding directives are needed to insure a large measure of conformism. A naive ethnocentricity which affects even such trivia as sports events, is not exclusively French. But dissatisfaction with working conditions created by an uncertain autonomy have driven many of the best talents away from the O.R.T.F. In spite of great and partly successful efforts at improving quality, its position as a truly public service is still contested and remains therefore almost as controversial as before the reform.

The most notable change in governmental control of the news media had only indirectly to do with the reorganization of the O.R.T.F. but might be indicative of future trends.

During the strenuous political campaigns of 1962 the government used its monopoly to insure a majority for the referendum on the constitutional amendment and to defeat the candidates of the opposition in the elections. The prestige of the President of the Republic and his talents as a performer on the television screen were pressed into service. Nonetheless, it is impossible to establish a positive correlation between the impact of television propaganda and voting; indeed, as in other countries, it is probable that governmental efforts, for being too ostentatious, provoked a boomerang effect in 1962. Some of the regions with the greatest number of TV sets voted against the government, while other regions where at that time television was not yet widespread lined up solidly behind General de Gaulle. The only positive evidence of the influence of television appeared to be an increase in political interest, since abstentions were on the whole less frequent in households with TV.[16]

16 Cf. René Rémond and Claude Neuschwander, "Télévision et Comportement Politique," *RFSP*, XIII:2 (1963), esp. pp. 345–46. On the basis of public opinion polls, Guy Michelat, "Télévisions, moyens d'information et comportement électoral," *ibid.*, XIV:5 (1964), pp. 877–905, has qualified some of the earlier findings without however invalidating them.

This trend continued during the presidential elections of 1965: the record low of abstention was partly attributed to the fascination with mass media and the role they played in the campaign. This time, however, the five candidates opposing the presidential incumbent were not only all given equal time on radio and television but also addressed their appeals to the electorate under the same conditions as de Gaulle. According to the calculations of the Minister of Information, this opened to the opposition candidates a total of six hundred minutes as against only twenty minutes for the President. Such a balance, or such a disequilibrium as others would say, resulted not from the reorganization of the O.R.T.F. but from the efforts of a National Control Commission which had been entrusted with supervising the entire operation of the presidential elections.

Quite obviously, the government desired to give to the first election of the Chief Executive by direct popular suffrage a maximum guarantee of fairness and respectability; moreover, it was no longer pressed, as it had been in 1962, by the possibility of a grave crisis of the regime. For these reasons, the government turned over the control of the elections to representatives of the highest judicial bodies in the country. Devoted to the principles of republican legality and desirous of formulating rules of the game that would be clear and command universal respect, the Control Commission insured for all candidates equal opportunities, which included equal access to radio and television time.[17] A new method of assigning time was introduced at the approach of the parliamentary elections of 1967. Now equal time was given to the candidates of the majority and to those of "the" opposition. This meant that the various parties and movements critical of the government had to share among themselves half of the totally allotted time. Protests against this arrangement were ignored.

Whether under these circumstances radio and television have influenced the vote in the presidential and parliamentary elections is again controversial.[18] The mere fact of owning a

[17] Cf. G. Rochecorbon, "Le 'contrôle' de la campagne électorale," *ibid.,* XVI:2 (1966), pp. 255–71.
[18] Cf. *Sondages,* XXVII:4 (1965), p. 19, and Williams, "The French Presidential Elections," esp. p. 28.

television set did not seem to make a difference. More detailed opinion polls revealed, however, that at the beginning of the presidential campaign about 20 per cent of those who watched TV declared to have changed their vote as a result. They explained that they had been motivated by the appearance on the screen of attractive and reasonable opposition leaders and the visible effect of age on de Gaulle. Later, when the effect of novelty had worn off, and especially before the run-off elections, most of the voters returned to traditional options without much regard for what they heard and saw on radio and TV. In the parliamentary elections of 1967 the government's advantage in the allotment of TV time apparently did not have a decisive effect in turning the elections in its favor, since it very nearly lost the elections (see Chap. VIII).

There is little doubt that the liberalized use of the mass media has contributed to a revitalization of political interest. An effort is being made to make the mass media responsive to such a change outside the drama of election campaigns. New feature programs are designed at least to alternate the habitual governmental monologue with dialogues and discussions; so far they have met with lively listeners' response. One of the difficulties for such a reorientation remains the division of the opposition. An effective presentation through the modern mass media presupposes a simplification of issues which is facilitated by a polarization of opinion into two opposing camps. It is too early to say whether such a polarization is on its way (see Chaps. VIII and IX). Moreover, in a period of rapid political transformation there is uncertainty as to who could be considered as the representative spokesmen for the traditional and who for the newly emerging political forces. The problem of control and of the flow of information is of necessity conditioned by the political modernization of the country.

# CHAPTER VII

# Articulation of Values and Interests:
# The Interest Groups

## INTEREST REPRESENTATION IN
## A FRAGMENTED SOCIETY

In every polity means exist to bring the demands and desires prevalent in the society to the attention of the decision-makers.[1] In France, as elsewhere, this function is served by a variety of structures. As in all modern states, the associational interest or pressure groups which specialize in the articulation of values and interests through a more or less permanent organization, occupy the foreground of the political stage. But other structures have by no means lost all importance. What have been called nonassociational groups, distinguished families, local or regional notables, prominent religious leaders, and especially the modern business firms or "industrial empires," exercise in France an influence which, although it is intermittent, often outweighs that of trade associations, trade unions, or other groups. In addition, interests are generated and articulated within governmental structures themselves. In France, the bureaucracy, both civil and military, does not simply react to pressures from the outside; its cleavages (for examples see Chap. V) and the frequent absence of political directives have

[1] See Almond and Powell, *op. cit.*, pp. 73 f. The discussion that follows adopts the framework established by these authors in Chap. IV of their book.

made it quite frequently into an autonomous force of interest representation.

For a truly realistic appraisal of the role of groups in the policy process one must investigate the actual and relative influence of the various organized and unorganized interests, the effectiveness of alliances and the impact of countervailing forces, both organizational and ideological.[2] Interest articulation by associational and nonassociational groups takes place at the boundary line between society and the political system. It is, therefore, entirely embedded in the political culture of the country. The political culture described in previous chapters, shapes, limits, and guides the pattern of group demands and activities. In turn, the groups influence the political culture in its evolution.

Discussions about the legitimacy of group activities do not only reflect constitutional and philosophical traditions. They are also determined by past experiences. Frequently, and not without reason, organized interests in France are held responsible for the fact that a society with egalitarian traditions has so often reproduced and aggravated existing inequalities. In other countries too the defense of the *status quo* might be the dominant concern of interest groups. But in the stalemate society that France has been for so long, such a position has had a special significance for retarding economic, social, and political development. Moreover, the ideological fragmentation of political life has determined the way in which demands are formulated and interest groups are organized. Once formed, the groups have done much to harden ideological divisions.

". . . if the general will is to be able to express itself, it is essential that there should be no partial society within the State and that each citizen should think only his own thought." This categorical condemnation by Rousseau of all intermediate groups has occupied an important place in French political theory and has been a factor in shaping legis-

[2] This point is made by Roy C. Macridis, "Interest Groups in Comparative Analysis," *The Journal of Politics*, XXII:1 (1961), pp. 25–45, and particularly in regard to the French situation by Jean Meynaud, *Nouvelles Etudes sur les Groupes de Pression en France* (Paris: Colin, 1962), pp. 384 ff. — an indispensable work for the student of French interest groups.

lation for more than a century. The individualism it expresses was shared by most of the philosophers of the French Enlightenment and fed on the observation of oppressive guild practices under the *Ancien Régime*. This attitude triumphed in the legislative enactments of the Revolution, especially the famous Le Chapelier law which outlawed all associations. The statute was rescinded only after more than a century (by a law in 1901), and even then with some reservations. However, the legal obstacles were frequently ignored; many categories of Frenchmen did not wait for the change in legislation to form groups and to constitute in fact the "partial societies" condemned by Rousseau.[3] But the necessity of achieving this by subterfuge was nevertheless bound to shape group practice and to spread doubts about the legitimacy of group activities.

Groups which seek to influence political decisions continue to incur public opprobrium. An outstanding public lawyer, member of the Council of State who became a cabinet member in the Fifth Republic, has quite recently characterized interest representation of whatever kind as a violation of the "still valid principles of 1789." [4] Until a few years ago, "pressure groups" (*groupes de pression*) and "lobbies" were political scare words, partly because public attention was focused on the showy activities of disreputable or unpopular groups. The first "modern" lobby in France, made up of many kinds of organizations and manipulating both parliament and bureaucracy almost at will, was the colonial lobby. Formed at the turn of the century, it was responsible for many of the colonial ventures of the Third Republic, and prolonged the costly wars of the Fourth. Other well-known lobbies were those of the munitions makers, the "merchants of death," and those of the interests which spread disease and vice by liquor or prostitution.

In reality, there has never been anything particularly scandalous about the defense of organized interests in France, nor

[3] See Georges Lavau, "Political Pressures by Interest Groups in France," in Henry W. Ehrmann (ed.), *Interest Groups on Four Continents* (Pittsburgh: Pittsburgh University Press, 1958, 1964), p. 60.

[4] Bernard Chenot, *Organisation économique de l'Etat* (Paris: Dalloz, 1951), p. 184.

has the pressure been truly irresistible. Indeed the structure and the organizational means of most associational interest groups are less solid than in many other countries. This is only partly caused by the legal and ideological obstacles that have been mentioned; more important is the general aversion to associational life (see Chap. III). In addition in a society which has never been as hierarchically organized as the state, industrialization was slow and the agricultural sector isolated — "Rather than a national market there was a conglomeration of small ones." [5] Accordingly, pressure groups were often more coherent on a local than on a national or regional scale. Yet their effectiveness on that level was limited by the centralization of governmental decision-making. This explains in part the difficulties encountered by interest confederations (the so-called *Spitzenverbände*), which in other countries have grouped quite effectively all of agriculture, labor, business, etc. These confederations must always mediate between and align for common action the naturally divergent interests of their member organizations. In France they have only been intermittently successful; even after organizational unity has been established, it is always likely to disintegrate again.

Weakness also results from the "cult of the small" which many groups, especially in business and farming, practice in order to establish their contested legitimacy. Internal cohesion must then be paid for by the defense of the least productive members and an alignment based on their requirements for survival. Moreover, the small and inefficient producers are usually most given to an "atomism" averse to all organization.

During the crisis-ridden last years of the Fourth Republic, the Union for the Defense of Shopkeepers and Artisans, launched by Pierre Poujade, mobilized the small businessmen threatened by the consequences of modernization and rationalization. Desirous as they were to resist authority, if need be by violence, they felt insufficiently protected by the existing interest groups, even though the latter were prepared to shield the marginal units in the economy. For a time Poujade succeeded in transforming the revolt of the injured interests into

[5] See Hoffmann, in *In Search of France*, p. 11.

a political movement which won 2.5 million votes in the 1956 elections. But the eventual failure of this and other flash parties demonstrates that there are boundary lines which group activities cannot transgress without risk either to themselves or to the society in which they operate.[6]

In more normal times, actual membership in almost all associations amounts to only a fraction of potential membership. At present, trade unions organize at most 17–20 per cent of eligible wage earners, and probably as little as 15 per cent. Only 17 per cent of the young have joined youth organizations. Not more than 25 per cent of the farmers belong to one of the numerous agricultural interest groups. There never has been a steady, if slow, progression of membership. Many of the important groups have known a mass influx of new members at dramatic moments of the country's social or political history, such as at the time of the Popular Front victories or the post-liberation era. But as soon as conditions become normal, "normal" individualism reasserts itself and leaves the associations with too small a membership to justify their claims of representativeness. The treasuries of many groups are often so depleted that they are unable to employ a competent staff. The modern pressure group official is a fairly recent phenomenon to be found only in certain sectors of the group system, such as business associations. The few organizations that count their members by the millions are likely to serve small interests or broad ideas: the home distillers of liquor, the friends or foes of the parochial schools, including the parent-teachers associations of the private and the public schools.

Political and ideological divisions add further to the fragmentation of group activities and augment the obstacles that stand in the way of effective articulation and defense of the interests. The trade-union movement and the agricultural organizations exemplify the difficulties which exist almost everywhere.

The French labor movement has never looked upon itself

[6] For more details on the Poujade Movement, see H. W. Ehrmann, *Organized Business*, pp. 183 ff., and Stanley Hoffmann, *Le Mouvement Poujade* (Paris: Colin, 1956).

as an interest group "like the others," nor has it been regarded as such by outsiders.[7] Whatever their political or philosophical persuasion, all of the major labor confederations want to rebuild society and polity on new foundations. Their pervasive anticapitalism feeds on many sources (forcefully expressed in the preamble of their respective bylaws): on Marxist concepts of the class struggle, on Christian or personalist indignation about the iniquities of the existing system, and even on preindustrial reflexes and resentments.

Most European trade unions have aspired to combine demands for the material betterment of their constituents with the fight for broader ideals of emancipation. But the heavy ideological baggage of French labor has encumbered normal trade union activities. Not infrequently, ideological commitment appears to serve as a compensation for weakness of organization and for the ensuing ineffectiveness of a divided labor movement. One attacks the existing economic system when one is unable to obtain limited reforms. On the other hand, union members are well aware that such lasting reforms as have been obtained are either due to legislation or to the intervention of the labor inspectors, the administrative field representatives of the state. Hence the relationship between improvements and union activities, especially as carried on by union members, appears tenuous at best.

From its beginning, the labor movement has suffered from particularly heavy membership fluctuations. The largest confederation, the Communist controlled *Confédération Générale du Travail* (C.G.T.), admits that its membership has dwindled from more than 6 million in 1945–46 to 1.7 million members in 1961, and that the number of union locals has been about halved. But membership figures published by labor are notoriously unreliable. In 1963 estimates of 800,000 for the C.G.T., 450,000 for the Catholic oriented *Confédération Française des Travailleurs Chrétiens* (C.F.T.C.), and at most

[7] For the French trade union movement see Henry W. Ehrmann, *French Labor from Popular Front to Liberation* (New York: Oxford University Press, 1947); Val Lorwin, *The French Labor Movement* (Cambridge: Harvard University Press, 1954); and the up-to-date account on both labor and business organizations in Jean-Daniel Reynaud, *Les Syndicats en France* (Paris: Colin, 1963).

380,000 for the anticommunist *Force Ouvrière* (F.O.), appear more realistic.[8] That the C.G.T. still attracts the largest number of wage earners and especially of industrial workers is largely due to the same reasons which explain the continuing electoral strength of the Communist Party (see Chap. VIII). But the C.G.T. has also fallen heir to the cherished traditions of the "heroic age" of French syndicalism. Its larger following and a capable staff enable it to provide the services which the membership expects, revolutionary commitment notwithstanding.

As late as 1964, yet another labor confederation, the *Confédération Française et Démocratique du Travail* (C.F.D.T.), was formed under conditions quite characteristic of the continuing ideological fragmentation of group life. A majority of unions affiliated with the C.F.T.C. wished to assert their complete independence from the catholic outlook. But since they were unable to persuade the entire Catholic labor confederation to join with them in a new endeavor, their attempt to renounce an ideological orientation led only to a new division, not to fusion.

Similar problems beset the numerically strong Federation of Teachers in which 80 per cent of the teachers in public primary schools are organized, all of them committed to the principle of *laïcism,* i.e., to the separation of church and state, almost all of them belonging to the left of the political spectrum. Yet its membership is so deeply divided along party lines and on minute questions of doctrinaire political orientation that the effectiveness of the organization is frequently impaired.

The competition between different and often antagonistic trade-union movements necessitates a special pattern of action. At places of work, trade-union "pluralism," as this fragmentation is euphemistically called, makes the open shop mandatory. Such pluralism determines bargaining procedures, as well as the relationship between the unions, the authorities, and the political parties. Existing legislation sanctions the fact that the same group of wage earners might be represented by different organizations. While this eliminates certain kinds of jurisdic-

[8] Reynaud, *op. cit.,* p. 127.

tional disputes, it also impairs the representativeness of the multiple trade-union movements.

A corresponding and long-standing division between agricultural organizations was more clearly political, although ideological overtones were not absent. Towards the end of the Second Empire, conservative and Catholic elements had formed one organization of farmers, including the large estate owners; after the establishment of the Third Republic, freemasons and republicans founded another. For a time both associations recruited in those regions to which they were politically attuned, both establishing credit institutions, insurance companies, producer- and consumer-cooperatives. For a time both had access to the Ministry of Agriculture, but when the Ministry came under the all but permanent control of Radical-Socialist ministers, the freethinkers were given a decided edge over their competitors. In addition, there also existed socialist and communist farming organizations and the fascist oriented "Green Shirts."

After the Second World War, it seemed for a moment that the time had come to form a large confederation grouping all interests. Founded upon the aspiration of a Socialist Minister of Agriculture who hoped to emulate Vichy's peasant corporation in a climate of freedom, the confederation claimed to group 80 per cent of those eligible. But before long subsidiary groups reasserted their autonomy and the peak association lost all importance. Some of the earlier political differences have been overcome. But the diversity of interests, the individualism and occasionally the sectarianism of their constituents explain the existence of close to five hundred rural defense organizations on the national level alone. This is an expensive structure, made possible only because many of the groups live in one way or the other on public subsidies. The most prominent rural defense organization is now the *Fédération Nationale des Syndicats d'Exploitants Agricoles* (F.N.S.E.A.). While politically neutral, it is frequently shaken by internal controversies about the proper future course of agricultural development (see also Chap. II).

Within several interest groups young members form an organization apart. But characteristically, this is not primarily a functional division, catering to the special needs of an age group, but rather another ideological alignment. The best known among these groups are the Young Farmers and the Young Employers. They attempt to elaborate a well-defined doctrine about new forms of capitalist enterprise and competition or about rural organization. The thinking of their most active members, like that of some of the leaders in the Christian trade-union movement, has often been stimulated by an updated and dynamic social Catholicism (see also Chap. III). Inside the larger interest organizations the activities of these groups meet with varied fates. Sometimes they are resented because their ideological commitment creates additional conflicts. While the *Jeunes Agriculteurs* have won leadership positions in the largest farmers' group, the *Jeunes Patrons* have all but withdrawn from the representative and exceptionally well-staffed business confederation, the *Conseil National du Patronat Français* (C.N.P.F.). The new split in the Christian trade-union movement is primarily the result of efforts by the younger leadership.

In all countries there is usually some overlapping between groups organizing the special interests of the various economic and social sections into which the population is divided and those groups promoting shared attitudes and common causes. But in France the mixing of both in the same organization has been carried very far, and such fusion has given special characteristics to the defense of all interests.

In addition to management, labor, and agriculture also such interest organizations as the students' associations, the ex-service men's, pensioners, and taxpayers' groups are riddled by ideological and political dissensions. The result is a form of interest articulation which is frequently far less satisfactory than one which is primarily pragmatic and instrumental.[9]

Given the ideological style of the country's political culture, it is not astonishing that there is a luxuriant growth of groups devoted solely to the promotion of causes. Some of them, such as the League for the Rights of Men, are centuries old. As already mentioned, the vigorous associations which, since the

---

[9] Almond and Powell, *op. cit.*, p. 89, point to the special difficulties that arise from this form of interest articulation.

beginning of the Third Republic, are aligned on the issue of public versus parochial education are still able to mobilize mass support. Other groups spring up and disappear in major or minor crisis situations. At times their impact on public opinion has been considerable; their emotional appeal is well suited for many audiences. Since many of them demand only a temporary commitment, they rarely need the permanent and qualified staff which only few French interest groups can assemble. On the other hand, civic groups demanding a sustained, cooperative effort from their members have only lately acquired prestige.

It has often been observed, in the United States and elsewhere, that multiple group membership has a moderating influence on the articulation and defense of interests. The leaders of one association have to take some account of the fact that their proposals must be acceptable to members who also belong to other groups.[10] No exact data are available on this phenomenon in France. However, there is evidence that in spite of the lower density of associational life multiple and overlapping membership in interest groups is a fairly frequent occurrence. But in France it appears that this escalates rather than moderates demands. For those who belong to different groups usually are also aligned in each of them with a definite ideological, political, or religious persuasion. Whether acting as parent, wage earner, or veteran, they will defend in each of their associations the ideals of the "spiritual family" with which they identify. This makes for more stubbornness and rigidity on the part of the membership and hence of the interest groups to which they belong.

In addition to the modern associational interest group more traditional structures, such as notables of all kinds, are still playing an important role in the articulation and defense of interests. In the past, the "bourgeois dynasties" (as leading families in business and banking used to be called), imposed their advice on the public authorities, controlled elections, and, if necessary, instigated and led revolts. Even today, some of the most important firms pay little attention to their own

10 See David Truman, *The Governmental Process* (New York: Knopf, 1951), pp. 509 ff.

trade associations. Since they have direct and satisfactory access to the centers of decision-making, they consider the cumbersome associational groups as an unnecessary concession to democracy. The moral, and sometimes political, influence of church leaders is exercised quite regularly outside the channels of the numerous organizations animated and controlled by the Catholic hierarchy. In rural regions, the mayors and other local officials derive their influence from their status as holders of official positions rather than from the associations to which they might belong.

### MEANS OF ACCESS AND STYLE OF ACTION

Interest groups are active in all the arenas from which authoritative decisions can be influenced: in the electoral process and in parliament; through contacts with the political executive and with members of the bureaucracy, and through those media which allow them to put their case before the general public or more specialized audiences.[11] By comparison with interest groups in other countries, the majority of the French groups appears less attuned to the intensive use of propaganda and of public relations. With some significant exceptions, few sectional interest groups will use the information media for broad-gauge appeals; cause groups have seldom the means to do so. In part such reluctance stems from the described uncertainties about the legitimacy of group activities. Organized business, for instance, has shunned for a long time all endeavors to create a public image of the community it represents. Partly this was due to the traditional secretiveness of the French businessman, partly to the conviction that, since France has become a business civilization only of late, the accomplishments of business and of its associations would hardly be appreciated by the public.

The setting of parliamentary and local elections which has been described earlier (see Chap. IV) have encouraged strenuous group activity during every campaign. The smallness of the constituency under most of the electoral systems that have

---

[11] For a general overview of group activities see Henry W. Ehrmann, "Pressure Groups in France," *Annals of the American Academy of Political and Social Science,* CCCXIX (1958), pp. 148 ff.

been used, the personalized relationship between representatives and electorate and, most of all, the flabbiness of party organization and discipline have at all times driven the groups to appeal directly to the candidate. Before the election, groups rather than individual voters put their demands to him. He was requested to pledge, often "on the dotted line," to defend the groups' concerns. His answers to such requests, whether positive or negative, was published in the newsletter which the group circulated among its membership. A candidate who in the first ballot had to face several competitors and could at best be elected by only a small margin of votes felt inclined to submit to such pressures. Even if he were not to honor his promises once he was elected, the din of organized groups during the campaign often deafened the candidate's political ears and prevented him from discussing larger issues. In this respect, however, the groups did little more than reinforce the traditional style of atomistic representation.

The role which groups played in financing election campaigns (and thereby in the selection of candidates) was admittedly important but also obscure, except for some widely publicized "scandals." [12] Candidates who obtained 5 per cent of the total vote in their constituency were and continue to be reimbursed by the government for certain specific campaign expenses. There is, however, no provision for the high costs of modern campaigning; control of total expenditures has always been lax and could easily be circumvented. In the absence of well-filled party treasuries, many candidates simply had to rely on group support which was likely to limit their freedom of action more than the mere signing of pledges.

In the Fifth Republic the scenario has not changed essentially. During election campaigns, groups still appeal to the candidates, and the candidates show deference or independence according to their temperament and lights. Although party discipline in the Gaullist Party, the U.N.R., is strict, its candidates are nonetheless encouraged by the party leadership to seek communication with and support from organized interests as a means of sinking stronger roots in their constitu-

---

[12] For details on some of them, see H. W. Ehrmann, *Organized Business,* pp. 219 ff.

encies. For similar reasons, many candidates of the opposition continue to cultivate group contacts.

What has changed is that both sides, candidates as well as associations, know well that the parliamentary arena has become far less useful for processing group claims. Since the main focus of decision-making has shifted to the executive and the bureaucracy, the opinion which deputies and senators might hold of a particular group has become a less important, though not entirely negligible, factor.

The example of Switzerland and of the American states shows that organized interests are able to play a prominent role also in a referendum campaign. But where the consultation of the electorate by referendum takes on a plebiscitarian character, as it has in France since 1958, groups might well judge it the better part of wisdom not to take sides in a political contest. This has been the tactic of all groups with few exceptions. The Communist-led C.G.T. enjoined its members in all but one of the referendums to cast a negative vote but it seems to have been only moderately successful. The groups formed to "Keep Algeria French" went down to resounding defeats in two of the verdicts of the electorate.

For most interest associations the presidential elections of 1965 were as embarrassing as the preceding plebiscites. They therefore avoided endorsing any candidate and did not participate in the campaign. Only the C.G.T. and the Federation of Teachers declared, somewhat platonically, their sympathies for Mitterand. However, the largest farmers' organization, the F.N.S.E.A., took a more forthright stand.[13]

The changes in the policy-making process of the Fifth Republic had deprived the F.N.S.E.A. of its customary channels of influence. It had also found out that resort to violence brought only limited success (for details see below). Hence it voiced its deep dissatisfaction with the agricultural policy of the regime at the beginning of the presidential campaign. It explicitly stated that as an interest group it was not qualified to endorse a candidate. But it also warned its members that

13 See, with many details on recent orientations and activities of the rural interest groups, Yves Tavernier, "Le Syndicalisme Paysan et la Cinquième République," *RFSP*, XVI:5 (1966), pp. 869–912.

the defense of their interests would be harmed if the farmers' votes were to back a hostile government, which they would do, as was generally understood, by reelecting General de Gaulle. The government took violent issue with the legitimacy of such a plea.

What effect the intervention of this interest group had on the outcome of the election is uncertain. As Table III (see above Chap. IV) shows, the farmers' vote and that of the rural population in general was far more favorable to de Gaulle than the national average (and slightly more so than during the referendum of 1962). It is nonetheless possible that without the widely publicized appeal issued by the F.N.S.E.A. a yet more favorable farm vote could have avoided the run-off elections which General de Gaulle considered humiliating. At any rate, it appeared that the government thought so when shortly after the elections it replaced the Minister of Agriculture: a popular politician from the Fourth Republic, pledged to classical price support of farm products, took the place of a reform-minded technician. Since F.N.S.E.A. obviously won a battle by engaging its forces in a presidential campaign, the lesson might not be lost on other interest groups.

In preceding regimes organized interests found parliament the most convenient channel for access to political power. When he wanted to inaugurate a policy of free trade, Napoleon III felt compelled to divest the elected representatives of all influence in the setting of tariffs since parliament was all too inclined to give in to the protectionist wishes of business. In the Third and Fourth Republics the highly specialized and powerful committees of both houses of parliament became often little more than institutional façades for pressure groups.[14] Open committee hearings, as they take place in Congress, were unknown. Instead, "study groups" brought deputies and group representatives together behind closed doors but in the very halls of the National Assembly. Under the influence of groups desiring to profit from their electoral support, deputies, irrespective of party affiliation, joined "friendly societies" (*amicales*) expressly formed to discuss the concerns

[14] See Williams, *Crisis,* pp. 374–77.

of various lobbies. For the associations and their leadership the *amicales* became convenient "super-parties." Quite frequently, by means of the *amicales,* groups were able to substitute bills of their own design for those submitted by the government. There have also been episodes when at the moment of important votes lobbyists filled the galleries of parliament in order to remind the people's representatives of the obligations they had incurred.

All this added to a climate of confusion and irresponsibility. There was no clear boundary line between the function of interest groups which is the articulation of interests, and the function of parties which is the aggregation of interests by sifting, moderating, and reconciling contradictory demands. It seems, however, that more often than not the actual impact of such penetration by the groups into the parliamentary arena was more apparent than real. Many of the bills and amendments which deputies moved on behalf of the lobbies lost out because of the general inefficiency of parliamentary proceedings. While in the election campaigns the absence of a valid party system increased the leverage of the groups, the situation was to some extent reversed in parliament. Since parties did not provide a shield behind which the deputies could transact business on behalf of groups, the identification of individual representatives as spokesmen for special interests was generally easy to make and became soon detrimental to their effectiveness. Some carefully concerted but discrediting lobbying by powerful groups resulted occasionally in resounding defeats: the ratification by parliament of the Schuman Plan for the European coal and steel industries over strenuous opposition by the business lobby is one example.[15]

It is true that interest groups gained considerable leverage by the myth they had created about themselves in the minds of deputies and senators. Pressures from organized groups were believed to be irresistible. Not to oppose them was considered a legacy of political wisdom handed down, lazily as it were, from generation to generation.

[15] For details on the defeat of the opponents of the Schuman Plan, see Henry W. Ehrmann, "The French Trade Associations and the Ratification of the Schuman Plan," *World Politics,* VI (1954), pp. 453 ff.

General de Gaulle and his closest collaborators, such as Michel Debré, have frequently lumped interest groups and political parties together in the category of "intermediaries" from which the state would not tolerate interference. The foremost reason for reforming and "rationalizing" parliament was the desire to reduce the role of parliament in the making and unmaking of governments. But many of the new rules, established by constitution and legislation (for details see Chap. X), also had the effect of diminishing the role of organized interests in the legislative process. By and large this has been accomplished, but it does not mean that interest groups have lost all influence on rule-making and policy formation.

The new arrangements have forced a change in tactics and, where such a change was not possible, lessened the status of those groups which in the past had concentrated their activities on parliament and on individual representatives. To be effective, all groups must now use the channels which the best equipped among those defending sectional interests had long found most rewarding, channels which give them access to the administrative process. Here, as in most modern democracies, both institutionalized procedures and the network of personal relations remain important.

The indispensable collaboration between organized private interests and the state is institutionalized in advisory committees, attached to most if not all administrations. They are composed mainly of group representatives who have thereby acquired the right to be consulted on administrative decisions affecting their constituents. Some of these committees have functioned since the Revolution, but their growth has been made particularly luxurious through legislation enacted since the two World Wars. On the national level alone, there exist now no less than five hundred "Councils," twelve hundred "Committees," and three thousand "Commissions," all bringing together group representatives and members of the bureaucracy. Contrary to what has occasionally been promised, in the Fifth Republic few of the advisory boards have been abolished, and many more have been added.

Hopes that by legitimizing interest groups in such a way pressures in other arenas would diminish proved vain. The advisory bodies are simply additional channels of influence and often, from the perspective of the groups, not the most important ones. It is controversial whether the consultation which takes place here leads to a democratization and humanization of administrative procedures or instead to an undesirable fragmentation of authority. Much seems to depend on the way in which bureaucracy uses these instruments of what in France is called "administrative pluralism." Where the civil servants merely take into account the opinions and the documentation presented to them before they reach an autonomous decision, the effect is beneficial. But there are also many cases where the authoritative decision bows entirely to the group's suggestions, so that in effect administrative functions are parceled out to socio-economic forces. Often administrators no longer dare to make decisions unless the groups are willing to assume responsibility for them. In certain situations, where an administration has belatedly resisted their wishes, groups have chosen the tactic of resigning noisily from the advisory boards in order to alarm their constituents and to arouse public opinion.

Although such occurrences were most frequent in the declining days of the Fourth Republic, they are not unknown at present. The courage of the administrator, just as that of the elected representative, is a more effective check on group pressures than the ostentatious style of a regime.

The routine contacts between group representatives and the bureaucracy offer to organized interests the most numerous and most valuable points of access. There is nothing scandalous about such contacts. From the perspective of the bureaucracy, interest groups are audience, advisors, and clients, foremost participants in the process of bargaining over governmental policy, and instrumentalities for the enforcement of its rulings. From the perspective of pressure politics, the administrative bureaus are a decisive center of power.

As has been explained above (see Chap. V), administrative decision-making in France is widely dispersed in spite of its formal centralization; different administrative *corps* have preserved a separate identity. Therefore, interest groups must intervene in a great number of bureaus and agencies, even when concerned with just one decision. To be effective, a group needs more than a bilateral relationship with a single administration — it must play on an extensive keyboard in order to touch all the points where its interests or values are affected. No generalizations are possible as to whether in these daily encounters the public interest emerges unscathed or whether the groups "colonize" parts of the administrative machinery to such an extent that organs of state are transformed into institutionalized pressure groups. Both extremes as well as a great many intermediate situations obtain.[16] The so-called vertical agencies, which like the clientele administration or the regulatory agencies in the United States are concerned with a single if sometimes composite interest, are most easily permeated by the views defended by the groups.

An official committee instituted in the early days of the Fifth Republic to investigate reasons for uneven economic development concluded:

> Under present conditions, characterized by vertical and water-tight compartmentalization of administrations, a great number of civil servants . . . have become accustomed to regard in good faith the defense of the interests which they are called upon to control a natural and essential aspect of their function, an aspect which for them tends to eclipse or to falsify their vision of the general interest.[17]

In the years that have elapsed since this report was published, little has changed. Hardly any of the recommendations offered by the committee have been acted upon.

It is quite natural that some interests have easier access to governmental bureaus than others. An affinity of views between group representatives and public administrators might be based on common outlook, common social origin, or education. The official of an important trade association who is not content with presenting the raw demands of his constituents but has already sorted them out and submits them in rational fashion gets easily a more sympathetic hearing in the bureaus

[16] For details, see H. W. Ehrmann, "French Bureaucracy and Organized Interests," pp. 541–43.

[17] *Rapport sur les obstacles à l'expansion économique* (Paris: Imprimerie Nationale, 1960), p. 24.

than an organization which seeks to defend atomistic interests by mobilizing latent resentment.

Since it is now far more advantageous to impress two well-placed administrators than twenty deputies, the weight of the best organized interests, equipped with qualified staff and useful documentation, has undoubtedly increased. This also holds true of such nonassociational interests as business firms or some prominent families.

Too complete a symbiosis between the public authorities and certain interests, to the exclusion of others, might result in that "quasi-corporatism" which is prevalent in Great Britain.[18] Periodic criticism of the civil servant as an unscrupulous technocrat originates often with spokesmen for interests which feel that they no longer get an adequate hearing.

In the absence of organized parties, organized interests have also brought pressure directly on the political executive. For a long time and for many groups the ministerial *cabinets,* the circle of personal collaborators of every French minister, have been an important target. For reasons to be explained (see Chap. IX), the functions and importance of these *cabinets* have, somewhat surprisingly, increased in the Fifth Republic. Hence qualified groups still seek and generally find access to the members of a *cabinet* and through them to certain ministers.

Inasmuch as the present regime has strengthened the position of the political executive, it has also enabled both the Prime Minister and the President of the Republic to function as arbiters between competing claims and to exercise stricter intra-administrative control over many agencies and ministries. This was not accomplished at once, and such controls as exist are unable to police all bargaining between public authorities and organized interests to ensure that it is in accordance with policy goals. But in many ways Algerian independence was a telling defeat of powerful interests: A lobby which for many years had been considered invincible and which, moreover, was closely allied to influential members of

18 The term was coined by Samuel H. Beer, "Group Representation in Great Britain and the United States," *The Annals of the American Academy of Political and Social Science,* CCCXIX (1958), p. 136.

an institutional interest group, the French Army, was successfully outmaneuvered. (See also Chap. IX.) Before and since
then all groups, of whatever kind, have had little if any leverage in decisions over which General de Gaulle has asserted
his presidential prerogatives. Colonial policies and European
integration, atomic development and major foreign policy
alternatives — on such and allied matters interest groups are
permitted to voice their opinion, but at least according to
appearances nothing else. The French business lobby is as
opposed to the entry of Great Britain into the Common Market as is General de Gaulle. But whether this opposition has
played a role in the determination of policy cannot be ascer-
tained easily.

In any system the style of group action is largely determined
by the means of access to power open to the group and by
the group's position in society. Their organizational frailty,
whose manifold causes have been discussed above, imposes on
many French interest groups a seemingly contradictory pattern of action.

On the one hand, most interest associations rely quite ex-
tensively on the state for some kind of support. Even at the
height of their anarcho-syndicalist opposition to the state,
labor unions carried on most of their business in publicly
subsidized buildings, the *Bourses de Travail;* to a large extent
this is still the case. At all times the Chambers of Commerce
and the Chambers of Agriculture have received ample if indirect governmental subsidies in recognition of the fact that
besides articulating the interests of their constituents they also
fulfill a number of official functions such as training of appren-
tices, controlling weights and measures, gathering statistical
information, etc. By having one foot in society and the other
inside the governmental structure, these organizations form an
institutional link between the state and the groups. The full-
grown corporatist experiment of the Vichy regime sought to
generalize such practices. It gave to entire sectors of economic
and social life an organizational structure which the country
had never known before because the ties established by voluntary associations had been too tenuous. When after the

liberation freedom of association was reestablished, many interest groups were not averse to a preservation of the framework which Vichy had created. Employers' associations, trade unions, and rural groups are enmeshed in the administration of the comprehensive social security system, public insurance boards, and the like.

On the other hand, the same interest group system exhibits occasionally a radicalism which has become rare in countries of similar development and is more generally found in an early industrial era. In part one is the consequence of the other. Groups want to demonstrate that their participation in administrative tasks and the public support they derive therefrom does not sap their militancy. To make this clear is particularly necessary when the plurality of ideologically divided organizations forces each of them to compete for the same clientele. In particular, trade unions and farmers' associations suffering from membership fluctuations try to mobilize potential members and marginal groups by inflated demands and by boldness of action. For groups that lack the means of using the information media such tactics also become a way to put their case before the public at large.

In a radical context even the defense of purely economic, social, or cultural interests takes on a political color. Here the poor boundary maintenance between the society and the political system [19] has even broader significance than it has, as previously noted, for the functioning of parliament. In order to intensify their political effectiveness, interest groups and parties, both too weak to act singly, organize alliances of more or less temporary duration but always adept in using a combative style. French history of the last decades is rich in episodes where a merger of lobbies and political movements has shaken the system. Their emphasis has usually been on protest rather than on demands for constructive action. Long standing historical traditions facilitate the transition from protest movements to militant organizations inclined to transcend the limits of legality.

The dramatic events of the great Revolution, the recurrent

[19] The phenomenon has been described in general terms by Almond and Coleman, *op. cit.*, pp. 37–38.

significance of street fighting and barricades in the upheavals
of the nineteenth century, and other romantically embellished
reminiscences have made "violence into a sort of second
nature of the French political temperament." [20] For the labor
movement the myth of the revolutionary strike seemed at one
time the only means of mobilizing workers for some kind of
participation.[21] For groups and individuals lawless action has
remained an outlet for frustrations imposed by the dominant
style of authority. Such action also betrays a pervasive distrust in the satisfactory processing of demands by the political
system. In addition, the use of violence is an attempt to obtain
by blackmail what one despairs of obtaining by moderate and
concrete demands.

Even though the Fifth Republic is committed to the
strengthening of governmental authority in every domain,
rebellions and political protest movements organized for the
defense of interests have increased considerably in number
and intensity since its inception. First in 1961, and periodically since then, agitation in various parts of rural France
reached the pitch of an extensive and violent *Jacquerie,* with
loss of property and lives. It forced the government to retreat
on some fundamental issues.[22] The labor movement, divided
though it was, resorted several times to strikes which were
avowedly motivated by political opposition to the government,
and which succeeded in paralyzing, even if only for a limited
time, most economic activities affected by the strikes.

The continuing unrest in the countryside is due to the painful adaptation of many agricultural regions and sectors to the
needs of a modernizing economy. Periods of despair alternate
with hopes that either the incorporation of French agriculture

20 See Rémond, *op. cit.,* I, p. 378.

21 See Crozier, *The Bureaucratic Phenomenon,* pp. 259–60. It was undoubtedly the organizational weakness of the French labor movement
which led Georges Sorel, an intellectual without trade union connections,
to conceive of the myth of the general strike as an instrument of mobilizing for class warfare. On the general significance of "anomie" see Eckstein, *op. cit.,* pp. 254 f. His brilliant analysis applies in every way to the
French situation.

22 For more details on the background and the setting of the 1961 movement, see Wright, *Rural Revolution,* pp. 167 ff.

into the Common Market or structural reforms will at least alleviate the most acute difficulties (see Chap. II and XI). Such alternation itself creates tensions which lead to spontaneous outbursts whenever hopes are disappointed. Rival groups feel that they risk losing all control over their membership if they do not take the lead in organizing rebellions and, if possible, in fomenting further trouble. As a consequence, the protest movements become steadily more political and more radical.

In many instances such a development is a consequence of the declining role of parliament in the policy process. In the past the Senate and National Assembly were the most valuable channels of influence for the rural defense groups. Such channels are now blocked, and in some instances so brutally that even the members of the majority have been embarrassed (see Chap. X). For many groups, especially those counting a large membership, contacts with the bureaucracy, open only to a small number of group leaders in Paris, cannot replace the leverage which these groups used to exercise in parliament and of which they boasted to their constituents.

Before 1958, the violence of group action was often due to the fact that the government lacked either the stability and strength to mobilize opinion behind the solutions which it proposed, or the ability to explain its actions. The government of the Fifth Republic, pursuing its policy of holding the public at arm's length, disdains to provide such information. The authorities are sometimes surprised by the bitterness of the reactions of the public which, partly because of the lack of communication, feels misunderstood and badly protected.

What has been described here are those manifestations of group action which are somewhat surprising in a country like France. But nevertheless in the Fifth Republic, just as in the regimes that preceded it, most interest articulation follows the pattern normal to a highly developed economy. Wherever there is access to the centers of rule-making — above all to the administration — contacts are frequent and of a routine nature. Compared to other European democracies, the organizational density of most associational groups remains weak — their prestige is proportionate to their strength in membership and resources.

## MUTATIONS IN THE GROUP UNIVERSE?

After the failure of the party system had led to the downfall of the Fourth Republic, hopes turned towards the interest groups, now less affected by public opprobrium than were the parties. From many sides associations of various kinds were hailed as the *forces vives* of politics, while the parties were regarded as moribund.

The simultaneous turn towards economic recovery and modernization facilitated the internal transformation of many groups and made it possible for them to reassess their goals. The integration of many firms into a national market from which they had been excluded, and the successful defense of the French economic position in the European Common Market diminished earlier feelings of insecurity. This in turn has strengthened the hand of those elements within the trade associations, agricultural organizations, and some trade unions which had long opposed restrictive practices and a merely defensive posture. Economic growth rather than the defense of marginal situations is now the focus of many group activities.[23] As a consequence, a competition for leadership positions has developed in many associations. Although the competition seldom leads to the complete victory of the modernization-minded elements, it has frequently opened a dialogue between generations. Men who were little used to talk back to their fathers or teachers now can argue with their elders inside the interest groups.

Those wishing to engage in political activities as well as the "aspirants" to political power (see Chap. V) have often found participation in group life more rewarding than membership in a political party. The new emphasis on groups has emboldened a French observer to liken present-day France to Tocqueville's America.[24]

[23] For interesting details about a new orientation of trade associations, see the (perhaps over-optimistic) picture drawn by Pitts, in *In Search of France*, pp. 276 ff. For the trade union movement, see Goguel, *ibid.*, p. 383.

[24] André Philip, as quoted by Hoffmann, in *In Search of France*, p. 70. In order to highlight the contrast between France and the United States, Tocqueville laid much stress on the merits of the "civil associations" he found in America.

The new leadership would deny emphatically that by turning their back on political parties and their confining dogmatism they have lost political interest. Groups have in fact taken on functions, such as civic and political education, which the parties no longer fulfill. During the early years of the Fifth Republic, the student movement, no longer satisfied with the mere corporative interests of its constituents, spoke out on questions of general policy, such as the war in Algeria, the defense of civil liberties, and the place of the rising generations in the nation.[25] Drawing on a tradition that reaches back to the *sociétés de pensée* of prerevolutionary times, the "clubs" have emerged as a new form of public interest organization. (For details see Chap. VIII.)

Many of the associations representing special interests have found it equally convenient to loosen their ties with political parties and party spokesmen in parliament. (It even holds true, though to a lesser extent, for the C.G.T. and other groups influenced by the Communists.) This enables the groups to enter into a new kind of intergroup alliance. Where in the past ideological commitment provided the cement for militant amalgamations of loosely organized parties and weak interest groups, now different groups unite for the pragmatic defense of common interests. Although so far organizational unity has nowhere been achieved, communication between the leadership of various associations has been facilitated. Strikes, at first in the public sector and of late also in private industry, have taken on many characteristics of the workers' movements in the United States: they have become primarily struggles for job security rather than complicated maneuvers in the class struggle.

The transformation of the groups and of their objectives has eased and regularized contacts between their associations and the administration. In the past such contacts were often rendered fruitless, at least insofar as trade unions were concerned, by the groups' principled opposition to the existing

[25] For an excellent description of the student movement during the early years of the Fifth Republic, see Meynaud, *op. cit.*, pp. 64 ff. For a general appraisal of interest group operations in the Fifth Republic see also the same author's, "Les Groupes de Pression sous la Ve République," *RFSP*, XII:3 (1962), pp. 672–97.

economic and social order. Such tensions are gradually being overcome.[26] Younger trade union leaders feel that at present their best interlocutors are neither the politicians nor the liberal intellectuals but the "uneasy technocrats" in the top bureaucracy. Even the C.G.T. has been invited and has found it possible to participate in the official committees and boards concerned with economic planning. The government has taken the initiative in attributing to organized interest groups a fairly large share in the new regional institutions. (To be discussed below, Chap. IX.)

These developments have given rise to hopes that a new form of "associational democracy" might be a suitable complement to the direct democracy which the new regime seeks to legitimize. Aversion to an obsolete party system perpetuating atomistic representation is common to the supporters of the regime and to many of its opponents. In their most advanced form, proposals for a more viable form of interest representation develop blueprints for an economic parliament. (For details see Chap. X.)

Yet the widespread fascination with the new look which many interest groups took on during the first years of the Fifth Republic has already been shaken by political realities. Even when preceded by a dialogue with the groups, the decision-making process of the regime is deliberately authoritarian and thereby limits the groups' participation in the process. Failure to modify governmental policies has discredited those group leaders who had hoped to demonstrate that a strategy transcending narrowly conceived special interest would yield results. As a consequence their prestige has diminished. Whether or not the traditional leadership is reconquering former positions of influence, the membership is reverting to the old distrust of the state and its officials.

Completely frustrated in its requests to be given at least a hearing before the enactment of comprehensive educational reforms, the student movement has become dispirited and divided. At many universities old sectarian political alignments, whether of the Left or of the Right, have reappeared

26 See the discussion by Alfred Grosser, in Robert A. Dahl (ed.), *Political Oppositions in Western Democracies* (New Haven: Yale University Press, 1966), pp. 299 ff.

and have made the movement largely ineffectual, unless it can foment outright rebellion.

The hopes and disappointments which the groups and their leadership have experienced since the advent of the Fifth Republic demonstrate quite clearly both the possibilities and limitations of interest articulation in a modern democracy. Undoubtedly parties do not have a monopoly of political action. Because parties and groups operate at the intersection between society and the polity, disillusionment with the political process is bound to set in when the decision-makers do not recognize how important the interplay of interests is for the setting of policy norms.[27]

But French interest groups have tried to do more. Their younger leaders thought they would be able to fill the political vacuum created after the collapse of the Fourth Republic. Legitimate representatives of economic and social forces though they were, they wanted to become the main actors on the political stage. The difficulties which these leaders met were only aggravated, not created, by the impatience of the regime with all "intermediaries." By experience and mentality, group leaders were unprepared for the roles they wished to assume. Interest groups, even when they formulate their demands in terms of the common good, are never apt to become the sole link between the citizenry and the democratic political process.[28] The leaders' attempt to ignore this truth led to the limited effectiveness of their efforts and to the resulting disenchantment of their constituents.

The participation of new elites in group life has been an important factor for the elites' own political socialization and has helped to preserve a democratic atmosphere in the Fifth Republic. But the eagerness of groups to participate in the political process is not a substitute for politics. In both a presidential and a parliamentary regime the selection and the democratic control of executive leadership requires effective party organization.

---

[27] Cf. the remarks by Louis Hartz, *Economic Planning and Democratic Thought* (Cambridge: Harvard University Press, 1948), p. 310.

[28] Very thoughtful on this point are Lavau, "Réflexions," pp. 832 ff., and Rémond, "Participation électorale et participation organisée," in Association Française de Science Politique, *La Dépolitisation,* pp. 95 ff.

# CHAPTER VIII

# Aggregation of Values and Interests: Political Parties

## THE PARTY SYSTEM

"The character and number of the political parties seeking to represent the various groups in a country are perhaps the chief determinants of how far the government acts through a stable system of interchanges between the key solidary groups and the political elite." [1] There is general agreement that French political parties have regularly prevented the functioning of such a stable system. Except for short and atypical periods they were "equally unable to make commitments in the name of their voters or to obtain legitimacy through transforming the voters' opinions and attitudes into impulses converted into governmental action." [2]

There are, however, divergent explanations of such inability. Should one conclude with General de Gaulle that the parties are merely a mirror of the perpetual French "political effervescence" and an expression of a "Gallic propensity towards divisions and quarrels" — an opinion he voiced in his speech at Bayeux and from which he has never departed? Is it

---

[1] Seymour M. Lipset, "Party Systems and the Representation of Social Groups," *European Journal of Sociology,* I:1 (1960), p. 53.

[2] Otto Kirchheimer, "The Transformation of the Western European Party Systems," in Joseph LaPalombara and Myron Weiner (eds.), *Political Parties and Political Development* (Princeton: Princeton University Press, 1966), p. 180.

the number of parties or their characteristics which are most to blame? Has the socio-economic structure of the country caused both the plurality and the characteristics of the parties? Or is the party chaos more apparent than real, hiding as it were behind opprobrious forms a basically stable division in the body politic? [3]

Answers to these questions are not only essential to an understanding of the perennial difficulties of democratic politics in France. They of necessity also determine the choice of remedies and of possible alternatives to the unsatisfactory functioning of the party system.

Some of the most knowledgeable analysts of election data have been struck by a chronic and seemingly unalterable division of Frenchmen into two camps, two large political "families," each motivated by a different political mood or temperament. Whether one wishes to identify these camps with the "Right" and the "Left" or christen them the "Party of Order" and the "Party of Movement" [4] is of less importance than the fact that if one views elections from this perspective, political alignments have remained surprisingly stable over long periods of history.

The party distribution in the first election held under general manhood suffrage (1849) shows that the proportions of votes going to the Right and to the Left were about the same as in the last elections of the Third Republic (1936) which led the Popular Front to victory. The conservative forces which backed General MacMahon in 1877 came from the same regions that supported the authoritarian-minded Poincaré in 1928. In the 1962 referendum and the elections that followed it the opposition to General de Gaulle was strongest where for more than a century republican traditions had had a solid foundation. Neither domestic upheavals nor international cataclysms have upset the geographical distribution or

[3] The possible influence of the electoral system has been dealt with above Chap. IV.

[4] The classical study of the party system in the Third Republic, François Goguel, *La Politique des Partis sous la IIIe République* (2 vols.; Paris: Editions du Seuil, 1946), tries to reduce party orientations to "order" and "movement." But in his conclusion, especially vol. II, p. 338, the author is inclined to soften the dichotomy which his work emphasizes so much.

the proportional strength of the two sides. An electoral system such as that of the Third and the Fifth Republics has apparently favored this simplification of political alignments. In the majority of constituencies the run-off elections have resulted in the confrontation of two candidates, each representing one of the two camps.

All this is not without significance but does not explain the malfunctioning of the party system. For a simple and stable division could have resulted in a pattern of two parties, or coalition of parties, alternating in power and opposition and hence giving valid expression to the voters' options. However, to discover simplicity and stability one must view French "political effervescence" from a distance sufficiently great so that the tensions between and within social groups and categories, between and within the coalitions and the parties, disappear from sight. Yet these tensions and their organizational expressions in fact shape political reality. "France contains two fundamental temperaments — that of the left and that of the right," Jacques Fauvet has stated quite correctly. But he had to add that she also contains "three principal tendencies, if one adds the center; six spiritual families; ten parties, large or small, traversed by multiple currents; fourteen parliamentary groups without much discipline; and forty million opinions." [5]

Any party system normally reflects some of the major characteristics of the political culture within which it functions. Historical circumstances but also constitutional arrangements will usually determine to what extent the party system neutralizes or, possibly, maximizes the difficulties created by a given political culture. In the French republics both traditions and constitutional practices have created or conserved a party system which has considerably aggravated rather than eased the inherent difficulties.

French parties, like parties everywhere, exist to fulfill a variety of functions. Most important among them are the aggregation of interests and demands and their transformation into policy; the mobilization of the citizenry for political participation and the integration of the citizenry into the system;

[5] Quoted here from Wright, *France*, p. 423.

the recruitment and selection of political leaders for executive and other posts; and the control of such leadership, especially the control of the government. Not all of these functions will be served equally well by all parties or at all times. What must be explained is why French parties have done so badly, over long periods, on almost all counts. Why have their structure, their style, and their orientation, all closely connected factors, been inadequate to their tasks and, in many cases, to their ambitions?

Except for the extreme Left and during some short-lived episodes, party organizations have remained as skeletal as were parties in many countries at the time of their nineteenth century beginnings. They developed in a largely pre-industrial and pre-urban environment, catering at first to upper-middle-class and later to middle-class elements. Their foremost, and frequently sole, function consisted in providing the organizational framework for the selection and election of candidates for political office on the local, departmental, and national level.

The slow and irregular industrialization of the country prevented, in spite of an early introduction of manhood suffrage, the formation of a disciplined working-class party which would have challenged the bourgeois parties to overhaul their own structure. The electoral system and a powerful upper house of parliament with a heavy overrepresentation of the rural population kept the workers in a position of electoral inferiority.[6] Before 1914, the Socialist Party was at best an incipient mass party, weakened not only by doctrinal dissensions in its midst, but by the workers' distrust of all institutions of the bourgeois state. Their distrust extended to the Socialist representatives in parliament, most of them of middle-class origin. When after the First World War the Communists were able to mount a well organized party, the split of the working-class vote between two mutually hostile camps attenuated the threat from the left. Hence the traditional parties could afford to preserve the loose structure they had previously adopted.

Current typologies of political parties distinguish between

6 See Kirchheimer, "The Transformation," pp. 178 f.

organizations that gradually emerge from groupings inside the legislature and those that are created outside the parliament among the voting population.[7] The French parties which have represented the majority of the electorate throughout long periods belong clearly to the first category, the internally created parties. Their major weight is to be found in their parliamentary representation; all truly important party activities occur inside the legislature. Political organization at the local and constituency level aims mainly at assuring the election or reelection of members belonging to various legislative blocks or factions in parliament. Up to the present, none of these parties can boast of anything like the constituency structure of a large British or continental party, a structure which is, of course, also unknown in the United States.

An internally created party is almost always less disciplined and ideologically less coherent than one that has emerged outside the legislature. Its organizational and hence its financial structure will usually be rudimentary, the very notion of membership in the party remains indeterminate, sometimes to the point of being meaningless. Where constituency parties have existed at all, they have been deferential to their legislative contingents; the elected representatives have usually been far more of an asset to the party than the party to them. For this very reason political leaders that were not Socialists or Communists have hardly ever emerged from the ranks of a party but from elective positions, either local or national.

During the election campaign the candidates can expect little financial support from the party (and this has remained true even for the Socialists). Between elections, those representing the traditional party formations are not amenable to any party directives coming from outside parliament. Even within a parliamentary group or fraction the formal institution of a whip is unknown. Whether the moral authority of a particular parliamentary party chairman is able to overcome the centrifugal trends of divided interests and loyalties depends on the circumstances. In most cases representatives vote,

[7] See Maurice Duverger, *Political Parties* (New York: Wiley, 1955), especially pp. XXIII–XXXVII. For a recent discussion of Duverger's criteria, see La Palombara and Weiner, *op. cit.,* pp. 8 ff.

on important as well as on unimportant matters, solely in accordance with the commands of "career, conscience and constituency." [8]

Occasionally, this has led to the expulsion from the party of a deputy (rarely of a senator) who had defied all too flagrantly a party directive. In a country with a developed party system, such as Great Britain or West Germany, the bolting of a party is usually tantamount to the end of a political career. In France, the party renegade if he chooses to do so, can stand for reelection in the same district which had sent him to parliament before and usually he has kept his seat under a new, and generally meaningless, party label. Some outstanding political leaders, such as Millerand and Pierre Laval, have in their long careers moved from the Left to the Extreme Right, always representing the same constituency.

One of the most decisive reasons for the survival of this form of representation and of party organization has been undoubtedly the voters' preference for it. An electorate which distrusts authority and wishes to be represented at the seats of power only in order to be protected against an always suspected arbitrariness of government is also suspicious of parties organized for reformatory political action. "For organization means power, and power means the oppression of the individual" — in these terms Lawrence Wylie has characterized the opinions of the villagers he so carefully observed.[9]

An egalitarian radicalism which puts a high valuation on "the people" and on the basic soundness of the public but distrusts the solidarity claimed by any organization in the name of collective interests will not easily propound party discipline. The strength of such radical traditions in France, and that of populism in the United States, is undoubtedly one of the major reasons for party weakness in both France and the United States.[10] In the case of France it is of particular

---

[8] See Williams, *Crisis and Compromise*, pp. 348 ff. This work remains an indispensable source for party history during the Fourth Republic.

[9] See Wylie, *Village*, pp. 330–331.

[10] This point is made by Samuel H. Beer, *British Politics in the Collectivist Age* (New York: Knopf, 1965), pp. 42 f., to explain the differences between party organization in Britain and in the United States. It is equally applicable to France, where the teaching of Alain (see above Chap.

significance that the two prevalent political orientations, the representative and the bonapartist (see Chap. I), have for all their mutual antagonism one thing in common: their aversion to well-established and strongly organized parties.

This explains why the same majority of voters who might criticize as senseless the games of "willful" politicians will reject the idea that their representatives be guided in their decisions by party directives (see Chap. IV). It also explains their low party identification. After a hotly contested election (1951) voters were asked whether the party for which they had cast their ballots deserved their entire confidence. Only 62 per cent of the Communist voters, 48 per cent of the Socialist voters, and only 37 per cent and 31 per cent of those who had voted for center and conservative parties answered in the affirmative.[11]

Accordingly, party membership, except during short and dramatic situations, has always been low. In 1962 it was estimated that of nineteen million voters not more than one-half million belonged to a party, and of these 300,000 were Communists. According to other estimates, less than 2 per cent of registered voters were members of a party. Among those younger than twenty-four, only 1.1 per cent admitted joining a party. Thirty years earlier the relation between electorate and party membership had been about the same.[12]

Organizational weakness and its underlying causes will easily result in a multipolar party system. But the primary cause of such division is past conflicts over interests and values, many of them but dimly remembered except for the resentments they caused and which have persisted. Historical traditions have determined whether constituencies are regu-

---

I) provided an "ultra-democratic" justification for party weakness. See especially his *Eléments d'une doctrine radicale*.

11 *Sondages*, I:2 (1952), pp. 5 ff. For other data on low party identification, see Converse and Dupeux, *op. cit.*

12 See Goguel and Grosser, *op. cit.*, p. 106, and Jacques Fauvet, "Le comportement des gouvernés," *Encyclopédie Française*, X (Paris: Sociélé Nouvelle, 1964), p. 226. Duncan MacRae, Jr., *op. cit.*, presents an interesting chart for the ratio between membership and electorate of major parties during the Fourth Republic. One only wishes the membership figures on which he had to base his calculations were more reliable.

larly on the right or the left of the political spectrum. Different property laws under the monarchy, clerical or secular administration during the *Ancien Régime,* differences in agricultural crops or in the speed of industrialization, religious affiliation — all these have shaped political alignments which frequently have perpetuated themselves long after the original causes have disappeared.

The violence with which partisans have clashed in the past, the bloodshed that has occurred time and again, has made reconciliation difficult not only on the level of party leadership but among party followers. When during a critical period of the Fourth Republic the headquarters of the Socialists and of the M.R.P., a party with a predominantly Catholic clientele, decided that the time had come to forge a closer unity between them, the *militants* (the party activists) in both camps found such collaboration with former enemies distasteful and sabotaged it as best they could.

Historical references provide justification not alone for the major division between Right and Left, but also for the equally important divisions within the two camps. On the Right one can still distinguish, among others, traditionalists (not all of them monarchists), "orléanists," i.e., conservatives with a credo of laissez faire, and bonapartists.[13] On the Left, there were the Jacobins and the Socialists before the Russian Revolution added the Communists. In many cases actual party labels have long become meaningless because they too can, in general, be explained only by historical circumstances, especially by the secessions which gave rise to ever new factions. Frequently party names were ideological in the sense of the word that conveys deception. The epithet *"Gauche"* was preferred by conservatives; groups that were nothing less than socialistic did not hesitate to use that adjective.

Because of the large number of weakly structured parties, most of them represent only a small section of the electorate. A party which, without risking ridicule, cannot claim to rep-

---

[13] See René Rémond, *La Droite en France* (Paris: Aubier, 1963), especially pp. 7 ff. He entitles the "prologue" to his work: "One or several Rights?" Mr. Rémond's excellent study is now available in an English translation, *The Right Wing in France: From 1815 to De Gaulle* (Phila.: U. of Penna. Press, 1968).

resent the interests of the entire electorate, or not even of a large sector, takes on the characteristics of an interest group. Instead of aggregating interests and values, the representatives of such a party merely articulate them. They thereby transmit to parliament, or, if they have the opportunity, to the government, the undiluted individualism of their constituents — another instance of the poor boundary maintenance discussed earlier (see Chap. VII).

Every party that operates from a limited base faces a variety of competitors seeking to draw strength from the same clientele. It can hope for no more than a marginal increase in bargaining power for the inevitable deals which it must conclude, in power or in opposition, with other small parties once the elections are over.[14] If such parties were to spell out the differences which separate them from their competitors in realistic and pragmatic terms, the contest would frequently appear merely as one between interest groups or between personalities. In order to avoid such a demonstration and still score over their competitors, parties will define even the most narrow political issues in lofty ideological and often esoteric terms. This is a general phenomenon in multipolar party systems. ". . . the more the number of parties increases, the more their identification becomes a problem; and the remedy to which each party has recourse in order to be perceived as distinct is a punctilious ideological and principled rigidity." [15]

The French habit of historical thinking and the general preference for an ideological style of politics enhances the behavior which extreme party division invites. It is only seemingly paradoxical that many parties have the characteristics of an interest group and yet indulge in ideological language. Since many French interest groups of whatever nature also conduct their propaganda in ideological terms, the style of parties and groups is frequently identical. This is caused by organizational weakness common to both, and by the desire

14 See Williams, *Crisis and Compromise,* p. 69.
15 Giovanni Sartori, "European Political Parties: The Case of Polarized Pluralism," in La Palombara and Weiner, *Political Parties,* p. 159.

to replace the lack of organization by strong, ultimative, and hence ideological, language.

As we have seen earlier, one expects an ideological under-pinning from externally created mass parties rather than from those based, as are the traditional French parties, on atomistic representation. But there is no true contradiction here either. After the elections and in the ensuing bargaining between parties, much of the ideological baggage is discarded. The gap between high-sounding principles and the need for pragmati-cally based coalitions becomes painfully obvious. It makes ideologies appear as subterfuges and convinces the voters that electoral contests are manifestations of sheer irresponsibility.

The inconveniences of the French multi-party system were compounded by the constitutional arrangements and parlia-mentary practices of the Third and Fourth Republics. To survive and to govern effectively, a cabinet needed more than just the absence of a majority willing to overthrow it, it needed a positive majority in favor of the government's policy and its legislative proposals (for details see Chap. X). This, however, was difficult to obtain where majorities consisted not of disciplined parties or of parliamentary groups kept in line by an effective whip but to a large extent of ephemeral coali-tions. Their cohesion or disruption depended on whatever problem was under consideration. As different problems came up, governments toppled or were condemned to immobility.

Neither Right nor Left was able to govern by itself for any length of time because it not only would invariably lose a temporary majority, but it also included at its extremes the groups that contested the legitimacy of the existing political or social order. In order not to risk the badly needed electoral support by these extremes, both right wing and left wing co-alitions had to make concessions to their own radicals and thereby narrowed the scope of possible action to such an extent that immobility ensued.

As a normal consequence of the existing party system, a center coalition has been in control of the government most of the time, no matter what the outcome of the preceding elections may have been. According to some calculations, during the period from 1789 to the advent of the Fifth Republic, France has been ruled by center governments for all but thirty years or for more than 80 per cent of this period. In a two or three party system, it is quite normal that the major parties move towards the political center in order to gain stability and cohesion. But where extreme party plurality prevails, the Center is a "swamp" instead of a cohesive political force.[16] It cannot pursue for long even moderate policies without losing necessary support, for there are no clear lines of division between government and opposition.

An opposition will behave responsibly if it knows that it may have to perform in the foreseeable future and that after taking over power it will have to live up, at least in part, to the promises it has made. French politicians belonging to the Center and temporarily without a cabinet post were free to use every means to weaken the government by steady criticism and eventually to cause its downfall. They knew that if they were to become part of the next shapeless center coalition they would probably never have to assume effective leadership but at most would share some peripheral responsibility behind the smokescreen of shifting coalitions.[17] At the same time, the policies of the Center threw substantial sectors of public opinion into permanent opposition, which strengthened the centrifugal strains on the system.

However unsatisfactory the results of a fragmented party system were, the fragmentation reflected a similar division of the electorate. This explains why from one election to the next the transfer of votes was in general extremely small and why all established parties, whatever their political color, had a fairly stable electoral following.[18] The disaffection from the party system as such was pronounced and often expressed in opinion polls both prior to and after the events of 1958. The voters made both the number of parties and their behavior responsible for the poor functioning of republican institu-

[16] The problem of the Center as a "swamp" has been analyzed at length by Maurice Duverger, "L'Eternel Marais, Essai sur le Centrisme Français," *RFSP,* XIV:1 (1964), pp. 33–51.

[17] See Sartori, *op. cit.,* pp. 157 f.

[18] See MacRae, *op. cit.,* pp. 230 ff., on the stability of party strength in the Fourth Republic.

tions. But at election time party loyalties seldom shifted. The strength of traditional alignments, frequently transmitted from one generation to the next, was generally unimpaired.

An exception to such stability was the successes of flash parties or surge movements. They were not unknown during various periods of the Third Republic but occurred with greater regularity in the Fourth.[19] The initial success of the Gaullist movement as an opposition party in 1947 and 1951, the upswing in favor of the followers of Mendès-France in the Radical Party between 1954 and 1957, the Poujadists in 1954–1956 were all different expressions of the same phenomenon. They were reactions against the immobility induced by a party system that was simultaneously too stable and too weak. They mobilized, if only for a short time, dissatisfied voters, drawing millions of them from the established groupings and a far smaller proportion from those who had abstained in the preceding elections. Typically, all these movements saw the need for a better structured and more active constituency organization and demanded a disciplined vote from their parliamentary representatives. But they all failed to bring about the attempted reforms, whereupon their forces dispersed usually as fast as they had assembled.

Only once, after the liberation of France in 1944, has there existed a serious chance for a thorough overhauling of the party system. The representative regime of which the Third Republic had been the prototype was thoroughly discredited. Three Parties, the Communists, the Socialists, and the *Mouvement Républicain Populaire,* emerged in the first elections of the new republic with a combined following of about 75 per cent of the electorate. All were intent on forming disciplined mass parties and on governing the country by an effective coalition government. Yet after a few transitional years the country reverted to the traditional forms of atavistic and atomistic representation and to the rule by shifting coalitions of the Center which now included the Socialists.

Undoubtedly uncontrollable pressures from the interna-

19 On the surge movements, see *ibid.,* pp. 268 ff., and the interesting table on p. 233.

tional environment were to blame in part. The initial majority lost its base when, as a natural consequence of France's alignment with the West in the cold war, the Communists were expelled from the government in the Spring of 1947. From then on the Communists remained, in terms of the popular vote, the largest single party. Since they were also committed to an almost constant and principled opposition, they and the trade unions affiliated with the C.G.T. kept at least that sizable fraction of the working class which they represented outside the polity. (For details see below.)

But other, domestic factors were equally responsible for the frustration of momentary hopes. The thinking of the resistance movement on matters of party reform had been unsure. Many of its most valid elements condemned not only the traditional party system but, in their quest for a new national unity, all parties as possible impediments to the emergence of the general will. They were seeking, often confusedly, for new forms of valid representation and thereby weakening the efforts for party reform.

General de Gaulle's attitude was of particular importance. As the generally acclaimed liberator of the country, he and probably he alone had the opportunity of "harnessing charisma as [the] foundation for a stable authority." [20] He could have done this by becoming, as soon as a democratic atmosphere was restored, the head of a solidly organized party which would serve as intermediary between himself and the electorate.[21] He refused to do so because, in accordance with conservative and monarchical thought, he wished to remain "above party." It can be seen that in this particular historical situation conservative and radical traditions merged once more in their common distrust of intermediaries. At the beginning of the Fourth Republic they were both inimical to a solid organization of political activity. As it turned out such a stance conformed to the fundamentally unchanged attitudes of large parts of the electorate.

[20] On the general political significance of such a situation, see Almond and Powell, *op. cit.*, p. 126.
[21] This point is made by Goguel in *In Search of France*, p. 399.

When a few years later General de Gaulle consented to preside over a new party (still christened a *Rassemblement* rather than a party), it was too late to spark a reform of the party system. Old habits had once more taken over parliamentary activities and political leaders were applauded when they inveighed against "monolithic," i.e., well organized and disciplined, parties. General de Gaulle's *Rassemblement* shared the fate of other "surge movements" described above.

Thereafter none of the parties eligible for a Center coalition could claim more than about 15 per cent of the vote, and many of these parties were again plagued by internal dissensions.[22] In the last elections of the Fourth Republic (1956), an *average* of almost ten candidates contested each available seat in parliament. In the same elections, the parties committed to fundamental opposition, whether from the Left or the Right, obtained 43.4 per cent of the popular vote.

In a heterogeneous society such as France, living through a period of intense internal and external pressures, multiple opinions and attitudes are bound to prevail. As before the war, the political parties did little to integrate and simplify them; instead they rigidified and crystallized existing antagonisms. In 1958 the problems introduced by decolonization and France's entrance into the Common Market culminated in a major political crisis which the party system lacked the resilience to face.

A discussion of the present party system and of the units composing it will make clear in what way and to what extent the parties, old and new, have responded to the events set in motion by the settlers' revolt in Algeria.[23] (See Table IV for the electoral strength and parliamentary representation of each party.)

[22] For a comprehensive analysis of the relationship between social class and political parties in the Fourth Republic, see the amply documented study by Maurice Duverger *et al.*, *Partis Politiques et Classes Sociales en France* (Paris: Colin, 1955). For party preferences of different social categories, see also the tables in MacRae, *op. cit.*, pp. 257 f. For more recent data see Alain Duhamel, "La Structure sociologique de l'électorat," *Sondages*, XXVIII:2 (1966), pp. 4–14.

[23] On the relationship between crises and party development see La Palombara and Weiner, *op. cit.*, p. 22 and *passim*.

**PRESENT-DAY PARTIES**

*The Communists* (*P.C.*). In all democratic countries the Communists are a "party not like the others." Their reliance on directives from Moscow is not equaled by whatever loose international ties other parties might have established. Because of the singular importance of France to the international position of the Soviet Union, the French P.C. has been ordered time and again, and at most dramatic moments, to alter its course abruptly, but always according to the demands of Russian foreign policy.

Yet a party which for more than twenty years has had an electoral following of between 20 and 25 per cent of the voters at all parliamentary elections and which is represented by more than twenty thousand city and town councilors and more than one thousand mayors throughout France, is also, and simultaneously, "a party like the others." Its very existence constantly impinges upon the rules of the political game,[24] and this is as true in the Fifth Republic as it has been in the past.

The P.C. has always been at least as disciplined and centralized as Communist parties elsewhere and as no other French Party has ever been for any length of time. This does not mean that the P.C. has been immune to the massive membership fluctuations which characterize all French organizations. Only to a small degree were such fluctuations the consequence of the periodic and ruthless purges of all "deviationists" from the party line. Rather membership rose and declined in line with general political developments and the party's abiilty to capitalize on upsurges of radical feelings. In the troubled aftermath of the First World War, the French Communists succeeded in doing what almost none of the other European communist movements had been able to bring about: the winning over of a substantial majority of the membership of the Socialist Party and of its valuable assets, such as the daily *L'Humanité*. However, by the time of the economic depression, what was left of the party was not much more than a bureaucratic apparatus and, around it, devoted party activists, *the mili-*

24 Goguel and Grosser, *op. cit.*, p. 109.

TABLE IV  First Ballot of French Parliamentary Elections, 1956–1967, and Seats Won in the National Assembly in Both Ballots[1]
(Voting in Metropolitan France)

| | 1956 | | | 1958 | | | 1962 | | | 1967 | | |
|---|---|---|---|---|---|---|---|---|---|---|---|---|
| Registered Votes, in millions | 26.77 | | | 27.24 | | | 27.53 | | | 28.3 | | |
| Abstentions, in % | 17.3% | | | 22.9% | | | 31.3% | | | 19.1% | | |
| Parties | Votes (In millions) | % of votes cast | Seats in Parliament | Votes (In millions) | % of votes cast | Seats in Parliament | Votes (In millions) | % of votes cast | Seats in Parliament | Votes (In millions) | % of votes cast | Seats in Parliament |
| Communists (P.C.) | 5.53 | 25.74 | 150 | 3.88 | 18.90 | 10 | 3.99 | 21.78 | 41 | 5.0 | 22.5 | 74 |
| Socialists (S.F.I.O.) | 3.18 | 14.80 | 94 | 3.17 | 15.50 | 44 | 2.31 | 12.65 | 66 | 4.2[3] | 18.8[3] | 116[3] |
| Radicals and Allied | 2.88 | 13.38 | 77 | 1.71 | 8.30 | 33 | 1.38 | 7.56 | 39 | | | |
| Gaullists (U.N.R.) | 0.95 | 4.42 | 21 | 3.60 | 20.40 | 212 | 5.85 | 31.90 | 233 | 8.5[4] | 37.8[4] | 242[4] |
| M.R.P. | 2.37 | 11.05 | 83 | 2.41 | 11.15 | 56 | 1.63 | 8.92 | 55 | 2.95 | 12.8[5] | 41[5] |
| Conservatives | 3.09 | 14.36 | 109 | 4.74 | 22.92 | 118 | 2.542 | 13.872 | 352 | | | |
| Extreme Right | 2.86 | 13.33 | 52 | 0.67 | 3.03 | 2[6] | 0.16 | 0.87 | 0 | 0.2 | 0.9 | 0 |

[1] Unaffiliated deputies and splinter groups not listed, except for Extreme Right
[2] Both pro- and anti-Gaullist Conservatives
[3] Allied in the Federation of the Left (see text for details)
[4] U.N.R. and Independent Republicans allied (see text for details)
[5] M.R.P. and anti-Gaullist Conservatives allied (see text for details)
[6] The impact of the Algerian war caused frequent changes in the affiliation of deputies belonging to the extreme Right.

*tants,* who had also lost most of their foothold in organized labor. After the changed tactics of Stalinist Russia made the formation of the French Popular Front possible, the party membership increased at least tenfold, to three hundred thousand. When after the liberation a heroic resistance record had blotted out the bitter memories of the Hitler-Stalin Pact, the party claimed a membership of close to a million, supplemented by numerous, large front organizations and the Communist-dominated C.G.T. Realistic estimates put the membership now at not more than three hundred thousand, a figure smaller than that of modern mass parties in other European countries but, as previously mentioned, probably larger than that of all other French parties combined.

The differences in motivation of the *militants,* of the merely dues-paying member, and of the communist voters vary considerably though they may overlap. For the activist the party, together with its traditions, its symbols, and its doctrine of class struggle, remains a "home," a sub-culture within which he moves most of his waking hours. His loyalty is affective, probably more so than it is rational. His devotion (and the impulsion coming from the party apparatus) permits the functioning of some seventeen thousand party cells of which less than one-fourth operate at places of work; more than one-third are rural cells; the rest are grouped according to residence.

That the P.C. has been able to enlist at various periods the active support of numerous intellectuals has been of some importance in a country in which intellectuals have often set the tone of political life. Before and after Stalin's death, the party leadership has frequently treated intellectuals with disdain. Yet, "the passion for responsibility, for devotion, for efficiency attracted to Communism all those who were incapable of bearing the weight of liberty and solitude . . . ," [25] and, one might add, those who, because of the general flabbi-

[25] Crozier in Graubard (ed.), *A New Europe?, op. cit.,* p. 612. On the reasons for the success of the French Communist Party in attracting members of the intellectual as well as the working-class elite, see Raymond Aron, *L'Opium des Intellectuels* (Paris: Calmann-Lévy, 1955), and Gabriel Almond. *The Appeals of Communism* (Princeton: Princeton University Press, 1954).

ness of the party system, did not find other outlets for their desire to become politically active.

For the Communist voters (5,030,000 in the 1967 elections) their ballot is above all an expression of protest and discontent. At least emotionally, a fairly large share of the Communist vote corresponds to the protest which millions of underprivileged citizens of the United States manifest by never casting a vote. But at the same time the P.C. appears to many voters to be the legitimate heir of radical movements and radical causes of the past, the only trustworthy defender of the small against the government, the church, the powerful and rich. The success of this appeal explains why a "class party" actually finds support among many socio-economic groups, in industrial as well as underdeveloped regions. In a country of frustrated egalitarianism, the P.C. has also capitalized on the fact that, unlike all other parties including the Socialists, Communist candidates for parliament are usually of working-class or at any rate of modest origin.

On the whole, the attractiveness of the party for the electorate has remained fairly stable not only in terms of its overall share in the total vote, but also in regional distribution. The one major setback which the P.C. has suffered since the war came in the election of 1958 (see Table IV). In the preceding referendum on the new constitution, millions of ordinary Communist voters, and especially women voters, had obviously not heeded the party's advice to vote "no," most likely because they had never felt any loyalty for the previous regime. This break in party loyalty was, to an extent, transmitted to the subsequent elections. But since then the party has slowly increased its vote in all elections, national and local, even though it has not quite reached the level it had attained in the Fourth Republic.

In the elections of 1962, about 70 per cent of the Communist vote came from working-class families, but less than one-half of the working-class population voted Communist. The substantial regional variations in the political alignment of French workers can once more be traced to historical traditions. Where Catholicism has remained strong, such as in the industrial centers of the East and certain districts of the North, Communists and Socialists combined have in the past obtained a little more than one-fourth of the working-class vote. However, in the elections of 1967, the P.C. registered notable increases in these and other industrial regions and hence has probably attracted more workers in regions where heretofore Communism was widely ostracized.[26]

The greatest concentration of Communist strength in the working-class vote remains in the unfashionable suburbs of large cities. Within the "red belt" almost encircling Paris, 1.5 millions live in districts administered by Communist mayors; the Communist vote amounts regularly to between 40 and 50 per cent of total votes cast and has grown even larger of late. There at least four-fifths of the vote comes from working-class families, and two-thirds of the working-class votes are cast for the P.C. The density of the working-class population favors an all-encompassing socialization by the Communist subculture. The number of those who read the Sunday edition of the *Humanité* in the red belt of Paris might reach the half million mark.

Other electoral strongholds of the P.C. continue to be, as they have been for a long time, certain rural departments in central and southern France. (In one of them, located in the Eastern Pyrenees, the party in 1967 won just short of 40 per cent of the vote.) In most of the underdeveloped rural regions, the P.C. appeals to the instincts and interests of the marginal farmers by extolling the virtues of the small family farm.[27] Rural interest groups, influenced by them, practice a neo-

[26] The estimates of Communist strength in the working class electorate are derived from Dogan, "Le vote ouvrier," and the same author's contribution to Léo Hamon, *et al., Les Nouveaux Comportements Politiques de la Classe Ouvrière* (Paris: P.U.F., 1962), pp. 101 ff. For a careful analysis of the Communist working-class vote before 1958 see Richard F. Hamilton, *Affluence and the French Workers in the Fourth Republic* (Princeton: Princeton University Press, 1967). For the results of the 1967 elections, see François Goguel, "Les Elections Législatives des 5 et 12 Mars 1967," *RFSP*, XVIII:3 (1967), pp. 429 ff., and Alain Lancelot, "Les élections des 5 et 12 mars 1967," *Projet* 15 (1967), pp. 549 ff.

[27] For an evaluation of earlier Communist strength among the farmers, cf. Henry W. Ehrmann, "The French Peasant and Communism," *American Political Science Review*, XLVI:1 (1952), pp. 19–34.

Poujadism which has been able to organize some of the farmers' revolts mentioned earlier (see Chap. VII). For long years the Communist weekly *La Terre* was the most widely read farm journal in the country.

During the last years of the Fourth Republic, the P.C. was, in spite of its continuing electoral appeal and its organizational strength, beset by the same kind of immobility that plagued other organizations and political life in general.[28] By appealing simultaneously to many groups, the party became enmeshed in the contradictions of an unevenly developing society and fell captive to the many, and partly conservative, forces whose support it sought. Its leadership was more entrenched and bureaucratic than that of almost any other Communist party, with the sole exception of the state party in East Germany. For many years neither the French nor the German party entered frankly upon the process of de-Stalinization. A sclerosis of doctrine and of party life was communicated to the entire organization by an overage leadership. While purges continued, they did not affect the true Stalinists. When Maurice Thorez died in 1964, he had been the party's Secretary General for 34 years.

During the years of the party's greatest immobility, not only its leadership and its activists but also its voters persisted in attitudes that set them apart from the main body of political opinion. Repeated polls revealed that on such questions as NATO and the unification of Europe, the Hungarian uprising, the Algerian war, or the chances of Mendès-France changing the political mores of the republic, Communist opinions were sharply different from those of most other Frenchmen. It is no exaggeration to state that the wall of mutual distrust which separated Communists from non-Communists confined the former to a political ghetto.

The advent of the Fifth Republic did not bring the outlawing of the Communists, whom General de Gaulle had long branded as "separatists." To the disappointment of many of

[28] This is the main argument of Roy C. Macridis, "The Immobility of the French Communist Party," *Journal of Politics*, XX:1 (1958), pp. 613–34. Although one can no longer speak of Communist "immobility" (see below in the text), the material discussed in the article is still of value.

his most ardent followers, General de Gaulle did not embark upon a course of action which he found repugnant since, given the strength of the P.C. in the electorate, in the trade-union movement, and in municipal government, it would have required quasi-totalitarian police control. Moreover, the referendum and the elections of 1958 seemed to indicate that electoral support for the Communists was ebbing. The electoral system which the new regime reintroduced was known to penalize, in the run-off elections, parties cut off by their isolation from alliances. Hence the number of P.C. deputies in the National Assembly was reduced in one sweep from 150 to 10. Finally, General de Gaulle may have assumed early that by moving away from the United States and by initiating a rapprochement with the Communist world he could tame and possibly paralyze the P.C.

But what happened instead was more than the slow recouping by the P.C. of its electoral strength (see above). With the stabilization of the regime after the Algerian war, it became clear that the opposition's announced goal of replacing the Gaullist government lacked credibility as long as the P.C., its followers, and its positions of strength were excluded from such effort. In the run-off elections of 1962, Socialist and Communist candidates, for the first time in 26 years, began to withdraw in each others' favor. In the presidential election the P.C. did not present a candidate of its own, having learned from previous experiences that it did not fare well when it stood alone in plebiscitarian contests. In the parliamentary elections of 1967, the alliance between the new Federation of the Left (see below) and the P.C. was perfected to the point that in some constituencies the Communists even withdrew candidates who had done better than their allies if this seemed necessary to beat the Gaullists. The disciplined Communist voters followed their party's directives almost to a man.

The result was that the Communists returned to the National Assembly with 74 deputies. Perhaps more important was the fact that the Communists had reentered the political stage as an accepted partner in opposition. Such reentry conformed to a changing public image of the P.C., and this in turn helped to promote a certain transformation of the party.

In a public opinion poll held more than a year prior to the 1967 elections, 60 per cent voiced the opinion that during the preceding decade the P.C. had become more conciliatory; only 22 per cent saw no change. Thirty-eight per cent, hence substantially more than the Communist electorate, favored the future participation of Communist ministers in government, with only 30 per cent opposed. Forty-eight per cent of all voters (and 50 per cent of the men among them) assumed that such Communist participation was likely within the next ten years, and 55 per cent believed that during the same time span a close unity of action between Communists and Socialists could be expected. Most striking proof of an end to the Communist ghetto was the voluntary admission by 42 per cent that they had Communists among their relatives and close friends.[29]

These attitudes were rather evenly distributed among many socio-economic groups and most regions. Even electoral preferences did not make a great difference. In the elections of 1967 such feelings came close to costing the government its majority. Electoral statistics seemed to indicate that in many cases middle-of-the-road voters, when faced in the run-off elections with a choice between a Gaullist and a left-wing candidate, Communist or Communist-supported, often chose the latter in order to voice their opposition to the government.

It may be assumed that, contrary to expectations, the new orientation of French foreign policy has made the P.C. more rather than less attractive. Since hostility to the United States and friendly gestures towards the Communist nations have been made legitimate by General de Gaulle and are no longer expressed solely by a political party suspect of foreign allegiance, the P.C. has become more than before a "party like the others." Cleansed of doubts of its patriotism, the party is able to assume the role of giving most resolute expression to the rather widespread dissatisfaction with the economic and social policies of the regime.

Simultaneously the party is undergoing certain internal changes. Polycentrism in Communist Eastern Europe and the

[29] See the data presented by the Institut Français d'Opinion Publique, *Les Français devant le Communisme* (mimeographed, Paris, February 1966).

Sino-Soviet split have finally also loosened the sterile mono-
lithism of the P.C. The acceptable limits for discussion within
the party and the organizations controlled by it, such as the
trade-unions and the Communist student movement, are somewhat less strict. A very cautious renewal of leadership seems
underway, though Thorez' successor, M. Waldeck-Rochet, is a
man in his sixties. Together with the party's success in elections and its newly shown flexibility in negotiations with its
partners, the changes that have occurred within the party have
made the P.C. once more attractive to the young.[30] Undoubtedly it has more young people among its members than other
parties, which in view of the fact that other parties hardly
recruit at all (see below) might not mean too much. But 44
per cent of a panel of young people between eighteen and
thirty years considered the P.C. the most dynamic of all parties; 68 per cent believed it had the greatest following among
youth. (For the Gaullist U.N.R. corresponding figures were a
disappointing 15 per cent and 6 per cent.) In the elections of
1967, 28 per cent of those who voted for the first time declared
to have cast their ballot for the P.C., hence far more than the
party's average among all age groups.

*The Socialists (S.F.I.O.).* In comparison with the solid Social
Democratic parties in other European countries, the French
Socialist Party has lacked muscle almost since its beginnings
in 1905. (The initials by which it is known express an idealis-
tic commitment to the cause of international solidarity; they
stand for *Section Française de l'Internationale Ouvrière*.)

The slow and uneven industrialization, paired with a reluctance to organize, has not only hampered the development of
labor unions. By the same token the S.F.I.O. has been deprived of that base of working-class strength which has come
to other Social Democratic parties from their affiliation with a
valid trade-union movement. Moreover, deeply engrained
syndicalist traditions which have survived in all "Latin" countries, prevented the existing trade-unions from collaborating

---

[30] For a careful but guarded study of this question, see various articles
under the heading "Questions au Parti Communiste" in *Esprit*, XXXIV:353
(1966).

too closely with any political party. Only when the Communists came on the scene was an end put to such prejudices.

Since very few socialist leaders had a working-class or trade-union background, the workers' distrust of the bourgeois and intellectuals representing them in parliament weakened the party. It is true that the S.F.I.O. has had throughout its history more than its share of renegades who bolted the party in which they had started their political careers, and who continued to hold elective office under another label.

Additional difficulties arose for the S.F.I.O. from the wide gap between a constantly reaffirmed Marxist ideology and a political practice which was frequently at odds with professed ideals. The problem as to whether and under what conditions a socialist party could participate in a bourgeois government was endlessly debated within the party, especially during the interwar years when Léon Blum was the party's respected leader. Outstanding intellectual and distinguished lawyer that he was, he had drunk deep from the wells of Marxism and of French democratic tradition.[31] His attempts to merge both amounted frequently to exercises in sophistry lost on the working-class audiences he addressed. The discussions would have been less poignant if the party had ever been strong enough to assume control of the government. Since its weakness reduced it to becoming at best one of several partners in a coalition government, doctrinaire principles were marshaled to replace the wanting power.

As late as 1962 the parliamentary group of the S.F.I.O. affirmed an earlier resolution adopted upon the urging of its present leader: the principle of revolutionary class struggle was to guide the party in the attainment of its goal, a socialist commonwealth built upon the foundations of working-class organizations.[32] Such ideological language has little to do with what the party is and does in fact. But it appears appropriate to hold together an extremely diversified following whose

[31] Joel Colton, *Léon Blum, Humanist in Politics* (New York: Knopf, 1966), gives a good account of the development of the S.F.I.O. during the long leadership of Blum. For the post-World War II period, see also Henry W. Ehrmann, "The Decline of the Socialist Party, in Earle, *op. cit.*, pp. 181–99.

[32] See *Le Monde,* December 12, 1962.

motivations for embracing Socialism are primarily ideological precisely because their actual interests diverge rather sharply.

It is estimated that today about one-sixth of the working class still vote the Socialist ticket and that about one-fifth of its dues-paying members are workers. Most of the working-class following of the S.F.I.O. is concentrated in a few regions but the party has a few strongholds elsewhere. Almost from its beginnings it has had a large following among the wine-growers of the South, fervent devotees of republican ideals, of anticlericalism, and of producers' cooperatives. The propor-tion of civil servants, especially of teachers, and of other people living on a fixed income is far higher in the ranks and among the voters of the S.F.I.O. than in the population at large. This makes for a deliberate but not particularly dy-namic following, especially since the young are no longer attracted by the party.

With a membership of not more than thirty thousand, the financial resources of the party are constantly strained. The Socialist press, rather widely read before the war, is reduced to almost nothing. Attempts to establish or revive communica-tions media to reach a wider public have regularly ended in failure.

In one respect only, albeit an important one, the Socialists outshine their Communist competitors: their positions in local government remain strong, due to experienced personnel and honored traditions. In 1961, forty-four mayors of cities over thirty thousand population in almost all parts of the country were Socialists (as against twenty-five Communists and twenty-six Gaullists); more than fifty thousand members of town and city councils are Socialists, substantially more than Commu-nists and Gaullists combined.[33] These positions of strength provide substantial patronage and help to keep the party together.

The parliamentary group of the party has frequently been divided on important questions; such as participation in vari-ous cabinets of the Fourth Republic and in the government formed by General de Gaulle in 1958; German rearmament; and the Algerian conflict, when certain Socialists sided with

[33] For these data, see Aubin, *op. cit.*, II, pp. 212 ff.

the most rabid partisans of the "Keep Algeria French" movement. Under the leadership of Guy Mollet the Socialist representation in the National Assembly has shrunk from 146 in 1945 to a mere 66 in 1962 (in the following elections they no longer ran as a separate entity). But Mollet, whose talents and tactics are quite similar to those of an American political boss, has nonetheless succeeded in overcoming all but one of the schisms that have threatened the party.[34]

His is clearly a holding operation which seeks to maintain the S.F.I.O. intact as an organization until the day when General de Gaulle disappears from the scene. The organization might be skeletal and the party's performance uninspiring; what counts for Mollet is its survival which can be guaranteed only if the party system as a whole is not altered.

The defeat which Gaston Defferre suffered when he attempted, at the approach of the presidential elections of 1965, to revamp the system demonstrated the solidity of traditional party structures.[35] The Socialist mayor of Marseilles was willing to run for the Presidency as the candidate of a broad but disciplined federation, open to all opposition parties and movements. He knew that the Communists would not join such a federation but hoped to attract all others, including the Catholic center party and, above all, the *forces vives* which had remained outside the regular party organizations (see Chap. VII). Defferre made it very clear that what mattered to him was not so much to be elected President as to change by his campaign the structure of political life. But this very design ran counter to the intentions of his own party.

When negotiations preparing for the federation broke down, the principal participants lent credence to assumptions that the old controversy of government aid to parochial schools had been the stumbling block. Because of the customary doctrinaire style of politics, the traditional party lead-

[34] The miniscule P.S.U. split from the Socialists in 1958 and has ever since been beset, like all leftist splinter movements, by unending internal dissensions. On the often faltering voting discipline of the Socialist deputies in the Fourth Republic, see Williams, *Crisis,* p. 93.

[35] See the interesting though not always reliable account by a close observer of these events, Georges Suffert, *De Deferre à Mitterand* (Paris: Editions du Seuil, 1966).

ers preferred that their unwillingness to come to an agreement took on the appearance of an ideological conflict. What had actually been unacceptable in Defferre's proposal was the necessity for the established organizations to merge irrevocably into a federation which sooner or later might become open to individual membership thus leading to the formation of a new mass party. (For the more modest federation formed afterwards by Mitterand, see below.)

*The Radical Party.* This most typical of all French political parties was rightly considered the very incarnation of the Third Republic; it showed astonishing staying power under the Fourth Republic, and has survived into the Fifth Republic.

Even during its height of power the Radical Party had no formal organization except on paper; its annual conventions were gatherings of politicians holding elective office on the national or local level, whose reelection was based on personal reputation and on the services they had rendered to their constituencies. For the financing of their campaigns they had to rely, unless they were independently wealthy, on funds distributed by interest groups. Organized business had recognized early that their subsidies should not benefit conservative candidates alone but at least certain radicals as well. The complete freedom from party directives and party programs which Radical representatives enjoyed made their parliamentary groups into a collection of individuals whose orientation toward day-to-day political decisions could differ widely. In general, a Radical Senator was far more conservative than his colleague in the lower house. This added to the confusion of coalition alignments — and made the party's phraseology all but meaningless.

Radical liberalism, which at times affects outright libertarianism, likes to trace its ancestry back to the Jacobins and to the republicans of 1848. Its political strength, however, dates from the era when it fought clericalism in all its forms. At times the fusion between ranking personalities in the Masonic Lodges and the Radical Party was complete. Once the separation of church and state was assured, the Radicals became, even before the First World War, the staunch supporters of the economic and social *status quo* attractive to the middle classes which were then rising to political prominence. A doctrinaire egalitarianism flattered small interests which explains the electoral strength of the Radicals in towns and countryside — mainly in areas of mediocre economic development in the South and the Southeast. But wherever circumstances demanded it, a principled Jacobinism was perfectly capable of adjusting itself to policies perpetuating differences of wealth and existing class structures. A leftist "sensibility," adverse to the concentration of power in the hands of the executive, was the main criterion by which ambitious and able leaders (or leaders-to-be) were recruited for a career in the Radical camp. The writings of Alain (see above) provided a convenient rationalization for an attitude seemingly coherent on a philosophical level but utterly contradictory in its political consequences.[36]

When the Fourth Republic came into being, the fate of the Radicals seemed sealed. A party that had identified itself completely with the discredited institutions and political mores of the Third Republic and that was still adverse to modern forms of party organization seemed unsuitable for the needs and the temper of the moment. Yet between 1948 and 1958 the Radicals furnished not only numerous cabinet members but also more Premiers than any other party; for a long time the speakers of both houses of parliament were Radicals (one of them still holds that post in the Senate of the Fifth Republic).

This astonishing comeback was a consequence of the permanent features of the political system and especially of the endurance of an unstable party system. The solid footholds which Radicals had established in local and departmental politics and historical loyalties, especially in the South, could

---

[36] See Alain, *op. cit.*, and the excellent criticism in Kirchheimer, "The Transformation," pp. 178 f. For the history and structure of the Radical Party in general see Daniel Bardonnet, *Evolution de la Structure du Parti Radical* (Paris: Mont Chrestien, 1960).

be turned into profitable assets when the style of the Fourth Republic, both within and outside parliament, came to resemble more and more that of the Third.

Most important, however, was the fact that Radicals, by composition and temperament, could play to perfection the role of the center, of the "swamp" whose importance in the French multi-party system has been described. After 1946, the Radical party's electoral strength never exceeded 10 to 11 per cent, but it was capable of participating in all government coalitions and soon became indispensable to most. Because it offered opportunity for office and power, it was again attractive to young and able men, although there was certainly no rejuvenation of ideas or methods. When the most outstanding Radical leader, Pierre Mendès-France, made a last ditch effort to give renewed vigor to the classical representative system, he was defeated by a coalition of enemies and of circumstances. In his attempt to reform the structure of his own party, he met with complete defeat. The Radicals split wide open, and Mendès-France left their ranks.

In the Fifth Republic, the Radicals have been confined to the camp of the opposition and have lost further strength in every national election while still holding on to important positions on the level of local government and politics. For them the newly formed "Federation of the Democratic and Socialist Left" has been a welcome means of concealing their weakness behind a larger coalition which has enabled some of them to win back parliamentary seats. Thus they too are able to "hibernate" until the political configuration of the post-Gaullist era becomes clearer.

*Federation of the Democratic and Socialist Left.* This organization is not properly speaking a political party, and it is uncertain whether it will ever become one. But it is also, at least for the time being, something more than a mere electoral and parliamentary alliance between the formations of which it is composed. During the last months of the presidential election campaign in 1965, the Socialists, the Radicals, and an umbrella organization of the most active political clubs, the Convention of Republican Institutions, entered into an agreement to back François Mitterand's candidacy. (For a discussion of the "clubs" as a novel political phenomenon, see below.) Their relative success at the polls (see Chap. IV) and their ability to achieve together what they did not dare seek separately, namely a partnership with the Communists, encouraged the signatories of the original agreement to remain united beyond the presidential elections.

None of the members of the Federation relinquished its identity; their organizations, where they existed, were not fused; decisions were and are made according to the federal principle giving to the three partners an equal vote, in spite of their widely differing strength in parliament and the country. But with the approach of the parliamentary elections of 1967, the Federation decided on a strategy which was different from that of earlier electoral cartels. Instead of agreeing, as had been done in the past, on a single candidate just for the run-off elections, this time the three member organizations of the Federation were represented in each constituency by only one candidate from the very beginning of the electoral campaign.

Such tactics were in part chosen to meet the challenge presented by the Gaullist majority when it decided on a single candidate for the first ballot. It is also obvious that they enhanced the solidarity of the partners. The deputies of the Federation, whatever their own political affiliation, owe their election to a majority whose components can no longer be easily distinguished. As a consequence, it has also become impossible to determine the respective strength of the Socialists and the Radicals in the electorate. In the first run, the Federation won 18.8 per cent of all votes cast, a slight decrease over the combined votes of Socialists and Radicals in the preceding election of 1962. (The third contingent, the Convention of Republican Institutions, did not exist as such in 1962.) If one compares the electoral strength of the Federation in various parts of the country (adding that of the small dissident Socialist Party, the P.S.U.) with the previous strength of the non-Communist Left, no dramatic gains or losses appear.[37] But such stability as was obtained amounted again

[37] See the useful maps in Goguel, "Les élections . . . 1967," pp. 462 ff.

to a relative success: the progressive emaciation of the Federation's components, underway since 1958, had been stopped.

In terms of the popular vote, the combined Left, i.e., the Federation, the P.S.U., and the Communists, had still only 43.5 per cent of the votes cast in 1967, little more than in the two previous elections and considerably less than the share of the electorate which the corresponding political forces had controlled in the Fourth Republic (60 per cent in the first, 56 per cent in the last elections). But the electoral alliance into which the Federation and the Communists entered for the run-off elections in 1967 yielded a substantial increase in the number of deputies for both: the Federation's and the P.S.U.'s contingent rose from 92 to 120,[38] and, as previously mentioned, that of the Communists from 41 to 73. This success was due to the fact that the voters, eager to present a united front against the Gaullist majority even at the price of strengthening the Communists in Parliament, followed the directives of the leadership of the Communist Party and of the Federation.

Since the 1967 elections, the cohesion of the Federation has been strengthened by its role as the core of the opposition to Gaullism. This alone would have enhanced the authority of its leader Mitterand. But his stature and standing profit also, and quite considerably, from the polarization of political life which has been underway since the presidential campaign of 1965. The fact (discussed above, Chap. IV) that Mitterand does not belong to any of the discredited traditional parties facilitates his role as the leader of a broad opposition; this in turn results in the greater visibility of the Federation over which Mitterand presides.

So far the Federation's program does not go beyond the generalities of its election platform. But the deputies belonging to it have pledged themselves to vote in accordance with the Federation's directives on all "important questions." The smallest of the three member organizations, the Convention, is most anxious to see the Federation develop into a more unified organization to which individuals can adhere directly. The Convention is in many ways the most dynamic group

[38] Of these it is estimated that the Socialists can claim about 76, the Radicals 33, the "Convention" 17, and the P.S.U. 4 seats.

and benefits from the fact that Mitterand belongs to it. Yet, at present it cannot be foretold whether its efforts will be successful. If this were the case, the result would be a somewhat modified version of Gaston Defferre's attempt to overhaul the party system. These efforts are, therefore, bound to meet with similar resistance from the established parties and especially from the party apparatus of the S.F.I.O. In the years to come, a development of the Federation beyond mere agreements between the national leaders or the parliamentary representatives might indicate whether or not a mutation of the party system is actually underway.

*The Democratic Center.* In forming the Democratic Center, the erstwhile presidential candidate Jean Lecanuet wished to emulate the step which his competitor Mitterand had taken in presiding over the Federation of the Left. Also, Lecanuet sought to capitalize on the simplification of party alignment which the mechanism of the presidential elections had suggested. He took the 3.7 million votes which in December 1965 favored a hitherto little-known politician as proof that there was room for a united non-Gaullist Center, just as Mitterand had concluded that he should bring together the non-Communist Left. But where Mitterand obtained a qualified success in terms of popular votes and a notable gain of seats in parliament, Lecanuet's efforts came to naught in both respects. In the National Assembly elected in 1967, the number of deputies affiliated with the Center had shrunk to a mere 42 as compared with the 120 seats of the non-Communist Left.

The main reason for such failure was that, contrary to his expectations, Lecanuet's efforts did not correspond to but rather ran counter to the prevailing trend. By taking a position neither for the majority nor for the opposition but hoping to arbitrate between both in some ill-defined manner, the Center did not acknowledge the bipolarity which had become as characteristic of the parliamentary elections as it had been of the preceding presidential contest. Hence the Center was unable to stem the decline of its component parts, a decline which had been underway for a considerable time.

The most prominent among the parties out of which Lecanuet had sought to fashion a new force was his own party, the *Mouvement Républicain Populaire* (M.R.P.). A few months after the 1967 elections, some twenty years after it had emerged for a time as the strongest of all political parties, it decided on its own demise. In 1946, it had attracted 28 per cent of the votes, surpassing for once the electoral strength of the Communists. Its rapid rise in the period after the liberation paralleled similar party developments in other Western democracies. The subsequent dwindling of its attractiveness points to the continuing peculiarities of French political culture.

The M.R.P. had drawn on old traditions of liberal French Catholicism (see Chap. III). Before the war and under the impact of the rising tide of European fascism, the movement had began to recruit from among those Catholic intellectuals and activists in the Catholic youth movement that were opposed to all forms of authoritarian conservatism. In the resistance it gathered support from many sides and from all social categories. During the first postwar elections, it was particularly attractive to women to whom the Third Republic had refused the suffrage.

The explicit purpose of the M.R.P. was to overcome the schism between the Republic and the faithful Catholics by offering a program of bold economic and social reform. Since it wanted to compete with the Socialists and Communists with whom it shared governmental office, it laid the foundation for a mass party, and at one time had a membership of over two hundred thousand. For a time it was also able to impose on its representatives in parliament a far stricter discipline than had been customary beyond the benches of the extreme Left.

The party furnished the governments of the Fourth Republic with five Prime Ministers and an impressive number of gifted and youthful Ministers. Since its support was sought by most cabinets, whatever their political orientation, the M.R.P. acquired the typical qualities of a French Center movement: soon enough it was wading, like the Radicals, into the "marais."

When the postwar eagerness for sweeping reforms had

receded, the M.R.P. was in part unwilling and in part unable to turn into the broadly based conservative mass party which the Christian-Democratic parties in Germany, Italy, and Belgium have become. Its voters deserted it by the millions as soon as the Gaullist movement assaulted the parliamentary system of the Fourth Republic and when traditional conservative forces reappeared on the political scene. By 1951 its electoral following had been cut by far more than half; in 1962, the last election in which the M.R.P. fought as an autonomous organization, its support had dwindled to less than 9 per cent of the votes cast. The membership of the party had become insignificant.

From its beginnings, the M.R.P. never wanted to be and never has been a "clerical" party. The Catholic hierarchy had no legal ties with the party; the clergy played no role in its organization. Yet, sociologically speaking, both its leadership and its following were as Catholic in sensibility and tradition as the Radicals were freethinkers. The electoral map of the M.R.P. showed that at the end of the Fourth Republic the party was left with only regional and mostly rural support — primarily in Alsace and in Brittany — and that its positions of strength coincided with the regions where the number of regular churchgoers was highest. Nationally, the voters of no other party or movement equaled those of the M.R.P. in faithfulness to the Church.[39] Quite naturally, such an image limited the audience of the party. Whenever the issue of parochial schools came to the fore, its commitment to a Catholic clientele forced the M.R.P. to part company with the Socialists and other natural allies with whom it agreed on matters of social policy or European unity.

Intraparty tensions weakened the effectiveness of the organization. They arose because its leadership and party activists, often operating from urban centers, were usually far more progressive than its mildly conservative voters in the countryside. Such differences became most visible in the Fifth Republic when at least part of the M.R.P. leadership changed

[39] See the details, partially based on survey materials, in René Rémond, *et al., Forces religieuses et attitudes politiques dans la France contemporaine* (Paris: Colin, 1965), pp. 75 ff.

gradually from conditional support of de Gaulle's policy to one of outright opposition to his European policy and his constitutional practices. Then the fact that most M.R.P. voters continued to back the government resulted in frequent split voting by M.R.P. deputies even on important questions.

Whatever electoral strength the Democratic Center still musters is inherited from the dwindling strongholds of the M.R.P. and from those Conservatives who have remained in opposition to Gaullist policies. Its following is concentrated in certain regions in the East, the West, and the Southwest of the country; there the farmers and upper income groups continue to vote for the Democratic Center.[40] In parliament it is represented by a number of able and experienced politicians who will regularly vote according to their own lights, although they may think alike about some questions of long-range concern, such as European federation and constitutional reforms. Organizationally the Center has become the classical "nonparty" of French conservatism. Little is left of the expectations which the M.R.P. had raised at the time of its founding.

For the time being, the Center can do little more than hope for the dislocation of the present majority, which is unlikely before de Gaulle's disappearance from the political scene. Only if the traditional multiparty system were to be restored could the Center hope to regain its classical functions.

*The Union pour la Nouvelle République* (U.N.R.). The U.N.R., thrown together hastily after General de Gaulle's return to power in 1958, is the one true novelty in French party politics. Novel it is first and foremost by the extent and durability of its success. It has already been the leader and the core of a stable governing coalition for a far longer period than has any other political movement in the history of French republics. When, only weeks after its birth, it won over 20 per cent of the vote and, more surprisingly, almost 40 per cent of the seats in the first parliament of the new re-

40 For details on the Democratic Center, see Jean-Luc Parodi, "Les paradoxes du Centre Démocrate," *RFSP*, XVI:4 (1966), pp. 957 ff.

public, it benefited largely from the floating vote which in the past had swelled, but never for long, other surge movements. The plethora of seats in the National Assembly, with which the U.N.R. found itself blessed after the run-off elections, resulted from a bandwagon effect which the electoral system chosen by General de Gaulle was expected to prevent. Yet, in the years that followed, there has not been a serious reflux of the U.N.R.'s strength.

As Table V indicates, parliamentary Gaullism has never been quite as successful as presidential, i.e., a clearly plebiscitarian, Gaullism. But at least in terms of the popular vote, the U.N.R. has increased its share in every parliamentary election. As for the Center and the Left, the electoral alliances of 1967 make comparisons difficult, but there is no doubt that with every election the party's following has become more "national" in scope. The U.N.R. is no longer exclusively strong in those regions north of the Loire River where traditionally the political Right had its dominant positions. From the beginning it had shown strength in the industrial North. But by now it has also made important inroads in the mountainous regions of the South-East and of the Center, of the U.N.R. which have long voted Left. According to some estimates, even at the 1967 elections not less than 1½ million of the U.N.R. voters were won away from parties of the Left

TABLE V  *Presidential and Parliamentary Gaullism * (in percentages of votes cast)*

|  | Referendum Sept. 1958 | Referendum Oct. 1962 | First Ballot Presidential Elections Dec. 1965 |
|---|---|---|---|
| Presidential Gaullism | 79.2 | 61.7 | 43.7 |

| First Ballot: | Elections Nov. 1958 | Elections Oct. 1962 | Elections March 1967 |
|---|---|---|---|
| Parliamentary Gaullism | 20.4 | 31.9 | 37.8 ** |

* Adapted from Alain Lancelot, "Les Elections des 5 et 12 mars 1967," *Project* 15 (1967), p. 556.
** This figure is apt to be slightly misleading since it includes the votes for the U.N.R.'s coalition partners (see below).

or extreme Left. As a result, the following of the U.N.R. is at present more evenly distributed throughout the country than that of any other party.[41]

The U.N.R. has therefore the characteristics of a "dominant" party, which France has not known since the beginning of the century when the Radicals occupied a similar position. But even during its apogee the Radical party never practiced the rigorous discipline to which all U.N.R. deputies have been subjected ever since the party was founded.

Other parties — de Gaulle's own R.P.F. (see below), the short-lived Poujade Movement (which in 1956 had won 52 seats), and others — have never been able to emulate for long the parliamentary discipline of the Communists. By contrast the U.N.R. has enforced compliance with its position in every vote of importance. Because of deep divergences over the solution of the Algerian conflict, this led to the expulsion from the party of some of de Gaulle's earliest and most prominent supporters. But unlike what happened to political apostates in the past, anathema from the U.N.R. leadership ended the careers of the dissidents. Not all were driven into exile as was Jacques Soustelle. But wherever they sought elective office, they were always soundly defeated. This has been enough to discourage any further thought of defection among Gaullist deputies and senators.

Even though the purges have eliminated some extremist firebrands, the Gaullist groups in both houses still comprise men of different backgrounds, temperaments, and even political orientations. Intense discussions among them are reported to be frequent. But the chairmen of the parliamentary groups have never experienced any serious difficulties when they seek compliance with the wishes formulated by the Prime Minister and by the President of the Republic.

As a disciplined force in parliament, the U.N.R. has been invaluable to the regime. It has never become, and never was intended to become, a modern mass party. General de Gaulle's aversion to all political parties had been confirmed

[41] For details see the election studies by Goguel and Lancelot quoted previously (n. 26) and François Goguel, "Bipolarisation ou Renovation du Centrisme?" *RFSP*, XVII:5 (1967), pp. 927 ff.

by the debacle of the *Rassemblement du Peuple Français* (R.P.F.) which he himself had founded in 1947 to attack the institutions of the Fourth Republic. As a mass movement, the R.P.F. had not been free of the rightist radicalism so distasteful to its leader. Its parliamentary representatives had not withstood the temptations of cabinet seats, finally the party succumbed to the centrifugal forces of day-to-day politics.

Since 1958 de Gaulle has kept all parties at arm's length, including his own. Nonetheless, the U.N.R. has prospered by its complete identification with the General's views and policies. It might have been possible at one time to develop the U.N.R. into the structured and disciplined conservative party which France has never known, but General de Gaulle has discouraged all attempts in this direction so that the U.N.R. remains what other French parties have always been: a cadre party, albeit a modernized and streamlined one. Its membership has been kept down to a maximum of eighty to ninety thousand and hence amounts to a very small fraction of the Gaullist electorate.

The upper echelons of the party hierarchy constitute almost without exception a "peer group." All of its members have belonged directly, or indirectly through a single intermediary, to General de Gaulle's entourage during the days of the Free French movement in London and Algiers, during the immediate postliberation period, or during the R.P.F. episode.[42] Since those troubled times have attracted men of widely different backgrounds to General de Gaulle, the ties that bind them to each other consist mostly of their personal loyalty to the leader.

The party activists, including the full-time party officials throughout the country are a rather unified social group, characterized by a solid middleclass background: businessmen, professionals, technicians, here and there local notables. The party apparatus is well equipped to furnish such services

[42] For details on this and on the structure and history of the U.N.R. in general see the excellent study by Jean Charlot, *L'U.N.R., Etude du Pouvoir au sein d'un Parti Politique* (Paris: Colin, 1967). For interesting biographical details (written in a lighter vein but entirely reliable) on the Gaullist leadership, see also the book by Pierre Viansson-Ponté, *The King and His Court* (Boston: Houghton Mifflin Co., 1965).

as information, propaganda material, and detailed advice to candidates and elected representatives at various levels of government. Political "activity" as such, especially debate and discussion taking place outside election campaigns, has a low priority if it is not frowned upon. General de Gaulle himself has never appeared at any of the annual party conventions. These are showy affairs with a flair for public relations but of little interest even to the party activists whose morale they are supposed to bolster. Speeches, frequently delivered by members of the government, are hardly ever followed by discussions since the voicing of political views might prove as divisive for the U.N.R. as it has been for other parties in the past.

Quite typically, the U.N.R. has never attempted, in spite of its impressive following, to have its own newspaper or to be identified with one. As has already been mentioned (see Chap. VI), its official organ, *La Nation,* is printed in a few thousand copies and is read by very few. Such unwillingness to commit party views to paper and to give them wide circulation can also be explained by the general reluctance of the movement to fix its line of conduct or to develop anything approximating a political doctrine.

What is the political orientation, the "Gaullism," of the U.N.R.? Even if it is defined primarily as the loyalty to a leader, even if it eschews ideology and professes to be "apolitical," this is in itself a political stance and one less novel than the U.N.R. claims. "The innermost thought of General de Gaulle is not all there is to gaullism," it has been said. . . . "But, on the other hand, the motives [of the millions of U.N.R. voters] have sometimes only a rather loose relationship with the essence of gaullism." [43] To explain the "essence" of the movement and the reasons for its attractiveness, one has to draw parallels to the various strands of French monarchical and other authoritarian traditions. But of all the isms of the past, Gaullism, and its accredited party the U.N.R., is the closest to bonapartism.

The aversion to parliamentary institutions; a preference

[43] René Rémond, *La Droite,* p. 279. See *ibid.,* pp. 280 ff. also for the following.

for seeing the general will expressed through referenda and other devices of plebiscitarian democracy; and the fusion of direct democracy with nationalism — these were the earmarks of authentic bonapartism. Another trait which gaullism shares with the regimes of the two Napoleons is an active personality cult — frequently characteristic of the political Right but in this case associated with a concern for social reform, which claims to be "of the people" rather than of the Right or of the Left. To be sure, it also is a "filtered" bonapartism, adapted to the times and modified by the personality of the present, but still essentially drawing on a tradition which, according to André Siegfried, has always been present in France even when it has been driven underground.[44]

If in spite of its denials the U.N.R. does have an "ideology," the party is able to manipulate it for maximum general appeal, hoping to catch all categories of voters. It has therefore the characteristics of the modern "catch-all" parties, although not all these parties are based to the same extent on personal loyalty to a leader as is the U.N.R.[45] Unlike the flash or surge movements of the past, the U.N.R. has done more than mobilize people who were previously, outside the political spectrum, nonvoters and the like. Rather its following appears to be a cross section of the electorate, distributed fairly evenly among all social groups, except that small businessmen and artisans still flock to it in greater numbers than other categories. Twenty-nine per cent of the workers declare their preference for the U.N.R. This corresponds roughly to the national average of votes which the party obtained from the general electorate in the last elections and might be compared with 26 per cent of the working class voting for the Communists and 21 per cent in sympathy with the Federation of the Left.[46]

The only group within the U.N.R. which has kept a certain autonomy and which, at the same time, prides itself on its ideological purity is the *Union Démocratique du Travail*

[44] Siegfried, *A Study,* pp. 98 ff.

[45] See Kirchheimer, "The Transformation," pp. 186 f.

[46] Société Française d'Enquête par Sondages, *Etude de l'attitude des Electeurs à l'égard des principaux Partis Politiques* (mimeographed: Paris, 1966), p. 9.

(U.D.T.). Its leaders regard themselves as leftist Gaullists and unfailingly interpret the practices of the regime in the sense of a Rousseauan democracy. Their personal loyalty to General de Gaulle puts strict limits on the autonomy which they claim; their lack of following restricts their effectiveness. As deputies a number of them occupy fairly important positions in the committees of parliament; but their efforts to swing legislation in a leftward direction are usually condemned to failure.

Neither the existence of the U.D.T. nor the emphasis which General de Gaulle himself has placed on social reforms introduced by the Fifth Republic has essentially altered the public image of the U.N.R. as a party of the Right. In a public opinion poll of 1965 39 per cent classified it as such; for 23 per cent it belongs in the "Center" and only 3 per cent regard it as being in the Left camp. But a remarkably high 35 per cent were unable or unwilling to classify the party at all.[47] This does not contradict what has been said previously about the attractiveness of the U.N.R. for the working class. In France, a substantial minority of the workers has frequently voted a conservative ticket, especially one with a bonapartist coloring. *Mutatis mutandis,* this is also true in Great Britain and West Germany.

Where the U.N.R. will go after General de Gaulle's demise is of paramount importance not only to the future of the party but to the regime itself. Once the deliberately authoritarian style of the leader is no longer to be reckoned with, the U.N.R. might move more clearly towards the center of the political spectrum. But when personal loyalty to a charismatic figure no longer balances centrifugal tendencies, will the U.N.R. be in a better position to preserve its unity than other center parties in the past? Will the majority of the party veer towards its own Right or its Left? Since the last elections both of these wings have begun to show restlessness. So far, and in spite of tenuous efforts, the U.N.R. has not been able to sink strong roots into local politics, the reservoir

---

[47] *Sondages,* XXVIII:1 (1966), p. 41. Another polling organization succeeded only a few months later in reducing in its sample the number of "Don't knows" to 17 per cent. But then 43 per cent classified the U.N.R. with the Right and 11 per cent with the extreme Right, see Deutsch, *et al., Les Familles politiques,* p. 113.

of national leadership. Opinion surveys indicate that the older generation rather than youth has sympathies for the party. Many young voters regard it as the least dynamic of the major political movements.

Such diffidence on the part of the young (and their previously reported sympathies for the Communist Party) are of particular significance since at the time of the next elections — assuming they will be held at a five years' interval — one out of 2 voters will be less than 32 years of age. One out of 3 will never have voted before the establishment of the Fifth Republic. For them the sins of the "old" parties, on which the U.N.R. still harps in its electoral propaganda, might have lost some of their abhorrent quality.

On the other hand, a new and quite able leadership group is emerging with the gradual disappearance from the scene of the Gaullist "old guard." By social origin, desire for modernization, and a generally technocratic bent, these party activists have an affinity with the graduates of the E.N.A. in the bureaucracy. A merger of both groups in the party leadership might give the party a more definite image and outlook. But whether this will result in a stable electoral following remains to be seen. To rejuvenate its image the party, late in 1967, rechristened itself as the *Union des Démocrates pour la Ve République.*

Like everybody else in present-day France, the leadership of the U.N.R. is convinced that time works for them. They believe that the longer the regime lasts, even under an aging leader, the more the electorate will be won over to the idea that stable parties, or at least stable coalitions, should face each other in government and opposition. When such a constellation prevails, the present leadership believes a united if flexible U.N.R. will no longer need de Gaulle to prove that the regime cannot exist without its stabilizing influence. For the time being there is little evidence to uphold such sanguine expectations.

*The Independent Republicans.* In none of the three parliaments elected so far in the Fifth Republic have the deputies of the U.N.R. commanded by themselves a majority of seats. The constitutional conflict of 1962 divided the conservative deputies, a group which had never been more than a loose affiliation of individuals. Those who sided with the President of the Republic established themselves in parliament as the *Républicains Indépendents* (R.I.). This party has furnished a number of ministers to the government and has regularly voted with the U.N.R. Even when its leader, Valéry Giscard d'Estaing, was rather unceremoniously dismissed as Minister of Finance, a post he had occupied under two Gaullist Prime Ministers, the party did not change its position of only slightly conditional support.

The new party was saved from showing the sparseness of its electoral following when President and Prime Minister insisted that even in the first ballot of the 1967 elections only a single candidate was to run for the majority in each constituency. Nonetheless, when the results of the run-off elections were in, the R.I. had increased the number of its deputies to 43 while the U.N.R. seats declined from 233 to 199. In many cases this shift reflected public confidence in mayors and other local leaders who, as candidates for the Assembly, preferred to be classified with the as yet shapeless formation of the Independents rather than with the more highly structured U.N.R.

Even before but especially since the 1967 elections, Giscard d'Estaing has seized many opportunities to distance himself from the U.N.R. and the government. He has criticized the authoritarian style of the regime, the "solitary exercise of power," rather than details of its domestic policies; its insufficient European commitment rather than its lack of ardor for federalist schemes for which he himself has little taste. But so far, the R.I. has not gone very far in developing a party organization in the country. A network of clubs, ambitiously called *"Perspectives et Réalités,"* has the aspect of study groups rather than of a political party. The party-sponsored periodical has been renamed programmatically and lengthily — *The Modern, Liberal, Centralist, European France* — without arousing much public interest.[48]

[48] On the various groups of Independents and on Giscard d'Estaing's efforts, see Marielle Bal, "Les Indépendents," *RFSP*, XV:3 (1965), pp. 537-55, and Marie-Christine Kessler, "M. Valéry Giscard d'Estaing et les républicains indépendants: réalités et perspectives," *ibid.*, XVI:5 (1966), pp. 940-57.

The attention which the communication media and elite opinion in Paris have paid Giscard d'Estaing bears little relation to his present influence. But it is a significant tribute to his ambition to be considered the favorite "outsider" for General de Gaulle's succession. Born in 1926, scion of an old family whose members have for a long time combined careers in banking with service to the state, Giscard d'Estaing became one of the most brilliant graduates the E.N.A. has produced since its founding. He is a member of the most distinguished corps of civil servants, the Inspectorate of Finance as were before him his father, his grandfather, and one of his uncles. (See Chap. IV.) Nonetheless, and this might be characteristic of the new elites he wishes to represent, highly qualified technician that he is, he sought elective office as early as 1956. Whether his groping for a new style of party leadership and of organization will bear fruit cannot be foretold. It is equally possible that the R.I. will revert to the traditional forms of French conservatism.

Except for unforeseeable circumstances, the R.I. and its leader have little interest in withdrawing support from the government and thereby bringing on new elections before General de Gaulle has left the political stage. Again, it is only after that event that one will be able to discern whether they, possibly together with their natural allies in the Democratic Center, will take their place in an altered party system or do their share in reinstating the system of former days.

### CONCLUSION: MUTATIONS IN THE PARTY SYSTEM?

The party system has been indicted, with many good reasons, for the malfunctioning of the parliamentary system in the Third and Fourth Republics. When after the end of the Algerian war, in 1962, the leadership of the old parties believed that the moment had come to prevent the new regime from changing too drastically the customary rules of the political game, they were soundly defeated. Yet, in spite of such discredit, many parties responsible for the previous stalemate have survived in more or less their old form, if sometimes under new labels; whatever little there is of party life and party organization has kept many of the old characteristics.

The one new organization, the U.N.R., has refrained from introducing a truly novel pattern.

An important reason for the survival of the traditional system is the fact that most political actors consider the present regime merely an interlude. Unable to fathom the future of the political system after de Gaulle, both the supporters and critics of the Fifth Republic are unable and unwilling to gauge what kind of party system will be needed to operate the institutional framework created in 1958 and profoundly modified since then. In the eyes of the "traditionalists," the thorough overhauling of the parties might be an unnecessarily high price to pay. The "modernists," on the other hand, hesitate to compromise their ideas by pushing too far and too fast experiments which cannot be tested reliably as long as General de Gaulle dominates the scene.

Such hesitation also explains, at least in part, why the political clubs have not played the role of political catalysts which many of their promoters assigned to them. When they were formed, first during the premiership of Mendès-France and then more numerously in many cities and regions after the establishment of the Fifth Republic, they appeared to be the most forthright attempt to soften up and possibly to explode and replace former party structures. They were the political expression of the same impetus which led to the formation of the *"forces vives"* in the group universe (see Chap. VII). Many of the clubs, indeed, wished to be considered as a form of general interest groups.

By their very name, the clubs drew on traditions of the French Revolution. At that time, when political parties had not yet come into being, the clubs had sought simultaneously to undertake the "patriotic" education of the citizenry and to direct their political activities. Since their renaissance in the 1950's, the clubs have wavered between the same two poles.[49] They have sprung up in all political groupings, from

[49] On the phenomenon and the development of the clubs see Jean-André Faucher, *Les Clubs Politiques en France* (Paris: 1965), and, vastly more reliable, Georges Lavau, "Les Clubs Politiques," *RFSP,* XV:1 (1965), pp. 103–13; and *ibid.,* XV:3 (1965), pp. 555–69.

the extreme Right to the Left. Most prominent political candidates have judged it opportune to secure the support of one or several clubs in the capital and in the provinces, if they have not encouraged their followers to found new ones. This can only be understood as a tribute to the potential significance of the clubs for future political developments, for none of them commands a substantial electoral following at present.

Most clubs have a total membership of not more than a few hundred and are actually, at least for the time being, adverse to mass recruiting. Usually, they pride themselves on their efforts to develop a coherent program, and in so doing they do not shun ideological commitment. To them this is not to be understood as a revival in new garb of the traditional doctrinairism of French politics, but as a recognition, in as pragmatic a fashion as possible, that all political solutions are based on attitudes and choices that ought to be defined rather than concealed. Some, but by no means all, of the programs and pronouncements of the clubs seem to justify such claims.[50]

For the time being, the most interesting aspect of the clubs is the role which they seek to play in political socialization and recruitment. While they have remained elite organizations with appeal to upper middle class elements, they have nevertheless brought together intellectuals and civil servants, businessmen and trade unionists, intellectuals and leaders of farmers' organizations. Some of the political "aspirants" (see Chap. V) have regarded the clubs as a more satisfactory outlet for their ambitions than parties. In some municipal elections, especially those at Grenoble (see Chap. IV), candidates were recruited, at least indirectly, through the clubs rather than through the parties.

Yet, for all their efforts and partial success, the clubs have been unable to channel their energies into the creation of those institutions which are needed for the running of a renovated parliamentary system. The undeniable though

[50] Most serious are the publications by the Club Jean Moulin; see its *Bulletin* and its cooperative volume, frequently quoted in previous chapters, *L'Etat et le Citoyen.*

possibly temporary stagnation of the clubs results partly from the very immobility of the party system which the clubs set out to overcome.

We have seen that until now a mutation in the party system has been effected neither from the inside by the parties themselves, whether old or new, nor from the outside. But parties are also shaped, and perhaps predominantly so, by the structure of the political system within which they operate.[51] There can be little doubt that the new institutional framework has resulted in certain changes in the number and functioning of parties. The regrouping and the simplification of the party system which have taken place is above all a consequence of the polarization which the new mode of presidential elections and the new rules of parliamentary procedure (see Chap. X) have favored. Under such conditions, even the electoral system reintroduced in 1958, which in the past often resulted in protracted atomization of both majority and opposition, has furthered the formation of what has been called political dualism, i.e. a clearer confrontation of majority and opposition.

Searching studies based on public opinion surveys have revealed some seemingly contradictory but not altogether surprising trends among the electorate.[52] When voters are asked to classify themselves as belonging to the traditional political "families," most are still quite prepared to do so: 16 per cent consider themselves of the Extreme Left, 19 per cent of the Left, 31 per cent of the Center, 17 per cent of the Right, and 7 per cent of the Extreme Right — here there is an interesting correlation to the 1965 votes for General de Gaulle, Lecanuet, and Mitterand (see Table III). Only 10 per cent refused to group themselves. But when the inquiry proceeded to obtain answers to questions which would have identified the respondents with definite political attitudes, it became clear that in every camp attitudes were represented

[51] This is the main thesis of the masterly analysis of the British party system by R. T. McKenzie, *British Political Parties* (2nd ed.; New York: Praeger, 1964).

[52] See Deutsch, *et al., Les Familles Politiques,* p. 14, and *passim,* and Denis Lindon, *L'Avenir de la Gauche* (mimeographed; Paris, October 1967).

which the opinion poll would classify as "revolutionary," "reformist," "moderate conservatives," or "convinced conservatives." To be sure, the distribution of these elements in the different groups varied. But, to give an example, even among those who counted themselves as belonging to the Extreme Left 41 per cent voiced opinions that could rightly be described as those of "convinced conservatives." As would be expected the ideological void was greatest among those classified as being in the *marais,* i.e. members of the Center who by their answers revealed that their political interest and their political socialization were minimal, a group which in the midst of "political dualism" has grown rather than shrunk. But at the same time the members of all the other political groups showed by the variety and diffuseness of their answers how little ideological content or commitment there is.

This lack of conviction could facilitate the emergence of large pragmatic parties, able to recruit an electoral following with widely divergent interests and values. Yet since traditional identifications have not been forgotten and since the parties representing them are still in existence, it would also be possible to revert to the kind of seemingly ideologically determined multi-party system that was described at the beginning of this chapter.

Under these circumstances it is not astonishing that the question whether the present incipient dualism can be expected to survive for long — whether or not it will ultimately lead to a classical or at least a modified two-party system — is widely and ardently discussed.[53] This question can be answered with a degree of certainty only if there were to emerge strongly articulated and disciplined parties which, both in power and in opposition, could be fairly sure of their own permanence. This however is not yet the case and, in the absence of such parties, the present trend towards dualism and towards the coagulation of disparate political forces is as-

[53] The best summary of the various points made in that debate is to be found in a symposium, "La France, va-t-elle au bipartisme?" *France-Forum,* No. 80 (1967), pp. 1–20. See also an article with the same title by Alain Duhamel in *Le Monde,* June 14, 1967. More sceptical about the chances for a classical or modified two-party system is the excellently informed article by Goguel, "Bipolarisation ou Rénovation," *op. cit.*

sured as long as such a trend is supported by the political system.

This is the reason why the current "political class" expects with anticipation, glee, or concern, as the case may be, the changes in the functioning of the political system which the post-Gaullist era will bring. But it might be doubted whether after General de Gaulle's disappearance the policy processes can function without that autonomous system of modern parties which the Fifth Republic lacks as much as has any preceding regime.

# CHAPTER IX

# Policy Processes — I

## THE PRESIDENT OF THE REPUBLIC:
## MULTIPLICITY OF FUNCTIONS AND OMNIPOTENCE

When General de Gaulle returned to power in 1958, it was generally expected that the Presidency of the Republic would be invested with a novel significance in the policy processes of the new republic. De Gaulle's Bayeux speech in 1961,[1] his subsequent writings, and the Gaullist propaganda in the following years constantly emphasized the need for a widely visible Chief of State. He was to be placed "above the parties" and empowered to represent effectively the unity rather than the diversity of the national community. In conforming to this concept and departing from earlier republican traditions, the text of the new constitution puts the office of the President first among the organs of government, immediately after the tribute to the principle of popular sovereignty, as if to symbolize what so far has, in fact, been the essence of the Fifth Republic: the alliance between the *homme providentiel* and the people.[2]

There is, however, a fundamental difference between the role which the constitution and those who had drafted it as-

[1] This speech of de Gaulle is indispensable for an understanding of his own constitutional thinking and that of his principal advisors. An English translation can be found in William G. Andrews (ed.), *European Political Institutions* (Princeton: Van Nostrand, 1966), pp. 40–43.

[2] See Philip M. Williams and Martin Harrison, *De Gaulle's Republic* (London: Longmans, Green, 1960), p. 214.

signed to the Presidency and the actual significance which
the office has taken on in the process of decision-making. Its
development presents a fascinating example of how within
a short time a conjunction of circumstances and of personality can thoroughly transform constitutional institutions and
their underlying ideas. (Ironically enough, but not at all acci-
dentally, the constitution of the Third Republic underwent
very early a similar and thorough transformation. But then
politics traveled in the opposite direction, namely towards
parliamentary omnipotence.)

Today national policy-making is almost totally dominated
by the Chief of State. The constitution had left the determination of policies to the Prime Minister and his government
(arts. 20–23), and the role of the President was to be that of
the guardian of the constitution, "who by his arbitration"
was to "ensure the regular functioning of the public authorities" (art. 5). In a brilliant exegesis of the constitutional text
he had authored in large part, Michel Debré explained that
it was the proper function of the arbiter to do little else than
to appeal to another power, be it parliament, the Constitutional Council, or the people. The President's right to dissolve parliament (art. 11) would permit nothing more than
"a short dialogue" between the Chief of State and the nation.
An electoral college, composed of local notables, should designate the President, for "the President who is elected by universal suffrage is a political leader bound by the daily work
of government and command." [3] In Debré's design this was
not to be the domain of the French President, who should
assume the executive powers of a constitutional dictator only
in times of grave trouble (art. 16).

That things have turned out so differently is partly due to
the fact that the heavily ideological concept of an arbiter
serving the cause of national integration "beyond politics" is
even more unrealistic today than in the nineteenth century
when it was developed as an underpinning for the constitu-

[3] A translation of M. Debré's address is to be found in Andrews, *op.
cit.*, pp. 43–55. For historical antecedents to Debré's constitutional thinking, see Nicholas Wahl, "The French Constitution of 1958: The Initial
Draft and Its Origins," *American Political Science Review*, LIII:2 (1959),
pp. 358–82.

tional monarchies of France and England. Neither the tensions generated by the Algerian war nor, in spite of some appearances, the personality of General de Gaulle, have lent themselves to the institution of a republican monarch whom Debré had described as the "keystone of a parliamentary regime."

Even before, and upon assuming presidential office, General de Gaulle introduced a new term to describe the task that awaited him. By claiming that he was not only Chief of State but also "France's *guide*," he undertook to play the role which Jean-Jacques Rousseau, in his *Social Contract,* assigned to him who will formulate for the people what the general will truly is. Such a function foreshadowed a permanent rather than the "brief" dialogue between the Chief of State and the people which Debré had foreseen for certain specified situations. In this dialogue, moreover, the *guide* would be able to make fullest use of modern communications media (see Chap. VI).

Less than a year later the speaker of the National Assembly explained to the U.N.R. Congress that certain policy domains, such as Algeria, foreign and military matters, were reserved to presidential decision-making and hence no longer subject to parliamentary scrutiny [4] since only the government, not the President, was responsible to parliament. The vertical separation of power thus established had no foundation whatsoever in the constitution, but it was generally accepted because a majority in the country and in parliament wished that at least one crucial question, that of the Algerian conflict, be solved by presidential fiat. The Hanoverian monarchy intended by Debré was rapidly evolving into the kind of consular dictatorship to which the Romans turned whenever the country was judged to be in danger.

From then on, a chain of events led to the gradual absorption of most decision-making by the Chief of State. The threat to the state which arose in 1960 from French settlers and in 1961 from mutinous army officers in Algeria, and the way in which the threat was met made it clear to all, including Prime Minister Michel Debré, that authority and legiti-

[4] See *A.P.* 1959, pp. 134–35.

macy had not been restored to the state but only to de Gaulle in person. The President himself became aware of the fact that the inefficiency of problem solution in the sectors to which he paid no attention (he liked to refer to them summarily as "the price of milk") endangered decision-making in the "reserved" domains. Because he was operating in a highly centralized system, the Chief of State was compelled, not only by choice but also by necessity, to hold a close rein on all matters. Soon the day came when a new Prime Minister declared that the concept of the two domains was no longer realistic.

Parallel to these experiences was de Gaulle's increasing use of and taste for the plebiscitarian approval of his actions and of his personality (see Chap. IV). When the referendum of 1962 laid the foundations for a popularly elected President, such a modification of the text and the spirit of the four-year-old constitution not only acknowledged the changes which "the circumstances" (a favored term in de Gaulle's vocabulary) had brought about, but also endowed the presidency with the legitimacy of a direct popular vote which, it was hoped, would accrue to the office when it was occupied by a less charismatic personality than General de Gaulle.

As was to be expected, the present Chief of State has transmitted his personal style to his performance in office. An elaborate ceremonial, combining modernity with tradition, distance even from his closest associates, discreetness in the preparation of decision, the formulation of unalterable policies in surprise announcements, all these are the expressions of personality traits that have become the paraphernalia of presidential and "solitary" powers.

Under such conditions, the question whether there exists an "inner circle" of presidential advisors gives rise to unending speculation. It is certain that in the intimacy of personal conversation the General solicits and listens to advice. And although over time the circle of those close to him has occasionally changed, at least three personalities have belonged to it almost permanently: the present Prime Minister Georges Pompidou, former professor of classics, high executive of the

Rothschild bank, member of the Council of State, collabora-
tor of de Gaulle since the days of the Provisional Government in 1944; André Malraux, prestigious intellectual
and writer, one-time communist sympathizer, fascinated by
de Gaulle since their first encounter during the war, and
since 1958 guardian of French *culture* in every government;
and Gaston Palewski, administrator-politician since the Third
Republic, deputy and one time Minister in the Fourth, diplo-
mat and cabinet member under de Gaulle whom he had
joined in the early days of the Free French in London.

The office of the Chief of State has been organized so as
to institutionalize the processes by which policy is not only
initiated and elaborated but frequently also executed. In
terms of function the staff at the Elysée Palace, composed of
a General Secretariat and the presidential cabinet, has become not unlike that of the Executive Office of the American
President, yet much smaller in size — a total of about thirty
persons.[5] Military personnel and political intimates of an
earlier period have been replaced almost entirely by high
civil servants. All the administrative *elite corps* (see Chap. V)
are now represented. The preponderance of members of the
diplomatic corps makes it easier for the Chief of State to
treat the Quai d'Orsay, the French Foreign Office, as he has
done for years, as an annex of his own office.

Staff members are not formally assigned to supervise each
of the administrative departments, but there exists a roughly
functional division. This leads frequently to parallel elaboration of policies by members of the Elysée staff and by the
Ministries. While this creates delays and confusion, as it does
in Washington, it also enables the President to let possibly
conflicting policy proposals confront each other until he
chooses between alternate solutions. Since it is known that
de Gaulle will not always side with his own staff, the competition between ideas, techniques, and priorities is frequently lively up to the moment of final presidential decision.

In line with the constitutional provision (art. 9), the Presi-

[5] For a description of the organization of the presidential staff, see Ridley and Blondel, *op. cit.*, p. 9, and André Passeron, "La Maison Civile du
Président de la République," *Le Monde,* Oct. 25 and 26, 1967.

dent chairs the Council of Ministers and does so as an active participant.[6] Cabinet meetings without him have become a rare occurrence. Debré's successor, Georges Pompidou, has interpreted the role of the Prime Minister as being primarily that of a chief of staff, and cabinet members have become the foremost technical advisors of the President (see also below).

Almost two years before the voters were asked to renew their confidence in General de Gaulle by electing him for a second term, the incumbent explained in starkly realistic terms the nature of his office and its significance for the policy process.[7] Almost every word of his interpretation of the constitution invites comparison with the totally different summary given less than six years earlier by the principal author of the text, Michel Debré. Compared with General de Gaulle's emphatically pragmatic explanation of what is, Debré's exposé of the constitutional construct had strongly ideological overtones. [Power], General de Gaulle said in 1964, "emanates directly from the people, which implies that the Head of State, elected by the nation, is the source and holder of this power." He insisted, " . . . that the individual authority of the State is entrusted completely to the President by the people who elected him, that there is no other authority — either ministerial, civilian, military, or judicial — which is not entrusted or maintained by him." As to the government, he described it as merely "sitting around him for the determination and application of policy and directing the administration."

During the same press conference General de Gaulle rejected, as Michel Debré had done before him but for different reasons, an American-type presidential system as unsuitable

[6] After the seven years of his first term, President de Gaulle during his press conference of September 9, 1965, ventured a statistical résumé of his activities: he had convened the Council of Ministers 302 times and inter-ministerial councils, bringing together several ministers on matters of common concern, 420 times. He had received the Prime Minister in his office 505 times, other members of the government 2,000 times, the Presidents of the Assemblies 78 times, chairmen or rapporteurs of parliamentary committees or parliamentary caucuses more than 100 times, top civil servants, experts, and group leaders about 1,500 times. See Andrews, *op. cit.,* pp. 61–62.

[7] In his press conference of January 3, 1964, *ibid.,* pp. 56–60.

for France. In fact, the differences in the policy process under the two regimes are enormous. There exists in present-day France no separation of powers and no effective provision for a system of checks and balances. By holding the threat of dissolution over parliament (art. 12) and by having at his disposal a number of other disciplinary devices which he can employ in conjunction with the government, the President is able to interfere directly with parliamentary organization and activities. He can invoke the jurisdiction of the Constitutional Council (arts. 56–63) when in his opinion parliament has transgressed its constitutional limitations. The control which the Council exercises over the constitutionality of legislation can in no way be compared to that of the American Supreme Court: it can never be invoked by a private citizen, nor can a minority in parliament appeal to it for a decision. The members of the Council are distinguished men but are selected primarily for political reasons. With minor exceptions, their relatively rare decisions have always strengthened the executive at the expense of parliament.[8]

In situations where the limited jurisdiction of the Constitutional Council cannot be or has not been invoked, the Chief of State has claimed that as guardian of the constitution he could sanction political practice by authoritative interpretation. In at least two widely discussed cases, the solution which he enforced was clearly in conflict with the wording of the constitutional text. Yet, in the absence of constitutional controls, his decisions could not be challenged effectively; both of them narrowed parliamentary prerogatives.[9]

The important role which the referendum has played in legitimizing presidential policies has already been discussed. The precedent created in the fall of 1962 and upheld by the Constitutional Council gives the President the initiative in the process of amending the constitution. (See Chap. IV.) It permits him to exclude parliament from this process by a di-

[8] See Maurice Duverger, *Institutions Politiques et Droit Constitutionnel* (Paris: Presses Universitaires, 1966), p. 653. Professor Duverger's treatise presents the most incisive analysis of constitutional law and constitutional practice during the Fifth Republic.

[9] *Ibid.,* p. 609 and p. 535.

rect appeal to the people. It is true that since 1962 the President has refrained from using such procedures; a minor constitutional revision has relied on concurring majorities in the two houses of parliament. But this does not preclude that in more dramatic situations the President's discretion could once more make the referendum into an instrument of extreme constitutional flexibility.

The enormous concentration of actual and potential power in the office of the presidency has so far taken place without invoking for more than a relatively short interlude the emergency powers attributed to the Chief of State by article 16. At the time the constitution was drafted, this provision was most arduously discussed. Its every word was fought over in a wrangle between the government and the Consultative Constitutional Committee which wished to safeguard as many guarantees as possible against the article's misuse.

In case of grave threat "to the institutions of the republic" (and in a number of other situations broadly and vaguely described), article 16 gives the President wider powers than even the Weimar constitution of Germany provided in its article 48 which served as a convenient cloak for legalizing the Nazi revolution. According to the constitution the French President may be indicted for high treason by a majority vote in the two houses of parliament and then tried by a High Court of Justice (art. 68). Since as soon as a state of emergency is declared parliament meets automatically and cannot be dissolved, a President who abuses his rights under article 16 could be brought to trial. But historical experience indicates that in a situation of dramatic tension he who holds power and controls the means of communication will be in the likeliest position to forestall an indictment by open ballot in parliament.

No other judicial controls limit the exercise of emergency powers as is the case in the United States.[10] While the French President must consult with other organs of government be-

---

[10] See, e.g., the well-known decision rendered during President Truman's administration: *Youngstown Sheet & Tube Co. et al. v. Sawyer,* 343 U.S. 579.

fore and during an emergency, he is under no constitutional obligation to heed the advice that might be tendered him.

Yet General de Gaulle has so far used his powers under article 16 only once, in 1961, at a moment when the rebellion of the generals in Algiers clearly justified such use.[11] The mutiny collapsed after a few days, not because a constitutional provision provided residual powers but because General de Gaulle's authority was unimpaired and hence left the rebels isolated and impotent. The fact that the state of emergency was not lifted until five months later violated, in the opinion of most, both the wording and the spirit of the text. Why this was done has never been made clear, particularly as the measures taken during the period (altogether sixteen acts of legislative character and of varying importance) did not infringe unduly upon civil liberties or other rights. The most likely explanation is that General de Gaulle wished to rehearse, as he has done frequently during his two terms in office, all available presidential roles to demonstrate that the period of executive weakness was gone forever.

Will the plenitude of powers inherent in the office become a danger to the democratic process under a President without the temperamental inhibitions of the present incumbent? To those who express such fears the defenders of the regime reply that the system is the very incarnation of democracy. Their arguments draw on the traditions of that plebiscitarian democracy which in France has frequently claimed preeminence over the model of a representative system (see Chap. I). According to their views, the dualism of parliament and executive checking on each other is crowned by what Frenchmen in the tradition of Rousseau like to call the monism of popular sovereignty. Its supreme manifestation is the popular election of the Chief of State. It is incumbent upon the President to stabilize the parliamentary system, always inclined towards "gallic effervescence," but his authority, this line of

---

[11] Excellent on that important episode is Martin Harrison, "The French Experiment of Exceptional Powers: 1961," *Journal of Politics,* XXV:2 (1963), pp. 139–58.

argument goes, is at all times subject to the commands of universal suffrage. Although the President is neither responsible to parliament nor subject to checks or controls by any other constitutional organ, he is nevertheless responsible to the sovereign people and to it alone. Elections and referenda become expressions of the general will and legitimize the concentration of power in one hand.[12]

If parliament were to withdraw its confidence from a government appointed by the Head of State, the presidential dissolution would invoke the voters' judgment. In other cases of conflict between parliament and the executive, the President can organize a referendum. If defeated, the President will have to abandon either his designs or his position, particularly as the constitution prescribes that a parliament elected after one dissolution cannot again be dissolved within a year following its election (art. 12). "Hence there is always a democratic way out," explained de Gaulle when he wanted to contrast this system with the recurring constitutional deadlocks in the United States.

In order to assure himself of the indispensable majority, President de Gaulle has "descended" into the political arena during all of the referendum campaigns and electoral battles that have been fought in the Fifth Republic. So far his personal popularity has been able to secure the approval he sought, even though the margin of success has been steadily reduced. (See Table V.) The test for the democratic quality of the established policy process will come if and when the verdict of universal suffrage disavows an omnipotent President during his term of office. The situation could be all the more critical as parliament is elected for only five years while the President is elected for seven without constitutional limitations on the number of his terms.

Until such a crisis has occurred and has been solved in accordance with the basic tenets of majority rule, the present setup has not established its claim of democratic legitimacy.

[12] For the most comprehensive statement of the Rousseauan justification of Gaullist practices, see René Capitant, "L'Aménagement du pouvoir exécutif et la question du chef de l'Etat," in *Encyclopédie Française*, X, pp. 142–62. Cf. also H. W. Ehrmann, "Direct Democracy," esp. pp. 891 ff.

## THE GOVERNMENT: RULE MAKING
## AND RULE APPLICATION

Since all powers proceed from the President of the Republic, the government headed by the Prime Minister has become essentially an organ of execution, notwithstanding a totally different description of its role in the constitution (art. 20). Its paramount function is to provide whatever is needed for the application of the policies conceived by the Chief of State. This means above all legislative enactments, whether they emanate from parliament or directly from the executive, and procurement of budgetary means either by parliamentary vote or by substitutes. The position which the government thus occupies resembles far more that of the cabinet in a presidential regime such as the United States, than that of a government in a parliamentary system such as Great Britain and the earlier French Republics.

In France as in most modern democracies the task of initiating legislation had long passed, from parliament to the executive. This function is now shared between the President and the government; but it is up to the President to determine in which affairs he wishes the government to exercise its share of rule initiation. Most notable however are the changes, even though they sometimes concern form more than substance, which the new regime has brought to the enactment of all legislative rulings. A number of constitutional provisions and of practices have seriously amputated the prerogatives of parliament (for details see Chap. X). By the same token and as would have been expected, broader legislative powers have accrued to the Executive. In many fields the government is able to implement presidential policies by legally enforceable enactments without recourse to parliament.[13]

The fact that no domain of governmental activity escapes presidential initiative and control does not mean that the members of the government are deprived of all autonomy and spontaneity. There is a great deal of interaction between

[13] For a succinct treatment of the complicated terminology of rule making in present-day France, see Ridley and Blondel, *op. cit.,* pp. 22 ff.

the President and the government, the presidential and ministerial staffs, and between the various cabinet members. The weekly meetings of the Council of Ministers under the chairmanship of the President have not only kept the decorum of earlier days, but are still a forum for deliberation and confrontation of viewpoints. The broader and more all-encompassing the executive powers of the President have become, the more patience General de Gaulle has shown for the reports presented by his Ministers and for the ensuing discussion.[14]

It is quite normal that these meetings are prepared by the more frequent gatherings of interministerial committees and by audiences which the President grants to the Prime Minister or to individual Ministers. Pompidou reportedly knows better than his more impetuous predecessor, Debré, how to distinguish between affairs of state which interest the President and those where the Prime Minister may, at least until further notice, act as chief executive rather than as chief of staff. He decides, accordingly, where and when the presidential staff or the Chief of State himself should be involved. Altogether he orders and expedites the flow of decision-making towards the President by minute preparation. Such working methods reduce the number of cases which the President has to arbitrate during meetings of the Council of Ministers.

Yet presidential arbitration is still invoked quite frequently to settle conflicts, such as those between the Minister of Finance as the holder of the purse and his ministerial colleagues who are "spendthrifts" by the nature of their functions. This is in itself a sign that even though ultimate decision-making is even more centralized than previously, the policy process has not suppressed the expression of a tra-

14 An excellent description of the sense and nonsense of Council meetings by a participant observer is given by Buron, *op. cit.*, pp. 218 ff. Interesting on the job of being a Minister under General de Gaulle is Bernard Chenot, *Etre Ministre* (Paris: Plon, 1967). De Gaulle himself has given an account of cabinet meetings during the time he headed the Provisional Government. (See *War Memoirs*, III, p. 143.) It seems that the proceedings are essentially unchanged and reminiscent of Lincoln's famous "The Ayes have it" when *his* "Aye" had been outvoted in a cabinet meeting.

ditional and natural clash of interests. The predominance of the *Rue de Rivoli* (that wing of the Louvre palace which houses the Ministry of Finance and of Economic Affairs) is of long standing and ensured by the excellence of its staff. Under the new regime, the authority of the Ministry has been on the increase for a variety of reasons: as mentioned previously, a developing economy is periodically in danger of overheating under inflationary pressures unless the Ministry of Finance exercises control; long tenure in office for the Minister has strengthened his authority with his own staff and thereby his effectiveness. Since most Ministers know that their projects have little chance of success if they incur the displeasure of the ubiquitous Corps of Finance Inspectors (see Chap. V), they will regularly seek the support of at least one of its members before the matter reaches the final stage of decision-making.[15]

Inasmuch as the Prime Minister is clearly more than a *primus inter pares* among his ministerial colleagues, the Fifth Republic continues and reinforces a development which has been underway at least since the end of the Second World War. The same is true of the expanding role which the General Secretariat of the Government plays in coordinating and accrediting policies. Its personnel has been astonishingly stable from one republic to another and forms the nucleus of the much larger Office of the Prime Minister. However, in contrast to former times, it has an influential counterpart in the General Secretariat of the President.

When the new regime was established, concern was expressed that the "dual executive" would inevitably weaken the authority of government and lead to serious conflicts between the President and the Prime Minister. Such conflicts have not arisen or at least have not come into the open because of the status which General de Gaulle has given to the presidency. The two incumbents in the office of Prime Minister have acted, as General de Gaulle has put it, "each in his own way and in a way that was not the same." But they have both subordinated their ideas and policies to those

[15] See Buron, *op. cit.*, pp. 214–17 for the relationship between the Ministry of Finance and the other administrations.

of the Chief of State and, from the very first, submitted the composition of their governments to General de Gaulle's approval. Pompidou has also been encouraged, undoubtedly by the President, to make himself more visible, not unlike an American Vice President. Hence he has appeared at certain critical political moments on television and has occasionally shared ceremonial functions with the Chief of State. Although General de Gaulle has refused to institutionalize lines of succession by constitutional stipulation or otherwise, he has offered Pompidou opportunities for serving an apprenticeship in the highest functions of state.

It falls to the Prime Minister, more than to any other member of the government, to provide the parliamentary majority which the system needs for correct functioning. He customarily defends the governmental, i.e. the presidential program, before the National Assembly, and at the approach of the elections of 1967 Pompidou also became the outspoken and quite authoritarian leader of the majority formed by the U.N.R. and the Independent Republicans. This role was all the more unusual for him as during his entire career he has had no other contact with politics than his devotion and usefulness to General de Gaulle.[16]

Governmental "stability" is one of the most striking differences between the present and the preceding regimes. In the eleven years and five months of its life, the Fourth Republic experienced a total of twenty cabinets and disquietingly lengthy periods of *crises* during which an interim government held office between the fall of one Prime Minister and the designation of his successor. In the Fifth Republic, there have been but two Prime Ministers and each of the cabinets over which they presided identified closely with the policy of a single Chief of State. The point has been made that to highlight these facts exaggerates the difference between the two systems. Before 1958, it is true, the combination of the French party system and the habits of the political class

[16] For a political biography of Pompidou (there exists none of Debré), see Merry Bromberger, *Le destin secret de Georges Pompidou* (Paris: Fayard, 1965). Less panegyrical but more succinct, Pierre Viansson-Ponté, *op. cit.*, pp. 229–33.

made the overthrow of ministries unavoidable; nonetheless, the same personnel appeared in many cabinets, and the permanence of policies was quite impressive. On the other hand, there has been a frequent and quite extensive reshuffling of ministerial posts under both Debré's and Pompidou's premierships. The important Ministry of Agriculture and Ministry of Education have not only changed hands but also policies many times. Even in the Ministry of Finance, the replacement of Giscard d'Estaing by Debré resulted in an overturn of orientation and, to a certain extent, of personnel.

Moreover, the very structure of the government and of the ministries has frequently been altered.[17] This in turn has resulted in uncertainties and a loss of effectiveness, so that at least in certain fields the permanent civil service or a ministry's clientele have complained that they were as little governed as before. During the first years of the regime additional confusion arose when unexpected presidential directives nullified policies developed by a ministry. Although for the time being this particular difficulty has somewhat subsided, it may be imminent in a system with a twin-headed executive.

Additional stability has accrued to the government of the Fifth Republic from another widely heralded innovation. Previously, as is normal in a parliamentary regime and mandatory in most, practically all members of the government held seats in either of the two houses of parliament; once their function in a cabinet had ended for one reason or other, they returned to their elective post. The new constitution stipulates that a position in the government is incompatible with parliamentary office (art. 23). Within one month of taking office, members of government must give up their seats for good until the end of the legislative period. In order to avoid frequent by-elections, the ballots for election to the National Assembly list in addition to the candidate a replacement who takes over the seat in parliament if it falls vacant because of such compulsory resignation or for other reasons.

[17] For the make-up of the first two Pompidou Cabinets, see Ridley and Blondel, *op. cit.*, p. 12. Since then the structure has again been changed substantially.

This provision satisfied Debré's dogmatic insistence on a clear distinction between the executive and the legislature. He was not alone in deploring that in the past all too often ministers had been guided by narrow constituency interests. In a system in which the lines between government and opposition were never clearly drawn, members of a government were also known to plot for the downfall of the cabinet to which they themselves belonged. Certain as they were of always returning to their seats in parliament, they did not risk much. But by such maneuvers they could hope to reach a better place in the ministerial hierarchy of a future government.

In the midst of antiparliamentarian sentiment such as prevailed in 1958, the incompatibility provision was heralded as a step towards the purification of political morals. But both General de Gaulle and Debré also hoped that it would attract technicians and civil servants to cabinet posts rather than politicians, so that the scope of "politics" in decision-making could be reduced by yet another device.

Both fears and hopes that the new arrangement might alter drastically the recruitment of parliamentary and ministerial personnel and thereby the conditions of the political process, proved unfounded. Whatever changes occurred were either temporary or were caused by general transformations rather than by a constitutionally decreed incompatibility. The cabinet which Pompidou formed after the elections of 1967 is composed of about thirty members, the customary size in France. Most of them are in charge of an administrative department. Others, the Ministers of State, have only a small staff assisting them in specific functions, such as administrative reform, scientific research, relations with parliament, etc. A third group, the Secretaries of State, are all attached to the office of a senior Minister and correspond therefore to an Undersecretary in the United States, but they too are members of the cabinet and participate in its working sessions, "sitting around the President," as General de Gaulle put it.

In their composition all the cabinets of the Fifth Republic have represented a political makeup reminiscent of the coalition building in the preceding regime and even of the "balanced ticket" in an American election. The various political tendencies within the dominant party — the U.N.R., the Independent Republicans and those without any party affiliation — have all received recognition in the distribution of more or less exalted posts in the cabinet.

In Debré's cabinet of 1959, well over one-third of the Ministers had never stood for parliamentary election, most of them being career civil servants. In 1967, all but two of the cabinet members had been candidates in the previous elections; the two exceptions were André Malraux as Minister of Cultural Affairs and Jean-Marcel Jeanneney, Minister of Social Affairs, a university professor and son of an eminent politician during the Third Republic. Even the Prime Minister ran for elective office for the first time in his life and won the election easily on the first ballot. By contrast two prominent members of the cabinet, the Ministers of Foreign Affairs and of the Armed Forces, who had run for the National Assembly in carefully selected constituencies were defeated; this, it is true, did not prevent them from continuing in the posts which they had held previously in Pompidou's cabinet. It is likely that Couve de Murville, who has been Foreign Minister since 1958, and who is the prototype of a high official in the diplomatic corps felt ill at ease as a political candidate.

A comparison between the present and the initial practices of the regime suggests that now an attempt is being made to build bridges between the executive and parliament rather than to separate them too rigidly. Members of the government (and their party, if they belong to any) are encouraged to have a firm rooting in a constituency, even though they must resign their seat in the National Assembly upon assuming their cabinet post. There are many indications that the voters expect, as they have in the past, special benefits from the fact that "their" deputy belongs to the government even while he is represented in parliament by a proxy. And in fact the Ministers of the Fifth Republic see to it that their constituencies are given special consideration. Moreover, a number of

Ministers have by now won local government positions, as mayors or members of the Municipal and Departmental Councils.

In part, this development reflects somewhat disappointing experiences with the technician-civil servants in the cabinet. It first became apparent to the ranking bureaucrats in their own Ministries, that a Minister with no support outside the civil service did not have enough political weight in the councils of government, especially in negotiations with the Ministry of France and the staff of the Elysée. Then some of the Ministers themselves understood what advantages for their own effectiveness and authority they could derive from a political mandate.

What might be described as a victory of politics over technocratic illusions does not mean that the present (and future) cabinets of the Fifth Republic will be manned entirely by members of the traditional "political class," as described earlier (see Chap. V). Rather, the personnel of the government represents a new breed and, with some exceptions, a somewhat youthful one. More than half of the present cabinet members belong to one or the other of the elite administrative corps. But during their careers, before as well as after 1958, they have wandered in and out of political appointments and sometimes elective office. The variety of their assignments indicates that they are temperamentally unwilling to be content with a life of bureaucratic routine. Of course, as members of the Council of State, the diplomatic, prefectoral, and other corps, they also enjoy the undiminished prestige of choice positions. If this amalgam of politics and of administration appears to be a significant development, the Fifth Republic has merely accelerated it, for it was well underway before.

Another traditional institution of governmental practice that has continued into the Fifth Republic draws its strength from similar trends. Each French minister has long surrounded himself with a group of personal collaborators, his *cabinet* (the ministerial *cabinet* is, of course, to be distinguished from the cabinet which is the government as a whole). The members of his *cabinet* have always served as the Minister's eyes and ears in the agency which he directs, whereas in other countries the top civil servants in each Ministry are entrusted with such a task. In the past, the frequent changes of government justified an institution which gave to the Minister some leverage with a bureaucracy always suspected of seeking to sabotage policy directives which it knew to be ephemeral.

But although under the present regime the life span of ministerial office has been lengthened, the ministerial *cabinets* have proven as indispensable as before — some Ministers have even enlarged their *cabinets* far beyond the legal limit of ten members. The particularities of French bureaucratic organization and the obstacles it puts in the way of innovation explain much of this phenomenon. Insufficient communication between different strata within the same agency leaves the holder of power so isolated that he is unable to overcome inflexible habits and to make a break in routine even when changes in the environment make such a break-through necessary. Here the members of the ministerial *cabinet* are called upon to overcome an isolation that would otherwise condemn an innovative Minister to impotence. For analogous reasons, the practice of attaching a *cabinet* to the office of those holding positions of command has become fairly generalized in large-scale organizations in both the public and the private sector.

At the ministerial level, the *cabinets* form a link between politics and administration and between administration and the outer environment; the latter comprising organized and potential interests as well as other administrations.[18] Before the war, and for a short time at the beginnings of both the Fourth and the Fifth Republics, Ministers frequently appointed their own political friends, journalists, or other "experts in communication," to *cabinet* positions. But gradually, for the sake of greater effectiveness, an increasing number of high civil servants has entered the *cabinets* and today dominates them. Their intimate knowledge of the workings of the bureaucratic machinery has proven indispensable. If they

[18] The literature on the *cabinets* is rich and interesting. Much of it is quoted in H. W. Ehrmann, "French Bureaucracy," pp. 545 ff., and "Bureaucracy and Interest Groups," pp. 279–80.

were mere line officials they might be unable or unwilling to overcome inertia; hence they are usually on detached service from other administrations and often belong to the elite corps whose mobility and interest in innovation have been described above (see Chap. V). In a period of sustained modernization their skills and working methods are in great demand. What distinguishes them from other civil servants, and this is especially true of those who have made careers in several different *cabinets,* is a special political sensitivity. The fact that the same quality characterizes the numerous Ministers who combine administrative experience with political office facilitates collaboration. In addition, a common social origin and educational background enhance lateral connections between the members of various ministerial *cabinets.*

All this explains why of late the *cabinets* have become a training ground and a source of recruitment for high political office, including junior Ministers in the government.

**THE CIVIL SERVICE:**
**MOTOR OR INSTRUMENTALITY?**

Because of its frank emphasis on the prestige and the procedures of the administrative state, and because of its dislike for "party politics," it was expected that the new regime would greatly increase the weight of the bureaucracy in the policy process. What has come about is, in fact, a seemingly contradictory but internally quite consistent development. On the one hand, the executive has subjected the bureaucracy to more stringent political controls, but, on the other, the domain open to decision-making by the technicians in the civil service has been enlarged considerably.[19] As Table VI shows, the number of civil servants rose rather steeply during the first years of the Fifth Republic; it continues to rise.

[19] This proposition was first put forward by Georges Vedel in his contribution to a roundtable concerned with "Technocracy and the Role of Experts in Government," organized by the Fifth World Congress of the *International Political Science Association* and held in Paris in 1961. Since then his thesis has been widely accepted as essentially correct. See also Victor Silvera, "Réflexions sur la stabilité gouvernementale et l'action administrative depuis 1958," *La Revue Administrative,* XVII (1964), pp. 545–55.

TABLE VI

| Full Time Civilian Public Employees * | 1956 | % Total Labor Force | 1965 | % Total Labor Force |
|---|---|---|---|---|
| National Government: | | | | |
| Civil Servants | 953,000 | 4.89 | 1,171,000 | 6.01 |
| Workers with civil service status | 156,000 | 0.80 | 139,000 | 0.71 |
| Local Government: | | | | |
| all levels | 437,000 | 2.24 | 552,000 | 2.83 |
| Total | 1,546,000 | 7.93 | 1,862,000 | 9.55 |

* These figures do not include those employed by nationalized enterprises, such as coal mines, railroads, and by the social security system (total of about 1,000,000).

Source: Roland Drago, *Cours de Science Administrative. Faculté de Droit de Paris* (Paris: Les Cours de Droit, 1966–1967), pp. 181–182.

Inasmuch as the rule-making power of the government has been extended, numerous rulings, whether of primary or secondary importance, have been formulated and codified by the civil service. At the start of the Fifth Republic, the staff of most ministries produced out of their desk drawers legislative texts which had been laid to rest there for months if not for years. For contrary to widespread belief, the bureaucracy had not been able to rule the Fourth Republic at will while ministries toppled; at the approach of every governmental crisis all projects of more than routine nature were shelved. During the first months after the promulgation of the new constitution and in conformity with its temporary dispositions (arts. 91, 92), a substantial number of long-delayed bills was enacted into law by the Council of Ministers.

Since then, top-ranking bureaucrats have prepared important policy decisions in every detail without consulting parliament or other elective bodies. Some of the measures for which the technicians in the government bureaus assumed *de facto* responsibility and about which there was little or no discussion in parliament, were the currency reform of 1958 and the host of economic measures accompanying it; the stabilization plan of 1961 with its far-reaching consequences; the thorough reforms of the court and social security systems. The complete revamping of the administrative structure of the Paris region, affecting more than nine million people and far more important than the changes introduced by Baron Haussman during the days of Napoleon III, was briefly debated in parliament, but in all essentials was shaped by governmental bureaus.[20] Many important *ad hoc* committees advising the government on long-range policy planning have been manned exclusively by civil servants. (It is true that by submitting the modernization plan to parliament at various stages of its elaboration, the government of the Fifth Republic took a step which the preceding regime had not dared to take for fear of seeing its objectives assaulted by special interests.)

Whether or not the animosity of the high bureaucracy towards parliament is actually greater than that of the population at large might be doubted (on this question see above Chap. V). But the lessening of controls and of interference by members of parliament is generally welcomed as a boon to administrative efficiency. Nationalized enterprise and the entire public sector of the economy have been freed almost completely from parliamentary supervision. The taste of the regime for secrecy and its preference for carefully channeled information correspond well to the working methods of the French bureaucracy. And even though a change of Ministers has been a fairly frequent occurrence, the civil service has on the whole welcomed the greatly increased governmental stability, as it has the ending of constant currency depreciation. While inflationary pressures are still felt (see Chap. II), they are less strong than in the recent past when they forced a constant revising and revamping of administrative projects. This explains why even those civil servants who were inimical to Gaullism on political grounds have in general greeted with satisfaction the restoration of governmental authority and the stabilization of financial resources.

But the restoration of authority has strengthened executive controls in many respects. For all his exaltation of technical

[20] The contrasting routes to metropolitan reform followed by Greater London and Greater Paris offered a striking example of the enormous differences between the policy process in present-day Britain and France. For London, see Frank Smallwood, *Greater London: The Politics of Metropolitan Reform* (Indianapolis: Bobbs-Merrill, 1965).

expertise and his depreciation of politics, one of the most articulate spokesmen of the regime, Michel Debré has long insisted that it was not the bureaucracy's role to rule but to serve a strongly governed state. The manner in which the Office of the President of the Republic issues policy directives and follows up on their transformation into administrative rulings corresponds to such a model. With increasing frequency the Elysée has overruled unceremoniously some long-established technicians and their coteries in a number of Ministries.

In the relationships between the Ministers, the members of their *cabinets,* and the administrative personnel, the lines separating the initiation and the execution of policies are of necessity less neatly drawn. For reasons that have been explained previously, there exists on these levels considerable homogeneity of functions and of mentality. Frequently a Minister and his staff become mere executive agents of presidential policies. But where leeway is left, the technician-ministers as well as the technician-civil servants (whether they be line officials or belong to a *cabinet*) become directly involved in establishing political priorities and thereby in decision-making.

Whether such an amalgamation of the political and the technical has resulted in greater bureaucratic efficiency cannot be determined in any generalized fashion. Seeming technical conflicts may lead to deadlocks in decision-making. The immobilism thus caused is no longer blasted apart, as it might have been in the past, by the dynamics of a frankly political decision coming from outside the bureaucracy.[21] And in fact, what appears as a disagreement over the most appropriate technical solution is frequently caused by controversies over fundamentals. The great problems which France has had to face and continues to face have divided the bureaucracy as they have other elites. The Algerian war and decolonization; European integration; foreign defense and atomic policies;

---

[21] This point was forcefully made by one of the outstanding technocrats in the high civil service, Bloch-Lainé. For his statement and a similar one by Viansson-Ponté, see Pierre Avril, *Le Régime Politique de la Ve République* (Paris: Librairie Générale de Droit, 1964), p. 196.

economic and social planning have been among such problems. The country's participation in the European Common
Market has had a considerable impact on administrative behavior and decision-making. French bureaucracy has shoul-
dered the new tasks with great talent and dexterity. But
where a choice between alternative solutions has to be made,
interagency disputes have arisen for which arbitration has not
always been available.

As has been explained earlier (see Chap. VII), validly organized interests are now concentrating their efforts almost
exclusively on the bureaucracy. An administration which is
exposed directly to unaggregated demands, without the shield
of political parties or of parliament, is frequently buffeted by
conflicting interests and in danger of losing coherence and
effectiveness in the process. Under these conditions the bureaucracy may find it more difficult, rather than easier, to live
up to its self-image as the guardian of the general interest.

So far the new regime has neither undertaken nor even announced a thorough reform of the country's administrative
structures. Hence the perennial trend towards an almost spontaneous centralization resulting frequently in the transfer of
decision-making to the next higher if not the highest echelon
has continued. There also is little counterweight to the compartmentalization of administrators into divided hierarchies
between which communication is often deficient. (For details
see Chap. V.) Individual efforts of some Ministers to overcome
such obstacles to political modernization have usually ended
in failure. It is quite characteristic that some pragmatic attempts to introduce more suppleness into administrative
procedures have been criticized high and low as infringements
upon standards of strict equality. From other quarters complaints are heard that the resulting uncertainties are an im-
pediment to investment and hence to economic development.

Nonetheless, the increasing involvement of the bureaucracy
in tasks concerned with the development of economic and
human resources has modified some of the rigidities in bureaucratic structures and working methods. It also has motivated the one major administrative reform which the new

regime has initiated, in addition to the reorganization of the Paris region.

When in 1962 the Modernization Plans began to attack seriously the imbalance in economic development between various regions (see Chap. II), it soon became apparent that the organization of the country into 90 departments, carved out in the eighteenth century, was cramping the needed effort. Conceived as a rational division of territory and as a counter-weight against excessive centralization, regionalism in France has a long and honorable tradition.[22] However, the Fifth Republic seems to have given no consideration to plans of merging departments and thereby undermining their power structure which is headed by the prefects. Quite to the contrary, whenever President de Gaulle has traveled through the French countryside, he has paid tribute to the particularities of each individual department and to its traditional elites, the prefects and the notables surrounding him. A true decentralization which would have made the prefects (or other newly created provincial authorities) less dependent on binding directives from Paris would have run counter to habits of centralization. It also would be unworkable as long as the resources needed for regional development have to be pumped in from the capital.

After many hesitations, a series of decrees issued in 1964 has attempted to enlarge the departmental framework and to co-ordinate the field services of the various Ministries concerned with regional development, without however undermining the authority of the prefect as representative of the central government. The country is now divided into twenty-one regions, each comprising several departments (see Map p. 22). In each region one of the prefects is designated prefect of the region. His very extensive responsibilities (which he carries on in addition to his normal duties as prefect of a department) consist in im-

[22] See Stanley Hoffmann, "The Areal Division of Powers in the Writings of French Political Thinkers," in Arthur Maas (ed.), *Area and Power, A Theory of Local Government* (Glencoe, Ill.: Free Press, 1959), pp. 113–49, and the fairly complete review of past thinking and efforts, by Lawrence Gladieux, "Regionalism in France," *Public and International Affairs,* V:1 (1967), pp. 135–57.

plementing the government's policy for regional development and the objectives set for the region by the Planning Office. It is he who supervises and coordinates the numerous field services of the national administrations, operating either on the regional or the departmental level.[23]

In order to enable the prefect of the region to discharge his manifold functions, a number of new institutions have been created, fashioned partly after the working methods of the Planning Office in Paris. They are undoubtedly the most original part of the new setup. On their effectiveness may depend not only the administrative success of regional development but also the possible significance of this experience for more far-reaching administrative reforms. The prefect of the region is materially assisted by a *mission,* a brain trust composed of high if generally young civil servants detached from various central administrations. In addition, he has to consult regularly the Regional Development Board, the CODER. Depending upon the importance of the region, the CODER is made up of between twenty and fifty members, half of them designated by interest groups, chambers of commerce, and the like, one fourth appointed by the Prime Minister, and the other fourth composed of traditional, elected leaders such as mayors and members of the departmental councils. One of the foremost tasks incumbent upon the regional prefect, his staff and his advisory body, is to decide on the proper distribution of the public investments available for regional development.

On paper this scheme looks like an ingenious if deliberately ambiguous blending of old and new. While it does not envisage a decentralization of powers, it provides for the deconcentration of functions. It could further the collaboration between the hierarchy of line officials and the younger technocrats whose training and interests are more functionally oriented, between local government authorities and organized interests, including the *"forces vives"* (see Chap. VII). If it

23 For a complete account of the new institutions, see Jean Hourticq, "La vie administrative dans les circonscriptions d'action régionale," *International Review of Administrative Sciences,* XXXI:1 (1965), pp. 8–12, with a summary in English, pp. ii–iii. For the earlier attempts at regional development, see Ridley and Blondel, *op. cit.,* pp. 226–32.

were fully implemented, the new regional organization could overcome existing rigidities and initiate better communications between all interested parties. Through the prefect of the region, it could make its administration into an agency of change and modernization in an area where both have become urgent.

It is too early to decide whether and to what extent the intended reforms will amount to more than organizational façades and generous declarations of intent. So far spontaneous and organized resistance to the arrangement has already made itself felt and has multiplied rather than abated. The fate of this reform might offer a fascinating example of the obstacles which a traditional mentality and corresponding structures are still able to put in the way of innovation.[24] Much of the resistance seems to come from the prefects of the single departments and of the subprefects in the *arrondissements,* the departmental subdivisions. To them the institution of a regional prefect, even though they share his training and career, is a violation of the principle of equality of all prefects before their common "sovereign," the Minister of the Interior. In the past, this equality has been safeguarded by the virtual isolation of each prefect in his department, an isolation which the regional institutions seek to overcome. Now the prefect of the region is suspected of seeking preferential treatment for his own department, since he controls the channeling of all economic information concerning the entire region to the Ministries in Paris. Certain prefects seem to fear that a long-established equilibrium, already endangered by urban growth and industrial deconcentration, will be further and definitely upset.

So far prefectural antagonism has condemned many of the regional brain trusts to ineffectiveness. In their opposition the prefects and their staffs can frequently count on local notables as their allies. The generally underrated solidarity between the prefects and the local government authorities (described

[24] For an account of the ongoing process see Pierre Grémion, "Résistance au changement de l'administration territoriale: le cas des institutions régionales," *Sociologie du Travail,* VIII:3 (1966), pp. 276–95. At an earlier stage of his careful inquiry, the same author had been far more optimistic, see his *La Mise en place des institutions régionales* (Paris: Centre de Recherche de Sociologie des Organisations, 1965).

above Chap. IV) has found new terrain in a common front against the staff of the regional prefect. Some popular mayors have publicly challenged (sometimes to the face of the visiting President of the Republic) the legitimacy of the CODER which the government is trying to accredit. All this means that until now the intended blending of the old with the new has resulted in a clash the final outcome of which cannot yet be foretold.

During the first years of the new regime, it appeared likely that the military bureaucracy, the career officers' corps, would claim a leading role in the political process. A number of generals stationed in Algeria had played an important part in the events which brought General de Gaulle back to power. At least some expected that their vision of a "forever French" Algeria and their views on the proper running of the French state would be given commensurate recognition.

The relationship between the French Republic and its standing army has been frequently beset by tensions. Both sides, the military as well as the political class, have felt mutually estranged. After the Dreyfus Affair had discredited the officers corps, the army retreated to the position of a "great mute," until its defeat in the Second World War brought it back to prominence in the armistice regime of Marshal Pétain. It is worth noting that political muteness, which should be the normal stance of the armed forces in a democracy, was frequently regarded in France as a remarkable phenomenon even by those who acknowledged it with relief.

The military and political events of the Second World War, followed by years of rear-guard fighting in colonial wars, threw the officers corps into deep crisis. It took long to heal the split between those who had sided with the Vichy regime and those who had fought for the Free French. When General de Gaulle attempted after the war to bring about the amalgamation of both sides with those who had participated as military men in the resistance movement, he failed. Instead, his own act of insubordination in June of 1940 became a lodestar for officers who wished to justify disobedience to authority by claiming a higher legitimacy for their actions. Many officers who found it difficult to adjust to the political and moral climate of post-war France found solace in the campaigns of Indochina and Algeria. Feeling more and more misunderstood by the political elites and by large sectors of the population, the "military society" grew apart from society at large. It formed a subsystem, with its own norms of behavior, values, and symbols.[25] However much the officers were opposed to Communism, their isolation resembled in many respects that of the working class in sympathy with the P.C.

It is however incorrect to assume that a homogeneous mentality distinguished the officers corps. The officers' ideas were frequently found to vary according to different experiences in the wars and in prisoner-of-war camps, or according to the services to which they belonged. Nevertheless, a lack of understanding for political realities, both national and international, characterized many of their divergent viewpoints. Their isolation from society was maintained and aggravated by a process of self-selection. Today almost 40 per cent of those attending officers' candidate schools are the sons of officers. But promotions from the ranks of noncommissioned officers are also a frequent occurrence. On a more limited scale, the career of an army officer has become, like that of other civil servants, a means of social promotion. For this reason, today's officers corps is more representative of the country's social structure than the officers of the past who came largely from aristocratic or upper bourgeoisie backgrounds. It is ironical that the feudally oriented army of earlier days had on the whole remained loyal to republican institutions, while a more democratic officers corps took it upon itself to challenge the democratic basis of both the Fourth and the Fifth Republics.[26]

A high army officer greeted General de Gaulle's return to power in terms which were indicative of the political role certain general officers felt entitled to play in this and any crisis situation: "At grave hours when the sovereign voice of

[25] See R. Girardet (ed.), *La Crise Militaire Française, 1945–1962* (Paris: Colin, 1964). For the mentality and politics of the officers corps during the period of the Vichy regime, see the study by Robert O. Paxton, *Parades and Politics at Vichy: The French Officers Corps under Marshal Pétain* (Princeton: Princeton University Press, 1966).

[26] See Hoffmann, in *In Search of France*, p. 52.

the people can no longer express itself, the ARMY suddenly becomes aware of what it is: the people under the Flag. Then the Army takes responsibility for the People." [27] (Capitals in the original.)

After it turned out that such was not the place General de Gaulle was willing to reserve to the army, the latter challenged the government once more, most dramatically in the Algerian uprising of 1961, only to find out at once that its isolation was complete.

The generals' ambition and the junior officers' dream of a new Algerian community uniting Frenchmen and Arabs had estranged the army activists from practically everybody: not only from the government authorities in Paris and Algiers but also from the white settlers, not only from liberal but also from right-wing politicians, and last but not least, from the conscript soldiers. The rebellion did not extend beyond a few elite units (if the Foreign Legion can be regarded as such). Their defeat not only sealed the fate of the putsch but put once more an end to the political role of the officers corps.

Undoubtedly the professional soldiers were more embittered against General de Gaulle than they had been against the political leadership of the Fourth Republic, since in their eyes de Gaulle had betrayed hopes which the previous regime had never truly raised. When rebellious officers and members of the military organizations carrying out terrorist acts were brought to trial, the defendants spoke the language of fundamental revolt against the existing state. The feelings they voiced were quite similar to those of the rightist extremists in pre-Hitler Germany. But while the German fanatics were hero-worshiped and, if convicted, regarded as martyrs by broad strata of public opinion, the French officers felt at best surrounded by indifference. The repeated plebiscitarian approval of de Gaulle's policies was tantamount to popular disapproval of an autonomous army position.

With the actual end of fighting in Algeria, special legislation drastically reduced the number of professional officers and men in the army, robbing them of a sense of career security. At

[27] Admiral Ortoli, "Général de Gaulle, soldat, écrivain, homme d'Etat," *Revue de la Défense Nationale,* IX (1959), p. 504.

present the total number of professional soldiers amounts to about 300,000 men. New recruitment of capable officer material has become difficult; voluntary resignations from the officers corps are said to be numerous, although exact data are not made available. But contrary to certain expectations (and again contrary to what happened in Germany after the First World War), the reintegration of officers into civilian life and occupations has generally been easy. This seems to indicate that the cleavage between the military and civil society has not been deep enough to prevent individuals from passing from one into the other.

Morale among those who have stayed on is not high. New weaponry, especially atomic, holds fascination for only a relatively small number of officers. For others, the failure of the high command to provide updated equipment and to overhaul the organization of the armed forces has meant simply more broken promises. The disengagement of the army from NATO forces seems to have been accepted with mixed feelings, since the officers corps was not of one mind regarding Atlantic defense policies.

If there is a latent crisis in the army, it is also far from acute. If opposition is voiced at all, it speaks the language of an interest group concerned with the security and welfare of its members. Fairly widespread dejection has facilitated the return to political muteness. Even the highest placed officers remain voluntarily distant from the process of policy formation.

# CHAPTER X

# Policy Processes — II

## PARLIAMENT: THE NATIONAL ASSEMBLY — FROM OMNIPOTENCE TO IMPOTENCE

The constitution-makers of 1958 had the announced ambition of endowing France with a "true" parliamentary regime, with "a Parliament," in the words of General de Gaulle, "intended to represent the political will of the nation, to enact laws and to control the executive, *without venturing to overstep its role.*" [1] Ever since the establishment of the Third Republic, constitutional and political discussions had centered on the question of the proper role of parliament in the policy process. The prevailing distrust of executive authority had tipped the balance in favor of tight and continuous supervision of the government by both houses of parliament. Techniques to make such supervision effective were developed early and steadily refined over time.[2] Their major purpose was to make the government dependent for its survival on a, however heterogeneous, majority of deputies. In both the Third and the Fourth Republic the power of the government to counteract a vote of censure, i.e., a threat to its own existence, by dissolving parliament and calling for new elections was constitutionally granted. But one early misuse of this right

[1] Speech of General de Gaulle of Sept. 4, 1958 (italics supplied), Andrews (ed.), *op. cit.,* p. 42.

[2] Williams, *Crisis,* pp. 208 ff., gives the most complete account of parliamentary activities in the Fourth Republic. For the same period, see also MacRae, *op. cit.,* pp. 181 ff. and *passim.*

by a military President (General MacMahon in 1877) had been enough to deprive this governmental privilege of its republican respectability and legitimacy. Hence it fell into disuse.

In the French republics the concept of parliamentary "sovereignty" included more than the right to cause the downfall of the government. It also left parliament at all times in complete control of its own proceedings and gave it the choice of topics to be debated. Its committees were entitled to alter the text of bills proposed by the government, even before they were considered by the Assembly. Like Congressional Committees, and unlike the corresponding bodies in the House of Commons, the standing committees of both houses were highly specialized which facilitated the access of interest groups to the center of decision-making. The constant watch which parliamentary committees kept over each of the ministries was all the more effective because the chairman of an important committee was often regarded as the most likely successor to the incumbent Minister. Such an assumption would hold even where committee chairman and Minister belonged to the same party.

Besides its other effects, the political harassment of the government led to the physical and mental exhaustion of its members — this has been described by many politicians of the period in their memoirs, and it perturbed Colonel Charles de Gaulle in his encounters with the leaders of the Third Republic.[3] Yet formal supremacy was not sufficient to give to the parliaments of the Third and Fourth Republics that power which institutions derive from an effective handling of their functions. Having sought to fuse parliamentary and executive functions, a parliament desirous of keeping the executive weak weakened itself in the process. Since there was no longer any clear focus for decision-making, the resulting loss of momentum communicated itself to all parts of the policy machinery, to parliament as well as to government.

The way in which parliament discharged its role as lawmaker illustrates the impotence of seeming omnipotence. In French constitutional doctrine, every single law is the expres-

[3] De Gaulle, *War Memoirs*, I, pp. 26 ff.

sion of the general will — by which the people through their representatives manifest their sovereignty. At least on the level of theoretical considerations, every statute takes on the same symbolic significance which the constitution has in the United States. Since only parliament can enact a law, only another act of parliament can rescind it.[4] But political realities have deprived the legislator of so exalted a place.

When after the First World War and especially during the depression of the Thirties a more active role was thrust upon the state, a parliament which lacked stable majorities proved unable to provide the needed legislation. In order to avoid chaos, it periodically abandoned its legislative authority to the government. During the interwar years, eleven governments obtained special powers from parliament to override existing laws and to enact new legislation by so-called decree-laws. "While decree-laws enabled the executive to act where the legislature would not, they encouraged evasion of responsibility by the deputies and of parliamentary control by the administration . . . the authority given was very widely drawn and still more widely interpreted."[5] Because of an unsteady party system, the composition and political orientation of a government never conformed for long with the wishes which the electorate might have expressed in the previous elections. To give but one example: although no new elections had taken place, in 1938 decree-laws annuled important parts of the social legislation which the Popular Front government had enacted two years earlier, and deputies who had turned over an essential part of their functions to an unrepresentative cabinet lost the respect of their constituents.

The constitution of the Fourth Republic sought to forestall such practices and their political consequences by addressing a stern prohibition to the National Assembly against delegating its legislative authority. But since the reasons for political disorder had not been removed and no disciplined majority

[4] For a classical (and remarkable) statement of the exalted role of the law in French constitutional thinking, see R. Carré de Malberg, *La Loi, expression de la volonté générale. Etude sur le concept de la loi dans la Constitution de 1875* (Paris: Recueil Sirey, 1931).

[5] Williams, *Crisis*, p. 270. See *ibid.*, pp. 271 ff. for interesting details on the practice followed in the Fourth Republic.

emerged in parliament, constitutional provisions were flouted. Using only slightly different techniques than before the war, parliament found ways to surrender its sovereign powers as the law-making authority to the executive. Yet as if to compensate for such weakness, it continuously shortened the life span of succeeding governments.

In line with previously developed Gaullist principles, the constitution of 1958 strove to put an end to the subordination of the government to parliament. The framers of the new text were in exactly the opposite position from that in which the founding fathers of the new Bonn constitution had found themselves about a decade earlier. After the experiences of the Nazi regime and of the Weimar Republic, the Federal Republic of Germany wished to give its parliament, the *Bundestag*, a central role in the political system,[6] while the Fifth Republic was to divest the National Assembly of such a role. Debré's acknowledged model was the political system of Great Britain where the place of parliament in policy-making is as well defined (though by custom rather than by law) as it is strictly limited. Whether Debré fully understood that such limitations are primarily an outcome of the party discipline which permits the Cabinet to control the majority in the House of Commons, is a moot question. He simply started with the assumption that the French voter could never be expected to send coherent majorities to the National Assembly.

Therefore the constitution and the so-called organic laws, enacted in conjunction with the constitution, fitted strict rules of behavior, something like a steel corset, on each individual deputy and on parliament as a body. This, it was hoped, would ensure what Debré and General de Gaulle have repeatedly described as the needed equilibrium between parliament and the executive.

Now the cabinet, not parliament, is effectively in control of proceedings in both houses and can require priority for bills which it wishes to push. While previously both the National Assembly and the upper house, the Senate, sat almost per-

---

[6] See Gerhard Loewenberg, *Parliament in the German Political System* (Ithaca: Cornell University Press, 1966), p. 432.

manently, they are now confined to sessions of closely regulated length (amounting to a maximum of six months), so that "the government has time to reflect and to act." [7] It is true that the constitution foresees the possibility of parliament's meeting in special session on a specific agenda at the request of either the Prime Minister or of the majority of the deputies (art. 29). But when in 1960 the required number of deputies expressed the wish to meet in a special session to deliberate on farmers' grievances, President de Gaulle advised the speaker of the Assembly that he would refuse to accede to this demand since in his opinion the deputies' request had been made under pressure from agricultural interest groups. As guardian of the spirit of the constitution he considered it his role to ward off such pressures when they were brought to bear on the representatives of the nation.[8] Hereby a precedent was set, requiring, in spite of the wording of the constitution, the assent of the President of the Republic to any demand for parliament to meet in special session.

It is still the parliament's function to enact laws. But the domain of the "law" is strictly defined (art. 34): major areas of modern life such as the regulation of civil liberties, the budget, important treaties, and at least the principles governing state intervention in economic and social life belong to this domain. But everything not specifically listed is subject to rule-making by the government. Such a distribution of tasks between the cabinet and the assemblies is designed to avoid what Debré has described with telling realism as the "double deviation of our political organization: a parliament overwhelmed by bills and rushing in disorder towards a multiplication of detailed speeches, [and] a government treating without parliamentary interference the gravest national problems."

While there were nineteen standing committees in the

[7] Speech by Michel Debré before the Council of State, reprinted in Andrews (ed.), *op. cit.*, p. 46. Other quotations from Debré's statement are taken from the same speech.
[8] For the text of the letter by the President, see *A.P.*, 1960, p. 640. Because of what he considered a flagrant violation of the constitution by the General, Vincent-Auriol resigned his seat on the Constitutional Council which he held *ex officio* as a former President of the Republic.

National Assembly of the Fourth Republic, their number is now reduced to six in each house. With a membership ranging from 60 to 120 representatives, the committees are made intentionally large so as to prevent interaction between highly specialized deputies or senators who could become effective counterparts to the Ministers. By the same token, the possible influence of pressure groups is diluted.

Both at the stage of deliberation by the competent committees and in plenary sessions, deputies and government are entitled to move amendments to a bill under consideration. But unlike what has happened in the past, the government has the power to force the final vote on a bill with only those amendments which it has been willing to accept. When the budget is being discussed, amendments which would reduce receipts or increase expenditures are out of order. Should parliament fail to accept the budget submitted by the government within the constitutionally allotted time of seventy days, the cabinet can enact the budget by ordinance — a procedure which so far has not been applied since parliament has hastened its deliberations to meet the prescribed deadline. Moreover no real difficulties have arisen because now parliament does little to alter the government's suggested budget. Unlike Congress and unlike the French parliaments of the past, but entirely in line with present British traditions, the National Assembly endorses most budgetary proposals as a matter of formality.

Among the parliaments of Europe the French Assembly has long been known more for its archaic than for its dignified aspects (although the latter are not entirely lacking). Hence a number of rules, which the new regime introduced and which were above all designed to rationalize and modernize the work of the elected representatives, were generally greeted with satisfaction. But, intentionally or not, these improvements were not associated with modern facilities which would make the work of parliament more efficient. Most deputies have neither working space nor staff. Their means of information are seriously limited: what they do not unearth by themselves has to be passed on to them by the government.

It is not surprising that the new constitution spelled out

in detail the conditions under which the National Assembly could overthrow a government. Since on the one hand the principle of parliamentary responsibility of the cabinet was to be maintained, and since on the other there was unanimous agreement that the previous frequency of cabinet crises was harmful to the policy process, possibilities for a vote of censure were left open but strictly regulated. Previously the constitution of the Fourth Republic stipulated that a government need resign only when a majority of the National Assembly had voted its downfall. That provision proved unrealistic; governments resigned voluntarily as soon as they had no positive majority behind them. Now the rule was given muscle and stated in more elaborate terms (arts. 49, 50). Yet more important: it was made clear that in the event of a motion of censure the President of the Republic would make use of his solemnly stated right to dissolve the National Assembly and to call for new elections (art. 12).

It is true that many of the reform proposals suggested before 1958 also envisaged the "automatic dissolution" of the parliament which had caused a cabinet crisis. What came as a surprise was that now the vote of censure, as it turned out, was the only means by which parliament could effectively criticize the conduct of government. As in the past, parliament can normally obtain information from the government by means of debate, confrontation of the Prime Minister or of members of his cabinet, written and oral questions, or formal investigations. However, backed by rulings of the Constitutional Council, the government made it clear that under the new regime the deputies would never have the right to express their appraisal of the information thus obtained by a vote or a resolution.[9] Such votes, the government explained, would bring back the practices of harassment which had proved so detrimental in the past because they had led to the gradual weakening of most cabinets. If the National Assembly wished to voice its displeasure with the government, it should gather

[9] For an English translation of some interesting phases of the discussion pertaining to the new standing orders of the National Assembly, see Andrews (ed.), *op. cit.*, pp. 377–85. The minutes of the entire debate fill 200 pages of the *Journal Officiel*.

sufficient votes for a motion of censure. As long as this major weapon was not wielded, no poisoned arrows should be shot in the direction of the benches occupied by cabinet members.

Such rules were quite obviously designed as a substitute for disciplined majority voting. Considered in their entirety, they did not necessarily make the role of parliament in the policy process a more limited one than that of the British "mother of parliaments" or of the *Bundestag* in West Germany. But from the very beginning of the Fifth Republic, the players on both sides, i.e., the members of the government as well as of parliament, adopted attitudes which narrowed the scope of parliamentary activities far more than might have been intended or necessary. The new constitutional provisions and standing orders were interpreted by the President, the Prime Minister, and the Constitutional Council with such harshness that the "no trespassing" signs which were erected always warned parliament, never the executive, to stay within its bounds. The government would argue that so painful a process of "reeducation" was necessary in order to forestall a return to the folkways of the political class. But on their side the deputies felt so uneasy in acting out roles that were new to them that they left unused many of the opportunities open to them for the exercise of their functions (see below).

The new imbalance between the executive and parliament has resulted in part from the preeminence of the President of the Republic in the policy process (see Chap. IX). The way in which General de Gaulle appointed the very first government of the new republic indicated that the flow of power and of policy initiative was to be channeled in unaccustomed ways. In a classical parliamentary regime, the head of state appoints the person who is likely to win the approval of parliament for himself and his program. In 1959, the newly elected President, General de Gaulle, simply let it be known that he had appointed Prime Minister and cabinet after having approved both program and personnel.[10]

It is true that Debré attempted to set a precedent by appearing before parliament, shortly after his appointment with

[10] For details, see Goguel and Grosser, *op. cit.*, pp. 207 f.

a declaration of policy which the Assembly could have rejected in the manner which the constitution prescribes for
the vote of censure. But his successor failed to follow the
precedent. After the elections of 1967 had left the government
with a rather precarious majority, Prime Minister Pompidou
refused, with the obvious approval of the President, to present
his program and the members of his government to parliament, even though the composition of the cabinet had been
changed substantially after the election. This brought the
procedures even closer to those prevalent in a presidential
system. Another formal step had been taken to limit the control of parliament over the sources of authority and the content of governmental policy.

As has been explained earlier (see Chap. IX), parliament
was anxious to have the President rather than the government carry the burden of responsibility for political decisions
until the Algerian crisis was resolved. Such a shift absolved
parliament from responsibility as well, since only the government, not the President, is accountable to the National
Assembly. But it also shook the very foundations of the parliamentary regime which the constitution was dedicated to
strengthening.

The legislative output of parliament under the new regime
has not been negligible. It is true that the number of laws
voted annually by parliament has been reduced rather drastically: an average of 80 laws per year between 1959 and 1965,
as compared with an annual average of 235 during the years
of the Fourth Republic.[11] But when laws are not counted but
weighed according to their importance, it appears that the
decline in numbers has affected enactments of very limited
interest which are usually voted upon without discussion, as
are private bills in the United States Congress.

The constitution had foreseen that in extraordinary situations normal legislative channels could be bypassed either by

[11] These and other data on legislative output are taken from François
Goguel, "L'Evolution du Pouvoir Législatif en France," an unpublished
report presented in April 1966 at Princeton University to a colloquium
on modern France, pp. 4 and *passim*. The account by Philip M. Williams, *The French Parliament, Politics in the Fifth Republic* (New York:
Praeger, 1968) has come to my attention too late to be considered.

a direct appeal to the people, the referendum (art. 11), or by the exercise of presidential emergency powers (art. 16). But unless these provisions are abused, they can shortcircuit parliament only in brief, dramatic situations and hence do not basically affect the balance between executive and parliament. What did prove detrimental to the latter's role in the policy process was the way in which the government handled the means at its disposal to exact voting discipline from the deputies or to obtain from parliament a temporary but sweeping transfer of legislative privilege to the executive.

Whenever the government wished to avoid a vote on a troublesome amendment, it made frequent use of the so-called "blocked vote" (art. 44) which compels parliament to vote on a bill only in that form which the government considers acceptable. An even more drastic means of obtaining acceptance of legislation for which there is clearly no majority in parliament is the possibility of making such approval a question of confidence (art. 49). Debré at one time stated that this procedure should be used rarely, but once more events exploded good intentions. Frequently the deputies were faced with a choice of either giving in to the government's wishes or censuring it. They also knew that a vote of censure would most likely lead to the dissolution of the Assembly, and that the subsequent elections would have all the characteristics of a plebiscite. Those who had voted the motion of censure would have to bear the onus of having opposed not only a government whose popularity might well have been waning, but the President of the Republic himself whose support waxed particularly strong whenever he could appeal to the electorate against the fomenters of disunity, the "old parties."

Important bills, such as that establishing France's nuclear striking force, have become laws in this manner. The preceding debate had made it clear that in the National Assembly of 1960 abstentions and negative votes would be numerous enough to defeat the government's intention of launching France on its career as a nuclear power. But since the motion of censure closing the debates was not carried by the required vote of half of the Assembly's total number of deputies, the Speaker could announce that "in consequence the bill for the program relating to certain military equipment [sic!] is considered adopted. . . ."

During the first two legislatures (1959–1966), parliament was induced seven times to authorize the government to pass, by executive ordinances, measures which were and are ordinarily in the domain of the law and should therefore have been voted upon by parliament (art. 38). This provision was fashioned after the practices which during the Third and Fourth Republics had enabled the legislative machinery to function by decree-laws in the absence of a coherent majority in parliament. To continue such practices under the changed conditions of the new regime was first considered advisable in connection with Algerian affairs. Later the authorization given to the executive concerned mostly more technical but equally important matters, such as the legislation necessitated by the association of France with the economies of the other Common Market countries. Between 1959 and 1965, almost 100 statutes, some of them of considerable significance, were enacted by the executive, as ordinances, as against 563 laws voted by parliament.

In other modern democracies, parliament can regulate a number of questions by broad enabling legislation and leave it to the government to fill in the necessary details. But in France, for a parliament struggling to regain its prestige and not to lose the foothold in the decision-making process which the constitution has provided, a further limitation of the parliamentary legislative function is of necessity more harmful than in a system where over the years the various organs of government have achieved mutual accommodation.

How far parliament has been eliminated from legislative policy-making became apparent when in the spring of 1967 the government combined a demand for new and rather sweeping enabling powers with a challenge to parliament to either accede to this demand or to vote a motion of censure. No crisis loomed on the political horizon, either national or international. The government was simply afraid that after elections that had severely curtailed its majority in parliament (see Chap. VIII), it might not be able to hold together the governmental coalition once it opened its bag of controversial bills, mostly concerned with long-postponed social and economic reforms. By combining the powers which it held under two articles of the constitution (articles 38 and 49), the government certainly was not violating the wording of the constitutional text. That it was acting against the spirit of the constitution was a reproach addressed to it not only by the opposition but by one of its own Ministers, Pisani, who resigned, with a resounding statement, from the government to which he had belonged in various capacities for over five years.[12]

In this as in other instances, the government demonstrated its unwillingness to open a dialogue with the deputies; it thereby curtailed the role both of its own backbenchers and of the opposition. Before the elections of 1967, the Prime Minister had declared that a reform of the social security system would need the widest possible public airing since it concerned the majority of Frenchmen. But this reform too was included among the measures on which the government was to rule by ordinance. Not only was a debate in parliament eluded in this way but, while the new legislation was in preparation, the official media of information — such as radio and television — never touched upon the problems, and the press was able to comment only afterwards.

Unwilling to make parliament a channel of information and as a sounding board, the government requires from parliament and from public opinion no other response than an expression of confidence. Since experience under previous regimes has shown that confidence in the government is difficult to obtain, and more difficult to maintain, parliament is still considered an incommodious rival rather than a partner in the exercise of power. The government has asserted that it is merely continuing a tradition developed by the decree-laws of the Third and Fourth Republics. But those traditions were the outgrowth of an instability which the new constitution had set out to correct by other means than by limiting the bounds of free debate and communication between the government and the governed.

In 1967 when the motion of censure was once more defeated, even if more narrowly than before, the government obtained automatically the powers for which it had asked.

[12] Edgard Pisani, "Sur une Démission," *Le Monde*, May 13, 1967.

Because opposition parties and public opinion were deprived of a forum, it was left to an interest group, organized labor, to express the hostility which governmental tactics and vaguely announced policies had aroused. A widely observed general strike of twenty-four hours was one of the instances (see Chap. VII) in which the trade-union movement resorted to a political action. This manifestation was particularly political in character as at the time of the strike the actual content of the reforms to be initiated by the government was not known. A movement of this kind indicates that the boundaries between political action and interest group activity are still as indeterminate as they often were in the past. The attitude which the new regime has taken towards parliament and its concomitant institutions, the political parties, goes far to explain such continuing confusion.

Another important milestone on the way to a decline of parliamentary powers was the referendum in the fall of 1962 which divested parliament of its role in the process of amending the constitution. The new constitution had stipulated that any revision of its provisions required the vote of an identical text by the two houses of parliament and its sanction by either a referendum or by a three-fifths majority of both houses combined (art. 89). By giving equal weight to the National Assembly and the Senate, this arrangement endowed the latter with somewhat surprisingly large powers. When President de Gaulle, under conditions described earlier (see Chap. IV), wished to inaugurate the election of the President by popular suffrage, he knew that the proposed change of the constitution would meet with resistance in parliament. To circumvent this difficulty, he submitted the amendment directly and without prior parliamentary debate or vote to a popular referendum. Article 11 which was invoked to justify this procedure was clearly not designed to amend the constitution. After a majority of the electorate had approved the text of the amendment, the Constitutional Council rejected an appeal by the Speaker of the Senate to declare the procedure unconstitutional. The Council declared that it lacked jurisdiction in cases where the *vox populi* had spoken.[13]

[13] For the text of the terse decision by the Constitutional Council, see *A.P.*, 1962, pp. 687 f.

In President de Gaulle's opinion, the popular verdict of 1962 meant that future amendments to the constitution could be submitted directly to the electorate for its approval, without recourse to parliament. So far he has not tested this proposition which would give great, and possibly dangerous, flexibility to the amendment process, but should another plebiscitarian situation arise, parliament might once more be deprived of its role in revising the constitution. Parliament also knows that it cannot count on being protected by the Constitutional Council which here as in other instances has usually limited parliamentary prerogatives.

The style and working methods of a parliament hemmed in on many sides by constitutional rules and by the authoritarian manners of the executive can be expected to vary greatly from those developed during times of parliamentary strength. In the past, as in other Western democracies, the political class (see Chap. V) was successful in giving to both houses of parliament a club-like atmosphere which neither acrimonious debate nor, on occasion, a duel between temperamental members could spoil. The longevity of the membership in elective office established solidarity between deputies and senators of all parties, with the sole exception of the Communists; political opponents would frequently address each other by the familiar *"tu,"* not always used between husband and wife when both belong to the upper bourgeoisie. New members of parliament were rapidly socialized into the established framework, its *esprit de corps,* and its style, which all contributed to making parliament into a subsystem of the political process.

In the Fifth Republic, the changes in personnel and radically changed expectations and attitudes have altered the atmosphere and have made internal socialization far less intense than previously. There is little likelihood that the uncertain habits of the present-day deputies will be passed on to their successors; moreover, majority and opposition have developed different concepts of their own roles. Many of the older deputies, except those belonging to the hard core of the U.N.R., still bear the marks of the previous system. They may have accepted some of the constitutional innovations as irrevocable, but they nevertheless expect that under another President of the Republic the exercise of parliamentary functions might become once more less frustrating than at present. In their eyes, the strict voting discipline exacted by the government is nothing short of dictatorial. They ridicule the members of the obedient majority party as the "boots" (*les godillots*) of the General. But even the behavior of the majority shows distinct traces of frustration.[14]

The boredom and indifference of many deputies can be measured by an absenteeism which is as rampant as ever, although the government has tried to counter it by granting rather degrading pay premiums for those who do attend. Such absenteeism is not restricted, as it is in the United States Congress, to plenary sessions but extends also to most committee meetings, which deputies and senators regard as futile. Even the parliamentary group of the U.N.R. finds it easier to produce unanimity than to compel attendance. Elaborate restrictions on the vote by proxy have been evaded with dexterity, so that it is practiced as frequently (and in many cases as scandalously) as before. The work load of the deputies belonging to the majority is very unevenly distributed. Whatever committee work there is, is managed firmly by the majority so that many opposition leaders consider their own participation a waste of time. One committee which has preserved a certain luster and importance is that of Finance and Economics, presided over by Giscard d'Estaing whose somewhat ambivalent position towards the government has been described (see Chap. VIII).

Altogether the deputies make meager use of those techniques and instrumentalities which are still at their disposal to control the government and to serve as a sounding board for public sentiment. For different reasons, both majority and opposition seem to compete in bringing about the self-effacement of the institution to which they belong.

One of the means by which members of parliament are able to extract information from the government and to search out

---

[14] For an interesting description of present-day parliamentary behavior, see the series of articles by André Laurens, "Le Métier de Député," *Le Monde,* Oct. 4, 5, 6, 8–9, 10, 1967.

dark corners of executive behavior is questions addressed to
the ministers. Written questions and answers thereto are published, as before, in the *Journal Officiel,* the French equivalent
of the Congressional Record. They continue to fulfill the
function of a gigantic service of free and official legal consultation. Often five thousand items are disposed of in a single
year.

In order to give prominence to more politically pointed,
oral questions, the new constitution stipulated that they and
the replies by the government be made a weekly priority item
(art. 48). The avowed intention in introducing this novelty
was once more the desire to emulate British practice. But it
was also hoped that the question period would take the place
of the "interpellation" by means of which, under previous
regimes, the deputies had harassed the government. The vote
taken at the end of frequently lengthy debates on such inter-
pellations had been a convenient way of gauging the cabinet's vanishing support. Hence the new standing order of
the National Assembly saw to it that the exchanges between
deputies and government arising from a question period could
never lead to a vote or a resolution.

In the eyes of representatives accustomed to embarrassing a
government rather than to scrutinizing its actions such an
arrangement deprived the question period of its major interest. Measured by their potential usefulness in as tightlipped
a regime as the Fifth Republic, oral questions have been an
unmitigated failure: there is none of the lively give-and-take
of the British model; sessions devoted to questions are usually
poorly attended; the deputies are inclined to clothe their
questions in lengthy speeches, just as the members of the government read lengthy answering statements prepared for them
by their staffs; and often Ministers will send an assistant to
represent them, just as President de Gaulle is known to have
prevented senior cabinet members from appearing before certain parliamentary committees. If so far neither opposition
nor majority has made appropriate use of the question period,
the reasons for such failure are to be found in the lack of
any tradition for a constructive dialogue between executive
and parliament. Both sides have difficulty in believing that a

confrontation, instead of precipitating the downfall of a government, could serve the ends of compromise and correction.

The possibility of controlling the executive machinery by *ad hoc* committees of investigation or of preparing legislation by other special committees has fared, if possible, even worse. Although committees of this kind have often been organized in the past, they have rarely been used effectively and have never been able to overcome administrative reluctance to disclose the truth.[15] At present their proceedings are strictly regulated. Committees can at all times exclude press and public from their hearings and do not need to publish their findings. Moreover, the majority is able to determine the membership at will, which makes the committees meaningless to the opposition. All this has meant that only a few trivial matters have been made the subject of investigations. Yet when an outstanding opposition leader, Pierre Mendès-France, returned to parliament after a forced absence of almost nine years, in his first speech he drew attention to the exaggerated secrecy of government operations, a secrecy which parliament has rarely been willing to pierce.

Also, parliamentary debates have lost much of their interest. Since victory or defeat for the government is seldom at stake, attendance is spotty. It is true that even before 1958 timidity and conformism had characterized many debates in the "House without Windows," the parliamentary building. If this trend has been amplified, it is not solely due to the government's ability to control the agenda. Only occasionally does a discussion on foreign policy still arouse some interest and provide arguments for debate in the information media.

Under present conditions, the relationship between the government and its own majority in parliament is of special importance. For, as in Great Britain, the opposition cannot really alter policy as long as the majority party does not lose cohesion. But there much political bargaining between the cabinet and its own backbenchers precedes formal policy an-

15 For the situation prevailing under the Third Republic, see Henry W. Ehrmann, "The Duty of Disclosure in Parliamentary Investigation: A Comparative Study," *The University of Chicago Law Review*, XI:1 and 2 (1943/44), pp. 1–25, 117–53.

nouncements and the submission of governmentally sponsored legislation. From the available information, partisan though it is, one gathers that the parliamentary caucus of the U.N.R., and to a lesser extent that of its long-time coalition partner, the Independent Republicans, are fairly regularly consulted by the government. At least certain "study groups" of the U.N.R. serve as links between the government and organized interests. Occasionally the study groups appear to have swayed a governmental decision; they claim to have played a role in shaping some of the agricultural reforms.[16] When the deputies of the majority plead with government and bureaucracy to show consideration for the interests of their constituents, their arguments have a certain weight because, as has been explained, the U.N.R. seeks a firmer footing in many electoral districts.

Quite generally deputies of all political persuasions pursue the traditional defense of constituency interests as energetically as ever. The decline in importance of other parliamentary activities, the new-old electoral system, and the centralization of executive decision-making in a period of rapid economic development encourage the most energetic representatives, young or old, to be first of all agents of their constituents in the capital. Even more than previously it is true that the deputy is "a lawyer with a monthly salary, an interpreter, an indefatigable broker . . . and also an extremely busy and often the most efficient social worker in his department." [17] As has been explained above (see Chap. VII), the deputy may no longer be sought out by those interest groups which have decided to seek direct access to the civil service, but many deputies find it worthwhile to negotiate in the name and for the sake of local government authorities.

[16] Interesting details and a careful evaluation are given in Charlot, *op. cit.*, pp. 153 ff. A far more sweeping assertion about the important role played by the U.N.R. backbenchers was made by the Chairman of one of the Assembly Committees, Professor René Capitant, in Association Française de Science Politique, *Le Parlementarisme, peut-il être limité sans être annihilé* (mimeographed; Paris, 1965), pp. 8 ff. and *passim*.

[17] Buron, *op. cit.*, pp. 81 ff. The enthusiastic and yet realistic account by the author who has been a long-time deputy and minister under both the Fourth and Fifth Republics, remains extremely valuable.

In a system where a local savings bank might need an authorization from Paris to finance the paving of a village street, the services of the deputy are highly appreciated. A number of representatives have made themselves the champions of regional development, acting either through the newly established CODER and through the prefects of the region (see Chap. IX) or through more conventional channels.

All such activities, however, are carried on by individual deputies or senators. Merit and prestige accrue to them and not to the party with which they are affiliated. With the sole exception of the Communists, the parties still lack the kind of organization that could provide even for the most rudimentary kind of social services.

## PARLIAMENT: WHICH UPPER HOUSE?

There were several reasons why the new regime wanted to create a "powerful second chamber." [18] Because they assumed that coherent majorities would never emerge in the "purely political body," as they called the National Assembly, General de Gaulle and Debré attributed to the upper chamber an important role in supporting the government. A house whose members were to be elected, as in the past, mostly by the municipal and department councilors would not only mirror "one of the fundamental aspects of French sociology" — namely the continuing existence of an inordinate number of small communes. It was also expected to bring into parliamentary activities an element of "administrative order." Whenever the National Assembly might yield to perennial temptations to overstep its boundaries, the government hoped to turn to the Senate for support.

Once more the hope of diminishing the realm of the political proved unrealistic. A thinly disguised lack of confidence in the representative expression of universal suffrage had to be paid for dearly. Almost from the beginning of the Fifth Republic the Senate has failed to play its assigned role. And the more it disappointed unwarranted expectations, the more

---

[18] Debré in his speech before the Council of State, in Andrews (ed.), *op. cit.*, p. 50. The quotations following in the text are either from Debré's address or from General de Gaulle's speech at Bayeux, *ibid.*, p. 38.

drastically it was excluded from any meaningful participation in the policy process.

The composition of the Senate and the methods of its election have remained essentially unchanged from what they were at the beginning of the Third Republic, when a republican leader called the upper house, not without scorn, the "Great Council of the *Communes.*" He might as well have spoken of the *petites communes,* for at all times the small communities have been heavily represented in the electoral college which designates the Senators for a nine-year term of office. (Like the Electoral College choosing the American President, this body never meets, its members voting, as it were, "at home.") All countries without a federalist structure are forever in a quandary as to which units of government or which elements of political life their upper chambers should represent. In a highly centralized system such as that of France, the difficulties are multiplied and lead to a continuous ambivalence towards the legitimacy of an indirectly elected assembly. This explains why every new constitution has determined anew the powers and functions of the upper house.

At present the delegates of municipal councils are still the predominant element among the electors: more than 100,000 of them cast their ballots together with about 3,000 members of the departmental councils, the next higher local government unit. (In this sea of votes, those contributed by the deputies of the National Assembly are without significance.) Because of the lilliputian size of so many local government units, 53 per cent of the delegates of the municipal councils represent units with less than 1,500 inhabitants, or 33 per cent of the total French population.[19] In the Senate itself, the sparsely populated regions are overrepresented: more than half of the 255 senators represent 40 per cent of the population.[20]

Because of the weight of the country's rural sector, the Senate has long been dubbed by its critics the "Chamber of

[19] See Duverger, *Institutions*, p. 584.

[20] In the upper house of a federal system such discrepancies are more functional than in a unitary system such as France, since even small or thinly populated states, "sovereign" as they are, might have a claim to "equal treatment."

Agriculture." Quite unavoidably, a body whose political roots are particularly strong in the economically least developed parts of the country tends towards parochial conservatism which is frequently out of touch with the problems of a rapidly modernizing country. Yet, in the past, the Senate has not invariably been found on the Right of the political spectrum. Its hostility to social and economic change has been balanced by a forthright defense of traditional republican liberties, and by a stand against the Catholic church and against demagogic appeals to latent antiparliamentary feelings.

In the Fifth Republic, neither the local elections which determine the membership of the electoral college nor the senatorial elections themselves have ever been touched by the Gaullist groundswell characteristic of all elections to the National Assembly. To speak here of a "revenge of the notables" is no exaggeration. The insufficient local implantation of the U.N.R. is more a consequence than a cause of this phenomenon. While classical "republican instincts" against a providential leader and a strong executive explain the hostility of many notables, especially south of the Loire River, even more fundamental sociological reasons bolster their resistance. The overwhelming majority of the electoral college — the mayors and municipal councilors of small towns in predominantly rural areas — feel that their status and influence are undermined by the personalization of political power, by the modern mass media and its use by the government, indeed by the well presented weeklies which more and more supplant the local press proper. These local notables transmit their own and their voters' outlook to senatorial candidates of similar leanings. In turn, numerous senators covet a seat in the upper house mainly because of the advantages they derive from it for the exercise of their functions as mayors or other local government officials.

All this explains why from the very beginning electoral support for the new regime has been stronger in the cities and urban areas than in the countryside and why the overrepresentation of rural areas in the Senate has been bound to weaken its Gaullist contingent. Although party labels in the upper house are often meaningless, it is nonetheless striking that the U.N.R. and the Independent Republicans which since 1962 have held a majority of seats in the National Assembly have never been able to claim more than thirty Senators as definitely committed to their cause.

The Senate, usually defending traditional positions, has disagreed with the government on many major policy decisions. In certain cases their opposition can be traced directly to the Senators' role of defenders of the least developed rural regions. A majority of Senators preferred price supports for agricultural products to structural reforms of rural holdings; they viewed the reorganization of the departments, the creation of CODER, with great misgivings. But it was the conflict over the revision of the constitution which in 1962 led to a pitched battle between the upper house and the President of the Republic.

The speaker of the Senate, Monnerville, a member of the Radical Party, used his constitutional position to denounce in the Senate and before the Constitutional Council the violation of the constitution by President and government. In the midst of the fight, the Senate reelected him as its speaker by an overwhelming majority. Reverting to a custom of heroic republican days, the Senate also decided that the speech in which Monnerville had attacked the government should be posted conspicuously in every town hall of the realm. The President of the Republic retorted with similar gestures and suspended all relations with the speaker of the upper house of parliament.[21]

Ever since then General de Gaulle and his Prime Minister have seen to it that the government is represented at Senate sessions not by the Minister with jurisdiction over the questions under discussion, but by a junior member of the cabinet, usually an under secretary. This provides a constant irritant to the Senators who react by rejecting or by amending copiously the bills approved by the National Assembly. However, this does not prove a lasting handicap to the government as it would have in the Third Republic when the Senate was

---

[21] These events are described in some detail by Jean-Luc Parodi, "Le conflit entre l'Exécutif et le président du Sénat," *RFSP*, XIII:2 (1963), pp. 454–59.

able to hold up any text in which it did not concur. The constitution provides that if there is disagreement between the two houses concerning pending legislation, the government can appoint a joint committee (art. 45). If the views of the two house are not reconciled, it is up to the government to decide which will prevail. A weapon originally designed to discipline an unruly lower house can now be turned against the Senate.

Between 1959 and 1965, 7 per cent of all legislation was passed over the opposition of the Senate. The number of bills ignoring the upper house have not only increased from year to year, they also have been those of greatest importance. The atomic striking force, the organization of military tribunals in cases of high treason, the plan for economic stabilization, the Fifth Modernization Plan, new statutes regulating municipal elections and strikes in public services have all been enacted in spite of senatorial dissent. This, of course, upsets the balance between executive and parliament from yet another side.

In view of such developments it is not surprising that proposals for a thorough reform of the upper house are heard frequently. At present the Senate does not really provide the balance which advocates of a bicameral system consider desirable; yet it is so unrepresentative of a modernizing country that to entrust it with additional powers is likely to lead to deadlock rather than to progress and growth.

From many sides it is argued that the most appropriate solution would be a chamber in which the major economic, social, and cultural interests of the nation would be represented. There has existed since 1924 an Economic and Social Council, which has functioned, under slightly different names and under a variety of statutes, almost continuously in spite of the constitutional vicissitudes of the period. Appointed either by major interest groups or by the government, the members of the Council deliberate on all bills which have an impact on economic and social matters and on the Modernization Plan. The Council also studies weighty problems before they have reached the stage of proposed legislation. After extensive debates in plenary sessions and committees, the Council formulates its advice, publishing if need be majority and minority reports. There is general agreement that since its beginnings, but especially since it was reconstituted in 1946, the Council's work has been generally of high quality; its debates have often been more interesting than those in parliament. But it is also general knowledge that neither in the past nor at present do government and parliament pay any attention to the Council's labors and advice. Its contribution to the policy process is negligible if not nil.[22]

Current proposals seek either to replace the present Senate by an assembly patterned after the Economic and Social Council or to combine the membership of both in some new way. In order to give more weight to the reorganized entity, it is suggested that it should not only have a voice but also a vote in the law-making process, even if in case of conflict between the two houses the National Assembly were to have the last word.

In European constitutional tradition, suggestions that the representatives of organized interests be invested with decision-making powers belong to the arsenal of authoritarian concepts. Corporatist chambers are usually devised as a defiance of the parliament based on universal suffrage. When General de Gaulle in his speech at Bayeux recommended that in the constitutional scheme, which he developed before his listeners, the second chamber should give "a voice to the great activities" of the country, the proposal was taken as additional proof that he was veering from the authentic republican tradition.

But in France more than elsewhere, anticapitalist syndicalism has frequently been very close to corporatist concepts, and the latter are shared by the socially most progressive industrialists. This explains why since 1958 conservatives as well as authentic liberals have backed the idea of transforming the upper house into a forum for interest representation.[23] The

[22] On the functioning of the Economic and Social Council, see J. E. S. Hayward, *Private Interests and Public Policy: The Experience of the French Economic and Social Council* (New York: Barnes and Noble, 1966), pp. 36–50. For a discussion of proposals for the future, see Duverger, *Institutions*, pp. 656–63.

[23] See e.g. the importance which Pierre Mendès-France attributes to the institution in *A Modern French Republic* (New York: Hill and Wang, 1963), pp. 78–81.

arguments advanced from both sides usually ignore the many and weighty reasons that have long been voiced against this solution. More than anything else, the proposals, and the urgency with which they are made, express a widespread uncertainty about the place of parliament in the policy process and about the idea of representation in a modern democracy. Quite typically, all sides profess the hope that an upper chamber of this kind would diminish the dominant role of the bureaucracy — a forlorn hope if past experience is a guide.[24]

From time to time General de Gaulle has spoken of the need to reform the Senate. Yet he has never indicated precisely what kind of reform he envisaged, nor how it was to be enacted. In his customary way, he is apparently waiting until an opportunity for action opens up. Except for a limited redistribution of Senate seats which would give more weight to the urban population, any change would require a constitutional amendment. It appears unlikely that the present Senate would agree to any reform which would drastically alter its composition. But without its approval, a constitutional revision could be enacted only by another unconstitutional referendum. This in turn could conjure up another crisis which might be altogether too high a price for a limited reform.

Nonetheless, the present controversies over the upper chamber of the future illustrate some of the difficulties which the regime faces in its endeavor to legitimize a new institutional framework.

**THE FUTURE OF PARLIAMENTARY GOVERNMENT**

From the outset, its functions and its freedom have been so circumscribed that the parliament of the Fifth Republic could hardly be regarded as "sovereign." In a number of essential respects, the new regime has departed from a classical

[24] When similar proposals were ventilated in Germany after the First World War, Max Weber expressed the contrary opinion: the position of the bureaucracy would be strengthened whenever it had to settle unavoidable conflicts between parliament and a chamber representing economic and social interests. See *Gesammelte Politische Schriften* (Tübingen: Mohr, 1958), p. 384.

parliamentary system. Parliament suffered a further decline of role and prestige when, instead of arbitrating between decisions that had been reached by the elected representatives and other organs of government, the President became the principal fountainhead of decision-making and when, instead of being elected by local notables, he competed with parliament for the direct suffrage.

In other European democracies there has also been a gradual decline of the role of parliament in the policy process. But for French deputies, at least for those who did not owe their seat to an identification with General de Gaulle, these drastic and sudden breaks with previous traditions were difficult to endure. Their experience was all the more traumatic as popular feelings in favor of a more important place for parliament were at first very slight and increased only gradually. Between 1959 and 1966, the number of those who regretted that parliament was playing so small a role rose from 31 to 43 per cent; in 1964 38 per cent declared that the question was without interest to them and 13 per cent refused to answer.[25] Sympathies for individual representatives might have been somewhat higher than for the institution as such, but in 1962 one-third of the population of voting age did not know the name of their deputy. Three years later only a little over one-fourth believed that regional interests were most effectively defended by deputies and senators. The majority considered local government and interest group officials more useful.[26]

The fact that many interest groups no longer seek access to parliament but turn to the bureaucracy deprives deputies and senators of their previously important part in the aggregation of interests. Finally, parliament has ceased to serve as the principal agency for recruiting the personnel for cabinet office. As has been mentioned most Ministers became candidates for election to parliament in the last elections; but many of them had first entered the government without having a parliamentary career behind them.

[25] See Brulé and Piret, *Les Transformations Sociales,* pp. 17, 18, and *Sondages,* XXVIII:1 (1966), p. 38.

[26] *Sondages,* XVII:1 (1965), pp. 69–72.

Functions remaining presently within the purview of parliament are not without importance but are regarded by most
representatives as vacuous.[27] Because of previous traditions,
the legitimization of policies and of laws initiated by the government appears tantamount to useless "rubberstamping,"
which in fact is what a disciplined majority in a parliamentary regime is expected to do.

Why the members of parliament fail to fulfill another important function, namely that of providing constant contact
between government and society, has been explained earlier.
Here the attitudes and role assumptions by both the executive
and the representatives, rather than the institutions, appear
to be at fault. But the result is that for the time being a new
disequilibrium is established, the preponderance of parliament has been superseded by that of the President of the
Republic — in his own words, "the only one to hold and to
delegate the authority of the state." [28]

It is true that deputies and senators seeking to escape frustration have turned their full attention to the defense of
constituency interests. By so doing they hope to regain prestige
and possibly authority for the institution to which they belong; this in turn preserves a democratic atmosphere. But
such activities also are keeping alive the habits of atomistic
representation, and on their reverse sides are those "games,
poisons, and delights" for which General de Gaulle has always
chided the political class.

In the end, the two branches of government may continue
to run on different tracks: a popularly elected President who
uses all the techniques of a plebiscitarian democracy, and a
parliament which, for lack of strong parties, perseveres in the
practices of an exclusively atomistic representation.[29] The
tension thus generated could result in renewed threats to
constitutional and political stability.

27 For an interesting discussion of this question, see Association Française de Science Politique, *Le Parlementarisme* . . . , *op. cit.*

28 So General de Gaulle in his press conference of January 1964, in
Andrews (ed.), *op. cit.,* p. 58.

29 This fear was voiced by Pisani in the declaration motivating his
resignation from his cabinet post in Pompidou's government, see above
n. 12.

# CHAPTER XI

# Political Modernization
# and Legitimacy

## THE DYNAMICS OF MODERNIZATION IN FRANCE

When political modernization is understood as the adaptation of the political process to changing functions, then even the most advanced countries are still modernizing.[1] In France as elsewhere, modernization takes place in an infinite continuum, and even though certain transitions deserve the scrutiny to which this and other studies have submitted them, they are never quite as dramatic as they might appear at certain moments to actors and onlookers alike. Why the French have a great ability for dramatizing the controversies generated by the modernization process has been explained in previous chapters. But similar and often identical controversies have occurred in numerous societies, reflecting everywhere reactions not only to political but also to intellectual, psychological, economic, and social problems.[2]

The particularities of the French political culture, while in no way preventing adaptation and change, have lent themselves to an alternation between periods of immobilism, when the process of modernization was blocked or unduly slowed, and "crisis-liquidation regimes." [3] Periods of purposeful ac-

[1] Cf. C. E. Black, *op. cit.*, pp. 7, 9. This essay by a historian has been very helpful in the discussion which follows.

[2] See also *ibid.*, p. 78.

[3] This term was coined by Almond and Powell, *op. cit.*, p. 310; see *ibid.*,

tivity have been followed by those of frustrating confusion and immobility. Decades during which nothing really new was tried were interrupted by brief and bold experimentation.

Frequently, the change from one stage to the other was abrupt instead of continuous and incremental. As a consequence, no French regime has had the capacity for thorough self-reform since the decline of the *Ancien Régime,* i.e., for almost two centuries. This in turn has magnified almost every political crisis, many of which centered around problems arising from modernization, into a constitutional crisis. It has also meant that each of the sixteen constitutional texts which France has known since 1791 has had to seek a new legitimacy for the institutions it established and the values it sought to represent. In one way or another each French constitution became a victim of French politics, yet this bestowed legitimacy on neither. Such discontinuity, to be sure, has proved traumatic and time and again a threat to democratic government. But discontinuity has also seemed unavoidable if one wanted to overcome a stability that was tantamount to stalemate. When pressures from the international environment left only the choice between permanent decline or adaptation to changing circumstances, stability was eventually sacrificed.

The Third Republic (1870–1940) offers a foremost example of the fact that longevity and staying power are not tantamount to that stability which permits the needed adaptation of institutions to newly accruing functions. At times it survived mainly because of the ineptness of its opponents. It operated differently in times of normalcy and in times of crisis, but it has been characterized with equal justification as a "system of democratic politics and nondemocratic government," or as offering "the paradox of a weak government with a strong state." [4] Its rapid collapse in the Second World War was largely due to a lack of modernization in the broad sense in which the term is employed here.

Those who believed that the significant demographic, eco-

---

p. 319 for a discussion of the Weimar Republic which is also helpful for an understanding of French politics.

[4] See Eckstein, *op. cit.,* p. 229, and André Siegfried, *De la IIIième à la IVième République* (Paris, Grasset, 1956), p. 251.

nomic, and social changes which the country underwent after the end of the war would result in a more or less automatic adaptation of political institutions and processes to the needs of the society saw their hopes frustrated, especially when it turned out that the party system remained obsolete (see Chap. VIII). When first the Indochina and then the Algerian war dramatized the problem of decolonization — another phase in the modernization process — the low threshold for crisis solution by the regime became apparent.

What remains to be examined is whether the Fifth Republic is merely another in the line of "crisis liquidation" regimes or whether it provides possibilities for more continuous change and for the acceptance of its rules as legitimate. This query is all the more pertinent since lessons of history seem to suggest that regimes which began, as did the Gaullist Republic, in a near-revolutionary situation, and which have centered around a charismatic personality, are usually of the most transient type.[5]

How a single person, General de Gaulle, has significantly altered the functioning of the political machinery has been described earlier (especially in Chaps. V, IX, and X). It is quite generally true that "functional change depends on the few, and may often be rapid and easy." [6] But whether the alteration of functions and of constitutional institutions will be accepted by the community will depend on whether more fundamental structural changes have been effected, such as changes in the way of doing things — transforming old customs and attitudes.

## LEGITIMACY FOR THE NEW INSTITUTIONS?

According to General de Gaulle's expressed beliefs, the twin problems of legitimacy and authority are deceptively simple, even if modern political science might characterize his beliefs as delusions. To him authority is characteristic only of the state and never of anything outside of it. All it takes to make this monopoly effective and thereby legitimate is that the state be strong. In periods when parties and other inter-

[5] See Eckstein, *op. cit.*, p. 274.
[6] See Black, *op. cit.*, p. 48.

mediary bodies are influential enough to besiege the state and
weaken its output, legitimacy ceases to exist.

In one of the most revealing passages of his memoirs, General de Gaulle has explained why when he, the guarantor of a
strong state, left the helm of government in 1946 sovereignty
and legitimacy lost actuality and became latent, waiting, as it
were, for the second coming of the saviour:

> Gone was that atmosphere of exaltation, that hope of success,
> that ambition for France, which supported the national soul.
> Every Frenchman, whatever his tendencies, had the troubling
> suspicion that with the General [Note: de Gaulle speaking about
> himself in the third person, as he frequently does] vanished
> something primordial, permanent and necessary which he in-
> carnated in history and which the regime of parties could not
> represent. In the side-tracked leader, men persisted in seeing a
> kind of capital of sovereignty, a last resort selected in advance.
> They supposed such legitimacy could remain latent in a period
> without anxiety. But they knew it could be invoked by common
> consent as soon as a new laceration threatened the nation.[7]

Such language suggests that upon returning to power, General de Gaulle himself considered it the foremost task of the
new regime once more to liquidate a crisis. When, especially
during the first years of the Fifth Republic, he consistently tied
legitimacy to his own person, he did so because he knew that
neither the new men, his collaborators, nor the new institutions commanded authority. Only the authority he had earned
by past deeds and merits enabled the state to overcome the
strains and centrifugal tendencies which, in General de
Gaulle's opinion, were artificially created by forces active from
outside the government.

In subsequent years, when circumstances made it no longer
necessary nor even possible to identify the new regime with
an acute crisis situation, the President of the Republic based
the claim for legitimacy on other grounds. Instead of personally acquired historical title, he now stresses that the quality of the constitution, the dignity, stability, and efficiency of
the regime will insure wide acceptance and survival after his
own demise. When he praises the institutions as being adapted

[7] De Gaulle, *War Memoirs,* III, p. 327.

to present-day conditions, he emphasizes their modernity. When he foresees that soon the constitution "with its effective separation of powers" and "with all that it entails will have become as second nature to us," he offers indeed a pragmatic and not necessarily undemocratic definition of legitimacy.[8]

What has not changed is General de Gaulle's conviction is that "politics" can be divorced from the "state" and consequently that the policy-making process in the Fifth Republic has nothing to do with the solving of political conflicts. In this sense he still considers himself, as have providential leaders before him, as a satisfactory substitute for both politics and participation. Yet, since politics cannot be eluded, the only true alternative is one between politics with and politics without popular participation.[9] There is no doubt that General de Gaulle has opted for a plebiscitarian version of the latter as the only means of controlling the political temper of his fellow Frenchmen. In this way he expects to insure the stability without which the regime can neither be strong nor legitimate.

For the time being, it appears that these propositions have found at least qualified support. Public opinion data gathered over recent years confirm that satisfaction with existing political institutions has been rising when it is measured by the way in which French citizens compare their own political system with that of other countries. Towards the end of the Fourth Republic, in January 1958, 39 per cent of the respondents thought that Great Britain was better governed than France, 58 per cent thought so when asked to compare their country with the United States, 52 per cent in comparison with West Germany, and 31 per cent with the Soviet Union. Seven years later, feelings had changed rather drastically: only 14 per cent regarded the political system of Great Britain superior, 30 per cent that of the United States, 21 per cent that of West Germany, 15 per cent that of the U.S.S.R., the last figure being considerably lower than the percentage of Communist voters

8 See various press conferences of General de Gaulle and especially that of November 27, 1967.

9 See Hoffmann, in *In Search of France*, p. 113, and also the same author's "Heroic Leadership: The Case of Modern France," in Edinger, *ed. Political Leadership in Industrialized Societies* (New York: Wiley, 1967), pp. 108–154.

in the electorate. There was, as would be expected, a high correlation between those who now approved of French political institutions and those who expressed satisfaction with the handling of the presidential duties by General de Gaulle.[10]

There has been at all times a more or less pronounced discrepancy between the popularity of the government and that of the President of the Republic. The government has frequently been out of favor with a majority of the electorate; satisfaction with General de Gaulle has hardly ever amounted to less than 50 per cent of those expressing an opinion and has usually, year after year, been closer to the 60 per cent mark. It is true that after fighting ceased in Algeria, the curve no longer reached 70 per cent as it had during the various crises precipitated by the war. Variations between social categories and even between regions have not been pronounced, although the South remains more reserved. The only real and continuing differences exist between the sexes and age groups: the General's popularity is far higher with women and those of retirement age; Frenchmen younger than thirty-four are considerably less favorably inclined than the national average.[11]

The reasons given at various times by those who express satisfaction with the overall record of the new regime are often imprecise and occasionally contradictory. But if one adopts as another common-sense definition of legitimacy a widely accepted title to rule, then General de Gaulle as a person as well as the present holder of the highest office in the new Republic has acquired such legitimacy. There is, to be sure, praise for his "honesty." But even praise for his personal qualities shades into pride in the status which his prestige has brought to France. It was explained earlier (see Chap. V) that General de Gaulle has laid so much stress on the "grandeur" of the nation, less because he has illusions about the international capacities of France than out of a desire to nurse Frenchmen back to self-respect and thereby to lower the

---

10 *Sondages*, XXVIII:1 (1966), p. 40. That between 30 and 46 per cent of the respondents refused to answer these questions which assume a fair amount of political information adds to the value of the sample. Of course, the answers given reflect also political developments in the countries with which France was compared.

11 See *ibid.*, pp. 22 ff., also for what follows in the text.

pitch of internecine bickering. Public opinion polls seem to indicate that he has been rather successful in this endeavor.

The renewal of respect at home and abroad is invariably credited to the "stability of the regime," "better government," and the like. Sixty per cent of the respondents concede that General de Gaulle has installed a *pouvoir personnel,* a term which carries extremely bad connotations in the language of republican traditions. But not much more than half of those who answers the question in the affirmative are of the opinion that this is a bad thing, to say nothing of those who completely deny that the new republic has established a "personal rule." The more concretely voters are asked to give reasons for satisfaction or dissatisfaction, the less wholehearted becomes the support not just of the government but of the regime as such. This is particularly true in regard to economic and social policies, and in spite of the fact that General de Gaulle (probably contrary to his personal inclinations) is displaying the statistical evidence of economic progress and well-being at ever greater length in his press conferences.

Yet it could be argued with some merit that even widespread displeasure with the regime in some domains, because it is coupled with a fairly general acceptance of the rules established for the processing of demands and of conflicts, does not deprive the republic of legitimacy. Just as satisfaction with the day-to-day results of public policy does not necessarily engender a more fundamental commitment to the system, so criticism of day-to-day operations does not necessarily destroy legitimacy. What is expected of modern representative government is that it govern efficiently *and* be able to claim representativeness. On both grounds the present regime appears to many of its constituents more satisfactory than preceding republican regimes.

Here one constitutional novelty stands out even though it was introduced by the violation of constitutional rules: the popular election of a President endowed with broad functions has met with wide approval because it can decide the outcome of a competition for power and politics (see Chap. IV). This is precisely what parliamentary elections in the Fourth and Third Republics were increasingly unable to do. There is hardly a political leader or movement which advocates at present that after General de Gaulle the institution of the popularly elected President be tampered with. Plans for a constitutional convention, discussed at length earlier by the Left and Extreme Left, are no longer heard of.[12] To have made the popular election of the Executive democratically respectable, after it had been tainted for more than a century by the suspicion of serving the ends of dictatorship, remains, for the time being, one of the historical achievements of the regime. In the country which continues to have the weakest of all party systems among the democracies of Western Europe, the direct election of the Head of State seems to compensate for some of the shortcomings of parliament as a representative body.

However, all judgments as to whether these steps towards a democratic system that is both stable and representative are provisional or lasting must be suspended as long as the system functions under the impulse of an extraordinary "heroic leader." Although there are of course speculations about his successor, there is only one certainty about him — he will be very unlike the present incumbent of the presidency. In every regime the transition from a heroic to a routine leadership is necessarily precarious. The American presidency and the papacy, among others can be cited as examples of how, with the help of long established traditions, something of an institutionalized or "office charisma" can be established which then can bestow legitimacy on the office holder whatever his personality. But such traditions are lacking in contemporary France. The personality of General de Gaulle, his views on history and government, and the way in which he regards his own role, past and present, make the conditions of transition only more hazardous.

It has been pointed out quite correctly that just as it makes a significant difference in a political system what expectations the members have as to what the government ought to do *for* them, so it makes a crucial difference what they believe the

[12] The sole exception to this acceptance of the new institution is Pierre Mendès-France who still considers it an unacceptable breach of republican traditions.

government ought to or can do *to* them.[13] It is generally admitted that nobody but General de Gaulle could have done to Frenchmen in metropolitan France and in Algeria what he did when he gave complete independence to Algeria (and to the French possessions in Black Africa). Nobody but de Gaulle could change the rules of the constitution (and thereby the rules of the political game, but without any essential infringement of civil liberties) as drastically as he has, especially when he transformed the functions of the President and the modes of his own election.

But it is the earmark of a democracy that it is legitimized more by its form than by its substantive results or by the self-restraint of its temporary ruler. General de Gaulle's vast authority has not been exercised constitutionally if one understands this term to mean (at the very least) that authority is exercised "within a framework of widely accepted and well-understood limits and rules, including, for example, the rule that authority inheres always in a collective structure." [14] At important junctures, not even the French cabinet ministers, to say nothing of the electorate, have understood either the rules which the Chief of State was about to establish or the limits which he set for himself.

Participation in decision-making by various elites inside and outside the government has remained narrowly circumscribed; participation by the citizenry, has been dispensed with. The only loyalty which the regime has asked from citizens has been an abstract and passive one, never an obligation or even an invitation to join a party or another organization. In this respect one might say that General de Gaulle has sided with Lord Bolingbroke, the British Tory of the early eighteenth century, who tried to form a party in order to destroy every future excuse for party, whereas it was Edmund Burke's desire to make party government a respectable instrument of honest men of principle.

To be sure plebiscitarian devices such as presidential-elections and the referendum have given the regime democratic representativeness. But here, as has been explained, involve-

---

[13] See Verba in Pye and Verba, *op. cit.,* p. 541.
[14] See Eckstein, *op. cit.,* pp. 198 and 235.

ment is fleeting. The hero has essentially ruled by seduction and by the kind of mild terror which he spread when he painted the alternatives to his rule in dreary if not repulsive colors: economic chaos and inflation, return to the tyranny of the "old parties," domination by either of the two superpowers.

That de Gaulle would rely on this time-honored plebiscitarian appeal during the early years of the regime, in an acute crisis situation, was almost to be expected. That he still utters such warnings,[15] while at the same time declaring that the new institutions are well established, expresses a lingering and possibly well-founded doubt as to whether there exists in fact a commitment to the system beyond that created by his own performance. Precisely because the performance has been stunning, politics have become more than ever a spectator sport. To be spectators "together" is pleasing to egalitarian instincts, even though the distance to the stage might vary slightly according to the price of the seats. The regime has shown little interest in changing Frenchmen from "political subjects" into political participants.[16] One might well conclude that the new institutions have acquired legitimacy at least partly because the pattern of nonparticipation on which they are built corresponds to the pattern of authority which has been described throughout this study as an important aspect of French political culture.

There are some indications that before leaving office General de Gaulle might once more organize a referendum, possibly on questions of foreign policy, and thereby attempt to bind his successor by another expression of the *vox populi* to the policies he wishes to see pursued.[17] But the problem of a transmission of legitimacy cannot be solved in this way.

General de Gaulle's disappearance will change the "field" so fundamentally that under his successor new problems, and

15 For instance, in the press conference of November 1967.

16 On this distinction, see Almond and Powell, *op. cit.*, pp. 58 ff.

17 Among the many rumors circulating in Parisian political circles one also hears that General de Gaulle would like to be the first in a chain of Presidents who in fact designate their successors by proposing them as candidates for subsequent elections. See *Le Monde*, October 1–2, 1967.

with them new alignments of political forces and a new leadership, will emerge. In this sense the present regime is and remains provisional, which might be another reason for its popularity. At the time the Third Republic was born Gustave Flaubert seemed to express widespread feelings when he rejoiced because "the provisional, the normal and true conditions for everything has become a constitutional reality."

It is not impossible that, as in the past, Frenchmen will seek to derive solutions from "the perfect" constitutional arrangement; in all likelihood they will attempt to fuse their latest experiences with earlier traditions. But what will prove all-important is whether the distribution of powers and functions throughout the system will be arranged so as to fill the needs of a country undergoing the stresses of rapid modernization.

### A MODERN DEMOCRACY? —
### CHANCES AND SHOALS

Present discussions about the future of French politics frequently envisage somewhat deceptively simple alternatives: should the regime develop into a better balanced presidential system or can a reformed parliamentary system provide both stability and representativeness? The constitutional framework created in 1958, even as amended by the referendum of 1962, leaves both possibilities open.

There is general agreement, extending from the present majority to the opposition, that the highly personal style which General de Gaulle has brought to the exercise of his functions will not survive him. But this does not necessarily mean that the office will be handled in a less authoritarian fashion.

The normal checks and balances of a full-fledged presidential system are constitutionally available or could be introduced by practice (e.g., an effective judicial review by the Constitutional Council or even the ordinary courts; restraints in the presidential prerogatives of declaring the state of emergency, of decreeing the dissolution of parliament, or of calling for a referendum). Such controls, however, are not legitimized by public approval simply because the electorate has not been made aware of their existence. If prior to 1958 the country was governed by a "false" parliamentary system, the subsequent experiences with a "false" presidential system might also have misled expectations and political thinking.

Under these conditions, the deadlock between parliament and executive (well known in the relationship between the White House and Capitol Hill) could become permanent and hence disastrous. In a country in which compromise between conflicting interests is still considered somewhat shameful, efforts aimed at establishing the needed concert could easily lead to a loss of authority for at least one, if not both, of the antagonistic forces.[18] If institutional arrangements leave the last word with the President, he might find it both easy and necessary to use his powers precipitously.

Undoubtedly the concentration of so much power in the hands of a President together with the lack of those checks and controls which are habitually generated by federalism can lead to misuse of presidential strength. The jacobinic strand in General de Gaulle's concepts and practice (see Chap. V) has only strengthened the almost automatically centralizing trend of French politics and government. So far timid and often frustrated attempts at regionalism have not been able to overcome ingrained habits which seriously limit possibilities for participatory activities. In a highly centralized system, the strains which invariably accompany modernization continuously push the resolution of conflicts to the top of the power pyramid.[19] The President (assisted by a bureaucracy subject to his directives) thus is confirmed in his self-appointed role as the sole defender of the public interest against the assault of conflicting demands.

The present regime has widely accredited the notion of a Chief Executive "above the parties": in a public opinion poll held in 1965, only 23 per cent regarded the President as the head of a majority party or coalition; 56 per cent thought that he should be free of all party entanglement. It is true that in this respect younger Frenchmen view the presidential office

18 See Hoffmann, in *In Search of France*, p. 114. His conclusions concerning the future of the regime were described by Goguel in the same volume, p. 403, as a "suspended judgment." Five years later, the judgment must remain similarly suspended.

19 Almond and Powell, *op. cit.*, p. 113.

with greater political realism. Not only did the younger age group, which has less sympathy for General de Gaulle than the rest of the electorate, approve of the implications of a more classical presidential system, but many of them considered it also quite normal that the future President be the candidate of a party.[20] Because of the future numerical preponderance of the younger generations in the electorate, such leanings might have great importance. It was on that very formula that Gaston Defferre, with the help of a group of young sympathizers and of the *forces vives,* sought to build his candidacy for public office in 1965, but was unable to overcome the resistance of traditional forces (see Chap. VIII). If the public mood of the younger generation were able to assert itself, such resistance might wear off.

In spite of present hopes and illusions, it is unlikely that any future President will be capable of counterbalancing the centrifugal forces in parliament without playing the role of a majority leader either directly or through an intermediary, such as the Prime Minister. Unless the warring factions of a coalition can be held together, no constitutional provision can prevent the continuing fluctuation of power between a splintered parliament and a providential leader posing as the savior from chronic disorder.

As long as the future of parties and the party system remains uncertain, it is also impossible to gauge whether parliament will ultimately be able to exercise the functions that belong to it in a modern democracy: to be an agency of effective representation and to control executive policy. In regard to both these functions, the present parliament as well as those of preceding regimes have been deficient. The modernization of society and especially the communications revolution have furthered to a certain degree the nationalization of political issues and consequently have helped to overcome some of the most blatant parochialism. Strictly enforced rules of parliamentary conduct and the demands of plebiscitarian elections have facilitated a simplification of party competition and alignments. But, particularly since the parliamentary elections of 1967, there is widespread doubt as to whether a coherent and

20 See *Sondages,* XXVII:4 (1965), p. 48.

representative majority will be available in the post-Gaullist era. (Conversely, it could be argued that if such a majority had existed prior to 1958, even the institutions of the Fourth Republic could have been made to work.)

The fate of the German Republic of Weimar shows that presidential elections are not enough to force parties and groups into greater cohesion. In pre-Hitler Germany, as in the Fifth Republic, only two candidates faced each other in the run-off elections of the presidential contest. Yet in Germany a splintered and rigid party system prevented the normal functioning of parliamentary institutions and finally of representative government. In France the old problem of the center might arise again, since the "swamp" has not really been drained (see Chap. VIII).[21] This would mean that, as in the past, a number of deputies whose votes are needed for the support of a coalition government would be sent to parliament by their constituents to pursue one set of policies, and then feel inclined to vote for and to follow other if not opposite policies. This obviously destroys the representativeness of parliament and the aggregative function of parties as well.

If the prognosis for French politics must remain suspended as long as the future of the party system is clouded, this would indicate that for all their importance constitutional arrangements and rearrangements can only have a limited effect. In the last analysis, problems of long-term structural changes must be resolved in terms of the inherited political culture of each society.[22] Hence much depends on the evolving attitudes and learning experiences of both the elites and the citizens. And while the recent past has shown that there is no automatic transfer of the modernizing trends in economy and society, political development nonetheless has received needed impulses from them. Whether such impulses are wasted or used depends on circumstances that might be altogether too unique for conceptualization.

Frequently, and not only in France, value systems have lagged behind economic and social developments, just as

[21] This is the sceptical conclusion reached by Goguel in "Bipolarisation," *op. cit.*
[22] See Black, *op. cit.*, p. 158.

national wealth and economic growth impinge on democratic structures only through the often delayed impact which they have on the general pattern of social forms.[23] Both value systems and social forms are of paramount importance for political modernization. When one seeks to generalize about French attitudes towards change, one can hardly avoid the pitfalls of such generalization. Tocqueville recognized in the Frenchmen of his time the traits which Caesar had drawn some 2,000 years earlier when he described the Gauls as *rerum novarum cupidi,* eager for all things new. Many of the great French novels of the nineteenth century are concerned with social change and illustrate masterfully the conflicts between traditional and modern values. Today, the same careful observer who has explained why the bureaucratic and bourgeois system of France has favored the blossoming of a highly individual culture clinging to its preindustrial ways considers it untrue that Frenchmen dislike change. "What they fear is not change itself, but the risks they may encounter if the stalemate that protects them (and restricts them at the same time) were to disappear." [24]

In more ways than one, the challenge of modernization and the attack on the structures of the stalemate are coming either from the outside or from developments which Frenchmen are no longer able or willing to prevent. The incorporation of the economy into the Common Market has done more than to sustain prosperity and to provide a more orderly set of relations with the country's ·neighbors. It has also afforded an opportunity to relieve the tensions generated by the modernization process within France. Many who originally feared competition in a larger market have defended themselves with remarkable success. The new conditions have forced many a French entrepreneur to abandon established routines; in both industry and agriculture obsolescent units are hard pressed. When such changes affect the tactics, outlook, and personnel of trade associations and other interest groups, the inputs into the political system are altered significantly.

Similarly, the demographic pressures, the onrush of the

---

[23] See *ibid.,* p. 89, and Eckstein, *op. cit.,* p. 188.
[24] Cf. Crozier, *The Bureaucratic Phenomenon,* p. 226.

younger generation, do not only alter the course of public investments. Such pressures also shake the foundations of an educational system which has remained the bottleneck in the modernization not only of social but also of political structures (see Chap. III), even though here as in other fields the social investments of the Fifth Republic still lag behind needs.

Whether these and other enforced breakthroughs are bringing about a different estimate of the proper role of government and politics in the process of change is a most important question. The answers to it are as yet inconclusive. There are indications that the old distrust of any reform action by the state is diminishing and that there is consequently less reluctance to seeing the capabilities of the political system increased. This is widely true in local urban politics. Young people who think that far too little, if anything, is done for them in their communities voice their complaints not with passive resignation but in an active desire to see reforms enacted.[25] Of course, an increased volume of demands is heightening tensions which may not always allow themselves to be dealt with in the detached, authoritarian fashion which President de Gaulle has adopted towards social protest movements (see Chap. VII).

Yet when demands for reform are put forward, they are no longer of necessity formulated as an attack upon the whole system. A wider acceptance of some of the ground rules of the political game makes it possible to bargain for a set of more or less limited objectives.[26] An empirical and pragmatic attitude towards the possibilities and methods of change seems to have attenuated the dead weight of past conflicts — this explains in part the astonishingly rapid healing of the wounds which the Algerian conflict had left. An abatement of the ideological expression of controversies does not indicate that conflicts have vanished. But their range appears narrowed, and the style in which they are contested is less dramatic and verbose. Almost all political parties, new and old, are trying

[25] See cf. *Jeunes d'aujourd'hui,* p. 47; 49 per cent of the respondents between 15 and 20 years of age, thought that little, and 30 per cent that nothing was done for their age group in their communities.

[26] Almond and Powell, *op. cit.,* p. 57, describe such a phenomenon as a "secularization" of political culture.

to find a style of action more appropriate to the prevailing temper. Their general unattractiveness might be caused by what could be termed a circular credibility gap: their organizational means are grossly inadequate to their tasks and pretensions, partly because of the diffidence with which parties are met.

Other situations described throughout this book indicate that the modernization process is hemmed in from many sides by traditional attitudes.[27] In many fields reforms have been diverted or halted altogether. On the other hand, some quite remarkable if limited social reforms have been received with so much indifference that a French sociologist, on the basis of several case studies, has only very recently remarked that "Frenchmen are very much interested in themselves and very little in their society." [28]

Because of such ambivalence, public reactions to frustrated expectations are unfathomable but could still result in a threat to democratic politics. If governmental stability, to which the citizens have become passively accustomed, were threatened anew, if deadlocks at various levels of government and of society were to develop, then it is not impossible that both elites and electorate would consider representative government inadequate. At that time the plenitude of unchecked power in the Presidency could become a threat, and the plebiscitarian possibilities of the office could be abused. Then the uncertainties as to which institutions and which rules have acquired legitimacy could become critical.[29]

However, such a crisis is unlikely now as the country does not currently face any major problems. Tensions generated by the internal modernization process and by the efforts at integrating parts of Europe, either functionally or constitutionally, will rise and fall. They will be nagging but diffuse,

[27] For a balanced and detailed over-all account of new and old in present-day France, see Tannenbaum, *op. cit., passim,* and the revised edition of Laurence Wylie, *Village.*

[28] Alain Touraine, "La société française: croissance et crise," in Société Française de Sociologie, *Tendances,* p. 474.

[29] In 1966, 48 per cent of respondents in a public opinion poll believed that the judicial system was functioning badly, 35 per cent that it was functioning well. It is true that four years earlier not less than 60 per cent had voiced distrust of the courts. See *Sondages,* XVIII:1 (1966), p. 51.

rather than systemic. They will create problems and possibly grave ones at that, but not *a* problem of the kind the Third Republic faced with the rise of Nazism and the Fourth with first the cold war and then the process of decolonization. The same is true, at least for the time being, for pressures arising from the international environment. The freedom and pronounced "independence" with which General de Gaulle has seemingly manipulated the international position and alignments of his country were made possible because of the small risks involved. This has facilitated a posture of assurance and given considerable latitude for expression. But a verbal legacy can either be lived with or liquidated without overwhelming difficulties.

The relative mildness of issues, the diminished load of problems fed into the political system should facilitate, though they do not guarantee, the ongoing modernization of French democracy. As long as French politics remain democratic, they will move rather more vigorously than the politics of other communities between the poles of cohesion and of diversity. This makes for their fascination. It also makes any prediction concerning the course of political change a hazardous undertaking.

# Postscript: Summer 1968

**THE EXPLOSIONS OF MAY**

In his customary New Year's address to the French nation, President de Gaulle saluted the year 1968 "with serenity" and boasted that "in the midst of so many countries disturbed by so much confusion, ours will continue to give an example of order." Without exception all political observers agreed with such an estimate. Before mid-year the country was shaken by one of the most violent social crises of its history — a history rich in such crises. While many of the consequences of the unforeseen explosions are as yet unpredictable, their impact on French politics and on the international position of France will be so great that an attempt will be made to explain the origins and the characteristics of the upheaval against the background of the analysis which the preceding chapters have furnished.[1]

With hindsight it appears surprising that the quite unusual expressions of social protest during the preceding winter had passed unnoticed. In a number of factories located near provincial universities, wildcat strikes had been launched by young workers who had only recently emigrated from the

[1] For reasons of space no references have been made to previous chapters. They suggest themselves. Hence this postscript should not be read first but last. Written without the benefit of historical distance, it is based mostly on interviews and personal impressions as well as on the daily and weekly press. Among the first analyses of the events in book form, still largely journalistic in content, the following might be mentioned: Jean-Jacques Servan-Schreiber, *Le Réveil de la France* (Paris: Denoël, 1968) and Pierre Mendès-France, *Pour préparer l'Avenir* (Paris: Denoël, 1968). Legions of other publications will follow.

countryside in the general process of the rural exodus. These strikes were usually vehement and almost uncontrolled by the trade unions. The traditional factory society had not yet achieved the socialization of these workers, who lived by themselves almost like foreign labor. But these workers found companionship among a politically conscious minority of students, some of whom had interrupted their studies to seek contacts in the working class.

Job insecurity played an important role in this flare-up of protest. It is estimated that at one time about 9 per cent (or 250,000) of those under 20 and employable were out of work, a far higher rate of unemployment than in the population at large. The sudden population growth of the post-war years had not been absorbed sufficiently when the young generation reached the labor market with rising expectations. It has long been known that by now France would be one of the most youthful nations of Europe. The prominent role which the young played in the events of May 1968 is, among others, an expression of the fact that almost 8 million — 15.8 per cent of all Frenchmen — are now between 16 and 25 years of age.

The fuse blew in the university system, which during the academic year 1967/68 tried to accommodate 602,000 students (compared with 170,000 at the beginning of the Fifth Republic). Undoubtedly the impact of events abroad was considerable. Student rebellions elsewhere, but especially in the Federal Republic of Germany, provided encouragement and a desire to emulate. In both the French secondary schools and the universities the groups that were to become most active in the revolt derived part of their membership from organizations that had opposed the war in Vietnam and were, with the beginning of the Paris negotiations, desirous of turning their energies elsewhere. Such activities by the political Left of the student youth resulted in a recrudescence of activities by the extreme Right. More than once the panicky moves by university authorities to reestablish order were motivated by the fear of a campus "civil war."

Far more decisive in the outbreak, however, was the basic inability of the entire educational system to overcome its own contradictions. These had grown more acute from year to year, not only because of the large influx of new students, but also because of the clash of modern needs with an archaic structure and with inappropriate methods of instruction and of selection. Because of the high degree of centralization, self-reform appeared ineffective and hence not worth attempting. The eight Ministers of National Education who have succeeded each other in the Fifth Republic all succumbed to the weight of the traditions they set out to bend according to their own lights. Their Ministry was weakly administered and unable as well as unwilling to overcome the resistance of the teaching profession which, although politically divided, was united in the defense of their corporate interests. Some of the tentative and controversial reforms had to be imposed by means that reinforced rather than diminished bureaucratic controls.

The first university to be closed because of student unrest was one only recently opened (in Nanterre, a northern suburb of Paris). In many respects the new campus reflected the errors inherent in authoritarian and centralized planning undertaken without consulting those affected. Its student body contained a higher than average number of students majoring in the newer social sciences. For them professional outlets in a not fully modernized economy appear uncertain especially as long as the civil service continues to recruit elsewhere for its prestigious positions.

After the closing of Nanterre the conflict was transferred to the Sorbonne in the heart of the capital. At times the breakdown in communications between authorities, faculties, and students was total — not surprising given the institutional arrangements. Such breakdown escalated the conflicts, while simultaneously the mass media (and especially the most flexible among them, the transistor radio) spread the news of all confrontations and heightened combativeness. The weakness of all organizations which could have interposed themselves between the government and the citizens in revolt was to give to the explosions of May the appearance of a revolution apt to threaten the existing regime. The absence of a valid student organization which would have been an intermediary between students and the authorities, was due partly to the long-standing unwillingness of the government to attribute useful functions to such an organization.

As a consequence of this lack of recognition, the national student movement (U.N.E.F.) had been torn for years by internal dissensions; its leadership was inexperienced and enjoyed little authority over its constituents. Five or more small groups represented various ideological tendencies which corresponded *grosso modo* to the New Left in the United States and in other countries. All were vigorously opposed to the Communists and their student organization — which after constant purges was leading a shadowy existence. When student unrest swelled and when it turned out that the university was the most vulnerable of all existing structures, the activist minorities found in battle a unity which debate and organizational efforts had denied them. They mobilized an army of sympathizers who were growing steadily more numerous and more radical in their demands. Protests about overcrowded facilities and antiquated methods of examination led step by step to a revolt against the entire system until lock-outs and sit-down strikes had swept most of the French universities and many of the Paris high-schools.

From the noblest of the *grandes écoles,* such as the E.N.A. or the *Polytechnique,* and the most conservative university departments to the most humble *lycée* for young girls hundreds of detailed and generous reform proposals emerged. They left no pedagogical stone unturned and attacked without exception the institutional basis, as well as the philosophy, of the system inaugurated by Napoléon and left basically untouched since.

But the sweep of the movement was far broader than earnest attempts at reform. To a small number of radical student leaders the assault on the university was only a tactical means for bringing down the government and the bourgeois society. The mood which developed among the students in the streets of Paris and in the buildings they occupied throughout the country was far less political in motivation. But it gave to the rebellion the cohesion which was needed to defy the authorities. A collective shedding of inhibitions, a determination to overcome alienation and isolation, a liberating psychological release, and finally a denial of all authority — that of the bourgeois father and teacher, of the clergy and of party leadership — were shouted, sung, and inscribed on the walls.[2] For the first time girls participated actively in a student movement. If the protest against capitalism and its democracy was prevalent, language and ideas were far more those of the utopian socialists of the 19th century than of Marxism or even Leninism. To be practical seemed irrelevant. "Be realistic, ask for the impossible," might well have been the most typical of the innumerable slogans intoxicating mildly or wildly tens of thousands of students.

Yet the surrealism of 1968 was not like its forerunner a literary movement. The "cultural revolution" and its "happenings" challenged and thus inevitably clashed with the state. Future historians will have to determine the part of conscious conspiratorial activities, of chance, of tactical, moral and intellectual errors, and of other circumstances which led to the manning of barricades and bitter street fighting in Paris, Lyons, Nantes, and Bordeaux.

Politically significant was the short-lived but intense solidarity which two-thirds of the Parisian population felt for the students as soon as the police went into action. A large majority blamed excessive brutality on the police, and more than half approved of the students' goals, even when the latter questioned the "basic tenets of the existing society," and applauded the professors who had sided with the youth against the authorities. Deeply engrained feelings of sympathy for those who had brought upon themselves police interference made the Parisians relive the insurrections of 1848 and of the Paris Commune — which the habit of historical thinking has engraved in popular memories, and not only of the proletariat. The feeling of broad support by the citizenry encouraged the students and their improvised leadership to stiffen resistance and to attack with increasing boldness. Particularly significant were the sympathies which high church officials and Catholic groups expressed for the rebels. They admonished the faithful

[2] A *"Comité Freud-Che Guevara"* might be singled out as quite typical. Its literature combines proposals for curriculum reforms with prescriptions for sexual liberation.

not to forget that the outbreaks were the manifestations of a search for new values which the Church felt bound to honor. They knew that some of the most militant elements among the students and young workers had come from or belonged to the various sectors of the Catholic youth movement. It is true that outside of Paris only a minority approved of the rebellion and that after two weeks of intermittent street fighting sympathies ebbed also in the capital.[3]

By the middle of May the student revolts had sparked another explosion: after young workers had taken the initiative for a sit-in strike in a nationalized enterprise near Nantes, a wave of labor conflicts engulfed large and small enterprises throughout France, until between 9 and 10 million workers were on strike (out of a total labor force of 17 million). When the workers discovered that under pressure the government was willing to promise sweeping university reforms, a long accumulated resentment about social injustices broke into the open. The feeling of having been denied a fair share in an expanding economy, the abnormally low rate of minimum wages, unpopular reforms, especially those of the social security system which the ordinances of 1967 had imposed without discussion, and also a widely felt need for recognition of trade union activities at places of work, motivated the workers' demands in private and public enterprises. The government had long ignored the discontent of the working class because it counted on the notorious weakness of the trade union movement. Now the workers astonished employers, government and trade union officials alike by their radical stubbornness and their unwillingness to abandon the fight for partial concessions. In a number of occupied factories the young workers were joined by students, an alliance which had never occurred previously. When in some instances both workers and students were savagely attacked by the police such experiences strengthened the newly established bonds. What the students and the strikers had in common were not only the symbols of

[3] These and all following public opinion data were gathered from various and partly unpublished polls taken by the *Institut Français d'Opinion Publique*. I wish to thank the staff of the Institute for their generous assistance.

the red flags hanging from occupied buildings and factories, but the determination to challenge all authority at the very place where it could be challenged most effectively.

One of the strikes, the longest of all, became by its nature a defiance of the government and of its control of mass communications. Strict governmental directives on how to handle the televised image of the students' rebellion, led to the strike of almost the entire personnel of the *Office de la Radiodiffusion-Télévision Française* (O.R.T.F.). The strike dramatized not only the often-denounced bureaucratic inefficiency of that operation but also the nagging and daily interference of various ministries with the handling of radio and television news and occasionally with programming. Earlier reforms had proved insufficient. While declining contemptuously an increase of material benefits offered to them by the government, the strikers demanded a complete overhaul of the structure of the O.R.T.F. which in their eyes had remained a decisive instrument for the manipulation of public opinion. In typical language the Office became another "Bastille" which had to be stormed if freedom of expression was to prevail.[4]

The violent explosions that shook the country had surprised the organized political forces opposed to the regime not less than the government. Far too weak and too divided to have caused any of the outbreaks, opposition parties and trade unions sought to control the movements or at least to profit by them in order to take over the government when it turned out that the regime appeared badly battered by the assault and unable to react to the challenge. As to parliamentary institutions, their brittleness had never been demonstrated more clearly: the debates which took place in the National Assembly while strikes and street battles were at their peak passed almost unnoticed. The rejection of a vote of censure by the majority did not solve any of the pressing problems. The imbalance between the executive and parliament had eliminated the latter from any role, positive or negative, in a crisis situation.

[4] The problem of the O.R.T.F. and proposals for its reform are competently discussed in Club Jean Moulin, *Que faire de la Révolution de Mai?* (Paris: Ed. Seuil, 1968), pp. 47–55.

For the Communist Party (P.C.) and the party-controlled trade union movement, the C.G.T., the threat which arose from the events was as much a threat to their very existence as it was for the government. The break between the Communists and the student movement occurred early. The more the students denounced the bureaucracy of party and C.G.T. as being deliberately moderate in demands and tactics and as traitors to the objectives of the upheaval, the more they in turn were accused by the Communists of anarchism and disorderly radicalism. The P.C. used the considerable means at its disposal to direct popular sympathies, and especially those of its own militants, away from the students. The greatest danger arose for the C.G.T. when its leadership was outflanked from the left in an increasing number of factories by the young workers, and soon not by them alone.

Members of the dissident Socialist Party, the P.S.U., and unions affiliated with the C.F.D.T. were doing all they could to carry out such a maneuver against the Communists. Since it has turned its back on the Catholic trade union movement the C.F.D.T. has attracted some of the most militant working class elements who seek to continue the French traditions of a labor organization not solely devoted to the defense of day-to-day interests. Under a new leadership the P.S.U. has remained numerically insignificant but has been concentrating energies on extra-parliamentary activities, inside and outside the university.

In order to channel the spontaneous outbreaks, the P.C. and C.G.T. organized a one-day general strike and several street demonstrations, always seeing to it that they were able to control them. After the sit-in strikes became widespread, the C.G.T. pressed the government to solve the conflicts as rapidly as possible by initiating on the national level an agreement between employers' associations and trade unions. But when the spokesmen for the C.G.T. returned to the factories to recommend the acceptance of the considerable gains in wages and benefits which the agreements had brought, they were received with catcalls and had to stiffen their demands. Whether the C.G.T. would have been able to interrupt essential services in the capital in order to force out the government is controversial. But there is no doubt that the trade unions did in fact not attempt such an action.

In the words of a careful and conservative commentator: "Not at any moment did the Communist Party and the C.G.T. further an uprising. Not at any moment did they wish to torpedo the Gaullist government whose foreign policy corresponds to their fondest wishes and which permits their progressive integration into French society. Obviously they would have taken care of the state if it had been handed to them. But their constant objective was not to 'make a revolution,' but not to let themselves be outflanked on their left by the students, by the Maoists, by the young workers . . ." [5] After days of careful maneuvering, the leadership of the C.G.T. did regain control over its membership and was able to counsel moderation.

Other factors than the influence of the P.C. must explain why on the whole the countryside remained calm and why the farmers did not participate actively in the various protest movements. The leading farmers' organization (the F.N.S.E.A.) was one of the few groups which kept calm in the midst of upheaval even though in the past the farmers had more than once engaged in violent outbursts of anger against the Gaullist regime. Undoubtedly in May the attitudes of the farmers and of their organization were in part determined by the fact that some of the more constructive reform proposals of the last decade have given them confidence in possibilities for orderly change. The hope that the government would do all to defend French farming interests in the continuing Common Market negotiations, was another factor for restraint. But also it appears likely, and the elections were to confirm such sentiments, that on the whole the rural world was out of sympathy with the methods and objectives of the revolt in the cities and industrial centers.

In quieter times the Federation of the Democratic and

[5] Raymond Aron, "Après la Tempête," *Le Figaro,* June 4, 1968. The events explaining the tactics of the C.G.T. and of the P.C. are discussed in detail by André Barjonet, *La Révolution Trahie de 1968* (Paris: John Didier, 1968). The author had been a leading official of the C.G.T. for 22 years until he resigned his post during the events of May.

Socialist Left had boasted of having formed a "counter government" modeled after the British shadow cabinet and ready to
take over when Gaullism would have to abandon power. But
when such a day seemed to be approaching, the Federation
lost much of its coherence. Conflicts between the organizations
affiliated with it and between the personalities making up its
leadership broke into the open. In spite of recent agreements
between the Federation and the P.C. the old problem as to
whether the Communists were to participate in a future "republican" government sharpened the more the crisis deepened.
At one point, and after considerable hesitations, François
Mitterand, whose popularity was declining faster than that
of General de Gaulle and of his Prime Minister, proposed that
the still prestigious Pierre Mendès-France become the leader of
a provisional government. But the latter was promptly disa-
vowed by the P.C. because he had never repudiated the students and their anti-communist tirades. The lack of a clear
alternative and the lack of an organized force of opposition
besides Communism proved to be an important asset for the
existing regime.

During the last days of May the legitimacy of the Fifth
Republic had worn as thin as that of the Fourth in 1958 and
as that of the Third Republic in 1940, except that this time
neither a colonial war nor a foreign invasion could provide
an excuse. During the decisive days it became apparent that the
institutionalization of the regime was still minimal. When some
Frenchmen took it upon themselves to change from "political
subjects" into political participants, the foundations of the
governmental and social edifice showed deep fissures. Once
more there seemed no other cure for chaos than the providential leader. He now was called upon to liquidate a crisis which
his own regime had brought about.

When the President of the Republic surveyed the disorder
which his government had not known how to prevent, he
typically sought to have recourse to a referendum—which
he announced in a televised speech. To him this institution
had always been the "most democratic" of appeals. In fact
it was the most personalized instrumentality of persuasion
and became even more so in an acute crisis. The referendum

which he proposed (according to art. 11 of the constitution) was to give him a vague mandate for "mutation" and "renovation," that is, for future reform legislation which the regime had not supplied and which now appeared indispensable. He added that if "massive" approval was not forthcoming, he would have to relinquish his office — a more plebiscitarian posture could hardly be imagined.

After the customary consultation, the Council of State declared unconstitutional the legislative texts that were proposed for the referendum. The precedent of the referendum held in 1962 had shown that such advice was not necessarily heeded by the Chief of State. But this time it became clear that the appeal presented by an aging and visibly diffident leader was ineffective. Disorders in streets and factories did not cease; centrifugal forces started tearing at the Gaullist majority in parliament; at least some of the younger high civil servants became restive and sought ways of facilitating the transition to a successor regime. Belatedly even the Communists seemed ready to profit by the occasion and expressed their willingness to participate in the next government.

If an inappropriate speech had accelerated the deterioration of the situation, six days later a new, and this time forceful, appeal made by the same speaker (but over the radio since the strikes made television facilities unavailable) proved to be the magic wand which needed to be waved to bring relief and, almost, order. Nothing illustrates better the high degree of personalization and, as it were, of verbalization of the Gaullist regime. There were certainly other than psychological factors in the equation which turned the tide. These other factors cannot be accounted for as long as little is known about the circumstances surrounding General de Gaulle's visit with certain army generals, about the role of the Prime Minister as de Gaulle's principal advisor during the decisive hours, and about the alternatives which the President of the Republic had in fact weighed.

On the day preceding the speech hundreds of thousands had demonstrated in the working class districts of Paris and demanded a new government. A few hours after the appeal, hundreds of thousands of the General's supporters, most of them middle class and led by the government, filled the Champs-Elysées with their shouts of joy and relief as if after a nightmare. (It reminded bystanders of the astonishing enthusiasm that greeted the French Prime Minister in 1938 when he returned to Paris after he had sealed at Munich the fate of France's ally, Czechoslovakia.)

Politically General de Gaulle's announcement that the government would abandon the plans for a referendum and instead dissolve the National Assembly and call for new elections (hence using art. 12 rather than art. 11 of the constitution) was a masterful stroke. Instead of crystallizing opposition against a plebiscite the regime now offered to the major political forces an opportunity to muster their strength in a traditional electoral contest, even though the circumstances were bound to give to the elections the significance of a plebiscite for or against the regime. The parliamentary opposition had long asked for the dissolution of an Assembly which only recently had once more defeated a motion of censure. Only the extreme Left demurred; but its slogan "Elections = Betrayal" conveniently isolated it from the overwhelming consensus of the body politic. Seventy-five per cent of Parisians approved of the dissolution of the Assembly at a time when 57 per cent welcomed General de Gaulle's decision not to resign from office.

By holding the election as soon as constitutionally possible, the government compelled all opposition forces to do their best to reestablish order, for to interfere with such a democratic device as general elections would turn to the electoral disadvantage of the troublemakers. Within a few days the overexcitement subsided with astonishing speed. Attendance at all but electoral meetings fell off. Most occupied premises, whether in universities or factories, were vacated without drastic police intervention. The time of explosions was over.

## RESTORATION WITHOUT REVOLUTION

The elections were fought in the most traditional forms perhaps more so than those of 1967 and 1962. An average of more than five candidates presented themselves in each of the 485 small constituencies; the electorate was composed of about 15 million women and 13 million men. The numerous electoral meetings were well attended at least in Paris. The discussion was generally low-keyed and without great interest. Even in the capital, not to speak of the provinces, most candidates mentioned the events of May as little as possible, as if not to touch fresh wounds. Because they were not yet twenty-one, many of those who had participated in these events were absent—as they would be on election day.

Candidates belonging to the right and left Center, including those presented by the Federation of the Left, insisted on their political independence. Their wish to be available for all possible governmental combinations furthered the party atomization that had been reversed seemingly in the preceding years. The true interest of the campaign however centered on the duel between the Gaullists [6] and the Communists, a duel which the Gaullists imposed on an almost unwilling opponent. Both President de Gaulle and Prime Minister Pompidou inaugurated the campaign by making the fight against the "totalitarian enterprise" of the Communists the main theme. This was a calculated, historical injustice committed in the interest of successful electioneering. They, and not they alone, knew well that all through the crisis the Communists had done all in their power to control the explosion and that without the discipline of the P.C. and the C.G.T. the regime might not have been saved.

The governmental tactics used against them did not prevent the Communists from hewing to their chosen line during the election campaign; they even amplified on their previous themes. Their attacks against the "personal power" of General de Gaulle were invariably followed by a far sharper criticism of leftist radicalism which they accused of becoming — by its violence of language and action — the accomplice of the regime. Communist propaganda regularly contrasted the absence of disorder in the strikes with the excesses committed by students and other left-wingers. Not communism was the alter-

[6] The Gaullist party as such, the former U.N.R., is now known by the initials U.D.-Ve. Its own candidates and those endorsed by it (Independent Republicans and some others) run for election under the designation U.D.R.

native to the Gaullist regime, they declared, but a broad coalition of workers and democratic forces for which the tricolor flag and the Marseillaise, not the red flag and the International anthem, were the appropriate symbols. By such language they sought to reduce the voters' fear of violence and disorder, while the Gaullists tried to capitalize on that very fear.

When one compares (see Table VII) the results of the first ballot of the 1968 elections not only with those of the preceding elections but also with various public opinion polls taken during the campaign, it becomes apparent that the Gaullist appeal proved far more successful than the protestations of loyalty proffered by the P.C. The losses of the Communists as well as those of the Federation became heavier while the campaign was in progress; the gains of the Gaullists and of their allies grew more pronounced until they took the proportion of a fair-sized landslide.

It is not possible as yet to determine with certainty where the 1.2 million new votes for the Gaullists and the candidates endorsed by them have come from. For the first time ever the percentage of votes for Gaullist candidates almost equalled that which General de Gaulle had obtained personally in previous contests (see Table V, p. 231). Hence the gap between "presidential" and "parliamentary" Gaullism seems all but closed. It appears likely that numerous voters belonging to the extreme Right and who had abstained from voting in 1967 have now lined up behind the Gaullist candidates, especially since the government, just in time for the election, granted an amnesty to a number of prominent Rightists who had been in prison since their mutinous opposition to de Gaulle's Algerian policy.[7]

But the increased support for the candidates presented by the government must be explained by a more general phenomenon. The dread of the recent and the fear of future disorders, an essentially negative reaction, rather than a mandate for

[7] In the first ballot of both the 1967 and the 1968 elections the abstentions amounted to about the same proportion (20 per cent of registered votes). But those who abstained have most likely come from different camps.

TABLE VII  *First Ballot of the Parliamentary Elections of 1968, and Seats won in the National Assembly in Both Ballots, compared to the Results of 1967 (Voting in Metropolitan France)* [1]

| | 1968 | | | 1967 | | | Differences in seats 1967–1968 |
|---|---|---|---|---|---|---|---|
| Registered Votes, in millions | 28.2 | | | 28.3 | | | |
| Abstentions, in % | 19.9% | | | 19.1% | | | |
| Parties | *Votes in millions* | *% of votes cast* | *Seats in Parliament* | *Votes in millions* | *% of votes cast* | *Seats in Parliament* | |
| Communists (P.C.) | 4.4 | 20.03 | 34 | 5.0 | 22.5 | 73 | − 39 |
| P.S.U. | 0.9 | 3.94 | 0 | 0.5 | 2.2 | 3 | − 3 |
| Federation of the Left | 3.6 | 16.50 | 57 | 4.2 | 18.9 | 118 | − 61 |
| Center | 2.3 | 10.3 | 29 | 2.9 | 12.8 | 39 | − 10 |
| U.D.R.[2] | 9.7 | 43.6 | 350 [3] | 8.4 | 37.8 | 242 | +108 |
| Conservatives | 0.9 | 4.1 | 12 [4] | 0.8 | 3.7 | 6 | + 6 |
| Extreme Right | 0.3 | 0.1 | 0 | 0.2 | 0.9 | 0 | − |

[1] Unaffiliated deputies omitted. Slight differences for the results of 1967 between this Table and Table IV (p. 211) result from changes in affiliation of a number of deputies between the elections.

[2] The Gaullist party as such (formerly U.N.R.) is now known by the initials U.D.-Ve.; its own candidates and those endorsed by it run for election under the designation U.D.R.

[3] This includes 296 Gaullists and 54 Independent Republicans who had received the endorsement of the U.D.R.

[4] Among them a number of Independent Republicans likely to vote with the majority.

any positive program has motivated the voters. Except for generalities there was little talk of such a program in the campaign. More than before the U.D.-Ve. (formerly the U.N.R.) has established positions of strength throughout the country, even where previously Gaullism had not been able to take firm root. North of the Loire river the belt of Departments where Gaullist candidates obtained more than 50 per cent of the votes extends now from the eastern border to the Atlantic.

While most of the Gaullist voters might still come from rural and urban middle classes, there has undoubtedly been a heavy inroad into the working class vote. Public opinion polls reveal that for the first time the working class vote for Gaullist candidates was at least equal and probably greater than that for the Communists.[8] Significantly, Gaullism was strengthened, and the Left correspondingly weakened in almost all regions where prolonged sit-in strikes had taken place. Possibly the strikers' wives and older workers who felt that they had been pushed too hard were now protesting by their votes against the experiences they had just lived through. The news and pictures of overturned and burned automobiles seemed to have been a particularly powerful motivation to vote for the party that promised order most unequivocally: the automobile has become throughout France the symbol of modest affluence and of mobility; its destruction was also taken as a sign of contempt for the skill and workmanship on which the French workers, even those in mass industries, still pride themselves.

In the population at large 46 per cent of women as against 35.5 per cent of men declared themselves for the U.D.R. Whereas the Communists still attracted 25 per cent of the male vote, only 18 per cent of the women were willing to vote for them. In addition differences in age still play a significant role: the Gaullist vote is far heavier among those older than 50, that for the P.C. among those younger than 50. There

---

[8] For these and for the figures following in the text see also Alain Duhamel, "Le Sondage de l'I.F.O.P.", *Le Monde,* June 28, 1968. Since between the poll and the election the number of Gaullist votes increased and Communist votes declined, the data given in the text must underestimate the actual differences.

is no such difference among the electorate of other parties. The fact that the elections took place about four years sooner than would be normal and before the heavy influx of younger voters was felt may have been a decisive factor in the result.

The losses sustained by the Communists and the Federation of the Left were about equal to the gains of the Gaullists, although there was no simple transfer of votes from the losers to the winners. The P.C. clearly paid the price for barricades it did not build and of picketing it had not encouraged. As a percentage of the total, the Communist vote was almost back to the low point reached in their serious defeat in 1958 (see Table IV, p. 211). Their slow comeback and especially their integration into French politics seem to have been interrupted once more. In spite of the mildness of Communist propaganda, in a crisis the P.C. is still suspect — clearly the reason why the party dreads social upheavals of almost any kind. The losses of Communist votes in working-class districts must have been particularly painful. On the whole its strength in the Paris Red Belt survived the shock, but even there votes declined substantially, while some of the traditional rural strongholds of the party were saved. Whether such electoral losses can be considered to be compensated in part by the hundreds of thousands of new members the C.G.T. boasts of having recruited remains to be seen: an influx into trade unions at the height of a strike movement has happened quite regularly, but has usually provided only ephemereal strength.

The Federation of the Left suffered severely from its inability to present through its leadership and its program a new image. Many and especially young voters complained that this formation turned out to be nothing but an agglomeration of political forces of the past, singularly inappropriate for representing them in the difficult days ahead. The electoral following of all of the Federation's national leaders declined sharply. In 1967 the Federation attracted more than 30 per cent of the electorate in eighteen Departments; of these eighteen, now only nine remained.

The only opposition party to increase its vote (by about 400,000) was the small P.S.U. to which many of the dissatisfied younger voters, be they Communists or Socialists, seem to have flocked. But in part such gains were merely the result of a greater number of candidates running on the party's ticket. In the end it did not return a single deputy.

The various candidates of the Center and those Conservatives who, because of their uncertain voting record in the defunct parliament, had not been endorsed by the government, lost on balance more than 400,000 votes. Hence the expectations of those who had reckoned that — at least in the first ballot — the electorate would strengthen the middle in order to stem the polarization of the electorate were not fulfilled.

The run-off elections transformed the Gaullist victory in the first ballot into an unprecedented triumph, the set-back of the Left into a disaster (see Table VII). In the future Assembly the disciplined Gaullist party forms by itself a large majority (296 seats of a total of 485). Although the conservative candidates belonging to the Independent Republicans (R.I.) have also increased the number of their deputies, their votes are no longer needed, which does not preclude the possibility that they may nevertheless be solicited. The control of parliament by a single party had not been achieved since the beginning of the Fifth Republic, nor has it ever been known in the history of any French republic.

To be sure the electoral system exaggerates voting trends. In popular votes the Left received in the second ballot about 6.1 million votes as against 6.7 million for the Gaullists. But it is nevertheless significant that the respective losses and gains for the majority and for the Left are distributed very evenly throughout the country.

The majority party has played the card of youth effectively. Among the new men whom the Gaullists are sending to parliament there are a number of very young candidates. Of the 13 deputies between 26 and 34 years of age, all but two are Gaullists. On the other hand votes cast for known personalities of the Left have declined without exception: Pierre Mendès-France was defeated, the leaders of the Federation and of the Socialist Party — Mitterand, Defferre and Mollet — saw their vote dwindle, as did many of their colleagues. In many constituencies it became obvious that the voters disliked the alliance between the P.C. and the Federation; this does not augur well for the future of an alliance forged so recently and which must be profitable to continue.

Undoubtedly the electorate has wanted to confirm its trust in General de Gaulle and his candidates, to express its disappointment in the performance of the opposition parties, and to state even more decidedly its dislike of the threat to stability inherent in the explosions of the preceding month. What the government has obtained is a brilliant success in its search for a vote of confidence by plebiscite. The vast improvement of its parliamentary situation is of far less if any importance. For even in its dying days the defunct parliament gave the government all the votes it asked for. No single bill of importance had ever been turned down. The reforms which the government is now promising were not enacted earlier simply because the government's policy then had no room for them. Hence the future of the Fifth Republic will clearly depend on the use which the government is going to make of the newly acquired popular confidence.

The real problems of French society and politics remain to be solved.

**PERSPECTIVES**

Once more Frenchmen have enacted the scenario, described by Tocqueville more than a century ago: "At one moment he [the Frenchman] is up in arms against authority and the next we find him serving the powers-that-be with a zeal such as the most servile races never display. So long as no one thinks of resisting, you can lead him on a thread, but once a revolutionary movement is afoot nothing can restrain him from taking part in it. That is why our rulers are so often taken by surprise; they fear the nation either too much or not enough . . ." [9]

The events of May, surprising a prosperous and rapidly modernizing country, have again dramatically demonstrated the perennial obstacles to a self-reform of the political and social system. The explosions have destroyed much that was rotten and some that was worthwhile. By themselves they could not bring about the needed reforms even if those who

[9] See Tocqueville, *The Old Régime* . . . op. cit., p. 211.

rebelled had had a clearer conception of what they wanted. The elections have merely suspended the crisis. As a reinstating phenomenon they have reestablished by and large the parliamentary *status quo ante* and lent to the regime the seal of renewed popular approval. But they did not provide legitimacy for the presumably sweeping overhaul of the economic and social structures which President and Prime Minister have promised for the immediate future. ("I am not at all embarrassed to be a revolutionary," General de Gaulle has declared over the radio, boasting of the reforms he had introduced in earlier times especially during the immediate postliberation period.[10])

It appears to be of secondary importance whether parliament will be associated in this enterprise, or whether the government will use the means of a constitutionally correct referendum, in order to emphasize the techniques of direct democracy, preferred by General de Gaulle and presumably catering to popular diffidence towards parliamentary institutions. If the President of the Republic were to retire from office before the expiration of his term in 1972 the recent electoral victory seems to assure that, unless a revolution were to change all predictions, a Gaullist regime would be in charge of assuring the succession and of initiating the mutations designed to liquidate the crisis.

Since the university structures were the first to crack, their rebuilding and those of the secondary schools are considered to be most urgent. From many sides autonomy for the individual institutions is recommended in order to overcome senseless, and as the recent events have shown, dangerous centralization which transmits local disturbances to the entire system. But, just as for the long-attempted administrative reforms, the main problem here consists of creating decentralized structures and true autonomy in spite of the traditional attitudes toward authority which reproduce automatically the trend toward centralization. The opposite tendency, a ferocious parochialism which in the past has been

[10] Among his "revolutionary" acts General de Gaulle included his 1967 speech in Montreal by which he sought to encourage Québec independence.

exemplified by a phenomenon such as Poujadism, is equally (if not more) inadequate to the needs of a modern society. Will the shock which society has received during the spring of 1968 be powerful enough to reverse such trends amidst hastily reestablished order?

The formula which the government and part of the opposition as well are constantly invoking is that of "participation." It probably corresponds to more than a political slogan although it has already been discredited by its overuse for political ends. The desire for effective participation was not absent from the strikes and from the street movements in May. It expresses a strongly felt if badly articulated need for communication and cooperation for which there has been little room in a hierarchically ordered political culture, as rich in privileges as it is in egalitarian pretensions.[11]

Yet the difficulties that are in the way of any meaningful participation have increased rather than abated. As long as the regime has not altered its authoritarian style — and how could the style be altered without a change of its leading personalities? — the young generation and the millions of voters, who even after an electoral defeat are still committed to the Left, will feel as excluded from the system as before. Hence psychological tensions detrimental to a climate of cooperation are bound to arise anew.

The two domains in which the explosions of May have occurred are particularly vulnerable. Even under the best of circumstances and after some changes have been introduced, the beginning of the next academic year, the *rentrée,* will have to face most of the old and many new problems: an even larger number of students and inadequate facilities, but also an increased number of political activists in universities and secondary schools who are preparing to renew the struggle. There are indications that an awakened and sharpened political sense will replace the somewhat lyrical exhibitionism of the spring.

Industrial peace is in no way assured. While most of the managers of the large modern enterprises are willing to abide

[11] See, also for the following, Raymond Aron, "Propos pour Adultes," *Le Figaro,* June 10, 1968.

by the agreements into which their associations have entered, many employers not only fear for the economic survival of their firms but are smarting under the loss of authority they believe they have incurred. Their mood is, if anything, even uglier than after the strikes which greeted the installation of the Popular Front Government in 1936 and which opened a long and debilitating period of social unrest. Then the government wore itself out in attempts to bring the warring parties together. Will the present regime be able to establish "dialogues" (another keyword of its vocabulary) not only to inaugurate better industrial relations but also to dissuade French business from proceeding with inflationary price rises?

The massive increases in labor costs will affect individual firms and the entire economy in a variety of ways that cannot yet be determined. The state will have to come to the aid of numerous enterprises, most likely in the form of direct and indirect subsidies which cannot easily be defended at a moment when the Common Market abolishes the last tariff barriers between the partners. But to postpone the further integration of the European economies would endanger the agricultural agreements on which the French farmers are counting.

The budgetary deficit will be at record heights when the growth of the GNP that had been scheduled to reach 5.5 per cent during 1968 may be down to 1 or 2 per cent. The rise in costs and, before long in prices, will seriously affect the trade balance and the franc must be defended possibly by drastic measures. That many small firms may be unable to survive sharpened competition at home and abroad and that large concerns will try to diminish labor costs by further mechanization could be considered salutary and even essential for economic modernization. But the spreading of unemployment at a time when the workers will notice that a large part of their recent gains are being lost in the upward spiralling of living costs could again exacerbate resentment. If this happens, new explosions are more likely than practices of participation.

The increase in resentment of group against group, class against class, generation against generation, and ideology against ideology has been covered up by the seemingly large consensus at the elections. Yet it may turn out to be the heaviest legacy of the recent troubles and a serious hindrance to the peaceful political change to which the regime is committed.

There can, finally, be no doubt that the international position of France will be affected by the events.[12] Even if the government were not to alter any of its European policies, if it were not to abandon but only to reschedule its plans for an atomic striking force, its weight in the concert of nations is bound to decrease. General de Gaulle's gestures in the foreign policy field, the advice he has offered freely to other nations, large and small, and even the material help extended to the new African states were all based on the image of France as a tranquil oasis in a troubled world, on the reality of a solid currency, and on the assumptions of social harmony. All this is gone, in large part because the government had postponed for too long and by inappropriate means the solution of urgent problems.

The primacy of foreign policy has been at all times one of the tenets of General de Gaulle's political conception. But to use his own terms: France will be France. The country has demonstrated that the passions and dreams, the values and interests of Frenchmen, in short French politics will not tolerate neglect.

[12] See André Fontaine, "Eclipse partielle," *Le Monde,* June 28, 1968 and especially Alfred Grosser, "La politique extérieure affectée?", *id.,* June 19, 1968.

# Suggestions for Further Reading

The footnotes of this book provide a rather complete bibliography of books and articles in English and French. The reader in search of factual information, either current or historical, will find indispensable the Paris daily *Le Monde* (of which a weekly "Selection" is available outside of France) and *L'Année Politique*, published every spring (Presses Universitaires de France). The journal of the French Political Science Association, *Revue Française de Science Politique*, contains a regular section *"Les Forces Politiques en France"* which is of great value.

The following bibliography lists, quite selectively, some books, all in English, which the reader may find useful when he wishes to familiarize himself with a variety of viewpoints on various periods and aspects of French politics.

Aron, Raymond, *France: Steadfast and Changing, The Fourth to the Fifth Republic* (Cambridge: Harvard University Press, 1960)

Aron, Robert, and Georges Elgey, *The Vichy Regime, 1940–1944* (New York: Macmillan, 1958)

Brinton, Crane, *The Americans and the French* (Cambridge: Harvard University Press, 1968)

Brogan, Denis W., *France under the Republic* (New York: Harper & Row, 1940)

Curtius, Ernst R., *The Civilization of France: An Introduction* (New York: Vintage Books, paperback ed., 1962)

Grosser, Alfred, *French Foreign Policy under de Gaulle* (Boston: Little, Brown and Company, 1967)

Hoffmann, Stanley, et al., *In Search of France* (Cambridge: Harvard University Press, paperback ed., 1965)

Kesselman, Mark, *The Ambiguous Consensus: A Study of Local Government in France* (New York: Knopf, 1967)

Macridis, Roy C., and Bernard Brown, *The de Gaulle Republic: Quest for Unity* and *Supplement to the de Gaulle Republic* (Homewood: Dorsey Press, 1960 and 1963)

Ridley F., and J. Blondel, *Public Administration in France* (New York: Barnes and Noble, 1965)

Siegfried, André, *France: A Study in Nationality* (New Haven: Yale University Press, 1930)

Thomson, David, *Democracy in France Since 1870* (New York: Oxford University Press, paperback ed., 1964)

Werth, Alexander, *De Gaulle: A Political Biography* (Baltimore, Penguin Books, 1965)

Williams, Philip M., *Crisis and Compromise: Politics in the Fourth Republic* (New York: Anchor Books, paperback ed., 1964)

Williams, Philip M., *De Gaulle's Republic* (London: Longmans, 1961)

Williams, Philip M., *The French Parliament: Politics in the Fifth Republic* (New York: Praeger, 1968)

Wright, Gordon, *France in Modern Times, 1760 to the Present* (Chicago: Rand McNally and Company, 1962)

# Chronology of Events

| | |
|---|---|
| 1789 | *July 14,* Fall of the Bastille |
| | *August,* Declaration of the Rights of Man |
| | *November,* Nationalization of Church property |
| 1791 | *September,* First constitution voted |
| 1792 | *September,* Abolition of Monarchy, First Republic |
| 1793 | *June,* Second constitution voted |
| 1794 | Fall of Robespierre |
| 1795 | Rule of Directory begins |
| 1799 | Coup d'état of 18 brumaire, Napoleon First Consul |
| 1804 | Proclamation of Empire |
| | Promulgation of the Civil Code |
| 1808 | Establishment of the University |
| 1814 | Abdication of Napoleon |
| | Constitutional Charter of the restored Bourbon Monarchy |
| 1815 | Napoleon's Hundred Days |
| 1830 | *July,* Revolution in Paris; fall of the Bourbon dynasty |
| | Constitutional Charter of the July Monarchy (Louis-Philippe) |
| 1848 | *February,* Revolution in Paris |
| | Proclamation of universal suffrage |
| | *June,* Bloody suppression of workers' insurrection in Paris |
| | Constitution of the Second Republic |
| | Louis Napoleon Bonaparte elected President |
| 1851 | Coup d'état by Louis Napoleon |
| 1852 | Proclamation of the Second Empire |
| 1867 | Napoleon III announces constitutional changes to inaugurate the "Liberal Empire" |

1870      Surrender of Napoleon III at Sedan; Government of National Defense

1871      *March to May*, Paris Commune

1875      Constitutional Laws of the Third Republic

1879–82   Educational reforms terminating clerical control and banning religious instruction from the public schools

1889      Movement in favor of General Boulanger collapses with Boulanger's flight

1890      Charles de Gaulle born in Lille

1892      High-tariff policy inaugurated by J. Méline, Minister of Agriculture

1897–99   Dreyfus Affair

1905      Law for separation of Church and State

1914      *July*, Assassination of the socialist leader Jaurès on the eve of the French mobilization for the First World War
            *September*, Battle of the Marne

1917      Clemenceau government with extensive wartime powers

1919      *June*, Treaty of Versailles

1923      *January*, Occupation of the Ruhr

1924      Electoral Victory of the "Cartel of the Left"

1934      Stavisky scandal
            Attempted coup d'état by the right-wing Leagues

1936      Electoral victory of the Popular Front

1937      Fall of the Popular Front government headed by Léon Blum

1938      Munich agreement on the dismemberment of Czechoslovakia

1939      England and France declare war on Germany

1940      *June 18*, General de Gaulle calls from London for continued resistance
            *June 22*, Pétain Government signs the armistice with Germany
            *July*, Vote in Vichy of constitutional laws establishing the French State

1942      *November*, Allied landings in North Africa; Germans move into unoccupied France

1944      *June*, Allied landings in Normandy
            *August*, General de Gaulle enters Paris

1945      The Constituent Assembly confirms General de Gaulle as head of the Provisional Government

1946      *January*, General de Gaulle resigns his office
            *June*, Speech at Bayeux, outlining General de Gaulle's constitutional ideas

*October,* Constitution of the Fourth Republic approved by referendum

1947     *May,* Dismissal of the Communist ministers from the government

*October,* A newly formed Gaullist party gains 40 percent of the votes in municipal elections

1949     NATO Treaty ratified by France

1951     Law (Barangé) granting state subsidies to parochial schools

Ratification of the treaty creating the Coal and Steel Community

1954     *May,* Defeat of the French Army at Dien Bien Phu by forces of Communist North Vietnam

*June,* Mendès-France government invested

*July,* Geneva Accords on Armistice in Vietnam

*November,* Nationalist insurrection in Algeria begins

1955     *February,* Mendès-France government falls on North African policy

*June,* General de Gaulle announces his total retirement from public life

1956     French troops participate in the attack on the Suez Canal

1957     Ratification of the Rome Treaties establishing the European Common Market

1958     *May 13,* Insurrection of French settlers in Algiers; formation of a Committee on Public Safety demanding the return to power of General de Gaulle

*June 1,* General de Gaulle government invested

*September,* Constitution of the Fifth Republic approved by referendum

*December,* General de Gaulle elected President of the Republic

1959     *September,* General de Gaulle proposes self-determination for Algeria

1960     *January,* Collapse of French settlers' revolt in Algeria

1961     *April,* Collapse of Army revolt in Algeria

1962     *March,* Cease-fire agreement for Algeria signed at Evian

*July,* Independence for Algeria approved by referendum

*October,* Amendment to the constitution, introducing the popular election of the President, accepted by referendum

1965     General de Gaulle reelected President of the Republic

1966     France leaves the North Atlantic Treaty Organization and demands the withdrawal of all foreign troops stationed on her territory

# The French Constitution of 1958

*(This abridgment includes only those parts which are referred to in the text of this book. A complete version of the constitution may be obtained from the Press and Information Division of the French Embassy, New York.)*

### PREAMBLE

The French people hereby solemnly proclaims their attachment to the Rights of Man and the principles of national sovereignty as defined by the Declaration of 1789, reaffirmed and completed by the Preamble to the Constitution of 1946.

· · · · · ·

### TITLE I — ON SOVEREIGNTY

*Article 2.* France is a Republic, indivisible, secular, democratic and social. It shall ensure the equality of all citizens before the law, without distinction of origin, race or religion. It shall respect all beliefs.

The national emblem is the tricolor flag, blue, white and red.

The national anthem is the "Marseillaise."

The motto of the Republic is "Liberty, Equality, Fraternity."

Its principle is government of the people, by the people and for the people.

*Article 3.* National sovereignty belongs to the people, which shall exercise it through their representatives and by way of referendum.

No section of the people, nor any individual, may attribute to themselves or himself the exercise thereof.

Suffrage may be direct or indirect under the conditions stipulated by the Constitution. It shall always be universal, equal and secret.

349

All French citizens of both sexes who are of age and who enjoy civil and political rights may vote under the conditions to be determined by law.

*Article 4.* Political parties and groups shall play a part in the exercise of the right to vote. They shall be formed freely and shall carry on their activities freely. They must respect the principles of national sovereignty and of democracy.

## TITLE II — THE PRESIDENT OF THE REPUBLIC

*Article 5.* The President of the Republic shall see that the Constitution is respected. He shall ensure, by his arbitration, the regular functioning of the governmental authorities, as well as the continuity of the State.

He shall be the guarantor of national independence, of the integrity of the territory, and of respect for Community agreements and treaties.

*Article 6.** The President of the Republic shall be elected for seven years by direct universal suffrage.

The procedures implementing the present article shall be determined by an organic law.

*Article 7.* The President of the Republic shall be elected by an absolute majority of the votes cast. If no such majority obtains on the first ballot, a second ballot shall take place on the second Sunday following the first ballot. Then only the two candidates who have received the greatest number of votes on the first ballot, after taking into account, if need be, better placed candidates who have withdrawn, may present themselves.

*Article 8.* The President of the Republic shall appoint the Prime Minister. He shall terminate the functions of the Prime Minister when the latter presents the resignation of the Government.

On the proposal of the Prime Minister, he shall appoint and dismiss the other members of the Government.

*Article 9.* The President of the Republic shall preside over the Council of Ministers.

*Article 10.* The President of the Republic shall promulgate the laws within fifteen days following their final adoption and transmission to the Government.

Before the end of this period he may ask Parliament for a reconsideration of the law or of certain of its articles. This reconsideration cannot be refused.

* [Adopted by referendum of October 28, 1962.]

*Article 11.* The President of the Republic, on the proposal of the Government during Parliamentary sessions, or on joint motion of the two Assemblies, published in the *Journal Officiel,* may submit to a referendum any bill dealing with the organization of the public authorities, entailing approval of a Community agreement, or authorizing the ratification of a treaty that, without being contrary to the Constitution, might affect the functioning of the institutions.

When the referendum decides in favor of the bill, the President of the Republic shall promulgate it within the time limit stipulated in the preceding article.

*Article 12.* The President of the Republic may, after consultation with the Prime Minister and the Presidents of the Assemblies, declare the dissolution of the National Assembly.

General elections shall take place twenty days at the least and forty days at the most after the dissolution.

The National Assembly shall convene by right on the second Thursday following its election. If this meeting takes place between the periods provided for ordinary sessions, a session shall, by right, be held for a fifteen-day period.

There may be no further dissolution within a year following these elections.

. . . . . .

*Article 16.* When the institutions of the Republic, the independence of the Nation, the integrity of its territory or the fulfillment of its international commitments are threatened in a grave and immediate manner and when the regular functioning of the constitutional public authorities is interrupted, the President of the Republic shall take the measures required by these circumstances, after official consultation with the Prime Minister, the Presidents of the Assemblies and the Constitutional Council.

He shall inform the nation of these measures by a message.

These measures must be inspired by the desire to ensure to the constitutional public authorities, in the shortest possible time, the means of fulfilling their assigned functions. The Constitutional Council shall be consulted about such measures.

Parliament shall meet by right.

The National Assembly may not be dissolved during the exercise of emergency powers.

. . . . . .

TITLE III — THE GOVERNMENT *

*Article 20.* The Government shall determine and direct the policy of the nation.

It shall have at its disposal the administration and the armed forces.

It shall be responsible to Parliament under the conditions and according to the procedures stipulated in Articles 49 and 50.

*Article 21.* The Prime Minister shall direct the operation of the Government. He shall be responsible for national defense. He shall ensure the execution of the laws. Subject to the provisions of Article 13, he shall have regulatory powers and shall make appointments to civil and military posts.

*Article 23.* Membership in the Government shall be incompatible with the exercise of any Parliamentary mandate, with the holding of any office at the national level in business, professional or labor organizations, and with any public employment or professional activity.

An organic law shall determine the conditions under which the holders of such mandates, functions or employments shall be replaced.

. . . . . .

TITLE IV — THE PARLIAMENT

*Article 24.* The Parliament shall comprise the National Assembly and the Senate.

The deputies to the National Assembly shall be elected by direct suffrage.

The Senate shall be elected by indirect suffrage. It shall ensure the representation of the territorial units of the Republic. Frenchmen living outside France shall be represented in the Senate.

. . . . . .

*Article 28.* Parliament shall convene by right in two ordinary sessions each year. The first session shall begin on October 2nd and last eighty days.

The second session shall begin on April 2nd and may not last longer than ninety days.

*Article 29.* Parliament shall convene in extraordinary session at the request of the Prime Minister, or of the majority of the members of the National Assembly, to consider a specific agenda.

* [The Constitution uses the term "government" in the narrow sense of the responsible ministry, the cabinet.]

When an extraordinary session is held at the request of the members of the National Assembly, the closure decree shall take effect as soon as the Parliament has exhausted the agenda for which it was called, and at the latest twelve days from the date of its meeting.

Only the Prime Minister may ask for a new session before the end of the month following the closure decree.

• • • • • •

TITLE V — RELATIONS BETWEEN PARLIAMENT AND THE GOVERNMENT

*Article 34.* All laws shall be voted by Parliament.

Laws shall establish the regulations concerning:

— civil rights and the fundamental guarantees granted to the citizens for the exercise of civil liberties; the obligations imposed by national defense upon the persons and property of citizens;

— nationality, status and legal capacity of persons, marriage contracts, inheritance and gifts;

— definitions of crimes and misdemeanors as well as the penalties applicable to them; criminal procedure; amnesty; the creation of new types of jurisdictions and the statute of the judiciary;

— the basis, the rate and the methods of collecting taxes of all types; the currency system.

Laws shall likewise determine the rules concerning:

— the electoral system for the Parliamentary and local assemblies;

— the creation of categories of public corporations;

— the fundamental guarantees granted to civil and military personnel employed by the State;

— the nationalization of enterprises and the transfer of property from the public to the private sector.

Laws shall determine the fundamental principles of:

— the general organization of national defense;

— the free administration of local communities, the extent of their jurisdiction and their resources;

— education;

— property rights, civil and commercial obligations;

— labor law, trade-union law and social security.

Finance laws shall determine the resources and obligations of the State under the conditions and with the reservations to be provided for by an organic law.

Laws pertaining to national planning shall determine the objectives of the economic and social action of the State.

The provisions of the present article may be developed in detail and completed by an organic law.

*Article 35.* Parliament shall authorize the declaration of war.

*Article 36.* Martial law shall be decreed in a meeting of the Council of Ministers.

Its prolongation beyond twelve days may be authorized only by Parliament.

*Article 37.* Matters other than those that fall within the domain of law shall be subject to rule-making.*

•  •  •  •  •  •

*Article 38.* The Government may, for the implementation of its program, ask Parliament to authorize it, for a limited period, to take by ordinance measures that are normally within the domain of law.

The ordinances shall be enacted in meetings of the Council of Ministers after consultation with the Council of State. They shall come into force upon their publication, but shall become null and void if the bill for their ratification is not submitted to Parliament before the date set by the enabling act.

At the expiration of the time limit referred to in the first paragraph of the present article, the ordinances may be modified only by law in those matters which are within the legislative domain.

•  •  •  •  •  •

*Article 40.* Bills and amendments introduced by members of Parliament shall not be considered when their adoption would have as a consequence either a diminution of public revenues, or the creation or increase of public expenditures.

*Article 41.* If it appears in the course of the legislative procedure that a private member bill or an amendment is not within the domain of law or is contrary to a delegation of authority granted by virtue of Article 38, the Government may request that it be ruled out of order.

In case of disagreement between the Government and the President of the assembly concerned, the Constitutional Council, upon the request of either party, shall rule within a time limit of eight days.

•  •  •  •  •  •

*Article 44.* Members of Parliament and of the Government shall have the right of amendment.

* [i.e., by the cabinet]

After the opening of the debate, the Government may oppose the examination of any amendment which has not previously been submitted to a committee.

If the Government so requests, the assembly concerned shall decide, by a single vote, on all or part of the bill under discussion, retaining only the amendments proposed or accepted by the Government.

*Article 45.* Every bill is discussed successively in the two assemblies with a view to agreement on identical versions.

When, as a result of disagreement between the two assemblies, a bill has not been passed after two readings in each assembly, or, if the Government has declared the bill urgent, after a single reading by each assembly, the Prime Minister is entitled to have the bill sent to a joint Committee composed of equal numbers from the two assemblies, with the task of finding agreed versions of the provisions in dispute.

The version prepared by the joint committee may be submitted by the Government to the two assemblies for their approval. No amendment may be accepted without the agreement of the Government.

If the joint committee does not produce an agreed version, or if the version agreed is not approved as provided for in the preceding paragraph, the Government may ask the National Assembly, after one more reading by the National Assembly and by the Senate, to decide the matter. In this case, the National Assembly may adopt either the version prepared by the joint committee or the last version passed by itself, modified, if necessary, by one or any of the amendments passed by the Senate.

·  ·  ·  ·  ·  ·

*Article 47.* Parliament shall pass finance bills under conditions to be stipulated by an organic law.

Should the National Assembly fail to reach a decision on first reading within a time limit of forty days after a bill has been introduced, the Government shall refer it to the Senate, which must rule within a time limit of fifteen days. The procedure set forth in Article 45 shall then be followed.

Should Parliament fail to reach a decision within a time limit of seventy days, the provisions of the bill may be put into effect by ordinance.

Should the finance bill establishing the revenues and expenditures of a fiscal year not be filed in time for it to be promulgated before the beginning of that fiscal year, the Government shall immediately request from Parliament the authorization to levy the taxes and shall make available by decree the funds needed to meet the Government commitments already voted.

The time limits provided for in the present article shall be suspended when Parliament is not in session.

The Court of Accounts shall assist Parliament and the Government in supervising the implementation of the finance laws.

*Article 48.* The discussion of the bills submitted or agreed upon by the Government shall have priority on the agenda of the assemblies in the order determined by the Government.

One meeting each week shall be reserved, by priority, for questions asked by members of Parliament and for answers by the Government.

*Article 49.* The Prime Minister, after deliberation in the Council of Ministers, may pledge the responsibility of the Government before the National Assembly with regard to the program of the Government, or if it be so decided with regard to a declaration of general policy.

The National Assembly may call into question the responsibility of the Government by the vote of a motion of censure. Such a motion shall be in order only if it is signed by at least one tenth of the members of the National Assembly. The vote may only take place forty-eight hours after the motion has been introduced. Only votes favorable to the motion shall be counted. It shall be considered adopted only if supported by a majority of the members of the Assembly. Should the motion of censure be rejected, its signatories may not introduce another motion in the course of the same session, except in the case provided for in the next paragraph.

The Prime Minister may, after deliberation in the Council of Ministers, pledge the Government's responsibility before the National Assembly on the vote of all or part of a bill or motion. In that case, the text shall be considered as adopted, unless a motion of censure, filed in the succeeding twenty-four hours, is voted under the conditions laid down in the previous paragraph.

The Prime Minister shall be entitled to ask the Senate for the approval of a general policy declaration.

*Article 50.* When the National Assembly adopts a motion of censure, or rejects the program or a declaration of general policy of the Government, the Prime Minister must submit the resignation of the Government to the President of the Republic.

. . . . . .

TITLE VII — THE CONSTITUTIONAL COUNCIL

*Article 56.* The Constitutional Council shall consist of nine members, whose term of office shall last nine years and shall not be renewable. One third of the membership of the Constitutional Council shall be renewed every three years. Three of its members shall be appointed by the President of the Republic, three by the President of the National Assembly, three by the President of the Senate.

In addition to the nine members provided for above, former Presidents of the Republic shall be members ex officio for life of the Constitutional Council.

The President shall be appointed by the President of the Republic. He shall have the deciding vote in case of a tie.

. . . . . .

*Article 61.* Organic laws, before their promulgation, and the rules of procedure of the Parliamentary assemblies, before they come into application, must be submitted to the Constitutional Council, which shall decide whether they conform to the Constitution.

To the same end, laws may be submitted to the Constitutional Council, before their promulgation, by the President of the Republic, the Prime Minister or the President of either assembly.

In the cases provided for by the two preceding paragraphs, the Constitutional Council must make its ruling within a time limit of one month. Nevertheless, at the request of the Government, in case of emergency, this period shall be reduced to eight days.

In these same cases, referral to the Constitutional Council shall suspend the time limit for promulgation.

*Article 62.* A provision declared unconstitutional may not be promulgated or implemented.

The decisions of the Constitutional Council are not subject to appeal. They are binding on public authorities and on all administrative and judicial authorities.

. . . . . .

TITLE X — THE ECONOMIC AND SOCIAL COUNCIL

*Article 69.* The Economic and Social Council, at the request of the Government, shall give its opinion on such Government bills, ordinances and decrees, as well as on the private members' bills as are submitted to it.

*Article 70.* The Economic and Social Council may likewise be consulted by the Government on any problem of an economic or social character of interest to the Republic or to the Community. Any plan, or any program-bill of an economic or social character shall be submitted to it for its advice.

* * * * * *

## TITLE XIV — AMENDMENT

*Article 89.* The initiative for amending the Constitution shall belong both to the President of the Republic on the proposal of the Prime Minister and to the members of Parliament.

The proposed amendment must be passed by the two assemblies in identical terms. The amendment shall become effective after approval by a referendum.

However, the proposed amendment shall not be submitted to a referendum when the President of the Republic decides to submit it to Parliament convened in Congress*; in this case, the proposed amendment shall be approved only if it is accepted by a three-fifths majority of the votes cast. The Bureau of the Congress shall be that of the National Assembly.

No amendment procedure may be initiated or pursued when the integrity of the territory is in jeopardy.

The Republican form of government shall not be subject to amendment.

* [i.e., a joint meeting of both Assemblies]

# Index

*Action Française*, 146
administration, 139–42
  centralization of, 11, 13, 84, 85, 138, 172, 340
  elite corps in, 249
  *see also* bureaucracy, ENA
agriculture, 26–28
  and governmental support, 41–42
  Ministry of, 136, 176, 182, 259
  and Common Market, 190–91
  and Senate, 295–97
  *see also* farmers, interest groups
Alain (Émile Chartier), 12, 93–94, 223
Algeria, 9, 221, 273, 286, 305
  crisis in, 46, 108, 139, 159, 162, 164, 193, 209, 215, 216, 232, 239, 247, 253, 267, 274, 284, 305, 308, 318, 334
  peace terms for, 110
  future of, 149
  independence of, 187, 311
  army mutiny in, 272–73
Allied Powers, 82
Alsace-Lorraine, 51
*amicales, see* interest groups
anti-clericalism, 48, 56, 72
Armed Forces, Ministry of, 261
Army, 188, 331
  officer corps of, 6, 270–75
*arrondissements,* 85
associations, 75–76. *See also* interest groups

atomic force, 285, 298, 343
Auriol, Vincent, 88
*Aurore, L'*, 155
authoritarianism, 66, 67
authority, attitudes toward, 10–14, 30, 44, 60, 66–68, 75, 78–80, 121, 324–25, 326–27

Balzac, Honoré de, 57
Barrès, Maurice, 127
Bayeux speech, 196, 245, 299. *See also* de Gaulle
Belgium, 229
Bismarck, Otto von, 3
"blocked vote," 285
Blum, Léon, 121, 139, 144, 219
Bolingbroke, Lord, 311
bonapartism, 8–9, 150, 202, 203, 234–35. *See also* Napoleon I, Napoleon III
Bossuet, Jacques, 148
Bourbons, 131
bourgeoisie, 5, 61–62, 331–32
  and working class 61–64
  and educational system, 69–72
  and interest groups, 76
  in parliament, 126–27
  in civil service, 133
Brittany, 51
budget, *see* finance
Burckhardt, Jacob, 106
bureaucracy, 131–42, 300
  and interest groups, 179–81, 184–88, 268

bureaucracy *(Cont.)*
executive controls of, 266–67
and parliament, 266, 278
and ministers, 267
and modernization, 268–69
*see also* administration, civil service, officers
Burke, Edmund, 4
business, private, 29–31, 33, 37, 116, 188, 341–42
business, government-operated, *see* public sector

cabinets, 97, 122, 158, 249, 250, 256, 260, 262–65, 267, 279, 281
lawyers in, 128–29
of Fourth Republic, 223
of Fifth Republic, 171, 260–62, 284
and censure vote, 281–82
and parliament, 301
*cabinets,* ministerial, *see* ministerial *cabinets*
Caesar, 17, 317
Camus, Albert, 79
Castro, Fidel, 161
Catholic Church, 2, 4, 47–57, 73, 179, 221, 296, 325–26
and anti-clericalism, 48–50. *See also* freemasonry
and working class, 55–56, 174
and press, 156–57
and Communist Party, 213–14
and M.R.P., 203, 228–29
*see also La Croix*
Catholics, 143, 148
in politics, 6, 50–51, 325–26
and 1965 presidential elections, 116–17
Catholic schools, 53, 55, 56, 73, 229
Catholic youth movement, 55
censure motions, 281–82, 285, 287–88, 327, 332
Chief of State, *see* President of the Republic
Center, 206, 207, 208, 224, 242, 333, 338

Chaban-Delmas, Jacques (Mayor of Bordeaux), 88, 91
Chambers of Agriculture, 188
Chambers of Commerce, 188
Chamber of Deputies, *see* National Assembly
Chambord, Comte de, 5
Chapelier law, Le, 171
Churchill, Winston, 148
civil service, 131–34, 139–42, 160, 259, 264–72, 331. *See also* bureaucracy
classes, 60–64, 68–71, 76. *See also* bourgeoisie, working class
Clemenceau, Georges, 148
clubs, political, 240–43
Coal and Steel Community, *see* Schuman Plan
CODER (Regional Development Boards), 270–72, 294, 297
Colbert, Jean Baptiste, 30, 34
Commissariat for Planning, 33–36. *See also* planning
committees
parliamentary, 277, 292
Finance and Economics, 290
Common Market, *see* European Common Market
*communes,* 82–85, 87, 88, 90, 91, 92
communication, mass, 87, 152–68, 287, 315
and 1965 presidential elections, 113–14
*see also* press, radio, television
Communist Party (P.C.), 50, 54, 86, 96, 114, 123–24, 193, 199, 200, 202, 207–08, 210–18, 226, 228, 237, 289, 294, 307, 324, 328–29, 331, 333–39
and working class, 63, 64
in local government, 91, 93
in 1958 referendum and elections, 110, 213
in 1965 presidential election, 113, 117
in Parliament, 125, 127
and de Gaulle, 150

Communist Party (P.C.) (*Cont.*)
  in trade unions, 174–75, 324
  and Socialists, 220, 221
  *see also* C.G.T.
"concerted economy" (*économie concertée*), 36
Confédération Française des Travailleurs Chrétiens (C.F.T.C.), 174–75
Confédération Française et Démocratique du Travail (C.F.D.T.), 175, 328
Confédération Générale du Travail (C.G.T.), 174–75, 181, 193–94, 208, 212, 328–29, 333, 337
Conseils Généraux, 83, 87, 89
Conseil National du Patronat Français (C.N.P.F.), 117
conservatives, *see* Right
constitution, 15, 120, 279, 304, 311
  of 1791, 7
  of 1793, 7
  of Third Republic, 246
  of Fourth Republic, 278–79
  of Fifth Republic, 46, 53–54, 105, 110–11, 148, 246, 250–54, 276, 279–85, 287–89, 306–07, 313, 330–31, 332
  1962 changes in, 149, 237–38, 297, 309–10. *See also* referendum of 1962
Constitutional Council, 164, 251–52, 282–83, 288–89, 297, 313
Convention of Republican Institutions, 224–27
Council of State, 135, 262, 331
Consultative Constitutional Committee, 252
Court of Accounts, 135
Couve de Murville, Maurice, 261
*Croix, La*, 156
Crozier, Michel, 78
Cultural Affairs, Ministry of, 2, 261
currency reform of 1958, 265

Debré, Michel, 17, 34, 132, 139, 147, 184, 246–47, 250, 256, 259–61, 279, 280, 285, 294
dechristianization, 51–52. *See also* Catholics, freemasonry
decolonization, *see* Algeria, Indochina
Defferre, Gaston, 56, 91, 221–22, 227, 315, 338. *See also* Socialist Party
de Gaulle, Charles, ix, 108, 142–51, 220, 269, 313, 321, 330–34, 339, 340
  memoirs of, 3, 145, 148, 149
  on French political culture, 4
  foreign policy of, 9, 149, 150, 320
  and referendums, 10, 101, 103–11, 125, 330
  and modernization, 33, 34, 38–39, 305–09
  on Fifth Republic, 88, 96, 245–61, 272–75, 284, 300
  and local politics, 91
  and elections, 95, 99–103, 112–18, 166, 167, 181–82, 242, 332
  founds R.P.F., 105
  and parliament, 121, 276, 279–80, 284–89, 291–92, 294–300
  *Edge of the Sword*, 146, 149
  charisma of, 150, 161, 330
  press conferences of, 159–60
  appeal of June 18, 1940, 161
  and party system, 184, 196–97, 208–09
  and interest groups, 188
  Bayeux speech of, 196, 245, 299
  and Communists, 215–17, 333–34
  and S.F.I.O., 221
  and U.N.R., 230–37
  and Prime Minister, 255–62
  and Third Republic, 277
  and problem of legitimacy and authority, 305–13
Democratic Center, 227–30
*départments*, 83, 84, 87, 88, 269, 297

deputies, 87–88, 94, 95, 97, 99,
    100, 121, 158, 225, 238, 281,
    290, 301–02, 338
  social origins of, 126–27
  election of, 122–28
  and constituency interests, 293–
    94
Dreyfus Affair, 6, 272
Durkheim, Emile, 75

*Echo de Notre Temps, L'*, 157
*École Libre des Science Politi-
    ques*, 132. *See also* Paris
    School of Political Science
*École Nationale d'Administra-
    tion* (ENA), 132–38, 237, 239,
    324
*École Normale*, 128
*École Polytechnique*, 132, 324
Economic and Social Council,
    298–99
economic development, *see* mod-
    ernization, economic
*Economist, The*, 157
education, 65–74, 318, 322, 340
  Ministry of, 66, 74, 136, 259
  parochial schools, 73, 178. *See
    also* Catholic schools
egalitarianism, 11, 13–14, 60–62,
    64, 66–67, 75, 121–22, 341
elections,
  municipal, 89, 90–93, 98, 298
  parliamentary, 94–103, 126, 332
    1849, 197
    1936, 197
    1945, 124
    1946, 124
    1956, 209, 211
    1958, 101, 124–26, 213, 216,
      337
    1962, 101, 112, 116, 126, 164,
      166, 213, 216, 332
    1967, 101–02, 126, 154, 160,
      167–68, 213–14, 216–17, 225–
      26, 232, 238, 258, 260, 284,
      287, 315, 332, 334
    1968, 332–39

elections (*Cont.*)
  presidential, 94–96, 103–05,
    111–18, 311
    1965, 112–18, 167, 181, 221, 242
    *See also* 1962 referendum
  participation in, 89, 100–01
  campaigning, 102–103, 113–14.
    *See also* communications
  interest groups in, 179–80
  party finances and, 200–01
electoral college, 105, 246, 295
electoral system, 97–103, 124, 198,
    242, 338
Élysée Palace, 249, 267
emergency powers, 252–53, 313
European Common Market, 27–
    28, 39, 41–42, 149, 188, 192,
    209, 268, 317, 329, 342

family, 57–60, 324–25
farmers, 41, 61, 86, 91, 162, 182,
    329, 342
  and economic modernization,
    25–28, 329
  and taxation, 37–38
  and governmental price sup-
    ports, 41–42
  and educational system, 68–69,
    71
  and parliament, 128
  in civil service, 133
  *see also* agriculture, interest
    groups
Fauvet, Jacques, 198
*Fédération Nationale des Syndi-
    cats d'Exploitants Agricoles*
    (F.N.S.E.A.), 176, 181, 182,
    329
Federation of the Democratic
    and Socialist Left, 216, 224–
    27, 329–30, 333, 337, 338–39
*Figaro, Le*, 155
Finance, Inspector of, 257
Finance, Ministry of, 135, 238,
    256–57, 259
finances, system of, 85–86, 281,
    342

Flaubert, Gustave, 313
*Force Ouvrière* (F.O.), 175
Foreign Legion, 274
Foreign Office (Quai d'Orsay), 135, 249, 261
foreign policy, 149–50, 217, 312, 343
*France-Soir,* 155
Free French, 72, 103–04, 144, 233, 272
freemasonry, 48–49, 55–56, 176, 222. *See also* anti-clericalism

Gambetta, Léon, 148
Gaullism, 93, 229–35, 331. *See also* de Gaulle
Germany
  Federal Republic of, 82, 165, 229, 279, 283, 322
  compared to France, 20, 21, 38, 40, 70, 98, 123, 307
  Democratic Republic of, 215
  Weimar Republic, 252, 279, 316
  Hitler, 252, 279, 320
Gide, André, 127
Giscard d'Estaing, Valéry, 238–39, 259, 290
*Grands Corps,* 136–37
Great Britain, 124, 145
  compared to France, 14, 21, 27, 38, 60, 67, 70, 83–84, 97, 113, 123, 126–27, 132, 137, 155, 162, 187, 200–01, 236, 255, 277, 281, 291, 292, 307
  House of Commons in, 122
  and B.B.C., 162–63, 165
  and Common Market, 188
"Green Shirts," 176
gross national product, 19, 37, 342

Haussman, Baron, 266
historical thinking, 14–17, 204–05, 325–26
Hitler-Stalin Pact, 212
Hugo, Victor, 127
*Humanité, L',* 154, 210, 214

ideology, 45–47, 121, 170, 172, 176, 193, 204–05, 222. *See also* style, political
*incivisme,* 80
individualism, 11–14, 78, 171, 173, 204
  of farmers, 28
  and business, 29–30
  and family structure, 59
  of deputies and senators, 294
Indochina, 273, 305, 332
industry, *see* business
inflation, 39–40, 266, 342
information, government control of, 163–68, 327
Information, Ministry of, 158, 164, 165, 167
intellectuals, 127–28
interest groups, 75–76, 130, 160, 169–95, 288, 299
  agricultural, 28, 173, 176, 177, 181, 189, 192, 214–15, 280, 329
  business, 29–30, 341–42
  legitimacy of, 170–71, 179, 189
  weakness of, 172–73
  membership in, 178–79
  and parties, 183
  and bureaucracy, 184–85, 193, 268, 301
  *see also* agriculture, associations, trade unions
Interior, Ministry of, 84, 271
Italy, 229

Jacobins, 2, 6, 8, 11, 13, 48, 203, 222–23
Japan, 82
Jeanneney, Jean-Marcel, 261
*Jeunes Agriculteurs,* 177
*Jeunes Patrons,* 177
Jews, 56
*Journal Officiel,* 291
Jouvenel, Robert de, 120
judiciary, 141–42, 167, 252, 266

Keynes, Maynard, 137

labor, distribution of, 21, 24, 25

labor unions, *see* trade unions
Lamartine, Alphonse, 127
Lasswell, Harold, 152
Laval, Pierre, 201
Lecanuet, Jean, 116, 117, 227, 242
Left, 98, 99, 110, 114, 116, 127,
    128, 150, 197, 199, 201, 203,
    205, 209, 225–26, 232, 235,
    236, 241–43, 310, 332, 336,
    338
  on Church/state relations, 50,
    54, 56–57
  *see also* Communists, Radicals,
    Socialists
legislative powers, 255, 256. *See
    also* ordinances, Parliament
legitimacy, 8, 98, 104, 117, 147–
    48, 254, 304–13, 330, 340
liberation, 32, 63, 207, 340
lobbies, *see* interest groups
local government, 82–93, 123,
    210, 220, 301, 318
Louis IX (Saint), 3
Louis XIV, 148
Louis XV, 11

MacMahon, General Marie de,
    197, 277
Malraux, André, 2, 127, 249, 261
*marais,* see Center
Marseilles, 91, 221
Marx, Karl, 2
marxism, 174, 219, 325
Masonic Lodges, *see* freemasonry
mass media, *see* communications
Mauriac, François, 127
Maurras, Charles, 146
mayors, 85–88, 90–93
  authority of, 86–87
Méline, Jules, 27
Mendès-France, Pierre, 5, 130,
    207, 215, 224, 240, 292, 330,
    338
Michelet, Jules, 3, 140
Michels, Robert, 119
middle classes, *see* bourgeoisie
military tribunals, 298
ministerial *cabinets,* 187, 262–64

Ministers, Council of, *see* cabinets
Mitterand, François, 113–18, 181,
    201, 222, 224–27, 242, 330,
    338
*Modern, Liberal, Centralist, Eu-
    ropean France, The,* 238
modernization
  economic, 18–25, 38–39, 135, 342
  agricultural, 26–28
  entrepreneurship and, 29–31
  public sector in, 31–34
  *see also* planning
  political, 45, 140–41, 268–72,
    303–05, 313–15, 317–20, 343
Mollet, Guy, 221, 338
*Monde, Le,* 156–57
Monnerville, Gaston, 297
Monnet, Jean, 33
Montesquieu, Baron de, ix, 15,
    44
Mosca, Gaetano, 119
*Mouvement Républicain Popu-
    laire* (M.R.P.), 116, 203, 207,
    228–30
municipal bonds, 85
municipal councils, 83, 86, 89,
    92, 295. *See also* local gov-
    ernment

Napoleon I, 7–9, 11, 65–68, 73,
    82, 106, 132, 146, 147, 160,
    324
Napoleon III, 9, 25, 30, 48, 80,
    104, 106, 111, 147, 148, 160,
    176, 182, 266
*Nation, La,* 154, 234
National Assembly, 120, 258, 327,
    332, 339
  in Third Republic (Chamber
    of Deputies), 123, 182–83
  in Fourth Republic, 89, 123,
    182–83
  in Fifth Republic, *see* Parlia-
    ment
  policy-making and, 276–83
  and Senate, 294–300
  elections to, *see* elections, par-
    liamentary

national character, *see* political culture
National Control Commission, 167
National Convention of 1792, 3
National Education, Ministry of, *see* education
NATO, 149, 215, 275

*Observer,* 157
occupation, Nazi, 153, 161
*Office de la Radiodiffusion-Télévision Française* (O.R.T.F.), 164–68, 327
officers, military, 270–75
ordinances, ministerial, 164–65, 286, 287, 326
Orleanists, 48, 203
*Ouest-France,* 155
*Ouvriérisme,* 63

Palewski, Gaston, 249
*pantouflage,* 134–35
Pareto, Vilfredo, 119
Paris, 25, 52, 91, 155, 266, 324–26, 331–32, 333, 337
Paris Commune of 1871, 2, 62, 325
Paris School of Political Science, 134
*Parisien Libéré,* 155
Parliament, 120, 129, 246, 251, 252, 286, 313, 327, 340
of 1792, 3
in Third Republic, 9, 48
in Fourth Republic, 9
and referendums, 108–09, 110–11
members of, 120–22, 126–30. *See also* deputies, senators
and communications, 158, 163–65
and interest groups, 181, 182–84, 191–94
in state of emergency, 252
and executive, 254, 255–60, 278–80, 283–89, 314, 340
ministers in, 259–61

Parliament (*Cont.*)
legislative function of, 278, 280–81, 284–87, 290, 298, 315
role in revision of constitution, 288–89
style and methods of, 289–94
questions in, 290–91
*see also* elections, National Assembly, Senate
parochial schools, *see* Catholic schools
*Parti Socialiste Unifié* (P.S.U.), 225, 226, 328, 337–38
parties, political, 75, 90, 91, 94, 121, 153, 187, 198–99, 201–02, 279, 294, 315–16, 318–19, 327
in Third Republic, 9
in Fourth Republic, 9
and parliamentary elections, 96–97, 99, 110, 332
and referendum voting, 110
and presidential elections, 117–18
candidates of, 123–24
and ministries, 139
and press, 155
and interest groups, 183, 189, 192–95
membership in, 202–04
surge movements, 207, 209
and president, 314
*see also* clubs, political; party system; specific parties
participation, in voting, 95–96, 99–101, 109–12, 334, 335
party system, 10, 94, 117–18, 198–201, 258–59, 310, 315–16, 338
weakness of, 16, 97, 196–97
and parliament, 125, 278
multipolar, 202–06
role of center coalition in, 205–06, 209
attempted reform of, 227
peasants, *see* farmers
Pisani, Edgard, 287
Péguy, Charles, 13
*Perspectives et Réalités,* 238

Pétain, Marshal, 272

Planning, General Commissariat for, 27–28, 33–36, 141, 270

Plans, Modernization, 34, 36–37, 266, 269, 298

plebiscitarianism, 7–10, 15, 103–04, 106, 112–13, 161, 181, 248, 253, 285, 307, 311–12, 315, 319, 331, 332. For individual plebiscites *see* referendums

Poincaré, Raymond, 197

policy-making process, 137, 307, 311
  political elite in, 120, 132
  and interest groups, 169–70, 181–82, 185–87
  president in, 245–54
  civil servants in, 264–71
  role of parliament in, 120–21, 191, 276–83, 300–02

political culture, 43–47, 62, 82, 341
  national character, 1–2, 10–14, 16–17, 57–60, 72, 78–80
  value systems, 43–44, 47–57, 58, 138, 177, 316–17, 341
  and bureaucracy, 131–32
  and interest groups, 170
  and party system, 198

polling, 46–47, 160–61

Pompidou, Georges, 248–50, 256–58, 259, 261, 284, 330

*Populaire, Le,* 154

Popular Front, 32, 62–63, 197, 212, 278, 342

population, growth of, 20–21

Poujade, Pierre, 172–73
  movement, 207, 215, 232, 341

prefects
  departmental, 85–86, 91, 92, 269–72
  regional, 270–72

President of the Republic, 88, 187, 245–59, 330–32, 339, 340
  and Parliament, 260, 283–89, 302, 314
  and government, 255–56
  and civil servants, 264, 266–67

President of the Republic (*Cont.*)
  and Speaker of the Senate, 297
  popular election of, 310. *See also* de Gaulle; elections, presidential; 1962 referendum

press, 103, 153–60
  conferences of de Gaulle, 159

pressure groups, *see* interest groups

Prime Minister, 187, 238, 255–62, 280, 283–84, 287, 297, 315, 330, 331, 332, 340
  in Fourth Republic, 17
  and Planning Commissariat, 36
  *see also* Debré, Pompidou

Protestants, 56–57

Public Health, Ministry of, 136

public sector of the economy, 31–33, 134


Radical Party, 83, 207, 222–24, 225, 232, 297

radio, 103, 153, 156, 161–63
  government control of, 162–64

Raspail, François, 127

*Rassemblement du Peuple Fran-çais* (R.P.F.), 232–33

referendums, 92, 103–08, 149, 254, 285, 311, 312, 313
  in Fourth Republic, 9, 104
  of 1958, 101, 106, 213, 216
  of 1962, 101, 104, 108, 110–11, 113, 116, 164, 166, 197, 248, 252, 288–89, 313, 331
  and presidential policy, 251–52, 330–31, 340

Regional Development Boards (CODER), 270–72, 294, 297

regionalism, 269–72, 214

Renan, Ernest, 14, 145

representation, 7–10, 15, 94, 98, 125, 202, 253

Republic
  Second, 127
  Third, 9, 46, 48–49, 62, 72, 94, 97, 103, 111, 123, 126, 144,

Republic (*Cont.*)
Third (*Cont.*)
145, 156, 171, 176–78, 228, 304, 320, 330
electoral system in, 98, 100, 102, 125, 198, 309
parliament in, 183, 276–78, 286–87, 309
party system in, 205, 207
constitution of, 246
Senate in, 295, 297–98
Fourth, 9, 33, 34, 73, 87, 89, 92, 94, 111, 123, 127, 130, 145, 157, 163, 307, 320
constitution of, 46, 104–05, 278–79
elections in, 95–96, 98, 100, 102, 125, 309
interest groups in, 172–73, 182, 185
parliament in, 182, 276–77, 281, 282, 284, 286, 287
fall of, 192, 331
party system in, 203, 205, 207–09
civil service in, 265
officer corps in, 273–74
Fifth, *see* specific subjects
republicanism, 12, 57, 176, 222
*Républicains Indépendents* (R.I.), 237–39, 258, 261, 293, 333, 338
resistance movement, 3, 50, 124, 147, 153, 208, 272
Revolution of 1789, 2, 4, 6, 7–9, 11, 14, 15, 47–48, 82, 83, 94, 131, 171, 189–90
Revolution of 1848, 62, 325. *See also* Paris Commune
Reynaud, Paul, 10, 125, 144
Richelieu, Cardinal de, 34, 146
Right, 98, 114, 127, 197, 201, 203, 205, 209, 231, 235, 236, 241–43, 296, 334, 338
and Church, 50, 54, 57
*see also* U.N.R., R.I.
Robespierre, Maximilien, 6, 146
Rochet, Waldeck, 218

Rousseau, Jean-Jacques, 7, 106, 119, 146, 147, 170, 171, 247, 253

Saint-Simon, Claude-Henri, 30, 139
Sartre, Jean-Paul, 127
Scandinavia, compared to France, 40, 98
Schuman Plan, 183
Secretariat of Government, 249, 257
Secretariat of the President, 257
*Section Française de l'Internationale Ouvrière* (S.F.I.O.), *see* Socialist Party
Senate, 120, 279–80, 288, 294–300. *See also* Parliament
senators, 87, 88, 95, 122–24, 158
Siegfried, André, 59, 235
Sieyès, Abbé, 17
Social Affairs, Ministry of, 261
social security system, 33, 37, 266, 287, 326
Socialist Party (S.F.I.O.), 63, 83, 114, 123–24, 154, 199, 200, 202, 203, 207, 218–22, 225, 227–29, 337–38
and Communists, 10, 13, 216, 217
*see also* Defferre, Gaston
Soustelle, Jacques, 232
Soviet Union, 210, 218, 307
stabilization plan of 1961, 265, 298
Stalin, Joseph, 212, 215
strikes, 42, 190, 193, 288, 298, 321, 326–29, 333, 336, 337, 341, 342
students, *see* youth
student movement, 194–95, 218, 321, 323, 326–27, 341
style, political, 4–6, 14–17, 46–47, 121, 188–90, 191, 341
violence as, 203, 323. *See also* strikes, revolution
suffrage, 83, 97, 114
Switzerland, 181

Sully, Duc de, 34

taxation, 37–38, 84–85, 93
teachers, 72, 87, 129
Teachers, Federation of, 175, 181
television, 103, 156, 158, 161–64, 166–68
*Terre, La,* 215
Thorez, Maurice, 215, 218
Tixier-Vignancour, Jean-Louis, 116
Tocqueville, Alexis de, x, xi, 17, 37, 45, 46, 47, 62, 82, 131, 192, 317, 339
town clerk, 86, 87
trade unions, 36, 64, 169, 173–77, 188–93, 208, 216, 288, 326–29, 337
 and parliament, 127
 and Socialists, 218–19
 *see also* interest groups
Turgot, Anne-Robert, 34
"tutelage" (*tutelle*) authorities, 84, 86, 91

*Union Démocratique du Travail* (U.D.T.), 235–36
*Union des Démocrates pour la Ve République, see* U.N.R.
Union for the Defense of Shopkeepers and Artisans, 172
*Union pour la Nouvelle République* (U.N.R.), 74, 117, 124, 154, 180–81, 218, 230–38, 240, 247, 258, 261, 289–90, 292–93, 297, 333–38
United States of America
 constitution of, 7
 compared to France, 11, 20, 21, 38, 40, 70, 75, 76, 83–84, 90, 97, 133, 137, 160–61, 178, 182, 186, 193, 200–01, 217, 249–51, 252, 254, 255, 258, 261, 277–78, 281, 284, 290, 295, 307
 party system of, 94, 117
 electoral system of, 99
 Congress of, 122

United States of America (*Cont.*)
 press, 157
 interest groups in, 181
urbanization, 24–25, 51–52, 87

Vichy regime, 6, 72, 104, 124, 176, 188–89, 272
Viviani, René, 48
Voltaire, François-Marie, 47, 52, 127

War, Ministry of, 146
Weber, Max, 149
women, 58, 142
 suffrage for, 97, 100, 109, 228
 and religion, 52, 157
working class, 61, 110, 133, 208, 326
 and religion, 49, 52
 and bourgeoisie, 62–64
 and educational system, 68, 69, 71
 vote, 116, 213, 336–37
 in parliament, 127
 and P.C., 214
 and S.F.I.O., 218–20
 and U.N.R., 235–36
World War I, 20, 50
World War II, 20, 31, 50, 272
Wylie, Lawrence, 201

youth, 321, 322, 325, 336, 337, 338, 341
 and farming, 28
 religious attitudes of, 53
 in family structure, 58–59
 and interest groups, 75–76, 176–77
 in local politics, 92–93
 and education, 193, 322–23
 and P.C., 218
 and U.N.R., 237
 and de Gaulle, 315
 *see also* education, student movement

*Zeit, Die,* 157
Zola, Émile, 127